Johann Wolfgang Goethe.

Heath's Modern Language Series

Goethes Faust

EDITED BY

CALVIN THOMAS

PROFESSOR OF GERMANIC LANGUAGES AND LITERATURES, COLUMBIA UNIVERSITY

VOLUME I: THE FIRST PART

D. C. HEATH & CO., PUBLISHERS

BOSTON   NEW YORK   CHICAGO

PREFACE

In undertaking this edition of *Faust* I was actuated chiefly by a desire to promote the study of the poem as a whole. It is not the place here to discuss the misconception which has prevailed so long, and to some extent still prevails, concerning the Second Part of Goethe's masterpiece. Enough that it *is* a misconception to regard it as a mass of riddles, allegories and deep abstractions requiring some sort of occult wisdom for their ' interpretation.' It is a mistake, too, to regard it as in any sense a senile afterthought, or as the product of decadent poetic powers, or as uninteresting. Let it not be supposed, either, that these sweeping statements of mine are only the confident proclamations of a new mystagogue who thinks that *he* has found the key. For the simple truth is that no key and no special order of intelligence are needed. The Second Part of *Faust*, to be sure, is not literature for children, or for the weak-minded, or for the very indolent, but — neither is the First Part. I only wish to urge here that any one who reads and enjoys the First Part (by which I mean the whole First Part and not simply the love story), should be able to read and enjoy the Second Part also. If he fails at first, his failure will be due probably to one of three causes: either he lacks interest in some of the large ideas that interested the maturer Goethe; or he has not made himself sufficiently at home in that dream-world of tradition which underlies the Faust-drama, or, possibly his vision has been obfuscated by one or more of those well-meaning but misguided persons whom the

(i)

late Friedrich Vischer called *allegorische Erklärungsphilister*. In any of these cases let him first correct the personal difficulty — a thing not hard to do — and then let him read the Second Part of *Faust* as he reads other good poetry: with a free play of intelligence to respond to its infinite suggestiveness, but without ever imagining that the text is a Chinese puzzle. Doing so he will find that he has gained a permanent source of high enjoyment — enjoyment of a kind (if his experience is at all like my own) that he will soon come to prefer greatly to that derivable from the painful tragedy of sin and suffering with which the First Part closes.

As to the animating spirit of my work it is needless to speak at length; that will appear best from the work itself. I have wrought as a philologist and a lover of definiteness. Taking for granted the fascinating power of *Faust* I have made it my aim to contribute to the understanding of it rather than to inculcate any particular views with regard to it. I have not been troubled by the solicitude one sometimes hears of in these days, that preoccupation with philological details, i. e., the attempt to get accurate knowledge of the particular matter in hand, could by any possibility in the long run injure the philosophical and æsthetic appreciation of the whole. On the other hand a multitude of warning examples made it both easy and necessary to keep in mind the dangers that arise from importing one's own ' philosophy ' into the poem in advance of a careful historical study of its genesis and a thorough philological mastery of the text.

My text aims to be an exact reprint of the Weimar edition. I hesitated somewhat about the use of the official spelling, but decided not to introduce it. I do not see how it is possible to devise sounder principles for the recension of Goethe's text than are those adopted by the Weimar editors. To depart from these principles in the matters of spelling and punctuation would have been opening the door to subjective caprice without accomplishing any discernible good whatever.

I have of course endeavored to profit by the labors of preceding editors, critics and expounders, of whom a list of the more important will be found in an appendix. In dealing with a subject like *Faust*, about which such mountains of literature exist, it is, in general, possible to attain originality only at the expense of either truth, usefulness or importance; and my aim has been to be useful rather than to seem acute or learned. I have, however, from first to last tried to work independently, i. e:, to go to first-hand sources of information and derive from them my knowledge and my impressions. In the notes I have as a rule avoided controversy and the rehearsal and discussion of conflicting views. My method has been to form my opinion from the data, then to read what the various commentators have to say, changing my own opinion where necessary, and then to present my final conclusion without argument. In dealing with matters of fact which I could verify I have not always been particular to name the writer who first called my attention to the primary source of information, but have proceeded, like most of my predecessors, on the Roman maxim *quod bene dictum est meum est*. On the other hand, in dealing with matters of opinion, or of fact that I could not verify, I have endeavored always to acknowledge all real obligation. Everywhere I have essayed the utmost brevity consistent with a satisfactory treatment of real difficulties. I have tried to waste no words in trivial, obvious or useless comment. Citations possessing only a curious or erudite interest, but not needed for scientific illustration, have not been admitted. I have also avoided any attempt to do the work of an etymological dictionary or a historical grammar.

According to my conceptions the one great purpose of the editor's notes to a classic should be to help the reader enter more perfectly than he otherwise might into the thought and feeling of the author. Philological lore which would have been news to the author and does not contribute to a proper understanding of the author's meaning, is, in general, out of place and entitled to no better name than pedantry.   The rule is, however, subject to this limitation : peculiarities of diction, which pertain to the author's individual style (the style is the man), may properly be made the subject of brief philological comment for the purpose of giving the reader, so far as may be, the author's exact point of view.

CALVIN THOMAS.

Ann Arbor, Mich., August, 1892.

PREFACE TO THE THIRD EDITION.

In revising my edition of *Faust* for the second time, after a lapse of fourteen years (a second edition was published in 1898), I have tried to work into it the sure gains of recent scholarship, and to do so without changing the essential character of the book. It was designed from the outset for the student — the able, advanced, ambitious student — making his first acquaintance with Goethe's great poem. I wished to be really helpful to such a person, rather than to win the encomiums of the *Goethe-Forscher*. The fruitage of the study of *Faust* is to realize it with the imagination and feel it with the soul. But first the text must be understood, and it is only there that a commentator can really be of much use. Critics whom I esteem have taxed me with being too matter-of-fact, and one of them tempers warm praise with the imputation of an *etwas nüchterne Geistesrichtung*. But this I deem a merit. No keen student of great poetry was ever very much helped by a commentator's

Quam mirabile! Who wants to visit the Parthenon with an effusive guide at his elbow telling him what to admire?

I have not found it necessary to rewrite the Introduction or to make many changes in it. On the whole it has stood the test of time and served its purpose very well. By rewriting I could certainly have made it different, but there was no reason to think that I could make it better for the purposes of the student. On the other hand, I *have* rewritten a good part of the commentary. There were some mistakes — not very many — to be corrected. Here and there a note was superfluous or liable to be misunderstood. In a number of cases, like that of *encheiresin naturae* in line 1940, discoveries had been made. In still others I was in duty bound to indicate the nature and scope of disputed questions and to supply references for the study of them. And then there was the subject of parallel citations, which constitute a salient feature of some recent commentaries. A scholar with time on his hands can soon fill a big note-book with quotations from ancient and modern authors which have a more or less striking resemblance to passages in *Faust*. There is simply no end to that sort of thing. But shall the erudite collector dump the contents of his note-book into a commentary on *Faust?* I do not think it best. Unless sternly held in check the commentator's *Citatenwut* soon becomes a distracting annoyance, instead of a help, to the student of poetry. A citation will always be in order if it throws light on a real and specific difficulty, or suggests the provenience of an expression; but not if it merely shows that different authors have had similar thoughts or expressed themselves in similar language. In dealing with this problem my principle has been to sow with the hand, not with the sack.

It is, however, undeniable that Goethe's language in *Faust* was strongly influenced here and there by his reading in out-of-the-way books. Wherever an influence of this kind has been clearly made out by the researches of scholars I have tried to make room in the Notes for the apposite matter; a certain number of suggestive citations that were either too long or too inconclusive to be incorporated in the Notes have been assembled in a new appendix.

Finally I call attention to my entirely new Bibliography in Appendix I. It has been prepared with great care, and ought, I should think, to prove useful.

C. T.

NEW YORK, January, 1912.

INTRODUCTION.

I.

IT was as early as 1769 that the mind of Goethe, then a youth of twenty, began to be haunted by the figure of the old magician Dr. Faust. During his sojourn at Strassburg, in 1770-1, he conceived the idea of a Faust-drama. Two or three years later he put pen to his work, little thinking, as he did so, that this particular poetic project would be the great task of a long lifetime, and would leave his hands some sixty years hence as the masterpiece of his country's poetry.

The general conception of the proposed drama, he tells us, lay clear in his mind at an early date; but from the first his procedure was unmethodical. The legend yielded, or could be made to yield, a hint for every mood: poetry, pathos, humor, satire, hocus-pocus — all were there. And so he worked in a desultory way, writing a passage here and a passage there, now a soliloquy, now a song, and again a bit of dialogue or a succession of dialogues, according as he had caught the vision of this or that interesting situation. Thus, without concern for acts or for a logical development of his plan, he allowed his work to take shape in a series of pictures, leaving the intervals to be filled in by the imagination. In this way a number of pictures (we may call them ‘scenes’) had been written down previous to his settlement at Weimar in November, 1775.

Then came a period in which the temper and circumstances of the poet were unfavorable to the continuation of the work. In 1788-9 a little more was written, and a part of the scenes on hand were revised for publication. These appeared in 1790 under the title of *Faust. Ein Fragment*. In 1797 the task was again resumed and during the next four years it made considerable progress. The work done at this time consisted partly in the writing of new scenes, partly in the revision and expansion of scenes already written but not published, and the welding of this new matter to the scenes of the published Fragment. During this process Goethe discovered that he could not complete his design within the limits of a single drama and so decided to publish, provisionally, a First Part. This First Part, still far from containing all that he had then written on the Faust-theme, appeared in 1808 under the title *Der Tragödie Erster Theil*.

Then ensued a long period of stagnation. At last, in 1825, *Faust* was again taken up to become, now, its author's chief occupation during his remaining years. The work done at this time was similar to that of 1797–1801, save that the proportion of entirely new matter added was much greater. Goethe died in March, 1832. The Second Part of *Faust* appeared in 1833.

The production that came into existence in this way holds a unique position in literature, there being nothing of its own kind with which to compare it. As a serious dramatic poem based on a tragical story and leading up to the death of its hero, it was called by Goethe a 'tragedy,' though the ordinary canons of tragedy do not, in the main, apply to it. On account of the magnitude of its scope it is often compared with the *Divine Comedy* of Dante. In some respects it resembles a medieval 'mystery.' But whatever it be called and however opinions may differ with respect to this or that detail, it is beyond question the most important monument of German poetry. No other is so much quoted by German writers, so much discussed by German scholars, so vitally related to the intellectual life of the new Germany.* Nor is it simply a national

---

* Egelhaaf, *Grundzüge der deutschen Litteraturgeschichte*, p. 112, speaks of *Faust* as "das Werk, ohne das unser Volk seine Kultur, der Einzelne sein eigenes Geistesleben sich kaum denken kann."

poem. In proportion as the genius of Goethe has of late won universal recognition, so *Faust*, as the most complete revelation of his mind and art, has become a world-classic whose power is felt everywhere by ' those that know.'

On account of this exceptional character the study of *Faust* is a difficult and peculiar study. The poem contains but little of abstruse thought — for Goethe was no ' metaphysician,' — but it does take us sooner or later into almost every conceivable sphere of human interest. Thus the philological reading of the text with its peculiarities of form and expression, its folk-lore and antiquities, its reminiscences of reading and observation, its frequent excursions into unfamiliar regions of thought, feeling and poetic vision, constitutes a task to which modern literature since Dante offers no parallel. And when the difficulties of the text are overcome, then there is the poem as an entirety. In a very real and important sense it has unity, and so must be studied as an artistic whole. At the same time it is by no means free from incongruities. Moreover, owing partly to its slow and desultory genesis, partly also to the very nature of the subject and of the poet's plan, different portions differ greatly in matter and style and in the kind of appeal they make to the reader's interest. The comprehension of these various parts, both in themselves and in their relation to the whole, is an important part of the study.

But the essential character of *Faust* is its symbolism, which presents living issues of modern culture in a setting of old popular legend. To acquire a right feeling for this symbolism, so as to make of it neither too much nor too little, so as to get out of the poem in the reading just what its author put into it, no less and no more, this is what is hardest and at the same time most vitally important. To aid here is the chief purpose of this Introduction. This object will be attained best, however, not by discussing symbolism in the abstract, but by describing minutely the genesis of the poem. To know what Goethe put into *Faust* we must study the origin of its different portions in connection with his contemporary moods and experiences. To understand the poetic artist we must first know the man thoroughly and then — watch him at his work. This is simply to follow his own well-known rule:

> Wer den Dichter will verstehen
> Muß in Dichters Lande gehen.

A famous passage from *Dichtung und Wahrheit* will serve as a convenient starting-point. In speaking of his first intimacy with Herder at Strassburg, which began in September, 1770, Goethe writes:

'Most carefully I hid from him my interest in certain subjects that had taken root with me and were now little by little trying to develop themselves into poetic forms. These were *Götz von Berlichingen* and *Faust* . . . The significant puppet-play legend of the latter echoed and buzzed in many tones within me. I too had drifted about in all knowledge and early enough had been brought to feel the vanity of it. I too had made all sorts of experiments in life and had always come back more unsatisfied and more tormented. I was now carrying these things, like many others, about with me and delighting myself with them in lonely hours, but without writing anything down. Especially, however, I hid from Herder my mystic-cabbalistic chemistry and what pertained to it, though I was still fond of busying myself with it in secret in order to develop it into a more consistent form than that in which it had come to me.' *

This passage calls for a retrospect in two directions. First we must see what that 'puppet-play legend' was that had so impressed Goethe in his youth. Then we must inquire into those personal experiences which led him to see in Faust a symbol of himself.

---

* *Werke*, XXVII., 320. References to Goethe's works are to the Weimar edition. *Werke* means the 'works' proper, or first 'Abtheilung' of the edition; *Naturwissenschaftliche Schriften* the second, *Tagebücher* the third, *Briefe* the fourth. Occasionally the Hempel edition, *Werke*, H., is referred to.

II.

THE DATA OF THE LEGEND.

The puppet-play referred to by Goethe was an outgrowth of an earlier popular drama performed by actors of flesh and blood. This popular Faust-drama made its appearance about the beginning of the seventeenth century, but in order to understand its character we must go still further back to the origin of the Faust-legend itself.

Of the actual personage whose life gave rise to the legend very little is known that is not matter of hearsay or of superstitious credulity. Modern scholars are well agreed, however, on the strength of several notices found in the writings of men who claim to have known Dr. Faust, that there was a man of that name who went about Germany in the first half of the sixteenth century and passed himself off on credulous people as a great magician. Philip Begardi, a physician who published an *Index Sanitatis* at Worms in 1539, speaks of Faust in this work as a notorious charlatan who had travelled about the country ' a few years ago,' calling himself *philosophus philosophorum*, etc., and cheating people out of their money by fortune-telling, necromancy, magical healing and the like.   Begardi was acquainted with many people who had been deluded by Faust's large promises and small performance.*

In an age when every one believed in magic it was natural that people should soon begin to credit Faust with actually doing the kind of things he said he could do.† Thus, even in his lifetime, his name came to be associated with marvellous feats of magic ; and

---

* The historical Faust does not greatly concern us. The notices relating to him are conveniently assembled by Tille at the beginning of his *Faustsplitter* ; also by Witkowski in the *Deutsche Zeitschrift für Geschichtswissenschaft*, Neue Folge, 1, 298 ff. — For exact bibliographical data concerning books referred to in this Introduction and in the Notes see Appendix I. at the end of the volume.

† Cf. Scherer, *Das älteste Faust-Buch*, p. vi-vii.

when, about the year 1540, he met with a violent death under obscure or mysterious circumstances, the mythopoeic imagination of the people was ready with its explanation: he had been carried off by the devil whose aid had enabled him to do his wonders. The myth once started, Faust speedily became a new representative of a type long familiar to European superstition, the type, namely, of the wicked magician who, for some transitory favor of pleasure, power, knowledge or the like, sells his soul to the devil. What was in circulation about former copartners of the devil began to be repeated, with local additions and variations, concerning Faust.* Thus grew up a mass of fables which, toward the end of the century, were collected, put together into something like a narrative and published as a *Historia von D. Johann Fausten dem weitbeschreyten Zauberer und Schwartzkünstler.†* This book appeared in 1587, at Frankfurt-on-the-Main. Its publisher was Johann Spies, who says in a preface that he had the manuscript from 'a good friend in Speyer.' The unknown author, apparently a Lutheran pastor, writes with a very definite and intensely serious purpose, which is to warn his readers against magic and the black art. The book is full of Bible quotations and bears on its title-page the motto: 'Resist the devil and he will flee from you.' The story told is in brief this:

---

* The following quotation will serve to show at once how early the legend had taken shape and in what kind of soil it grew. It is from the *Sermones Convivales* of the Basel preacher Johann Gast. The book was printed in 1543. Gast writes of Faust: 'I dined with him in the great college at Basel. He had given the cook birds of different kinds to roast. I do not know how he got them, since there were none on sale at the time. He had a dog and a horse which, in my belief, were devils, as they could do everything. Some said the dog occasionally took the form of a servant and brought him food. The wretch met a terrible end, for he was strangled by the devil.' Later notices also give to Faust a 'black dog which was the devil.'

† Of the original Faust-book, first edition, there are now known to exist, according to Engel, *Zusammenstellung der Faust-Schriften*, p. 59, only five copies. It is, however, obtainable in various reprints: (1) in facsimile, *Das älteste Faust-Buch, mit einer Einleitung* von Wilhelm Scherer, Berlin, 1884; (2) *Das älteste Faustbuch, mit Einleitung und Anmerkungen* von August Kühne, Zerbst, 1868; (3) *Das Volksbuch vom Doctor Faust,* in Braune's *Neudrucke deutscher Literaturwerke*, Halle, 1878.

Faust, the son of a peasant living near Weimar, is brought up by a rich uncle at Wittenberg, where, in due time, he studies theology at the university and takes his degree with distinction. Being, however, of a 'foolish and arrogant' (*we* should say, a bold and original) mind, he gets the name of 'speculator,' and begins to study books of magic. Soon he repudiates the name of a '*theologus*' and becomes a '*Weltmensch*,' calls himself a 'doctor of medicine,' 'astrologer,' etc., and goes about healing people with herbs, roots and clysters. Having thus 'taken eagles' wings' to himself, and resolved to search into all things in heaven and earth,' he carries his madness to the extent of trying to evoke the devil. Going into the woods near Wittenberg, at night, he succeeds, after much ado, in raising a subordinate devil who appears in the guise of a monk. Faust demands that this spirit shall come to his house the next day at midnight, which the spirit does. Then, after various preliminary 'disputations,' in one of which the spirit gives his name as Mephostophiles,* the pair enter, at Faust's solicitation, into an agreement. Mephostophiles agrees to bestow upon Faust the form and nature of a spirit, to be his faithful and obedient servant, to come to his house whenever wanted, and there either to remain invisible or to take any desired shape. In return, Faust agrees that after a certain period, fixed later at twenty-four years, he is to belong to the devil, and that meanwhile he will renounce the Christian faith, hate all Christians, resist all attempts to convert him, and sign this covenant with his own blood.

For a while Faust remains at home seeing no one but Mephostophiles and his famulus, an 'insolent lubber' called Christoph Wagner, who had formerly been a worthless vagabond. At first Mephostophiles amuses Faust and Wagner (who is in his master's secret) with various manifestations, and feeds them on princely food and drink purloined from the neighboring castles. So Faust leads 'an epicurean life' day and night, ceases to 'believe in God, hell, or devil,'† and 'thinks that soul and body die together.' He desires a wife, but marriage being a Christian ordinance, the devil objects and finds other ways to gratify his lust. He also provides a great book dealing with all sorts of magic and 'nigromancy.' Faust's curiosity being excited, he asks his familiar all sorts of questions con-

---

* On the forms of the name see note to line 242+, of the text.

† Chap. X. This curious feature of the legend which makes Faust skeptical with regard to hell and the devil even while he is on intimate terms with an envoy of hell and is daily doing wonders in the devil's name, is worthy of special notice.

cerning the spirit-world. Long 'disputations' ensue respecting
hell, the hierarchy of devils, the fall of the recreant angels, etc.
Mephostophiles' account of Lucifer's former estate brings Faust to
tears of remorse over his own folly; still he will not repent and
return to God and the church, but persists „in allen seinen opinioni-
bus und Meynungen." Presently the devil refuses to answer further
questions, whereupon Faust becomes a calendar-maker, and turns
his attention to physics and astronomy. In such pursuits seven
years pass.

In the next eight years we hear of only two adventures. Faust
desires to visit hell, and Mephostophiles brings it about that Beelzebub calls for him at midnight, takes him up into the air in an ivory
chair, puts him asleep and lets him dream of hell in the belief that
he is really there. Afterward he ascends into the sky in a car
drawn by dragons and spends a week among the stars. In the
sixteenth year he conceives a desire to travel on earth; so Mephostophiles converts himself into a 'horse with wings like a drome-
dary,' and bears him to all parts of the world. In this way he
visits many lands, seeing their sights, enjoying their pleasures, and
performing all sorts of conjuror's tricks. At Rome he plays pranks
upon the pope. At Constantinople he visits the Sultan's harem in
the role of Mahomet. At the court of Charles V. he counterfeits
the forms of Alexander the Great and his wife. Again he conjures
a stag's horns upon the head of a knight, swallows a peasant's cart-
load of hay, and saws off his own leg and leaves it in pawn with a
Jew. Toward the end he spends much time in revelry with certain
jolly students. On one occasion some of these wish to see Helena
of Greece, whereupon Faust produces her for their diversion.
Later he takes Helena as a concubine and has by her a son Justus
Faust, who foretells future events for his father.

As the end of his career approaches Faust regrets his bargain
and bewails his fate in bitter tears and lamentations. The devil
tries to console him, but insists inexorably on the contract. On
the last day of the twenty-four years, having previously willed his
property to Wagner, Faust goes with his boon companions to an
inn near Wittenberg, treats the company to good food and wine,
informs them ruefully of his situation, and tells them that the devil
is to come for him at midnight. They then separate. At the
hour named the students hear a terrible sound of hissing and
whistling, and in the morning on going to look for him they find
'no Faust,' but only his mangled body lying on a heap of refuse.

The gist of this story, as seen by those who created it, is the awful fate of a bad man who is led by the study of magic into dealings with the devil. The league with the devil is not the root, but the fruit of Faust's badness, which consists, primarily, in an unholy intellectual curiosity. A promising theologian, he is not content with traditional theology, but wishes to know 'all things in heaven and earth.' This desire itself is sinful. Men should be content with what is revealed in the Word. Faust essays to get the desired knowledge by the study of magic, but this study is sinful. Knowledge and power may, to be sure, be got in that way, but they are got by the devil's help and men are commanded to resist the devil instead of making friends with him. Hence the logic of the catastrophe. Faust's wicked desire is gratified. For a while he lives as a superior being and lords it over time and space. But he does this by the devil's aid and the devil must have his pay, and his pay is the soul of his dupe.

Speaking broadly and from a modern point of view,* what we see in the Faust-legend is the popular Protestant theology of the Reformation period expressing itself upon the great intellectual movement of the Renaissance; upon the new spirit of free inquiry, of revolt against narrow traditions, of delight in ancient ideals of beauty. Faust is a representative of this spirit. It might seem at first as if there were but little likeness between him and the great humanists, but there are two traits which connect him with them, namely, his interest in secular science and his love of antique beauty. The lovely pagan Helena, as well as physics and astronomy, is one of the devil's tools for entrapping the soul of Faust. In this connection it is noteworthy that a very early tradition connects Faust with the University of Erfurt, then the great seat of German humanism.† There he is represented as lecturing upon

---

* On the historical import of the Faust-legend, cf. Erich Schmidt, *Charakteristiken*, pp. 1-37, Witkowski's article above referred to, and Scherer's Introduction to his facsimile edition of the original Faust-book.

† Cf. Scherer, *Geschichte der deutschen Litteratur*, 1st ed., p. 273.

Homer and calling up the shades of Homeric heroes to illustrate his lecture. Again he participates in a discussion on the utility of Latin comedy as reading-matter for the schools. In this Faust we see a genuine colleague of the humanists.

Thus it would seem as if the legend, in working out the character and career of Faust, had intentionally made him a wicked secular counterpart to Luther. At least the parallel, as drawn by Scherer,* is very striking. Both Luther and Faust are occupied with the old humanities at Erfurt, but Luther turns his back on the sensuous lures of paganism and meets his need of woman's love by marrying him a wife in accordance with divine ordinance, while Faust yields to lawless passion, rejects marriage at the devil's advice, and takes Helena as a paramour. Both live at Wittenberg, the cradle of the Reformation, Luther as the reverent student and expounder of the Bible, Faust as a despiser of scripture and a searcher after forbidden knowledge. Both visit Rome, where Luther is shocked by the prevailing license, Faust cynically amused to find that others are no better than himself. Luther shies his inkstand at the devil, Faust makes friends with him; Luther is a devout believer, Faust a reckless skeptic.

For a time the Faust-narrative proved very popular and new editions and translations came out in rapid succession.† In 1599 G. R. Widman published the story with an elaborate commentary, and his account, it would seem, became the chief source of the subsequent versions.‡ Widman differs in many particulars from the original Faust-book, but the details do not concern us here. In general he gives to the legend a more decidedly anti-Catholic tinge and deprives it of its poetry. In his hands Faust loses the character of a titanic philosopher who 'takes eagles' wings to himself'; he is, rather, a promising youth led into bad ways through

---

* *Faust-Buch*, p. xxi.

† For exact bibliographical data, see Engel, *Zusammenstellung*, p. 57 ff.

‡ Widman's work is reprinted in Scheible's *Kloster*, II., 273 ff.

contact with the magic of the Catholic church. The episode of
Helena Widman only refers to in a foot-note; he will not offend
chaste ears and hearts by relating it. In 1674 a new edition*
of Widman's work was published by C. N. Pfitzer, a Nürnberg
physician, and Pfitzer's book was re-issued in abbreviated
form early in the following century by an anonymous editor
styling himself 'a man of Christian sentiments' (von einem
Christlich Meynenden).† This little book was widely sold and must
have been familiar to the boy Goethe at Frankfurt.‡ Indeed it
was here, or in Pfitzer, that the author of *Faust* found the hint for
his Gretchen. On the strength, probably, of some tradition that
had escaped or scandalized Widman, Pfitzer and his anonymous
successor tell of Faust's falling in love with a poor but beautiful
servant-girl. At first Faust tries to seduce her; then when her
virtue turns out to be proof against his wiles, he proposes to marry
her. From this purpose he is frightened by the devil, who gives
him the fair Helena in the girl's stead.§

But it was the popular Faust-drama, more than the narrative,
which kept the subject alive for the German people during the
seventeenth and eighteenth centuries, as it was also the drama, in
the form of a puppet-show, which impressed the young Goethe with
the significance of the legend. Of this drama as performed by
living actors no text is extant. Indeed it was not a drama in a
critical or literary sense, but a popular show presented from age to
age by strolling companies, with variations and improvisations to
suit the time or the views of the manager. But in spite of their
variety these shows were of the same general type and conformed

---

* Reprinted by A. von Keller, Tübingen, 1880.

† Reprinted, with a good Introduction by Szamatólski, as No. 39 of Goeschen's
Deutsche Litteraturdenkmale. This reprint is from a copy of the year 1725, the earliest
known.

‡ It is now known that Goethe's main reliance, for the legend, was Pfitzer. This is
shown by the records of the Weimar library. Cf. Pniower, *Zeugnisse und Excurse,* p. 82.

§ Szamatólski, p. 23.

broadly to a traditional text which now appears to have been derived from Marlowe's *Faustus* as brought to Germany by English players and performed there early in the seventeenth century.* Marlowe's *Faustus* was written in 1589, the poet getting his knowledge of the story from the translated English Faust-book which appeared before Feb. 28, 1589.† The play follows the legend closely in spirit and in details. It begins, after an expository chorus, with a soliloquy in which Faustus expresses his dissatisfaction with philosophy, law, medicine and theology, and resolves to study magic. He is warned by a good angel that he will do this at the peril of his soul, but he is captivated by the vision of the wonderful things he will be able to do and enjoy as magician, and so decides to ' conjure though he die therefore.' Going into the woods at night he brings up a spirit, Mephistophilis, with whom he arranges terms of service for twenty-four years, promising to give, at the end of that time, his body and soul to Lucifer. Then follow the disputations, travels and tricks, as in the legend. Again and again Faustus would fain repent and save himself, but is always persuaded that he cannot, that it is too late. At the last, in an agony of remorse and fear, he is carried off by devils.

Thus we see that Marlowe takes the theology of the legend as he finds it and gives us a simple tragedy of sin and damnation. His Faustus is a depraved soul that wilfully follows the lower instead of the higher voice, and suffers the consequences he had himself foreseen. The poet, to be sure, makes his hero doubt the reality of hell,‡ but this skepticism sits lightly upon him, and we feel that under the circumstances he has no right to be skeptical. The compact is a plain matter of purchase and sale. Faustus has had before him an emissary of hell in bodily form, and this emissary has assured him that heaven and hell are supreme realities. Nevertheless he says to himself

---

* Cf. Creizenach, *Geschichte des Volksschauspiels vom Dr. Faust*, chapters 1 and 2.

† Cf. Zarncke, in *Anglia*, IX., 610.

‡ " Come, I think hell's a fable "; act II., sc. 1.

"The god thou serv'st is thine own appetite,"

and forthwith proceeds to sell his soul for a mess of pottage. The pottage is purveyed in accordance with the agreement, and the devil gets his own.

There is reason to think that Marlowe himself treated his subject rather seriously, making but little use of clown scenes and hocus-pocus to amuse the crowd. These things, however, were called for by the popular taste, and after Marlowe's death, in 1593, his text underwent extensive interpolations of that kind. It was this *Faustus*, thus amplified, which was taken to Germany and played there, with other English plays, by English actors.* The earliest performance of which we chance to have a record was at Graz in 1608.† Very soon the subject was taken up by companies of German actors who, whether they really owed anything to Marlowe or not, at least followed the same general line of treatment. Of this German Faust-play as performed in the seventeenth century our knowledge is scanty, more ample, however, for the eighteenth century. By that time it had become a spectacular extravaganza in which the clown, under the various names of Pickelhäring, Hans Wurst, Harlekin, Crispin, Casper, (his part was usually taken by the manager of the company‡) was the main center of interest. The story of Faust, while its serious import was not altogether lost sight of, was treated as a convenient thread on which to string all sorts of grotesque and grewsome *diablerie*. Thus a performance given at Frankfurt in 1767 (Goethe was then in Leipzig), was advertised as a 'grand machine comedy,' with specific attractions like these: (1) 'Faust's dissertation in his museum (study) as to whether he shall pursue theology or 'micro-

---

* At these performances it was customary for the clown to speak German, while the other actors used English — an arrangement which tended from the outset to give the clown at once a factitious importance and an episodical character. Cf. Creizenach, p. 69.

† Creizenach, p. 45.

‡ Creizenach, p. 148.

mancy' (necromancy).' (2) 'Faust's remarkable conjuration at night in a dark wood, whereat various infernal monsters, furies, spirits (among these Mephistopheles) appear amid thunder and lightning.' (3) 'Crispin makes fun with the spirits in the magic circle.' (4) 'Faust's contract with hell; the document carried off by a raven through the air.' (5) 'Crispin opens a book in Faust's library and little devils come out.' (6) 'Faust's journey through the air with Mephistopheles,' and so on. At the last Faust is carried off to hell by furies and the play concluded with a ballet of furies and a 'grand display of fire-works' representing hell.*

But it would be a mistake to suppose that such performances as this were still common as late as 1767. Long before that, the old popular plays with their prominent clown, their coarse humor, their fondness for fantastic supernaturalism, their indifference to literary standards, had fallen into disrepute in high-toned circles. An artificial taste had grown up which looked to the classical drama of France as the model of all excellence. Dr. Faust and his theatrical associations had become ridiculous and vulgar; so that it required the boldness as well as the insight of a Lessing to take a stand against the swelling tide of correct but vapid imitations of the French and to come to the rescue of the old German plays. In his memorable seventeenth *Literaturbrief*, published in 1759, Lessing argued that the spirit of the English drama, rather than the French, was best adapted to the German people. 'In our tragedies,' he insists, 'we want to see and think more than the timid French tragedy gives us to see and to think. The grand, the terrible, the melancholy, works better upon us than the nice, the delicate, the love-lorn.' Later in the same letter he writes: 'Our old plays really contain much that is English. To take only the best known of them: *Dr. Faust* has a number of scenes such as only a Shakespearian genius would have been able to conceive. And Germany was, in part still is, so enamored of its *Dr. Faust*.' After this

---

* Creizenach, p. 11, 12.

Lessing gives a specimen of a Faust-scene such as he would like to see.

The effect of Lessing's letter was to rescue the Faust-theme from the disrepute into which it had fallen and to make it seem available for the higher purposes of poetry. A new Faust-tragedy thus became, as Schröer expresses it, a problem of the age.* Lessing himself, as is well known, attacked the problem, and it is matter for lasting regret that his *Faust* never saw the light, though Providence had better things in store than any solution which he could have offered. There is no evidence, however, that Goethe was directly influenced by Lessing's letter, though he must have read it. He came by his interest in the subject in his own way, the way of the puppet-play. To this we must now turn.

When the old popular Faust-play was retired in disgrace from the theaters, that was by no means the end of it; it found refuge with a class of men who cared very little for critical theories of the drama, namely, the showmen who amused the young with their wooden puppets. The play soon fell altogether into the hands of these men and by them the earlier dramatic tradition has been continued more or less intact down to our own time. In the early years of this century these plays became objects of scientific interest, so that reports of performances, and in due time complete texts, began to find their way into print. To-day we have a considerable collection of them,† differing a good deal of course in minor *dramatis personae* and in details of plot, but still conforming to the same general type. Unfortunately none of these plays, as we know them, can be identified with the one which Goethe saw. Indeed he may have seen more than one. Still, by a comparison of those we have,

---

* In the Introduction to his edition of *Faust*, p. xxiii.

† Six were printed forty years ago by Scheible, V., 732 ff. These and several others, eight in all, were studied by Creizenach in 1878. Since that time has appeared *Das Schwiegerlingsche Puppenspiel vom Doktor Faust*, herausgegeben von A. Bielschowsky, Brieg, 1882. The latter is based on a stenographic report of a performance given at Brieg in 1877. It is supplied with a good Introduction, and contains, in six parallel columns, a conspectus of the plots of five puppet-plays and Marlowe's *Faustus*.

we can form at least a rough mental picture of the 'legend' that was 'buzzing' in his thoughts at Strassburg in 1770.

Some of the plays begin with a prologue in hell. Charon complains to Pluto that he does not get souls enough for his ferry. Pluto promises to increase his custom by sending devils to mislead men. In one case he promises specifically to have Mephistopheles beguile Dr. Faust of Wittenberg into the study of magic. Most of the plays, however, begin with a brooding soliloquy of Faust, in which he explains why he has taken to magic. Usually it is because he has found no satisfaction in theology. A supernatural voice at his right warns him, while one at his left encourages. In the next scene, as a rule, Wagner comes in and announces that two students have just brought a mysterious book, a *clavis de magica* or the like. Faust is delighted and Wagner now secures permission to employ a fellow-servant for the coarse house-work. The clown comes and is engaged by Wagner for this position. Faust now proceeds to conjure with the book, but in his study instead of in the woods. Various devils appear and Faust selects the swiftest, Mephistopheles, with whom he contracts for twenty-four years' service, signing the paper in his own blood. He then demands diversion and Mephistopheles spirits him away to some princely court, usually that of the Duke of Parma. After he is gone the clown comes, gets into Faust's magic circle, cites the devils to appear, and amuses himself with them. Faust now conjures for the amusement of the court, calling up apparitions of Alexander, David and Goliath, etc. Meanwhile the clown has followed him and contrives to betray the secret of his new master's power. Faust becomes an object of suspicion and is compelled to go away. Then he appears as a penitent. He would return to God, but Mephistopheles beguiles him with the gift of Helena. After this we have a scene in which the clown, as watchman, calls out the hours of the night. At the stroke of twelve Faust is carried off by devils or furies.

We come now to our second retrospect. Goethe tells us, it will be remembered, that he had 'drifted about in all knowledge and early enough come to feel the vanity of it'; also that he had 'made all sorts of experiments in life and always come back more unsatisfied, more tormented.' And then there was his 'mystic-cabbalistic chemistry.' Let us see precisely what these experiences had been, which formed the soil that nourished the roots of *Faust*.

III.

PREPARATORY EXPERIENCES OF GOETHE.

In the fall of 1765 the boy Goethe was deemed ready to leave his father's house in Frankfurt for the university. His own desire was to study the old humanities at Göttingen, but his father insisted upon Leipzig and the law. To Leipzig he accordingly went; cherishing the secret purpose to trouble himself but little with jurisprudence, but to devote himself to those studies which best promised to develop the poet in him.* Half diverted from this purpose by Professor Böhme, to whom he brought letters from home, he took up certain law-lectures only to find them a bore and presently to drop them: he knew, or thought he knew, all that the lecturer saw fit to impart. He began a course in logic, but the study appeared to him frivolous; instead of teaching him to think, it taught him to pick his old simple thoughts to pieces. With philosophy it went no better; that too seemed a matter of words. 'Of the subject in hand,' he writes, 'of the world, of God, I thought I knew about as much as the teacher himself.'† His highest hopes he set on the famous Professor Gellert, but Gellert proved to care more for good handwriting than for poetry. A course in Cicero's *De Oratore*, under the distinguished Ernesti, turned out a little, but not much, more helpful. 'What I wanted,' Goethe writes, 'was a standard of judgment, and this no one seemed to possess.'‡

---

* *Werke*, XXVII., 50 ff.
† *Werke*, XXVII., 53.
‡ *Werke*, XXVII., 67.

What wonder if, under such circumstances, having failed to find a single line of appetizing study, the young student should fall into a pessimistic frame of mind respecting the whole round of academic pursuits? What wonder if it may have seemed to him, in an occasional savage mood, that the learning of the learned was little else than a hypocritical farce of words paraded as a cover for ignorance; a floating bog of conventional verbiage, in which a firm standing-ground of positive knowledge was nowhere to be found? We must of course guard against reading too much of the later Goethe into the life of the youngster at Leipzig. It was no doubt later that moods like these threw their deepest shadow; but even now he began to feed on the very food in all the world most fitted to beget them. In a letter of Oct. 12, 1767, he calls the sentiment *plus (que) les mœurs se raffinent, plus les hommes se dépravent*, a 'truth most worthy of reverence.' This wonderful 'truth' came to him, no doubt, from the great apostle of nature, Jean Jacques Rousseau.* The sentiment is the burden of Rousseau's famous prize Discourse of 1750, and if the main thesis so pleased our young philosopher of seventeen, it is fair to presume that he was no less captivated by the diatribes against the learned which abound in the same essay. Rousseau's doctrine was that civilization is corruption. Its arts and sciences and other boasted refinements have substituted for the good simplicity of nature a bad web of conventionalities, prominent among which are the idle researches and the hair-splitting quibbles of the learned.

Thus Goethe found in Rousseau the antithesis: nature *versus* traditional book-learning.† He heard a voice telling him with passionate eloquence, that the life of the scholar, 'poring over miserable books,' is contrary to nature. And this voice found in

---

* Careful search has failed to discover these exact words in Rousseau's writings, but the Rousseau tinge is unmistakable. The young Goethe, who often wrote French at this time, seems to be stating in language of his own an idea that he had got from reading a French book.

† Or, as Fischer puts it in German, *Urnatur gegen Unnatur.*

his own being a responsive chord which a little later was to be heard vibrating in the great symphony of *Faust*.*

Outside the university, too, the Saxons quarreled with the young Frankfurter's opinions, his poetic taste, even his clothes, his manners and his language, and insisted on making him over without convincing him that they were right and he wrong. At the end of a year's residence we find him writing that he begins to be 'rather dissatisfied with Leipzig.' He has quite fallen out with 'society,' and delights to shut himself up in Auerbach's Hof with his new friend Behrisch and laugh at the Leipzig people.† This Behrisch was a droll genius with a cynical bent and a talent for persiflage. He was eleven years older than Goethe. Memories of these conferences in Auerbach's Hof and of jolly times in the 'cellar' below, lingered in the mind of the younger man and were turned to account in *Faust*. They furnished hints not only for the scene 'Auerbach's Cellar,' but also for the student scene, § in which, in its earlier form, Mephistopheles talks very much as we can imagine Behrisch to have talked, with his youthful auditor's approval, on these occasions. There is evidence, also, that Behrisch contributed in less innocent ways to the initial conception of Mephistopheles. In an extant letter to him Goethe imagines himself playing the very part toward a virtuous girl which Faust plays toward Gretchen.‖ Besides these things there is nothing in

---

* E. g., lines 386–446, 1064–1125.

† *Briefe* I., 82. On the locality cf. the general note to the scene 'Auerbach's Cellar.'

§ Lines 1868, ff.

‖ Letter of Nov. 7, 1767, *Briefe*, I., 133. The writer, be it remembered, sins only in thought, but his language is noteworthy. The seduction of a virtuous girl is an 'affair of the devil' which he, the writer, were he not afraid, would undertake to carry through after 'fourteen days' preparation' (cf. *Faust*, line 2640). And Behrisch is his 'teacher.' The passage ends thus: "Und der Ton und ich zusammen! Es ist komisch. Aber ohne zu schwören ich unterstehe mich schon ein Mädgen zu nennen. Genug Monsieur, alles was sie (Sie) von dem gelehrigsten und fleissigsten ihrer Schüler erwarten können." Note the " schon " and cf. *Faust*, line 2645.

Goethe's Leipzig life that has an obvious bearing upon his great poem. His law studies continued to bore him as often as he gave them a chance. In a letter of October 12, 1767, he writes his sister in a cynical vein of the courses he is pursuing. After dilating on the shortcomings of his teachers and the stupidity of their subject-matter he exclaims: 'So you see how much complete knowledge a *studiosus juris* can have. I'll be hanged if I know anything!' By this time, however, his poetic ardor, which for a time had left him completely in the lurch, had returned in full force. His passion for Annette Schönkopf caused him to seek relief from the torments of a jealous lover by depicting the type in *Die Laune des Verliebten*, his earliest play; while reminiscences of Frankfurt life in its lower strata led to the conception of a second drama, *Die Mitschuldigen*. He also found at last helpful guidance and congenial occupation at the home of the artist Oeser. He was learning many other things, if not much law, when, in the summer of 1768, a severe internal hemorrhage sent him home.

Returning to Frankfurt he found himself doomed for a long time to the role of an invalid. A dangerous illness held him in its grip, bringing him more than once to the brink of death, deepening his character and giving to his thoughts a serious cast. 'In my illness,' he writes to Annette Schönkopf, 'I have learned much that I could have learned nowhere else in the world.'* This alludes, no doubt, to his religious experiences under the tutelage of the pious Fräulein von Klettenberg, the 'beautiful soul' whom he afterwards immortalized in *Wilhelm Meister*. This good lady interested herself deeply in his spiritual condition, and tried to have him make his peace with God in her way. He tells us that he proved but a stubborn pupil, since he could not persuade himself that he had been a very great sinner.† Still, subsequent letters of his show

---

* *Briefe*, I., 183.
† *Werke*, XXVII., 201.

that he was for a time much affected by these pious ministrations.*
He became for a season very devout, and this period of quickened
religious feeling has left its mark here and there upon the language
of *Faust*.†

Of importance also were the studies in magic and alchemy which
he now took up. His physician was a member of Fräulein von
Klettenberg's pietistic coterie, and a believer in alchemy. He
claimed to have a panacea which he had made but dared not use
for fear of the law. He also gave out that his wonderful remedy
could be made, indeed, since there were personal moral factors
involved, could best be made, by each one for himself; and he was
in the habit of recommending certain books that would be helpful
in this direction. In December, 1768, Goethe was taken suddenly
and violently ill so that he despaired of life. The anxious mother
persuaded the doctor that now, if ever, was the time for the cure-all.
Reluctantly the doctor administered his salt and the patient forthwith began to improve. ‡ This was enough for Fräulein von Klettenberg. She became at once deeply interested in the wonderful
medicine, and through her Goethe says he was himself ‘inoculated
with the disease.’ He set about reading the doctor's books and as
soon as possible equipped a laboratory and began a line of fantastic
experiments with retort and crucible.

The first of the books read was Welling's *Opus Mago-Cabbalisti-
cum et Theosophicum*. This is a German treatise dealing with
alchemy, magic, astrology, etc. The first part treats of salt, the
second of sulphur, the third of mercury. It is illustrated with cabbalistic drawings and has various appendixes relating to the philosopher's stone. The whole is intensely Christian, the argument

---

* ‘I am as I was, save that I am on a somewhat better footing with our Lord
God and his dear son Jesus Christ’; letter of April 13, 1770, *Briefe*, I., 232.

† E. g., lines 771-85, 1178-85, 1210-19.

‡ This story of the wonderful medicine, supposed by Loeper (Goethe's *Werke*, Hempel
edition, XXI., 352) to have been sodium sulphate or Glauber's salt, is found in *Dichtung
und Wahrheit*, bk. 8.

being based throughout on quotations from the Bible.   Its intellectual character will appear from this specimen: ' So then it must
surely and incontestably follow for the adept (Naturgeübten) that
fire, salt and gold are at the root absolutely one and the same in
kind, and that the red solar and the white lunar sulphur are in
their basis and origin identical, namely, spiritual gold and silver;
and that he who knows these two sulphurs, and knows how to find,
compound in the right proportion, unite and fix them, must neces-
sarily come to see the splendid, radiant, indestructible and immortal
body of the man Adam.' *   Reminiscences of Welling's jargon
freely adapted † meet us here and there in *Faust*.

Once embarked on this line of study, the young convalescent
with time on his hands began following up Welling's references to
older authorities and so was led to concern himself with Paracelsus,
Van Helmont and others.   A work that gave him particular
pleasure, he tells us, was the so-called *Aurea Catena Homeri*, ‡ in
which he found ' nature represented, though fantastically, in a
beautiful concatenation.' This conception of nature as a grand
harmony of interconnected parts, each with its own relation to the
activity of the whole, underlies Faust's vision of the macrocosm.

But the most important result of these lucubrations was doubtless, as Loeper suggests, § the idea of a spiritualized nature, the
conception of the world as a living manifestation of divinity.   This
conception fell in well with his own early prepossessions.   As a boy
he had felt that ' the God who stands in immediate relation to
nature, recognizing it as his work and loving it, was the real God.' ∥
At the same time the Bible taught him that this Creator of the
world could enter into close relations with men.   And so as a boy

---

* Page 30.

† Treated "nach eignem Belieben," as Goethe says in *Dichtung und Wahrheit;
Werke*, XXVII., 204.

‡ Cf. *Aurea Catena Homeri*, von Hermann Kopp, Braunschweig, 1880.

§ Goethe's *Werke*, Hempel edition, XXI., 350.

∥ *Werke*, XXVI., 63.

he had actually built an altar and burned incense in order to 'draw near' to the great World-God in 'good Old Testament fashion.' And now he found his mystical alchemists teaching, or rather assuming as a matter of course, that nature is altogether spiritual; that the stars and planets, as well as lesser terrestrial objects and chemical substances, were each controlled by an indwelling spirit which could variously influence and be influenced by the human mind. Paracelsus tells of an *Archeus terrae*, or Lord of earth, whom he conceives as a director of nature's laboratory; Giordano Bruno of a central *anima terrae*. The same conception of an Earth-spirit is found also in other writers known to have been read by Goethe. Now the knowledge of all these spirits — astrology proper is constantly mixed up with alchemy and demonology — was regarded by the cabbalists as the supreme science. It was called 'natural magic,' and was held to be far nobler than the vulgar art of conjuring up devils. To this high art Goethe's Faust applies himself at first, but he is also an adept in the lower magic.

It would be idle to inquire how far the young Goethe believed in this lore; * enough that he found here that which the poet in him could feed upon. His scientific and philosophic intellect was all unschooled, and Spinoza had not yet come to clear the air for him. Might there not be something in it, after all, this occult wisdom that had for ages occupied the best minds in Europe ? Might not this wonderful Nature, could one but properly get into communication with the divinity that speaks in her visible forms, have some strange high secret to tell; some simple, universal, joy-giving message that should put an end to the 'uncertain lot of humanity,' ren-

---

* At the end of the eighth book of *Dichtung und Wahrheit* Goethe himself attempts to describe retrospectively the peculiar Weltanschauung at which he had now arrived. He calls it a mixture of Hermetism, mysticism and cabbalism, on the basis of neo-Platonism. For a while he seems to have taken it very seriously, but he very soon drifted away from it.

der the weary plodding of the schools absurd, and make man a partaker in the life of the gods?

It was under the spell of such vague, vain dreams as these that the puppet-play magician, who had devoted himself to magic out of disgust for traditional learning, began to acquire for Goethe a new and personal interest: he saw in Faust a symbol of his own strivings. In a letter of Feb. 13, 1769, he compares himself with a 'night-brooding magus,' and says further on: 'A great scholar is seldom a great philosopher, and he who has laboriously turned the leaves of many books despises the easy simple book of nature; and yet there is nothing true but what is simple'. Add to this that Goethe speaks of *Faust* as a subject that 'had (already) taken root' in his mind at Strassburg in the autumn of 1770, and we shall have no occasion to doubt the accuracy of the poet's memory when, in a letter to Zelter, written June 1, 1831, he dates the first conception of *Faust* back to the year 1769.

But the moment the young dreamer began to identify himself with Faust, that moment it was all up with the wickedness of the old magician. For the son of the eighteenth century could see no damnable perversity in any man's aspirations for higher, clearer, surer, simpler, more inspiriting knowledge than he had thus far found. Nor could the possession of power, as an accessory of knowledge, seem to him anything else than an unmixed blessing. And so the Faust of the legend soon began to take on the features of a misunderstood and maligned searcher after truth. Here, too, Goethe was helped by his reading. One of the books read with great interest at this time, he tells us,* was Arnold's *Kirchen- und Ketzerhistorien*. From this he learned that many a famous heretic whom orthodox tradition has labelled 'crazy' or 'godless,' was in reality a man of the highest purposes, who taught what he taught because he believed it to be the truth. Thus he was led to ponder on the sad fact that it is the man of exceptional insight and nobility

---

* *Werke* XXVII., 217.

of motive whom the people are most prone to crucify, or to pillory posthumously as a monster of wickedness.* An instance of this was presented in Paracelsus, with whom, as we saw, Goethe was led to concern himself in this year of fruitful idleness at Frankfurt.

Paracelsus was born about 1490. Setting out to learn the healing art (his father was a physician) he applied himself to the usual studies, but soon became disgusted, forsook the schoolmen and went to live among the miners of Tyrol. Here he studied chemistry, mineralogy and the facts of disease, in his own way. Acquiring reputation thus, he was in the prime of life made town-physician of Basel and soon after appointed to lecture on medicine at the University. Here he bitterly denounced the traditional medical learning of the day and insisted on the importance of studying facts rather than old opinions. The violence of his assaults upon venerable authorities soon involved him in trouble and he was forced to leave Basel. He then entered upon extensive wanderings which lasted many years. In 1541 the Archbishop of Salzburg offered him a home and protection. He accepted the offer, but died that same year.

Here was a new picture for the mental gallery of our young poet: A gifted youth impatient of tradition; his father a physician devoted to the old, blind routine, himself an ardent seeker after higher things; this youth as man driven from his university chair by ignorant prejudice for telling the truth as he had learned it at first hand in the school of nature; for years a wanderer on the face of the earth; a moment of settled, orderly activity with high hopes for the future, then, death. — Insensibly the features of the legendary Faust blended in Goethe's mind with those of the actual Paracelsus.

Such, then, were the musings which Goethe took with him when, in the spring of 1770, with health nearly restored, he again left home to resume his law studies at Strassburg. Had these musings

* Cf. *Faust*, lines 590-3.

taken dramatic form? Had he made any progress in the elabora-
tion of a plot? Was the figure of Gretchen already in his mind?
Probably not; at least there is no evidence to that effect, and the
letter to Zelter above referred to does not imply anything of the kind.
Of one thing, however, we may be sure: Had he commenced writing
at this time, the result would have had little similarity in form or substance to the earliest scenes of *Faust* as we know them. To produce these he needed that general awakening and liberation which
came to him at Strassburg, chiefly through the influence of Herder.
Thus far he had been but little affected by the new ideas that were
beginning to make themselves felt in the field of German letters.
At Leipzig he had fallen naturally into the ways of the French
'school,' that is, he had learned to think of poetry as the accom-
plishment of the cultivated, a matter of regularity, rhetorical point,
and elegance of diction. He had himself written two plays in
alexandrines, and a number of songs that speak more of the conscious craftsman than of the glowing soul. And whatever he had
written had usually been praised by admiring friends.

But now at Strassburg, after he had been there some five months,
enjoying life in a congenial and stimulating society, studying a little
law, and a little medicine, and reading this and that in a desultory
way, he came for the first time into contact with a man of powerful,
keen, original intellect; a man who, though only five years older
than himself, was already the author of published writings which
showed him to be the peer of Lessing in knowledge and critical insight. And this man did not praise him at all, but ridiculed him
and found fault with him at every turn. For Herder the Frenchified
German poetry of the day was simply an abomination. In his published writings he had attacked the prestige of the word 'classical,' and insisted that the essence of poetry is 'singing nature.'
Especially he had dwelt upon the idea that good poetry must be
deeply rooted in the national character of the people. Every people,
he had argued, expresses itself first in poetry, which is thus the

mother tongue of humanity. Its mission is to speak from the heart and to the heart of the people in the people's language.

The views of Herder were somewhat extreme and one-sided. He undervalued the formal, artistic side of poetry, and his conception of 'nature' and 'the natural,' like that of Rousseau and the eighteenth century sentimentalists generally, was more or less fantastic and unsound. Still, considering the time and the prevailing taste, his ideas were wholesome. In any case, set forth as they were with a dogmatic positiveness that would brook no opposition or qualification, they could not fail to make a deep impression upon Goethe. At Herder's instigation he began to collect popular songs and to study Ossian and Homer, and very soon he had caught the full force of that intoxication which was to be known to posterity as the 'storm and stress period.' French authors and French taste were abjured as antiquated and worthless. Nature, originality, force, — these were the new watchwords. Down with the rules and conventions that hinder the free flight of genius! — such was the battle-cry.

We see now why Goethe hid his interest in *Faust* from Herder. It was not that he was ashamed of the subject, for that, as being intensely German, was of the very kind to commend itself to him under the new light; but he dreaded harsh and unsympathetic criticism. So he kept his musings to himself, but continued to ponder and to read on the theme, as leisure offered itself in the intervals of his academic pursuits and his visits to Sesenheim. For we have now reached the period of his romance with Friederike Brion, which was also in its way a part of his preparation for *Faust*. Friederike, a girl of eighteen, was the daughter of a Lutheran pastor living at Sesenheim, a few miles from Strassburg. Being introduced at the Brion house by a fellow-student, Goethe at once fell in love with Friederike, who was also pleased with him. For a while the romance was allowed to take its course with no thought of the future, but presently Goethe saw that all his own interests, both higher and lower, required him to retreat. For this act of unromantic perfidy, which common sense has always found it easy to justify, his own conscience did not acquit him. There is a faint echo of remorse in the fact that for some time to come he is very deeply interested as poet in a certain tragic situation, namely, that of a simple, naïve girl with a 'superior' lover whose worldly plans would be interfered with by marriage. The situation recurs in four of his early plays. In the first, *Götz von Berlichingen*, the tragic nemesis falls only on the perfidious lover : Weislingen is poisoned and Marie gets a better husband. In *Clavigo*, Marie dies of a broken heart, while her worthless lover is killed by her brother. In *Egmont*, the lover remains faithful, but Clärchen, having given her honor and therewith her worldly all, for love's sake, voluntarily follows Egmont to death. In *Faust*, the tragic pathos is thrown altogether upon the girl : she suffers an appalling fate, but her lover goes unpunished save by his own conscience.

In August, 1771, Goethe returned, as a licensed practitioner of law, to Frankfurt, where he remained until the following May, when he went to Wetzlar. In speaking of this period he says that *Faust* 'was already well under way,'* an expression which, while it does not prove that anything had yet been written down, does suggest that the plan of the work must have been pretty clearly worked out by that time. This accords, too, with a statement of Goethe in a letter written to Wilhelm von Humboldt, March 17, 1832, in which he says that the 'conception' of *Faust*, clear from the first in the days of his youth, had lain in his mind over sixty years.† What was this conception ? We shall find abundant evidence of vacillation and change affecting both plot and characters. We know that the poet's 'plan' in a certain sense grew with his

---

* "War schon vorgerückt"; *Werke*, XXVIII., 98.

† "Es sind über 60 Jahre, dass die Conception des *Faust* bei mir jugendlich, von vorn herein klar, die ganze Reihenfolge hin weniger ausführlich vorlag."

own growth, and that the bulk of what was to go into the poem could not have been foreseen at this time. What, then, was that ' general conception ' to which he was fond of insisting in his old age that he had remained faithful from the first? The question can only be answered conjecturally and with more or less liability to error. It must be answered, too, in rather general terms. Stated in the form of a project the plan was something like this:

The legend will furnish the external setting and costume of the drama, and the puppet-play, with its popular tone, its free use of the supernatural, and its indifference to conventional technique, will supply a rough outline of the action. But the characters will speak the thoughts and feelings of Goethe and his contemporaries. First, Faust will be introduced as a young university teacher, chafing under the limitations of his knowledge, and hence devoting himself to magic. This Faust will proceed to conjure with a book as in the puppet-play. At this point, however, Goethe will deviate from the legend. His Faust will call up neither a number of devils from whom to chose the swiftest, as in the puppet-plays and in Lessing's *Faust*, nor yet the ' prince of hell ' as in the Christlich Meynenden narrative, but, instead, the Earth-Spirit, a personification of terrestrial nature in her restless, awe-inspiring, inscrutable energy. Then, just as the prince of hell in the legend refuses, on the ground that he is a sovereign, to do Faust's will, but promises to send, and then does send, a minion of his to be the magician's servant,* so Goethe's Earth-Spirit, as a being of higher order, will spurn Faust's friendly advances, but will after all send a spirit of inferior rank, with whom the magician *can* enter into relations of intimacy. As the Earth-Spirit vanishes, Faust will be interrupted by his famulus Wagner, to whom he will proceed to lay down the law anent the foolishness of the book-worm's ideals. Mephistopheles will then appear in the form of a dog, and, so the poet now intends, remain in that form for a while as Faust's familiar before taking human shape.

---

* Scheible's *Kloster* II., 80.

Then, somehow, an alliance between the two is to be provided for, but the poet has not now in mind, in 1772, an agreement like that introduced later in lines 1692 ff. As friend and servant of Professor Faust, Mephistopheles will be given an opportunity to advise a newly-arrived freshman with respect to academic life. Very soon, however, Faust will leave his professorship to assume the rôle of a gay young cavalier seeing the world with his friend. First he will appear in Auerbach's Keller and perform there various tricks ascribed to him in the legend. Then he will fall in love with Gretchen. Led on by imperious passion, but without becoming a conscienceless villain, he will ruin her and cause the death of her mother and brother. Fleeing arrest he will be away from her for a time, and then, learning somehow that she is in prison for child-murder, will return in a frenzy of remorse to liberate her, and will thus be a witness to her half-insane ravings and her death in the prison. Then (the transition not yet provided for), he will go to a princely court and do conjurer's tricks for the amusement of the great. Somehow (the scene not yet clearly motivated), he will be united with Helena and have by her a marvellous son. At last he will find a settled activity of some large and useful kind, and die happy in the thought that his name will live after him and that coming generations will profit by the good work he has done.

And will this Faust be saved? Suffice it to say, for the present, that he is at any rate not to be damned as in the legend. A young poet of a serious turn does not deliberately send his own soul to hell. Moreover this poet is a Pelagian in theology. He tells us so expressly in explaining how he came to drift away from the pietists.* They believed in total depravity, he did not; they in passive reliance on divine grace, he in active self-help. This Pelagianism now underlies subconsciously his conception of Faust. God is the Eternal

---

* At the beginning of the fifteenth book of *Dichtung und Wahrheit*. The passage is important for the understanding of *Faust*. See also below p. lix and cf. the note to lines 328-9.

Pardoner. If a man means well and 'strives,' he will not be lost for following the impulses of his nature whereof God is the author. He may go wrong, but his wrong-doing will be a mistake, and God pardons mistakes. Still this matter of his hero's final 'salvation' is not now prominent in his thoughts. As man and as poet he is interested deeply in this world, but not much in the legendary heaven and hell. In fact, as we shall see,* he has substituted for the supernatural powers of tradition, conceptions of his own, which render the question of 'salvation' in the traditional sense all but meaningless. At any rate it is perfectly certain that he has never intended for a moment that his Faust, like that of the legend, should go to perdition at the last.

Regarding Goethe's preparation for the first stage of his poem as now complete, let us see how the text as we know it took shape under his hands.

IV.

THE GENESIS OF THE FIRST PART.

1. *The Pre-Weimarian Scenes.*

The portion of Faust now to be considered had its origin in the most fervid period of Goethe's youthful storm and stress, being contemporary with the grandiose titanism of *Prometheus*, the brooding Weltschmerz of *Werther*, the stormy passion of *Clavigo* and *Stella*, and the wild satirical humor of *Satyros* and *Pater Brey*. It was for the poet a time of utmost mental tension, of swiftly changing moods and manifold excitements; of high-soaring dreams and thoughts of suicide; of lonely, rapturous communions with nature and of enthusiastic friendships. It was the time also of his love for Lili.

Work with the pen upon *Faust* is commonly thought to have begun in 1773, but it is quite possible that certain scenes were writ-

---

* Below, p. lix.

ten down in prose the preceding year. Not until early in 1773, however, is Goethe known to have employed anywhere the Hans Sachs *Knüttelvers*, or doggerel tetrameter, which is the prevailing meter of the earliest scenes of *Faust*. That the composition was in progress during 1773 we have at least two indications: first, a remark of Goethe in a letter from Italy dated March 1, 1788, to the effect that the writing out of *Faust* was a very different thing then from what it was fifteen years before; secondly, the fact that Goethe's friend Gotter, in a jocose letter of July, 1773, asks for a copy of *Faust* as soon as its author shall have ' stormed it out.'*

The year 1774 furnishes several notices relating to *Faust*. In the summer of that year Goethe recited to F. H. Jacobi the ballad of the ' King of Thule.'† Boie visited Goethe in October, 1774, and was much impressed by certain scenes of *Faust* that were read to him. Dec. 20, 1774, Knebel wrote to Bertuch: ' I have a mass of fragments from him (Goethe), amongst others some belonging to a *Dr. Faust*, in which there are some very fine things indeed. He pulls the bits of manuscript out of every corner of his room.' For the year 1775 we have various notices, partly in Goethe's own letters, partly in those of his friends, which show that *Faust* was progressing and had already acquired a good deal of celebrity in literary circles. After the poet's settlement in Weimar no further progress can be traced for some twelve years, during which he became another man.

---

* "Schick mir dafür den Doctor Faust,
        Sobald dein Kopf ihn ausgebraust!"

   Goethe met Gotter at Wetzlar in the summer of 1772. The verb "ausbrausen" suggests that Gotter knew not only that his friend had a *Faust* under way, but also something of its character. Had Goethe, who returned to Frankfurt in the fall of 1772, read from his prose Faust-scenes to Gotter at Wetzlar? Did Gotter know by hearsay that the new *Faust* would be ' stormy'? Or did he simply assume that anything written by the Goethe whom he had known would be ' stormed out'? Cf. Herbst, *Goethe in Wetzlar*, p. 154.

   † *Dichtung und Wahrheit*, bk. 14. There is no certainty, however, that the ballad was originally written for *Faust*. Cf. Kögel in *Vierteljahrschrift für Litteraturgeschichte* I., 59.

The chaotic Faust-manuscript which Goethe took with him to Weimar in November, 1775, has never been found, and its character and contents were until quite recently matters of speculation. Very lately, however, through a lucky accident, the loss of the original manuscript has been in part made good. At some time during his early years at Weimar, Goethe loaned his *Faust* to Fräulein Luise von Göchhausen, a maid-of-honor at the court, and she transcribed it at length in a manuscript book of literary extracts. Here the copy remained unnoticed among the effects of the Göchhausen family until January, 1887, when it was accidentally discovered by Erich Schmidt, who at once published it.* The copy shows verse and prose mixed up together in true Shakespearian style. The word 'act' or 'scene' is not employed, but each separate dramatic picture is headed with a sort of stage-direction indicating the situation. There is evidence that the copying was done with very great care.

The Göchhausen *Faust* consists of some twenty 'scenes,' of which all but the first three pertain to the tragedy of Gretchen. It begins with a scene substantially identical in form and matter with the present lines 354–605; containing, that is, Faust's first soliloquy, vision of the macrocosm, dialogue with the Earth-Spirit, and dialogue with Wagner. Next comes a conversation between Mephistopheles and a student. The text is mainly that of the present lines 1868–2050, but instead of the cynical comments on law and theology, we find the devil warning the youngster against girls and gaming, and recommending him to Frau Sprizbierlein's boarding-house. After this comes 'Auerbach's Cellar,' the first eight lines in verse as in the final version, the remainder of the scene, except the songs, in prose. The matter of the dialogue corresponds pretty nearly to that of the later version, but one noteworthy fact is that here Faust and not Mephistopheles performs the tricks. The

* *Goethe's Faust in ursprünglicher Gestalt* nach der Göchhausenschen Abschrift herausgegeben von Erich Schmidt. 8. Abdruck. Weimar, Böhlau, 1910.

next scene is a short one of four verses containing a dialogue between Faust and Mephistopheles about a cross they are passing.
The lines were rejected in the revision and published with the Paralipomena. This is followed by the tragedy of Gretchen, substantially as we know it from the final revision. The earlier scenes,
Faust's meeting with Gretchen, his rakish talk with Mephistopheles
about her, their visit to her room with the jewels, her girlish glee
over the ornaments, the talk about the greedy priests, the scene at
Martha's house with the Padua story, the dialogue about bearing
false witness, the promenade and summer-house scenes, — all these
are, aside from spelling and insignificant textual differences, the
same and the same in sequence, as in the present text. Directly
after 3216, however, comes the lyric monologue „ Meine Ruh ift
hin," followed by the catechism scene and the scenes 'At the Well'
and 'Zwinger.'* Next comes the scene 'Cathedral' with the explicit heading 'Obsequies of Gretchen's Mother.' After Gretchen's
swoon comes the speech of Valentin, lines 3620–45, then a short
dialogue between Faust and Mephistopheles comprising the present
lines 3650–59, and then the verses 3342–69. Then follow the
prose scene, but without the heading 'Dismal Day,' the witch scene
at the place of execution, and the final scene 'Prison,' the latter in
prose throughout and without the consoling 'voice from above' at
the end.

At first it was generally assumed that this so-called 'Urfaust'
told the whole story respecting the progress of Goethe's great poem
up to the time of his removal to Weimar. Very soon, however,
it became evident that such is not the case. There is matter in the
First Part which is not in the Göchhausen manuscript, but is
shown by evidence of style and language to be of early origin.† The
probability is that the sheets which came into the hands of Fräu-

---

* On the meaning of this untranslatable word see the general note to the scene
'Zwinger.'

† Cf. *Vierteljahrschrift für Litteraturgeschichte*, II., 545 ff.

lein Göchhausen were a 'clean copy' of such scenes and parts of scenes as Goethe himself at the time regarded as complete. Other sheets containing bits of dialogue and partly elaborated 'concepts,' the meaning and connection of which would hardly be clear to any-one but himself, were retained by him. It is also very likely that he took with him to Weimar, in various stages of mental elabora-tion, Faust-scenes that he had not written down at all.

But while we must be on our guard against supposing that no-thing in the poem can be of pre-Weimarian origin unless it is found in the Göchhausen manuscript, the 'Urfaust' is still of very great importance, since the study of it shows us clearly how the Faust-theme had presented itself to the poet in his early years, and what aspects of it had interested him. In the first place there had risen prominently into the field of his imagination the figure of Faust pre-vious to the compact. This Faust he had conceived, partly on the basis of the puppet-play, partly on the basis of personal experience, as a youngish professor oppressed by a sense of the vanity of his learning, and sick at heart of shamming knowledge before his stu-dents; as a man who is not troubled by the devils and spooks of the theological small fry about him, and so has none of their reasons for dreading magic; a man, however, who does believe in the divinity of nature, and, being possessed of vague longings for wonderful knowledge, power and happiness, supposed to be obtainable through communication with elemental spirits, has de-voted himself to magic, to see if he can get into such communica-tion. This initial conception the young artist had then developed with true poetic instinct by means of two powerful contrasts: Faust the pigmy in presence of the Earth-Spirit, a symbol of the vast, inscrutable, unfeeling energy of nature, that nature which had seemed to Werther 'an eternally devouring monster'*; then, Faust the giant in presence of Wagner, the contented book-worm happy in chewing the cud of traditional learning.

---

* "Ich sehe nichts als ein ewig verschlingendes, ewig wiederkäuendes Ungeheuer"; First Part of *Werther*, letter of Aug. 18.

Then, in the second place, the poet had caught and fixed a vision of the same Faust after the *salto mortale* with Mephistopheles. This Faust he had conceived as a rakish seducer, subject, however, to qualms of conscience and fits of high sentiment; a 'supersensual, sensual lover'; a wanderer without home and without ties, who yields all too easily to the pull of lawless passion and then, when he learns of the ruin he has wrought, falls into a paroxysm of rage and remorse.

Then, thirdly, there was the figure of Gretchen, whose tragic story, unfolded in a series of powerful pictures, had soon overshadowed all else in the poet's interest.

These were the principal features of the *Faust* that Goethe took to Weimar. Incidentally, however, he had found in the theme an opportunity to record some of his reminiscences of academic life. The dialogue between Mephistopheles and a newly arrived freshman offered a superb setting for his satirical humor, while a scene of coarse revelry in Auerbach's Cellar suggested itself naturally both on legendary and on personal grounds. It is possible that these student scenes, which in the Göchhausen *Faust* are here and there somewhat boyish, were the first portions of the poem to be thought out.

Turning now from what is in the 'Urfaust' to what is not in it, we note first that the transition from the first to the second Faust, from the disgruntled professor to the ready libertine, the introduction of Mephistopheles and the motivation of his permanent connection with Faust, are still to be provided for. Secondly, there is a noteworthy gap in the love-tragedy: it is necessary to account for Faust's long absence from Gretchen during the time of her extremity. 'Insipid joys'* have been promised, but the picture has yet to be filled in. Thirdly, all that part of the action which was to follow the death of Gretchen is still untouched.

---

* Prose scene, 'Trüber Tag,' line 10. The 'Urfaust' has " in abgeschmackten Freuden" instead of the later " in abgeschmackten Zerstreuungen."

And when we pass from the matter of plot to that of portraiture, we are struck, first of all, by the fact that the character of Faust is here somewhat hard and unamiable.   He discloses but little suscep-tibility to the higher and holier moods of humanity.   One is not quite prepared, to be sure, for his sudden depravity as lover of Gretchen, but the dissonance is much less sharp than in the final version, since nothing has gone before that makes such rakishness unthinkable.*   Goethe has imagined a man whose disgust with study and sense of limitation have become an acute disease, so that he is ready to break with the moral order; and then, in adjusting this conception to the legend, the poet has chosen to ally his Faust with that particular devil of his own acquaintance whose whisper-ings were referred to above.†   There was no inner necessity for so doing.   There is no natural connection between an unsatisfied craving for knowledge and — libertinism.   ' I would fain be a god, but cannot, so I will be a Don Juan,' is not good psychology, not a natural evolution of character, and in introducing it into *Faust* Goethe prepared difficulties for himself.   It is, of course, to be ad-mitted that the idea of a disappointed dreamer resolving some day in desperation to quit his brooding and enjoy himself in the world, is in itself perfectly natural; only one does not expect the leopard to change his spots instantly on escaping from the cage.   It may be added, too, that the difficulties just referred to reside not so much in the mere fact that the professor becomes a sensualist as that, in so doing, he passes into a new world.   The first Faust is the hero of a symbolical action, who has to do with magic books and Earth-spirits, but the second is the hero of a perfectly natural love-story. As we shall see further on, this early interlocking of two worlds in one and the same action was destined to make trouble.

Consistently with what has just been said, Mephistopheles ap-pears in the ' Urfaust ' as a rake's friend who has nothing about him,

---

* That is, no such passages as lines 614-22, 762-84, 1009-10, 1178-85, 1194-1201,1210-23.
† Page xxv., foot-note.

except perhaps his magic horses, to suggest that he is not an ordinary human reprobate. His relation to Faust is that of a despised but indispensable servant. There has been as yet no thought of a compact like the one finally introduced. Faust can terminate his relation with Mephistopheles at any moment.* Mephistopheles is not concerned to win Faust by making sensual pleasure attractive, but only to do as he is bid and in so doing to expose his master to the torments of conscience. Faust uses his servant as an abettor of his lust, but professes to despise him and occasionally denounces him as a beast and a monster.† At the same time he insists that he ‘must’ do the bidding of this servant.‡ Such a relation is rational only upon one supposition, namely, that Mephistopheles is a personification of that instinct which leads a man to follow his sensual promptings when he knows that his conscience will presently put him on the rack for it. In this way only can we understand this early Mephistopheles, this ‘tormentor’ who has not yet received any of the touches that make his later self, in the words of Freytag, the ‘most lovable of all devils.’§ His character, as well as that of Faust, awaits the deepening, broadening and sobering of Goethe’s own nature, which came with his first decade in Weimar.

2. *The Fragment of* 1790.

As was said above, there is no evidence of progress upon *Faust* between 1775 and 1788, though Goethe’s letters and journals for this period give us a very complete record of his doings.‖ The reasons for this stagnation of the work are well known. They are to be sought at first in the manifold distractions, later in the engross-

---

* Line 2638.

† Lines 3207, 3536.

‡ Lines 3072, 3360.

§ *Technik des Dramas*, p. 48.

‖ The oft-repeated statement that portions of the *Helena* were read in the Weimar court circle in 1780 is erroneous. It goes back to Riemer’s *Mittheilungen* II., 581, but Riemer misconstrued a passage in Goethe’s diary which referred to Hasse’s oratorio of *Helena*. Cf. Kuno Fischer, *Goethe’s Faust*, p. 249.

ing duties of the new life; then also in the gradual alienation from his former self which came with the momentous change that took place in his character and his conception of the poetic art. The storm and stress subsided. Practical work exercised its sobering influence. Intercourse with people of high refinement led to a better opinion of form, in life as well as in art. His love for Frau von Stein brought new ideals of womanhood and opened new vistas of poetic creation. He began to look back with little pride or pleasure upon the insurgent, formless, extravagant productions of an earlier day. His feeling for nature underwent a change. Journeys to Switzerland and the Harz, scientific observation, a riper knowledge of Spinoza's philosophy, and, finally, the mere lapse of time, begot a calmer attitude in presence of the world's mystery. The awful Sphinx became the benignant Teacher, and the chief lesson she had to teach was the lesson of bit-by-bit development, which led him to recognize his own kinship with all that lives.*

Thus we understand why it was that the Weimar courtier, when the spirit moved him to higher poetic creation, was not led to complete the old projects, but to begin new ones like *Iphigenie* and *Tasso*, which accorded better with his present moods. And we see, too, why even these new projects could not advance to a satisfactory completion: the needed leisure and serenity of mind were lacking. The poet felt himself 'entangled in a net' and the inner conflict between the artist and the man of affairs produced at last a dissonance in his life which he himself refers to as a 'terrible malady.'† Release became imperatively necessary.

On escaping to Italy in September 1786, he took with him his manuscript of *Faust*, but it is a year and half before we hear of any work upon it. By that time his 'intellectual new-birth' was

---

* Cf. Kalischer, *Goethe's Verhältniss zur Naturwissenschaft* in the Hempel edition of the works, XXXIII., p xlix., ff. ; also Thomas, *Goethe and the Development Hypothesis* in the *Open Court* for March 15, 1888.

† *Werke*, Hempel edition, XXIV., 143. Cf. Thomas's *Goethe's Tasso*, p. xxxii.

accomplished: the dissonance had disappeared and he had once more 'found himself as poet.' Feb. 16, 1788, he writes from Rome with regard to his literary work: ' Now there is almost nothing more before my nose but the hill *Tasso* and the mountain *Faustus*. I shall not rest day or night until both are finished. For both I have a singular inclination and, of late, wonderful prospects and hopes. All these resumptions of old ideas, these returns to subjects from which I thought myself estranged forever, and to which I hardly dreamed of being equal, give me great delight.'*

Under date of March 1, 1788, in the *Italienische Reise*, we read: ' It has been a fruitful week that seems to me in the retrospect like a month. First the plan of *Faust* was made, and I hope I have been successful in this operation. Of course it is a different thing, writing the piece out now from what it was fifteen years ago. I think it will lose nothing in the process, especially since I believe I have now rediscovered the thread. As to the tone of the whole, too, I am of good cheer. I have lately worked out a new scene and, if I smoke the paper, I should think no one would be able to pick out the old matter.'†

This new scene, as we know from Eckermann,‡ was the

---

* Letter to Karl August; *Briefe*, viii., 347.

† This passage has given much trouble. Goethe speaks here of ' making the plan of *Faust*,' as if he had not had a plan before, and further on, as if to reinforce this implication, remarks that the principal scenes had been written down "gleich so ohne Concept." And yet in his old age, as we have seen, he insisted repeatedly that the conception of *Faust* had lain clear in his mind from the days of his youth. The seeming inconsistency is to be explained in this way : The early plan was vague and general on its philosophical side. The young poet, starting, as always, from a mental picture rather than an abstraction, had conceived a *career* and had portrayed incidents of it here and there. But the *meaning* of the career, and the inner logic of his hero's development had not been thoroughly thought out, and in painting his separate pictures he had paid little attention to these things. When he resumed work in 1788, this was the matter that troubled him and necessitated ' making his plan ' anew. Years before, he had provided mentally for a thread of dramatic logic on which his beads were to be strung, and had then lost that thread. Now, in 1788, he felicitates himself for a moment as he *thinks* he has *re*-discovered the old thread. In fact, however, he will find that the old thread is worthless and that he must provide a new one. See below p. lix.

‡ *Gespräche mit Goethe*, under date of Apr. 10, 1829.

'Witch's Kitchen,' whereby the poet, now sojourning in the Villa Borghese at Rome, had attempted to explain the transition from the first to the second of the somewhat incongruous Fausts whose pictures he found peering out at him from the old, yellow, thumb-worn, unstitched manuscript that he had brought with him from the foggy north. He had given his learned professor an elixir of youth, which was at the same time a love-philtre, and had thus transferred to the devil, in some measure at least, the initial responsibility for Gretchen's ruin. Had this been his intention from the first? Doubtful and yet possible. One reads the Göchhausen *Faust* in vain for any suggestion that its hero was thought of as an old man. He has been teaching ten years, which suggests a man in the prime of life. All the emotions of the first Faust are those of youth, specifically those of the youthful Goethe; while those of the second Faust are such as the young Goethe felt *would* have been his, had he been the villain which he was not. The legend makes Faust devote himself to magic soon after taking his degree. On the other hand, the popular drama, needing a definite point of time for its action, and fixing its attention mainly upon the awful fate of Faust at the end of the twenty-four years, naturally introduced him as an oldish man. One of the puppet-plays begins: 'Countless years I have now been brooding,' etc.* So the artists, notably Rembrandt, conceived Faust as an oldish man and this conception has become the familiar one. Thus Goethe had good legendary grounds for introducing his incipient magician as a man well along in years; and while it is very doubtful whether that was his intention at first, still he found nothing in what he had written which was flatly opposed to such an assumption.† This assumption being made, the rejuvenation of Faust's passions by means of a love-potion presented itself as the simplest motivation of his conduct toward Gretchen.

---

* The opening of the Schwiegerling puppet-play ; see above p, xxi.

† For the teacher of only ten years' experience *might* be thought of as having begun to teach somewhat late in life.

Besides this scene, in spite of Goethe's fine resolutions, *Faust* seems to have made no more progress for some time to come. He may have written some portion of the scene 'Forest and Cavern' while still in Italy, but this is uncertain. The 'hill' prevailed over the 'mountain' and continued to prevail long after his return to Weimar in June, 1788. By midsummer, 1789, *Tasso* was at last complete, and not long afterwards, it would seem, *Faust* was again taken up. By this time, however, Goethe had given up the thought of finishing the work immediately. Just why, we can at least guess. The 'plan' proved after all difficult to manage. The happy creative mood, the joy in the resumption of old projects, which had come to him for a moment in Italy, were not now always at his command. Absorbed in reminiscences of the south, he could not always go out of himself at will and return to the thoughts and feelings of his early manhood. Perhaps the magnitude and the technical difficulties of the subject oppressed him. Nevertheless, his *Faust* had been promised for the new edition of his works just then going through the press of Göschen at Leipzig; and so it was that he decided to half-satisfy the public and his own conscience by revising and printing a portion of the scenes on hand under the title *Faust. Ein Fragment.* This Fragment appeared then in 1790, comprising, with two 'Singspiele,' the seventh volume of the new works. Facing the title-page is an engraving by Lips, after Rembrandt, representing Faust as an old man gazing at a radiant cabbalistic circle in his window.

Comparing, now, the Fragment with the Göchhausen *Faust*, we see at once that no little work had been done in preparing the former for publication. Various kinds of changes are to be noted: (1) minor orthographical and verbal changes in the interest of a more correct and refined diction; (2) corrections made in the interest of literary congruity; (3) suppression of old matter; (4) addition of new matter, and (5) versification of prose. To go somewhat into details, we note that, excepting changes of the first

kind, the significant omission of the stage-direction which made
the Earth-Spirit appear 'in repellent form' (cf. the note to line
481+), and the substitution in line 519 of the verse

Es wird mein schönstes Glück zu nichte!

for the original

Nun werd ich tiefer tief zu nichte!

the first scene, lines 354–605, is kept intact. After that, however,
comes a passage not found in the Göchhausen manuscript and comprising the present lines 1770–1867. Then follows the student
scene considerably modified: the talk about girls, gaming and
Frau Sprizbierlein's boarding-house has been suppressed, and in
its place we have the famous lines on theology and law. After the
exit of the student and the satirical comment of Mephistopheles,
lines 2049–50, Faust reappears and we have the brief dialogue,
lines 2051–72, which is not in the 'Urfaust.' Next comes
'Auerbach's Cellar,' in verse throughout, and with the rôle of magician assigned to Mephistopheles, Faust being converted into a disgusted spectator. Next, the scene 'Witch's Kitchen,' already
spoken of; then the tragedy of Gretchen as in the Göchhausen
manuscript (minor verbal changes excepted) up to 'Zwinger,' before which is inserted the present 'Forest and Cavern.' After this
come the scenes 'Zwinger' and 'Cathedral,' the Fragment ending
with Gretchen's swoon in the church. The Valentin monologue
and the three prose scenes which end the Göchhausen manuscript
are all omitted from the Fragment.

So we see clearly that the Fragment was the result of a deliberate selection, much being withheld. On what principle was the
selection made? Obviously the poetic power of the scenes was
not the main criterion. Goethe was not intent on giving the public random specimens of his best work on the Faust-theme. His
aim was rather to present those scenes with which he was satisfied;
those which, both internally and in their connection, he felt to be

in full harmony with his plan as it now lay in his mind; so that at some future time he could complete the drama by a process of filling in, without retracting or greatly modifying anything that had once been published. Secondarily, of course, he wished the Fragment to be as intelligible as possible in itself. Accordingly he inserted the lines 1770–1867, beginning abruptly with

Und was der ganzen Menschheit zugetheilt ist,

thus providing a needed setting for the student scene* and at the same time making it clear that Faust's motive in allying himself with the devil for a grand tour of the world is to be a desire not of pleasure simply, but of experience. With the introduction of this idea the career of Faust acquires at once a new interest: we see that he is not a mere sensualist, but a man bent on draining the cup of life to its dregs. He is to leave his bookish pursuits and participate to the fullest in the life of men, share in all its weal and woe, and end the mad voyage with the shipwreck which is called death.† In this strange program of Faust (one hardly knows whether to call it grand or grandiose) we see a poetic reflection of Goethe's own youthful

"Yearning for the large excitement that the coming years would yield."‡

As to what should precede line 1770, it is, of course, not to be supposed that the mind of the poet was at this time a blank. Some sort of 'concept' he no doubt had, but as to the nature of it we are

---

* But this setting is not the one originally conceived. In the 'Urfaust' Mephistopheles is made to appear 'in dressing-gown with a large wig on'—which shows that the dialogue had not been thought of as taking place just before the pair set out on their travels. The situation in the poet's mind had been rather something like this: Mephistopheles has become Faust's domestic servant and acts as a sort of famulus. In that capacity, he one day, in his master's absence, receives a caller and mystifies him when he sees that the boy takes him for the famous Professor Faust. Cf. *Vierteljahrsschrift für Litteraturgeschichte*, II., 552.

† Line 1775; cf. below p. lix. and also the note on lines 1765-75.

‡ Cf. the significant passage at the beginning of *Dichtung und Wahrheit*, bk. 9.

quite in the dark. One thing only is clear: the compact as finally drawn up had not yet been thought of. This is shown by the soliloquy in lines 1851–67. The Mephistopheles who speaks here is still the 'tormentor.' He would not have been made to use such language as he does use if he had been thought of as having but lately entered into a solemn agreement to serve Faust for life and to let his chance of final reward depend on his *satisfying* his master with some form of pleasure.

But if we find it hard to guess how far and in what way the editor of the Fragment had mentally, for his own purposes, filled up the gap between lines 605 and 1770, we can at least understand the difficulties that beset him. The intellectual preparation of Faust for his savage revolt against the moral order, and that, too, in harmonious connection with a deeper and nobler conception of his character, the introduction of Mephistopheles in such a way as to let it appear thinkable that a man like Faust would wish to form an alliance with him for life, the dramatic motivation of this alliance itself (since a professor might easily give up his calling to 'see what life is' without formally leaguing himself with the devil) — all these were poetic problems which it was easier to postpone than to solve. And so, postponed they were — to be taken up ten years later and carried to a solution, which, if not perfect in all its details, is, in a large view of the matter, admirable.*

And when the poet came to deal with his student scene, he saw that some of it was rather puerile; so he struck out this part and replaced it with those genial but penetrating comments upon the routine study of law and theology;† comments drawn no longer from the shallow cynicism of an all-too-knowing student, but from the deep heart of the century. So, too, the original 'Auerbach's Cellar' appeared to him now as out of tune with his lofty argument.

---

* But the useless and incongruous soliloquy, lines 1851–67, might have been consigned to the Paralipomena.

† Lines 1970 ff.

Faust as a sardonic, self-complacent practical joker was not the Faust that now filled his imagination. Then the scene was too boisterous. It was necessary to lift it out of the plane of a local student burlesque into the sphere of poetry. So he cast the whole of it into verse, toned down its coarseness and gave to Mephistopheles the rôle that had been Faust's.

When the love-tragedy was reached there was still the grand difficulty of explaining Faust's desertion of Gretchen. The presence of Valentin in the Göchhausen *Faust* shows that he was a part of the plan from the beginning. We may suppose the original idea to have been something like this: When Gretchen's shame becomes known to her brother, several months after her fall, he attacks her seducer and is killed in the quarrel. Faust flees to avoid arrest. While he is away Gretchen's child is born and drowned by the frantic mother, who then wanders about for some time as a homeless vagrant before she is imprisoned and condemned to die. All this, think of it as we may, must take several months. Meanwhile, Faust, in ignorance of her fate, was to be 'lulled in insipid joys' by Mephistopheles. But how was this to be managed? To make Faust, as the possessor of a conscience, and after all his high protestations of love, leave Gretchen and be away for months without an effort to see her, and that after having caused the death of her mother and brother, was very unnatural. His rage on the discovery of her plight would be but small atonement for such conduct. And then, what were those 'insipid joys' to be? Had the 'Walpurgis-Night' been thought of from the first? Probably not, since the festival of the witches occurs on the eve of May-day, while Gretchen's fall takes place in the season of blossoming daisies, and in the cathedral scene she is far on the way toward motherhood.*

Here was a tangle which it was not easy to straighten without sacrificing the dignity and consistency of Faust's character; and

---

* Lines 3790-3. Cf. the introductory note to the scene 'Cathedral.'

the poet was not yet, in 1789, ready to do what he did finally, namely, make the sacrifice in cold blood and totally disregard the requirements of his realistic love-tragedy. He preferred to postpone the difficulty, by omitting from the Fragment not only the 'insipid joys,' but also Valentin and the three concluding scenes.

The only new matter in the Fragment, beside what has now been spoken of, is the scene 'Forest and Cavern,' and of this the significant lines 3345–69, beginning

Was ift bie Himmelsfreud' in ihren Armen!

are found in the Göchhausen *Faust*. We may therefore safely regard these verses as the nucleus of the whole scene, and look to them for its germ idea. Doing so we see clearly what Goethe was here concerned with: it was to show the libertine Faust suffering the pangs of conscience. He saw, however, and saw no doubt much earlier than 1789, that so important an idea demanded fuller treatment; it was not enough to despatch it in a few words spoken by his hero while on the way for one of his nocturnal visits to his paramour. Hence came the thought of taking Faust out into the woods where he himself in earlier days had been wont to seek relief from over-tension of feeling. In the sixth book of *Dichtung und Wahrheit*, he describes a secluded spot in the woods near Frankfurt to which he resorted with an elderly friend. On one occasion the friend begins to explain how the ancient Germans, as described by Tacitus, were also given to communing with the mystic divinity of the woods. Whereupon the boy interrupts: 'O, why does not this precious spot lie in the depths of the wilderness? Why may we not hedge it in, in order to consecrate it and ourselves and separate both from the world! Surely there is no more beautiful worship than that for which no symbol is needed, that which springs from our heart simply through communion with nature!' — From such experiences came the dramatic idea of letting Faust retire to the woods to commune with himself in his guilty unrest and be joined in due time by Mephistopheles, who should ridicule his scruples and urge him to go back to the city and 'enjoy' himself in the embraces of Gretchen.

The general conception of the scene as thus described was very likely of early origin. But when the preliminary soliloquy of Faust, Faust alone with the woods, came to be worked out in 1788 or 1789, (for the perfect iambics can hardly have been written earlier), the task found a poet whose thoughts were no longer fixed so much upon the dramatic requirements of the scene, not so much upon the angry pathos of the dialogue about Gretchen which was to follow, as upon the opportunity offered for giving expression to his own maturer feelings of sympathy with, and gratitude to, the Universal Mother. Thus the soliloquy took its present form. In a serene and exalted mood, Faust returns thanks to the Earth-Spirit, conceived as the giver of all things, for the high feelings he has been permitted to enjoy. Then, by way of leading up to the coming dialogue, he deplores the fact that the spirit has also sent Mephistopheles, who, with his sneering, 'converts the good gifts into nothingness.'

Having completed the scene in this way, Goethe inserted it in the Fragment where it obviously belongs, namely, *after* the scene 'At the Well,' in which it is clearly intimated that Gretchen's honor is lost. Later, however, he transposed the scene to its present position. The reasons for this change are discussed below.

3. *The Completion of the First Part.*

Such was the 'Fragment' that came from the press just as Europe was beginning to vibrate to the first throes of the Revolution. It made no great stir in literary circles, but among the few who saw in it the 'torso of a Hercules' was Schiller, whose correspondence with Goethe now becomes, after the completed text itself, our main source of knowledge respecting the progress of the poem in the next stage of its genesis. This correspondence gives us, to be sure, but little information with regard to any details of construction; its chief value consists in the light it throws upon the spirit and manner in which Goethe proceeded to the completion of the First Part. The most important notices bearing upon this subject will now be brought together.

In a letter of Nov. 29, 1794, Schiller writes enthusiastically of his interest in *Faust*, and of the pleasure it would give him to read some of the unpublished scenes. Goethe replies that he does not dare untie the package containing them; he could not copy without elaborating, and for that he has not the heart. Still, he adds, if anything could induce him to go on with the work, it would be Schiller's interest in it. Jan. 2, 1795, the younger poet renews his request still more urgently, but to no effect; then he ceases importuning and two years pass. June 22, 1797, Goethe suddenly announces that he is going to resume *Faust*, and if not complete it, at least forward it a good bit. To this end he is now separating what has been printed and disposing it 'in large masses' together with 'what is already finished or invented' (but not printed), and so preparing to carry out his 'plan which is properly only an idea.' This 'plan' is precisely what is now engaging his thoughts and he finds that he is tolerably agreed with himself. 'Our ballad-study,' he continues, 'has brought me back to this misty, foggy path, and circumstances counsel, for more than one reason, that I wander about in it for a time.' Schiller at once replies expressing his delight, and the next day, June 24, Goethe writes that really his return to *Faust* is a measure of prudence. Since, after all, he is not to go to Italy, as he had hoped, but has another northern winter in prospect, and does not wish to bore himself and his friends with idle brooding over his disappointment, he is pleasing himself with the idea of a return to the 'world of symbol, idea, and fog.' 'At first,' he proceeds, 'I shall only try to finish the large masses that have been invented and half worked out, fit these to what has been printed, and so go on to the end of the circle.' June 26 Schiller writes at some length of *Faust*, of the embarrassing magnitude of the subject, of the difficulty involved in finding a poetic frame to contain it, in holding the balance between understanding and reason, jest and earnest, and in adapting the philosophical part to the popular legend. To this Goethe replies the next day thanking Schiller for his observations. 'As was natural,' says he, 'they coincide very well with my own plans and purposes, save that I shall take things somewhat more easily with this barbarous composition, and try to touch, rather than to satisfy, the highest demands. Thus probably reason and understanding will knock one another around like two prize-fighters, only to lie down peacefully at nightfall. I shall take care that the parts be agreeable and entertaining, and afford something to think of. As to the whole, which will always remain a fragment, our new theory of the epic may come in play.'

In a few days, however, the 'air-phantoms of *Faust*' are dispelled by southern reminiscences, and we hear no more of it for several months. Dec. 6, 1797, Goethe writes: 'Pray keep to your *Wallenstein*. I shall probably go at my *Faust* next, partly in order to be rid of this tragelaph,* partly to prepare myself for a higher and serener mood, perhaps for *Tell*.'† Feb. 3, 1798, he is 'thinking somewhat more earnestly of *Faust*,' and sees in it occupation for a year. April 11 he is working at it and finds the vernal mood good for a 'rhapsodical drama.' May 5 he reports good progress made on *Faust*, and remarks upon a 'curious case' that has turned up in connection with his work. 'Some of the scenes,' he observes, 'were written in prose, and they are, in comparison with the rest, quite intolerable in their naturalness and force. So I am now trying to put them into rime, whereby then the idea will appear as through a vail, and the immediate effect of the monstrous

---

* Τραγέλαφος, 'goat-stag,' 'fantastic animal.'

† Goethe was then meditating an epic on the Tell-saga.

matter will be subdued.' (This refers, of course, to the scenes 'Dismal Day,' and 'Prison'; the former resisted the transmuting process and was finally left in prose. See below, p. lxiv.)

Shortly after this date, the Schiller-Goethe correspondence becomes silent respecting *Faust* until the summer of 1800, when we have several references to it. At this time, however, it is the incident of Helena that is on the anvil. Sept. 13, 1800, Schiller counsels his friend not to be disturbed over the 'barbarization of the beautiful forms and situations' (i. e. the blending of the Faust-legend with the antique), and suggests that this hint may be of use in connection with the Second Part, — which is the earliest reference to any plan of making two parts. We may conjecture that the expedient had presented itself to Goethe not long before in connection with his work upon the Helena incident. This, in his earlier plan no doubt an episode, as in the puppet-play, had now come to stand forth in his imagination as the culminating point of the entire action. It needed, therefore, to be elaborated at length. Once suggested, the idea of a Second Part may have commended itself the more on account of Schiller's example in *Wallenstein.*

In the spring of 1801 we hear of another period of creative activity. March 11 *Faust* is 'progressing slowly.' Apr. 6 Goethe 'hopes that soon nothing will be lacking in the great gap (i. e. between lines 605 and 1772) except the disputation'; but this, he adds, is a 'work by itself, which will not be easily extemporized.' Here the Faust-notices of the correspondence end, nor do we get much light from any other sources extraneous to the text about the further progress of the poem. In his *Tag- und Jahreshefte* for 1806, Goethe enters the record Fauſt in ſeiner jetʒigen Geſtalt frag= mentariſch behandelt"; which means, seemingly, that the First Part as we now know it was then finally got ready for the printer. It appeared in the spring of 1808, constituting Volume 8 of the first Cotta edition of Goethe's works.

What now is to be learned from these notices? That which

impresses one most in reading them is the cynical tone in which
Goethe speaks of the Faust-theme. Was this cynicism genuine or
was it only a jocose affectation? Did the poet really regard his
great work as a 'monstrosity,' and if so, on what ground? To
what extent did this quasi-contemptuous attitude really influence the
work done in completion of the First Part? The importance of
these questions is obvious. If Goethe himself did not regard his
work as artistically coherent, and took no pains to make it so, then
all attempts to read coherency into it are a sheer waste of time. On
the other hand, if he did regard it as a work of art built on a consistent plan, then we want to know just what he meant by calling it
a 'tragelaph' and a 'barbarous composition.'

With respect to the first point, the genuineness of the cynical
feeling, there is but little room for serious doubt. Some allowance
may be made indeed for the play of humor, but the derogatory ex-
pressions in the Schiller correspondence are too numerous and
pointed, and the evidence of the text itself in the 'Walpurgis-
Night' and the 'Intermezzo' is too cogent to be put aside as insignificant. Goethe evidently felt that the *Faust* he was creating was
going to be a peculiar affair with which he might take liberties. It
would lack a certain kind, and that the most common kind, of
artistic congruity. That is, it was a 'monstrosity.'

The general grounds of this feeling are not hard to discover.
With his present classical predilections he could feel, as poet, but
little sympathy with vagueness and extravagance. He was fresh
from the composition of *Hermann*, and the qualities he most admired in poetry were definiteness, plasticity, well-regulated technique. In his *Faust*, however, he saw a dramatic work which he
had begun in a spirit of reckless indifference to the rules and requirements of the drama. The supernatural, that is, the very pinnacle
of improbability, had been assumed as a matter of course and made
the basis of the action, and the action itself was to consist of
selected chapters from the miscellaneous experiences of a life-time.

The underlying story was a mass of silly superstitions which could only be lifted into the sphere of serious poetry by being treated as symbolical of things real. And yet he had linked with the fantastic supernaturalism of the legend a terribly pathetic love-story which was not symbolical at all, but had been made to stand on its own merits as a picture of life. His hero, Faust, he had introduced as a man animated by vague perfervid longings for the impossible — at first by a fantastic feeling for nature, then by an equally fantastic *Weltdurst*. This hero he had then turned into a rake-unable-to-help-himself. All this must have seemed to the Goethe of 1797, the mature literary artist, the experienced scientific investigator, traveller and man of the world — slightly ridiculous. And yet he knew that a quarter of a century before, he had wrought his very soul into that same *Faust*.

Besides this, he had written in his youth with no very clear idea as to what the end of his play was to be or to signify. There is not a spark of evidence that he ever intended to send his hero to perdition in the traditionary way. Nor is there any more evidence that he intended to save him. He had simply abandoned tradition altogether and invented a mythology of his own which took no cognizance of heaven or hell. His hero was to drain the cup of life to its dregs and then ' go to ruin ' — not to hell, but to the general ruin which awaits all mankind at the end of their terrestrial voyage. It was to be the tragedy of life's fitful fever lived through in delirium and followed by sleep. What was to come after this sleep had not been provided for. We may indeed be very certain that the young Goethe had never planned to let his Faust die a debauched and demoralized sensualist. The youth who at Frankfurt was dreaming of large and useful activity for himself, and who so admired Möser's *Patriotische Phantasien*, had no doubt provided in his own mind that his Faust should find at last some field of usefulness and die happy in the sense of having lived to some purpose ; but what was to come after that he had not included in his dramatic

scheme.   He held the view, no doubt, that God would take care of
souls like his and Faust's, but for dramatic purposes he probably
had expected to leave his hero right where the human tragi-comedy
does actually leave us all when the curtain goes down, — in the
hands of Providence.

But now the question presents itself, and no doubt the same
question presented itself to Goethe in his mature years : What was
to be the import, and what the dramatic interest, of such a tragedy?
A drama requires more than fulness of life followed by the quietus
of death; it demands struggle directed to a particular end, and a
catastrophe in which the struggle is decided.

With all these considerations in mind, we can understand the
feelings with which, in the plenitude of his powers, Goethe took up
again his long neglected *Faust*.   We can enter into his thoughts as
he surveys the old manuscript and the pages of the printed Fragment.   He cannot go on in the manner or in the spirit of his early
beginning.   He must complete the poem, if he completes it all, by
engrafting his present self upon it.   This, to be sure, will leave it a
' monstrosity.'   The plot will contain incongruities, the characters
will be inconsistent with themselves, and all that.   Still it will have
the consistency of his own life, and an organic, if not a tectonic
unity.   Its unity will be that of a spreading, gnarly oak, rather than
that of a smart new villa.

And now, what is the nature of this new graft?   Or, dropping
metaphor, when the poet of 1797 has matured his plans, what is it
that he purposes to do?   In the first place, he will go no further
with his invented mythology, but will plant himself on the firm
ground of legend.   He will bring his hero into relation with the
God and the devil of tradition.   He will make this hero's career
symbolize, in one of its phases, the triumph of idealism over sensualism, and this final triumph and salvation of Faust he will fore-
shadow by means of a prologue in heaven.   In conformity with this
purpose, he will convert his devil from a ' tormentor ' into a se-

ducer, whose problem it shall be to win Faust by making sensuality satisfy him completely. And as for Faust's wild longings and strange conduct, he will let the prologue intimate that *this* Faust is a wanderer in the dark, who is to be duly led out into the light. That is, Faust's career will be made to symbolize, in another phase of it, a clarifying and chastening process.

Let us now come to the details of the filling-in, following, for the sake of convenience, the order of the completed text, though the new passages and scenes were by no means written in that order. First came, in all probability, the three preliminary poems, but the consideration of these will be taken up in another connection.

The first scene of the Fragment closed with what is now line 605, and the immediately preceding speech of Wagner consisted simply of the two lines 596–7. The next four lines beginning with the slightly illogical „ doch Morgen," were inserted on the final revision for the purpose of intimating the time of the action and foreshadowing the walk of Faust and Wagner upon Easter day. There is no hint in the 'Urfaust' or in the Fragment, that the action of the play had been thought of as beginning at Easter. This definite fixation of the time came from the happy idea of letting Faust, in his despair over the Earth-Spirit's rebuff, be recalled from suicide by the religious memories of his youth. The date fitted in well, also, with the plan which Goethe had early conceived of introducing into *Faust* a picture of a popular holiday. It fitted also with the love story of Heinrich and Gretchen, whose idyl takes place in the season of blossoming daisies. Again, it comported well with the ' Walpurgis-Night,' which comes on the eve of May 1. The poet seems to have forgotten, however, that it did not comport with what he had written in the scene ' Cathedral,' provided that was to stand before the ' Walpurgis-Night.'

The next new passage is the second monologue of Faust, lines 606–807. The artistic motive that guided the hand of the poet here is easily discerned : It was his purpose to deepen and ennoble the character of Faust, to bring him nearer to our sympathies and to give his pessimism a more real and human tinge. It is but a shallow criticism of this fine monologue to insist that men do not in actual life commit suicide because they find themselves denied certain knowledge they would like to possess. Realism is not to be our poet's watchword hereafter, nor is his hero's trouble so easily summed up.

Of the scene 'Before the Gate,' little needs to be said here. There is evidence, not altogether conclusive, that something of the kind had been imagined in the early Frankfurt days, though the poet then had in mind a later season than Easter.* What he now did was to adapt the scene to the new date and bring out of it at last the poodle. So also the first of the two scenes headed 'Study' gives evidence, up to line 1322, of early origin, though the ensuing dialogue is probably one of the latest portions of the First Part. As to the second scene 'Study,' that is, the part of it preceding line 1770, with which the Fragment breaks in abruptly, it is difficult to separate the new matter from the old. Some passages convey a strong suggestion of Goethe's youth, but the most of the lines were probably written in 1801.

We come next to the transposition of the scene 'Forest and Cavern.' The grounds of the change are not easy to see. It is perfectly certain that the scene was written under the presupposition that Gretchen's honor is lost, but as it stands, it must be read on the assumption that she is still innocent. Perhaps the change grew out of a desire to remove the coarse implication of a vulgar *liaison* involving repeated visits of Faust to Gretchen. It is quite clear that the poet originally conceived the relation of the pair as precisely like that of Egmont and Clärchen, but in his old age he seems to have thought he had so ordered matters as to convey the impression that Gretchen had sinned but once. In line 12066-7, the saints say of her :

---

* See Kögel in *Vieterljahrschrift für Litteraturgeschichte*, II., 559.

Die sich einmal nur vergessen,
Die nicht ahnte daß sie fehle.

It may be remarked here that the omission from the scene 'Cathe-dral' of the original heading which made known that the occasion was the funeral of Gretchen's mother, was in line with this idea of putting Gretchen's character in a more favorable light. Still, the text was never thoroughly revised with reference to the point, as witness line 3675. Again the transposition of 'Forest and Cavern' may have been suggested by a feeling that the serene and lofty mood of Faust in the opening soliloquy hardly befits the con-firmed libertine. It may have seemed more poetical and more creditable to Faust to depict him as wrestling with himself and with the devil over the wrong that he is *about to do* under the influence of a dæmonic passion than to represent his fine compunctions as all about the gross question of repetition.

Upon the whole, however, the transposition must be regarded as unfortunate. For, in the first place, as the scene now stands, there are several passages that do not read naturally,* and then, one wonders why the jubilant and prosperous lover of the preceding scene has suddenly become a hermit in the woods.

Our attention is next claimed by the completed Valentin scene, the early conception of which was described above. In the Göch-hausen manuscript this scene is found after 'Cathedral,' which lacks line 3789, with its allusion to Valentin. The transposition of the scene intensifies the pathos of Gretchen's agony in the church, since she thus appears burdened with a double guilt. Then, too, the scene 'Cathedral' had been conceived as taking place some months after Gretchen's fall; it could not therefore come before the death of Valentin if that was to be thought of as occurring just be-fore Walpurgis-Night.

Finally, we have to do with the prose scene and the carnival on

---

* Lines 3249, 3328-9, 3336, 3360-1.

the Blocksberg. It will be remembered how Goethe himself felt that the prose scenes, because of their savage force of expression, were 'intolerable in comparison with the rest.' He tried, we must infer, to put both of them into verse, but failed with the scene 'Dismal Day,' which left its isolated oddity all the more conspicuous because the versifying process succeeded well with the final scene 'Prison.' Besides being in prose, too, the scene 'Dismal Day,' presupposed a different use of the poodle legend from that which he had now adopted in the earlier part of the play. Again, it had been written on the assumption that Mephistopheles would appear as in some special sense an envoy of the Earth-Spirit, which idea had now been given up. But in spite of these things, with a few trifling verbal changes, — in went the prose scene just as it stood. The 'tragelaph' had to be disposed of!

But we have not yet touched the real heart of the 'intolerableness' alluded to by Goethe. The 'force and naturalness' of the prose scene are not out of harmony, but quite *in* harmony, with 'the rest,' if by the rest we mean the love-tragedy to which it belongs. The prose, as prose, would produce but a slight jar if the scene came directly after the cathedral scene: the reader's inference would be that only prose could adequately express Faust's rage. Even the other incongruities mentioned, though a few strokes of the pen would have removed them, would probably never have troubled anybody but philologists. The real dissonance lies not in the prose scene at all, but in the scene which Goethe had now written and designed to precede it. Taken by itself as a separate work of art, the 'Walpurgis-Night' is in its way admirable, but viewed in its connection as a link in the drama, it can only be explained as a wanton freak of poetic cynicism. We are, of course, to assume that the revels of the Brocken are the 'insipid diversions' referred to in the prose scene, though Faust has not found them insipid. But they take place in the spring before Gretchen is a mother, and must therefore have been ancient history at the date of the prose scene. What has Faust been doing in the meantime? And then why this frenzied rage at Mephistopheles for ' lulling him in insipid diversions' when he has been taking part in them with the zest of a person whose conscience is in no need of diabolical ' lulling'? The man who has been joining in the lewd mirth of naked witches is not the man to be thrown into a fury by hearing of the sad fate of a girl whom he has seduced. And why should Faust on the Brocken refer to his love in elegiac tone as a distant memory, and why should he have a vision of the beheaded Gretchen when it is but a day since he left her alive and well? And why should hopeless confusion be brought into the chronology of a natural order of events?*

To these questions there is no answer that is altogether creditable to Goethe's poetic conscience. It pleased his fancy to write the ' Walpurgis-Night' as an *étude* in the uncanny and the gross, and a satire upon contemporary men and tendencies that he did not like. In painting the picture he simply gave the rein to his present humor with no serious concern about the inner or the outward harmony of what he was now writing with the love-tragedy that he had written a quarter of a century before. The result, as we have it, is undeniably a blemish in the poem. The idea of the scene may be accepted as good. The Faust of the legend visits hell. Mephistopheles as a purveyor of sensual pleasures would naturally wish to take his patron sooner or later to the grand festival on the Blocksberg. Goethe had all along intended some such picture for the interval between Valentin's death and Faust's discovery of Gretchen's plight. Thus the idea of the scene came naturally enough. Nor is it reasonable to find fault with the poet for not attuning the ' Walpurgis-Night' as a whole to the high pathos of the love-tragedy: that would have been poetically out of the question, and,

---

* As the text stands we go backward in time when we pass from the cathedral scene to the Walpurgis-Night, or else lines 3790-3 have to be ignored. Cf. the introductory note upon the cathedral scene.

besides, he was now no longer a master of high pathos. It is simply pedantic, too, to condemn austerely the element of personal satire; one may enjoy that, especially where it has some broad universal import, and one may even put up with a little nonsensical mystification. But the poet might have spared us the wanton degradation of his hero's character, he might have taken a little more pains to harmonize the scene technically with what goes before and what comes after, and he might have found some other place in his works for the trivial and obscure personalities which make up a good part of the 'Intermezzo.'

But while we may fairly charge the author of *Faust* with carrying his cynicism too far in this portion of his work, we should not let our impatience lead us to take the wrong side on the main issue. Many able critics have made the mistake of siding with the young Goethe against his maturer self. They have praised the youthful realism, which we see at its best in the Gretchen scenes, as worthy of all admiration, and have treated his later manner as an aberration from the right path. It is this mistake which was chiefly responsible for the long eclipse of the Second Part and for the undue exaltation of the love-tragedy. Many readers, stopping with the First Part, and further influenced perhaps by the prominence of Gretchen on the stage, have been led to think of her as the heroine of the play in the same sense that Faust is its hero. To such persons the 'Walpurgis-Night' could hardly seem anything else than a dark enigma to be dimly comprehended perhaps on the one supposition that the tragedy was to end with the First Part and Faust to be sent to perdition for his conduct toward Gretchen.

The truth is, however, that the love-story is only an incident of the 'little world.' It is an episode which the young Goethe, enamored of the lifelike pictures he was creating, and not yet clear as to the ethical import or the poetic requirements of his theme, had permitted to grow into a drama by itself; a drama which, admirable as it is in its kind, has nothing to do with the legend and

would read as well if published separately under the title of
'Heinrich, Gretchen and Iago.' In his riper years, Goethe came
to see clearly that pathetic realism was not the element in which a
poem based on the Faust-legend should live and move. Humor,
the poetic revivification of Tradition's dream-world, with here and
there a bit of playful symbolism, — this was to be the element. It
was not a question of the merits of realism *per se*, but of the requirements of this particular theme. And on this question there is
to-day no room for doubt that the Goethe of 1800, much wiser in
every way than the Goethe of 1775, was entirely right. It was not
for him therefore to be over-anxious about introducing a discordant
passage into the pathos of his love tragedy. He had invited the
world to think of his hero as a 'good man' and had made some
effort to rescue this hero's title to that name. But he must have
felt, as every reader feels, that the effort had not been altogether
successful. In spite of the 'Witch's Kitchen,' in spite of Faust's
'I must,' and in spite of the devil, one feels that the seducer of
Gretchen is detestable, and the more so for his fine sentiment. It
was not possible to save the dignity or the consistency of his character. Why then make the attempt, especially since he was to be
presented as a 'wanderer in the dark'? Why introduce him in the
rôle of a solemn puritan among the mythical lubricities of the
Brocken? Why not let him rise to the humor of the situation and
enjoy himself like a man fully alive to the greatness of his opportunity? And why trouble about matters of time and space and
quotidian probability, since all such bonds were to be thrown to the
winds in the remainder of the poem?

Some such thoughts as these, we can imagine, had flitted
through the mind of the author of the 'Walpurgis-Night.' *

---

* Cf. G. Witkowski's little book, *Die Walpurgisnacht.* Leipzig, 1894. This
excellent essay discusses the scene thoroughly from the genetic and also from the æsthetic
point of view, taking on the whole a little more favorable view of it than is taken in the
text above. All that can reasonably be said in defense of it is there very well put.

V.

THE COMPLETED FIRST PART.

But now, the letters to Schiller tell us also another story. They tell us, namely, of earnest ponderings on the 'plan,' the 'idea,' of *Faust*. In spite of his cynical references to the theme, the poet felt that what he was creating was, with all its barbarism and 'monstrosity,' a work of art. He probably did not realize at this time, as he did in his latter days, that this *Faust* was to be the great work of his life. When he published the First Part, too, he probably thought it very doubtful whether he should ever complete the work, and this doubt, this feeling that very likely the 'tragedy' would always remain a fragment, may have made him more indifferent than he otherwise would have been to the imperfections just discussed. But, on the other hand, there is no good reason to doubt that when he published the First Part he felt that what he had put into it was, notwithstanding its incongruities, in harmony with his general plan and hence sufficiently consistent with itself. 'For,' as he observes in *Dichtung und Wahrheit*, 'the inner content of the matter treated is the beginning and the end of art.' Now it is of prime importance in the study of *Faust* to understand this 'inner content,' which gives to the whole its unity and consistency. For the purpose of bringing this clearly into view we will now enter upon a brief analysis of the completed First Part.

The first two of the three preliminary poems have nothing to do with the action and so need not occupy us here. The Prologue, however, is vital. It indicates clearly the general character and final outcome of the action. We are not to have a drama of sin and damnation, as the legend would suggest, but a drama of intellectual clarification. The dialogue acquaints us with Faust as a man of high ideal aspirations, a 'good man,' a 'servant' of the Lord, whose service, however, is just now 'confused.' But the Lord promises that he shall be led out 'into the clear' — a phrase which does not refer to Faust's final reception into heaven, though that, too, may be implied, but to the clearing up of his 'confusion' on earth. Mephistopheles, appearing here as a cynical 'wag,' thinks that Faust's high yearnings are so much nonsense, and craves permission to 'lead him in *his* way,' i. e., to give him a taste of earth's pleasures; he is confident that he can soon make Faust 'eat dust with pleasure,' i. e., be satisfied with an animal existence. The Lord gives him permission to try his arts upon Faust during the latter's earthly life, but forewarns him that he will fail. Mephistopheles accepts the offer jauntily. He does not care for 'dead men'; it will be reward enough for him, in the event of success, to be allowed to boast of his triumph over the Lord.

We are now introduced to Faust in his 'confusion.' He is out of humor with life and is chafing morbidly under the necessary limitations of *human* existence. Nominally and at first, that which troubles him is his lack of certain knowledge that he thinks he needs for his own peace of mind as man and as teacher; but when he describes the nature of his longing, we begin to see that it is for something not attainable by mortals. This superhuman character of his yearnings becomes more apparent farther on: he would fain be an elemental spirit, dreams of 'flowing through the veins of Nature and enjoying the life of gods,' and of 'soaring away to new spheres of pure activity.' Later we find him pining to fly away after the sun like a bird, and to be wafted through space in a magic mantle. In other words, he is not content to 'stand before Nature simply as a man.' He feels his human existence as a galling fetter, instead of seeing in it an opportunity for free activity. Just this is his 'confusion,' and the 'clearing up' is to consist in the transformation of this attitude toward life into another which may best be described by the phrase *resignation without apathy*.

But to return to the argument. Pursuing his superhuman vagaries, Faust has devoted himself to magic. With the aid of a book that he has somehow secured he succeeds in calling up the Earth-

Spirit, but when he meditates a friendly approach to this being of a higher order, he is met with a rebuff which tells him plainly that the coveted knowledge, the wished-for footing of intimacy with divine power, the high destiny of godlike activity and unmixed happiness, are not for the like of him. Then Wagner appears and the dialogue with him shows us Faust's idealism in a somewhat saner form (his love of truth and hatred of shams), though he is still somewhat quixotic in the fury of his assault upon Wagner's harmless academic windmills. With the exit of Wagner Faust is thrown back upon himself. He had set his supreme hope on the spirit-world and this has failed him; what is there left? In his despair he is led on to a mournful indictment of life in general. The *misère* of his existence vanquishes the will to live and he resolves to die; but as he sets the poison to his lips he hears the Easter music which reminds him of a youth made happy by a religious faith that is now no longer his. The sweet memory stays his hand. The next afternoon he takes a holiday walk with Wagner, in the course of which his brooding pessimism, his rooted conviction of the badness of man's lot, is still further brought to view. At nightfall he returns in a serener mood, but with the fateful poodle.

Then follow the scenes which lead up to the compact with the devil. Mephistopheles, appearing as a gay young squire, advises Faust to quit his brooding and go out into the world to see what life is. Faust repeats his litany of wretchedness and curses the whole round of man's pursuits and ideals. It is here that his ' confusion ' culminates. Mephistopheles again urges that he seek a cure for his malady by testing the pleasures of earth, and offers to be his companion or even his servant in such an experiment. Faust is desperate. He feels certain that the devil's lures cannot bring him the peace he craves; he is bored in advance by the program suggested to him. Still he cannot go on in the old way — he has reached the very end of his course. He has meant well, but his high cravings have brought him only disappointment and pain.

So, in a spirit of reckless desperation he closes with the devil's offer, not as one expecting to enjoy the new life, but as one bent on probing to the utmost all the facts of man's miserable estate. Jumping the life to come, he will at least find out what this life is like in all its forms and phases. In consenting to be amused in the devil's way he merely stipulates that there shall be no rest, no cessation, in the wild ' reel' from one experience to another. Accordingly the pair make a solemn agreement with each other. Faust is to have during the remainder of his life the prompt and active service of Mephistopheles, but in the next world the relation of master and servant is to be reversed. This last, however, only on one condition: Faust must be ' satisfied with himself.' Only when he shall ' stretch himself upon a bed of ease,' completely absorbed in the pleasure of the present moment, shall Mephistopheles have the right to claim him as his own.

With respect to this compact, a few comments will be in order. In the first place there is the obvious improbability that a sane man, who really believed that he possessed an immortal soul, would ever *admit* that he was satisfied with any earthly pleasure, if he knew that that admission would forthwith send him to eternal perdition. Goethe has attempted to deal with this difficulty formally by making Faust give his solemn assurance that he will be honest. But he has dealt with it more vitally by giving us to understand in more ways than one that the stake of Faust's soul in the life to come is a somewhat formal matter, a part of the costume required by the legend. Of course we may not say boldly that Faust does not believe in immortality, but he is at heart a skeptic for whom the question is at least an open one. At any rate it is not the life to come, but this life, which troubles him, and it is in this world that the real interest centres both for him and for us. And indeed for the devil also — which is the real reason why he facetiously says to the Lord in heaven that he does not care for dead men. We must not think of Goethe's Mephistopheles as a malignant fiend,

artfully and hatefully leading his victim in the way of pleasure, saying to him with each experiment, ' Is not this enough?' and standing ready with his bludgeon in case of an affirmative answer.   He
is rather a gentleman of culture,* who represents a certain view of
life, and the question is whether he will succeed in making his view
acceptable to Faust.   If Mephistopheles wins, then Faust's idealism will be quenched in some form of pleasure, and the modern
ethical interpretation of such an outcome will be : Eat, drink, and
be merry, for to-morrow ye die.   If Faust wins, two contingencies
are conceivable.   Either he will go on to the end tugging at the
chains of his human nature and feeling that existence is a burden,
in which case the conclusion would mean that man's life is indeed,
as the Buddhists and Schopenhauer conceive it, a thing of evil, and
that the saddest part of it consists of those lofty aspirations that
whisper to men of their superiority to the brutes that perish ; or,
on the other hand, his idealism will continue invincible to the end,
but be ' cleared up,' chastened and directed into channels that will
give to life dignity and value.   In that event — but the ethical philosophy of *Faust* is a large subject, the consideration of which
comes properly in connection with the conclusion of the Second
Part.

When the compact is signed, Faust, of course, does not know
which of these contingencies is to happen.   He only feels sure that
Mephistopheles will not win ; for, though he talks of going to wreck
and ruin, that, as we have seen, does not refer to damnation in-
curred through the devil's triumph.   Nor, so the fiction requires us
to assume, does Mephistopheles know what is coming.   Though
his defeat has been foretold on the highest authority, he still counts
on victory.   But if neither of the parties to the agreement knows
how it is to end, the Lord in heaven knows, and by virtue of the
Prologue *we* know — at least in a general way.

---

* In his later stage, of course.

Thus bound together, the two set out to visit first the 'little world' and then the 'great.' The little world is the life of common men, the great world, the Emperor's court. They go first to Auerbach's Cellar, where Faust is bored. Mephistopheles perceives that his comrade's youth must be renewed, and takes him accordingly to a witch, whose elixir of youth turns out to be at the same time a love potion. Then comes the story of Gretchen. Faust (thanks in part to the magic) seems to drop into his new rôle all too easily, so that we begin to think that as lover he is approaching perilously near to Mephisto's goal. But no: under all the lover's raptures there is constantly felt — our poet takes good care of that — the prick of conscience, and no man can be completely 'satisfied' with the things of sense so long as he is inwardly troubled by that silent envoy of the supersensual world, the monitor that 'makes cowards of us all.' Faust remains 'conscious of the right way,' and when the wrong is done, the ruin wrought, and he returns from the orgies of the Brocken (even here his thoughts are fantastically haunted by the figure of the wronged Gretchen), we find him to his honor still capable of acutest suffering. He has coveted the full experience of man's weal and woe, and now there is wrung from him the line of awful pathos,

> Der Menschheit ganzer Jammer faßt mich an.

In these words are summed up, so far as Faust is concerned, the whole import of the Gretchen tragedy. He has not yet been led into 'clearness,' on the contrary, his 'confusion' seems to have become more confounded. But the wagers are not yet decided, and the 'great world' is still to come. *Faust* does not end, and its author never dreamed that any sane being would try to imagine it as ending, in the prison-cell of the dead Gretchen. To suppose, as many have done, that the Second Part was an afterthought is to make the most radical and pernicious mistake that can possibly be made in the interpretation of the poem.

VI.

THE PRINCIPAL CHARACTERS.

1. *Faust.*

The foregoing pages have shown clearly enough that the character of Faust has its root and its development in the personal experiences of Goethe; it owes to the legend only the externals of costume and historical setting. Of course, we may not say in any
literal sense that Faust is Goethe — the identity of the poet with
his hero must be understood in the light of Goethe's well-known
artistic methods. He never deliberately depicted himself, but his
works were in a very eminent degree personal 'confessions.'
Faust is only one of several poetic creations which are, to employ a
figure used by Goethe respecting his *Tasso*, 'bone of his bone and
flesh of his flesh'; the chief difference being that Faust gives us the
poet in his development from youth to age, while Werther, Tasso,
Meister, reflect particular phases of his history. In all alike, however, what we have in the fictitious hero is not the veritable
Goethe, but only actual moods of his transfigured and potential-
ized for the purposes of his art. It is by no means to be assumed
that what Faust says and does under his circumstances is what
Goethe would have approved under like circumstances, could they
have been realized. What we have is always a poetic rendition of
actualities, not a photograph, and still less an allegory requiring to
be deciphered in detail with reference to particular incidents in the
poet's life. This is not to be construed as denying that the poem
may contain here and there an almost literal transcript from biog-
raphy. Take, for example, the incident of the flower oracle, the
lover's pursuit and the captured kiss in the summer-house: this
certainly sounds very like a chapter from Goethe's romance at
Sesenheim. So there are many passages in the poem in which the
details are such that a well-informed reader will inevitably think his
own thoughts; but in few of them is it possible to prove anything

or to separate the basis of fact from the fabric of fancy. Such readings between the lines are, when reasonably managed, well enough in their way and may now and then throw an interesting side light upon particular scenes. In general, however, it is not biographical details of any kind, but the broad features of Goethe's inner history that we must expect to find reflected in Faust. What this saying means has been so fully brought to view in the foregoing discussion that nothing further on the subject is necessary.

2. *Mephistopheles.*

In this most unique and powerful of Goethe's creations, just as in the case of Faust, we have to do with an evolution. He meets us first as a wag and a rake's friend. But for his name and an allusion to magic horses, the 'Urfaust' conveys no suggestion that Mephistopheles is a supernatural being. The 'devil' in him is the devil of sensual promptings, and his relation to Faust is that of a tormentor in the guise of an obedient servant. Later, Goethe invests him with all sorts of legendary trappings derived rather from the devil-myth in general than from the Faust-legend in particular. This devil-myth is, as is well known, a highly composite affair. The Jewish 'adversary' and prince of demons, Satan, the Persian god of darkness, Angra-Mainyus (Ahriman, Arimanes), the serpent-story of Genesis, the monstrous imaginings of the apocalyptic writers of the Old and New Testaments, theological speculations about Titan-angels at war with God, attributes of Greek, Roman, and Germanic divinities, — these are some of the sources from which 'the devil' of medieval Christian demonology had been elaborated by popular and learned superstition.* From such traditionary sources Goethe draws at will, adding conceptions of his own as suits his purpose. As an adversary of divine power, Mephistopheles is a spirit of negation: God affirms and creates,

---

* Cf. Roskoff, *Geschichte des Teufels*, I., 186 ff.

the devil denies and destroys. He is therefore the natural lord and patron of destructive agencies, great and small. Fire, as the enemy of life, is his natural element. Against the divine regime 'let there be light,' he is a prince of darkness and a champion of primeval chaos. He has the lameness of Hephæstus, the hoof of Pan, and the two ravens of Odin. In accordance with the familiar popular conception he is a lover of witches.

Passing from these externals, which are legendary, to the intellect, which is modern, we find the essence of his character to consist in his cynical hostility to all idealism. 'Man in his high endeavor,' is for him a laughing-stock. Moral scruples, sympathy, supersensual love of woman or of nature, are the ridiculous antics of the human grasshopper that would fain fly but cannot. At first his cynicism is bitter earnest; he meets Faust's pathos of high feeling with a pathos of contempt for high feeling. In the later scenes, as throughout the Second Part, he is a more genial devil, and his cynicism takes the form of clever satire.

Concerning his indebtedness to actual personages much has been conjectured and but little proved. We have seen reasons for thinking that the initial conception owed somewhat to Goethe's Leipzig friend Behrisch. From *Dichtung und Wahrheit* one would infer that the living model of Mephistopheles was, if anyone, J. H. Merck, with whom Goethe became intimate directly after his return from Strassburg. Merck was a man of extensive knowledge, fine critical perception, easy, self-assured social bearing, and altogether solid character. Goethe describes him as tall and gaunt (so was Behrisch likewise), and as having a prominent pointed nose and eyes that continually peered here and there, giving to him a certain 'tigerish' expression. He further imputes to him a propensity for biting satire and a capricious habit of treading on people's toes regardless of the hurt. This personage Goethe expressly credits with having exerted a 'very great influence' upon his own life, and he refers to him repeatedly as Mephistopheles Merck. But it is a question whether these Mephistophelean traits of Merck are not largely a matter of fanciful retrospect. Goethe, to be sure, is not the only one who ascribes horns and claws to this youthful friend of his, but Merck's letters and extant critical writings, and the total impression of his character derived from contemporary sources, offer little suggestion of the peculiar diabolism that shows itself in Mephistopheles.*

And the same thing is to be said of Herder, whom Herman Grimm regards as the living prototype of Mephistopheles.† Grimm's theory is that Herder became for Goethe at Strassburg the starting-point for the poetic conception of an overweening, remorseless, destructive critic, a critic that knows it all, sees through you and over you, and delights in showing up the vanity of your enthusiasms. Grimm supposes, then, that this conception was borne in mind by Goethe until Merck came to give it individuality and speech. To this theory as guardedly set forth by its author, one cannot deny a measure of plausibility, only we must not look for anything of the actual Herder in Goethe's devil. Herder was no cynical enemy of idealism, but himself one of the towering idealists of his century. If he ridiculed Goethe's enthusiasms it was not in a spirit of contempt for enthusiasm *per se*, but out of devotion to what he thought a better enthusiasm of his own. Another point deserves to be noted with regard to Grimm's hypothesis. The only Mephistopheles that we can even imagine to have been much influenced by Herder is, of course, that of the early pre-Weimarian scenes. But the Göchhausen *Faust*, not known when Grimm wrote, shows us that this Mephistopheles was by no means an incarnation of omniscient, overweening critical intellect. He is a kind of devil of whom there was no spark in Herder, and who did not need to be suggested by a Herder, the species being only too common among the sons of Adam. Finally, it is highly probable

---

* Cf. Loeper in the Hempel edition of Goethe's works, XXII., 292 ff.
† *Vorlesungen über Goethe*, 25te Vorlesung.

that the initial conception of Mephistopheles had already taken root in Goethe's mind before he knew Herder at all.

The truth is that Goethe's famous creation owes very little, and nothing that is clearly definable, to any actual personage. Mephistopheles is simply the natural, and in view of Goethe's poetic methods, necessary pendant to Faust. The pair are in their way but another instance of that dualism of poetic conception which meets us elsewhere as Götz and Weislingen, Clavigo and Carlos, Orestes and Pylades, Tasso and Antonio. Over against the extreme of titanic idealism seen in Faust, the poet sets an extreme of earthly sensualism in Mephistopheles. The devil of any age or people is the enemy of what that age or people regards as supremely good. So in a time of emotional expansion like the storm and stress era, when ' feeling is everything' and supernal unrest the accepted sign of the soul's nobility, the devil is naturally a person who throws cold water upon all high sentiment. Our poet needed no models, and no suggestion beyond what was furnished by his widening acquaintance with life, and his observation of the inner contrasts of his own being. The habit of critical self-inspection early became a part of his nature. It was as if he were accompanied by an inward Mephistopheles, that now confronted his flight of feeling with cold common sense, now whispered of the base while he dreamed of the noble, and again turned his pathos of emotion into ridicule. All men carry their devil with them and Goethe was no exception. He once said to Eckermann that there was no crime but envy, of which he could not imagine himself to be guilty. Bearing this in mind and remembering also Goethe's way of potentializing his own moods in his fictitious heroes, his way of raising these moods, so to speak, to a higher power, and carrying out their consequences to a logical end, — remembering this we have, broadly speaking, all that is needed to explain the character of Mephistopheles both in its inception and in its development.

3. *Wagner.*

The legend, as we saw, gives to Faust a famulus in the person of an 'insolent lubber' called Christoph Wagner, who is in his master's secret and becomes his heir. This Wagner also regularly appears in the puppet-plays, having there a somewhat colorless and unimportant rôle. Goethe makes use of him for a contrast to Faust of a different kind from that offered by the Earth-Spirit or Mephistopheles, that, namely of a practical, self-satisfied book-worm. The young Goethe, who slighted his lectures at Leipzig and Strassburg, was, of course, acquainted with fellow-students who attended steadily to their work and were not given to repining over the inadequacy of the official academic fountain for quenching the diviner thirsts of human nature. In sombre moods the species no doubt exasperated him, and so when he came to depict it in *Faust*, he threw a touch of satire into the portrait, and made qualities appear despicable that are not so very despicable after all. For it is a mistake to regard Wagner as a type of the paltry pedant. There is nothing of the pedant about him. He makes no offensive parade of lean and wasteful learning, nor is there anything in him to suggest that he cares only for the letter and not for the spirit. He is a zealous student, a little tactless and importunate, a little *naif* in his ambition to know everything, but otherwise quite worthy of respect. He knows what he wants and his wishes are creditable to his head and heart. Faust, in his irritation, calls him the 'poorest of the sons of men,' but humanly speaking, Wagner is a promising youth who will make his mark in the world, in fact, does make it. He is quite right to care for the things that pertain to his future vocation and Faust's bitter rhetoric does him injustice. Wagner is not digging after mysterious, unnamable treasures, but after bait to catch fish; he has a right, therefore, to be pleased when he turns up an angleworm. The point of these remarks is to caution against the common error of reading the Wagner scenes as if Faust were an oracle of absolute wisdom, and Wagner a ridiculous shallow-pate.

It is Faust who is in the wrong, and his 'clearing up' will bring him, not further from but nearer to, the humble, practical, human idealism of his famulus.

4. *Gretchen.*

The later Faust-books, as was noted above on page xvii., contain an account of Faust's falling in love with a servant-girl. Whether this story is really, as Scherer supposed,[*] the 'germ' of Goethe's Gretchen is at least doubtful; Kuno Fischer [†] thinks the hypothesis unnecessary and even absurd. Of one thing at any rate we may be sure, and that is that nothing more than the merest hint can have been obtained by Goethe from this source; for the story is told in two sentences in the Christlich Meynenden Faust-book, and has no resemblance whatever to the love-tragedy in *Faust*. This last cannot be said, however, of a certain other narrative which has lately been put forward not only as the probable 'original' of the Gretchen story but also as evidence that the Faust-book used by Goethe was that of Pfitzer.[‡] In a long note to his second chapter, by way of parallel to Faust's youthful profligacy, Pfitzer tells a story, not found in Widman, of a young student Apion, who falls in love with a girl named Amee, wins her favor by means of presents and then dishonors her. The mother, trusting her daughter and busy with her house-work, knows nothing of the relation. The maid Caride knows, however, and threatens to betray Amee, but is quieted by Apion's silver. In her shame, Amee is deserted by her betrayer and in due time gives birth to a daughter, who is put to death by Caride, with the young mother's consent. After two years the crime is discovered and both Amee and Caride are beheaded, while the mother is banished for not taking better care of her daughter.

The similarity of this story to that of Gretchen is so striking as to suggest more than a possibility that Goethe may have read it.

---

[*] *Faust-Buch*, p. xxviii.

[†] *Goethe's Faust*, p. 150.

[‡] *Goethe-Jahrbuch*, VII., 278. On the Pfitzer book, see above, p. xvii.

Still, there are certain facts that should not be ignored. First, the story is not told of Faust at all. Secondly, the main elements of the recital are not so unheard of in life or in literature as to compel the supposition that Goethe needed this particular tale to set his imagination at work. Finally, as we have seen, Gretchen is only one of a group of similar portraits painted by Goethe in his youth. His mind was long haunted by the vision of an artless, naive girl with a superior worldling for a lover. Any theory that attempts to account for the origin of the conception of Gretchen must also account for the Marie of *Götz von Berlichingen* and the Clärchen of *Egmont*.

In any case, therefore, we cannot suppose that Goethe's creation owes more than a bare suggestion to his reading in Faust-lore. Nor does it owe very much that is definable to any maidens of flesh and blood. Some have thought, and even argued vehemently, that the portrait of Gretchen is based upon reminiscences of the Frankfurt Gretchen described so vividly in the fifth book of *Dichtung und Wahrheit*.* But this is not very probable. Even supposing this early love to have been as fervid as would appear from *Dichtung und Wahrheit*, the episode was ancient history at the time when the Gretchen scenes in *Faust* were written. Ten years had passed with their kaleidoscopic succession of sweethearts, and the young Goethe was preeminently a poet who wrought from the issues of the living present. It is more likely that the Frankfurt Gretchen was copied from her namesake in *Faust*.

With better reason we may assign to Friederike Brion the chief influence, among actual maidens, in shaping the conception of Gretchen. The reasons for this opinion have already been given.

In these pages we have called Goethe's heroine uniformly by the name of Gretchen, but he himself calls her also by the name of Margarete. As a rule the name Gretchen is used where she appears

---

* E. g., Schröer; cf. the Introduction to his edition of *Faust*, p. xl. ff.

alone, as in the scenes, 'Gretchen's Room,' 'Zwinger,' 'Cathe-dral.' In the dialogue scenes, excepting 'At the Well,' she is introduced by the poet as 'Margarete,' though the characters speak of her as 'Gretchen,' 'Gretel,' 'Gretelchen,' and 'Margretlein.' Reasoning on this fact, before the discovery of the Göchhausen manuscript, Schröer was led to imagine a later origin for the 'Gretchen' scenes, as if the image of his heroine in certain pathetic situations had lingered on in the poet's mind after he had composed the dramatic dialogue. But the 'Urfaust' hardly supports this view. In general it uses the names as they are used in the final version, but with the important exception that in the catechism scene we have 'Margrete' in the heading, then 'Gretgen' twice in the text following, then a single 'Margrete,' and the rest of the way only 'Gretgen.' That is, the names are used fortuitously in the same scene.

Faust.

Eine Tragödie.

Zueignung. *1789*

Ihr naht euch wieder, schwankende Gestalten,
Die früh sich einst dem trüben Blick gezeigt.
Versuch' ich wohl euch dießmal fest zu halten?
Fühl' ich mein Herz noch jenem Wahn geneigt?
5 Ihr drängt euch zu! nun gut, so mögt ihr walten,
Wie ihr aus Dunst und Nebel um mich steigt;
Mein Busen fühlt sich jugendlich erschüttert
Vom Zauberhauch, der euren Zug umwittert.

Ihr bringt mit euch die Bilder froher Tage,
10 Und manche liebe Schatten steigen auf;
Gleich einer alten halbverklungnen Sage
Kommt erste Lieb' und Freundschaft mit herauf;
Der Schmerz wird neu, es wiederholt die Klage
Des Lebens labyrinthisch irren Lauf,
15 Und nennt die Guten, die, um schöne Stunden
Vom Glück getäuscht, vor mir hinweggeschwunden.

Sie hören nicht die folgenden Gesänge,
Die Seelen, denen ich die ersten sang;
Zerstoben ist das freundliche Gedränge,
20 Verklungen ach! der erste Widerklang.
Mein Leid ertönt der unbekannten Menge,
Ihr Beifall selbst macht meinem Herzen bang,
Und was sich sonst an meinem Lied erfreuet,
Wenn es noch lebt, irrt in der Welt zerstreuet.

(3)

Und mich ergreift ein längſt entwöhntes Sehnen   25
Nach jenem ſtillen ernſten Geiſterreich,
Es ſchwebet nun in unbeſtimmten Tönen
Mein liſpelnd Lied, der Aolsharfe gleich,
Ein Schauer faßt mich, Thräne folgt den Thränen,
Das ſtrenge Herz es fühlt ſich mild und weich;   30
Was ich beſitze ſeh’ ich wie im Weiten,
Und was verſchwand wird mir zu Wirklichkeiten.

Vorspiel auf dem Theater.

Director, Theaterdichter, Lustige Person.

Director.

Ihr beiden, die ihr mir so oft,
In Noth und Trübsal, beigestanden,

35   Sagt was ihr wohl in deutschen Landen
Von unsrer Unternehmung hofft?
Ich wünschte sehr der Menge zu behagen,
Besonders weil sie lebt und leben läßt.
Die Pfosten sind, die Breter aufgeschlagen,

40   Und jedermann erwartet sich ein Fest.
Sie sitzen schon mit hohen Augenbraunen
Gelassen da und möchten gern erstaunen.
Ich weiß wie man den Geist des Volks versöhnt;
Doch so verlegen bin ich nie gewesen;

45   Zwar sind sie an das Beste nicht gewöhnt,
Allein sie haben schrecklich viel gelesen.
Wie machen wir's, daß alles frisch und neu
Und mit Bedeutung auch gefällig sei?
Denn freilich mag ich gern die Menge sehen,

50   Wenn sich der Strom nach unsrer Bude drängt,
Und mit gewaltig wiederholten Wehen
Sich durch die enge Gnadenpforte zwängt,
Bei hellem Tage, schon vor Vieren,
Mit Stößen sich bis an die Casse ficht

Und, wie in Hungersnoth um Brot an Bäckerthüren,   55
Um ein Billet ſich faſt die Hälſe bricht.
Dieß Wunder wirkt auf ſo verſchiedne Leute
Der Dichter nur; mein Freund, o! thu' es heute!

Dichter.

O ſprich mir nicht von jener bunten Menge,
Bei deren Anblick uns der Geiſt entflieht.   60
Verhülle mir das wogende Gedränge,
Das wider Willen uns zum Strudel zieht.
Nein, führe mich zur ſtillen Himmelsenge,
Wo nur dem Dichter reine Freude blüht;
Wo Lieb' und Freundſchaft unſres Herzens Segen   65
Mit Götterhand erſchaffen und erpflegen.

Ach! was in tiefer Bruſt uns da entſprungen,
Was ſich die Lippe ſchüchtern vorgelallt,
Mißrathen jetzt und jetzt vielleicht gelungen,
Verſchlingt des wilden Augenblicks Gewalt.   70
Oft wenn es erſt durch Jahre durchgedrungen
Erſcheint es in vollendeter Geſtalt.
Was glänzt iſt für den Augenblick geboren;
Das Echte bleibt der Nachwelt unverloren.

Luſtige Perſon.

Wenn ich nur nichts von Nachwelt hören ſollte;   75
Geſetzt daß ich von Nachwelt reden wollte,
Wer machte denn der Mitwelt Spaß?
Den will ſie doch und ſoll ihn haben.
Die Gegenwart von einem braven Knaben
Iſt, dächt' ich, immer auch ſchon was.   80

Wer sich behaglich mitzutheilen weiß,
Den wird des Volkes Laune nicht erbittern;
Er wünscht sich einen großen Kreis,
Um ihn gewisser zu erschüttern.
85   Drum seid nur brav und zeigt euch musterhaft,
Laßt Phantasie, mit allen ihren Chören,
Vernunft, Verstand, Empfindung, Leidenschaft,
Doch, merkt euch wohl! nicht ohne Narrheit hören.

Director.

Besonders aber laßt genug geschehn!
90   Man kommt zu schaun, man will am liebsten sehn.
Wird vieles vor den Augen abgesponnen,
So daß die Menge staunend gaffen kann,
Da habt ihr in der Breite gleich gewonnen,
Ihr seid ein vielgeliebter Mann.
95   Die Masse könnt ihr nur durch Masse zwingen,
Ein jeder sucht sich endlich selbst was aus.
Wer vieles bringt, wird manchem etwas bringen;
Und jeder geht zufrieden aus dem Haus.
Gebt ihr ein Stück, so gebt es gleich in Stücken!
100   Solch ein Ragout es muß euch glücken;
Leicht ist es vorgelegt, so leicht als ausgedacht.
Was hilft's, wenn ihr ein Ganzes dargebracht,
Das Publicum wird es euch doch zerpflücken.

Dichter.

Ihr fühlet nicht, wie schlecht ein solches Handwerk sei!
105   Wie wenig das dem echten Künstler zieme!
Der saubern Herren Pfuscherei
Ist, merk' ich, schon bei euch Maxime.

Director.

Ein solcher Vorwurf läßt mich ungekränkt:
Ein Mann, der recht zu wirken denkt,
Muß auf das beste Werkzeug halten. 110
Bedenkt, ihr habet weiches Holz zu spalten,
Und seht nur hin für wen ihr schreibt!
Wenn diesen Langeweile treibt, —
Kommt jener satt vom übertischten Mahle,
Und, was das allerschlimmste bleibt, 115
Gar mancher kommt vom Lesen der Journale.
Man eilt zerstreut zu uns, wie zu den Maskenfesten,
Und Neugier nur beflügelt jeden Schritt;
Die Damen geben sich und ihren Putz zum Besten
Und spielen ohne Gage mit. 120
Was träumet ihr auf eurer Dichter=Höhe?
Was macht ein volles Haus euch froh?
Beseht die Gönner in der Nähe!
Halb sind sie kalt, halb sind sie roh.
Der, nach dem Schauspiel, hofft ein Kartenspiel, 125
Der eine wilde Nacht an einer Dirne Busen.
Was plagt ihr armen Thoren viel,
Zu solchem Zweck, die holden Musen?
Ich sag' euch, gebt nur mehr, und immer, immer mehr,
So könnt ihr euch vom Ziele nie verirren, 130
Sucht nur die Menschen zu verwirren,
Sie zu befriedigen ist schwer —
Was fällt euch an? Entzückung oder Schmerzen?

Dichter.

Geh hin und such' dir einen andern Knecht!
Der Dichter sollte wohl das höchste Recht, 135

Das Menschenrecht, das ihm Natur vergönnt,
Um deinetwillen freventlich verscherzen!
Wodurch bewegt er alle Herzen?
Wodurch besiegt er jedes Element?
140   Ist es der Einklang nicht, der aus dem Busen dringt,
Und in sein Herz die Welt zurücke schlingt?
Wenn die Natur des Fadens ew'ge Länge,
Gleichgültig drehend, auf die Spindel zwingt,
Wenn aller Wesen unharmon'sche Menge
145   Verdrießlich durch einander klingt;
Wer theilt die fließend immer gleiche Reihe
Belebend ab, daß sie sich rhythmisch regt?
Wer ruft das Einzelne zur allgemeinen Weihe,
Wo es in herrlichen Accorden schlägt?
150   Wer läßt den Sturm zu Leidenschaften wüthen?
Das Abendroth im ernsten Sinne glühn?
Wer schüttet alle schönen Frühlingsblüthen
Auf der Geliebten Pfade hin?
Wer flicht die unbedeutend grünen Blätter
155   Zum Ehrenkranz Verdiensten jeder Art?
Wer sichert den Olymp, vereinet Götter?
Des Menschen Kraft im Dichter offenbart.

Lustige Person.

So braucht sie denn die schönen Kräfte
Und treibt die dichtrischen Geschäfte,
160   Wie man ein Liebesabenteuer treibt.
Zufällig naht man sich, man fühlt, man bleibt
Und nach und nach wird man verflochten;
Es wächs't das Glück, dann wird es angefochten,
Man ist entzückt, nun kommt der Schmerz heran,

Und eh' man ſich's verſieht, iſt's eben ein Roman.   165
Laßt uns auch ſo ein Schauſpiel geben!
Greift nur hinein in's volle Menſchenleben!
Ein jeder lebt's, nicht vielen iſt's bekannt,
Und wo ihr's packt, da iſt's intereſſant.
In bunten Bildern wenig Klarheit,   170
Viel Irrthum und ein Fünkchen Wahrheit,
So wird der beſte Trank gebraut,
Der alle Welt erquickt und auferbaut.
Dann ſammelt ſich der Jugend ſchönſte Blüthe
Vor eurem Spiel und lauſcht der Offenbarung,   175
Dann ſauget jedes zärtliche Gemüthe
Aus eurem Werk ſich melanchol'ſche Nahrung,
Dann wird bald dieß bald jenes aufgeregt,
Ein jeder ſieht was er im Herzen trägt.
Noch ſind ſie gleich bereit zu weinen und zu lachen,   180
Sie ehren noch den Schwung, erfreuen ſich am Schein;
Wer fertig iſt, dem iſt nichts recht zu machen;
Ein Werdender wird immer dankbar ſein.

Dichter.

So gib mir auch die Zeiten wieder,
Da ich noch ſelbſt im Werden war,   185
Da ſich ein Quell gedrängter Lieder
Ununterbrochen neu gebar,
Da Nebel mir die Welt verhüllten,
Die Knoſpe Wunder noch verſprach,
Da ich die tauſend Blumen brach,   190
Die alle Thäler reichlich füllten.
Ich hatte nichts und doch genug,
Den Drang nach Wahrheit und die Luſt am Trug.

Gib ungebändigt jene Triebe,
195 Das tiefe schmerzenvolle Glück,
Des Hasses Kraft, die Macht der Liebe,
Gib meine Jugend mir zurück!

Lustige Person.

Der Jugend, guter Freund, bedarfst du allenfalls,
Wenn dich in Schlachten Feinde drängen,
200 Wenn mit Gewalt an deinen Hals
Sich allerliebste Mädchen hängen,
Wenn fern des schnellen Laufes Kranz
Vom schwer erreichten Ziele winket,
Wenn nach dem heft'gen Wirbeltanz
205 Die Nächte schmausend man vertrinket.
Doch in's bekannte Saitenspiel
Mit Muth und Anmuth einzugreifen,
Nach einem selbstgesteckten Ziel
Mit holdem Irren hinzuschweifen,
210 Das, alte Herrn, ist eure Pflicht,
Und wir verehren euch darum nicht minder.
Das Alter macht nicht kindisch, wie man spricht,
Es findet uns nur noch als wahre Kinder.

Director.

Der Worte sind genug gewechselt,
215 Laßt mich auch endlich Thaten sehn;
Indeß ihr Complimente drechselt,
Kann etwas Nützliches geschehn.
Was hilft es viel von Stimmung reden?
Dem Zaudernden erscheint sie nie.
220 Gebt ihr euch einmal für Poeten,
So commandirt die Poesie.

Euch iſt bekannt, was wir bedürfen,
Wir wollen ſtark Getränke ſchlürfen;
Nun braut mir unverzüglich dran!
Was heute nicht geſchieht, iſt morgen nicht gethan,   225
Und keinen Tag ſoll man verpaſſen,
Das Mögliche ſoll der Entſchluß
Beherzt ſogleich bei'm Schopfe faſſen,
Er will es dann nicht fahren laſſen,
Und wirket weiter, weil er muß.   230

Ihr wißt auf unſern deutſchen Bühnen
Probirt ein jeder was er mag;
Drum ſchonet mir an dieſem Tag
Proſpecte nicht und nicht Maſchinen.
Gebraucht das groß' und kleine Himmelslicht,   235
Die Sterne dürfet ihr verſchwenden;
An Waſſer, Feuer, Felſenwänden,
An Thier und Vögeln fehlt es nicht.
So ſchreitet in dem engen Breterhaus
Den ganzen Kreis der Schöpfung aus,   240
Und wandelt mit bedächt'ger Schnelle,
Vom Himmel durch die Welt zur Hölle.

Prolog im Himmel.

Der Herr, die himmlischen Heerschaaren, nachher Mephistopheles.

Die drei Erzengel treten vor.

Raphael.

Die Sonne tönt nach alter Weise
In Brudersphären Wettgesang,
245   Und ihre vorgeschriebne Reise
Vollendet sie mit Donnergang.
Ihr Anblick gibt den Engeln Stärke,
Wenn keiner sie ergründen mag;
Die unbegreiflich hohen Werke
250   Sind herrlich wie am ersten Tag.

Gabriel.

Und schnell und unbegreiflich schnelle
Dreht sich umher der Erde Pracht;
Es wechselt Paradieses-Helle
Mit tiefer schauervoller Nacht;
255   Es schäumt das Meer in breiten Flüssen
Am tiefen Grund der Felsen auf,
Und Fels und Meer wird fortgerissen
In ewig schnellem Sphärenlauf.

(13)

Michael.

Und Stürme brauſen um die Wette,
Vom Meer auf's Land, vom Land auf's Meer,   26a
Und bilden wüthend eine Kette
Der tiefſten Wirkung rings umher.
Da flammt ein blitzendes Verheeren
Dem Pfade vor des Donnerſchlags;
Doch deine Boten, Herr, verehren   265
Das ſanfte Wandeln deines Tags.

Zu Drei.

Der Anblick gibt den Engeln Stärke
Da keiner dich ergründen mag,
Und alle deine hohen Werke
Sind herrlich wie am erſten Tag.   270

Mephiſtopheles.

Da du, o Herr, dich einmal wieder nahſt
Und fragſt wie alles ſich bei uns befinde,
Und du mich ſonſt gewöhnlich gerne ſahſt,
So ſiehſt du mich auch unter dem Geſinde.
Verzeih, ich kann nicht hohe Worte machen,   275
Und wenn mich auch der ganze Kreis verhöhnt;
Mein Pathos brächte dich gewiß zum Lachen,
Hätt'ſt du dir nicht das Lachen abgewöhnt.
Von Sonn= und Welten weiß ich nichts zu ſagen,
Ich ſehe nur wie ſich die Menſchen plagen.   280
Der kleine Gott der Welt bleibt ſtets von gleichem Schlag,
Und iſt ſo wunderlich als wie am erſten Tag.
Ein wenig beſſer würd' er leben,
Hätt'ſt du ihm nicht den Schein des Himmelslichts gegeben;

285 Er nennt's Vernunft und braucht's allein,
Nur thierischer als jedes Thier zu sein.
Er scheint mir, mit Verlaub von Ew. Gnaden,
Wie eine der langbeinigen Cicaden,
Die immer fliegt und fliegend springt
290 Und gleich im Gras ihr altes Liedchen singt;
Und läg' er nur noch immer in dem Grase!
In jeden Quark begräbt er seine Nase.

Der Herr.

Hast du mir weiter nichts zu sagen?
Kommst du nur immer anzuklagen?
295 Ist auf der Erde ewig dir nichts recht?

Mephistopheles.

Nein Herr! ich find' es dort, wie immer, herzlich schlecht.
Die Menschen dauern mich in ihren Jammertagen,
Ich mag sogar die Armen selbst nicht plagen.

Der Herr.

Kennst du den Faust?

Mephistopheles.

Den Doctor?

Der Herr

Meinen Knecht!

Mephistopheles.

300 Fürwahr! er dient euch auf besondre Weise.
Nicht irdisch ist des Thoren Trank noch Speise.
Ihn treibt die Gährung in die Ferne,
Er ist sich seiner Tollheit halb bewußt;
Vom Himmel fordert er die schönsten Sterne,
305 Und von der Erde jede höchste Lust,

Und alle Näh und alle Ferne
Befriedigt nicht die tiefbewegte Bruſt.

Der Herr.

Wenn er mir jetzt auch nur verworren dient,
So werd' ich ihn bald in die Klarheit führen.
Weiß doch der Gärtner, wenn das Bäumchen grünt,   310
Daß Blüth' und Frucht die künft'gen Jahre zieren.

Mephiſtopheles.

Was wettet ihr? den ſollt ihr noch verlieren,
Wenn ihr mir die Erlaubniß gebt
Ihn meine Straße ſacht zu führen!

Der Herr.

So lang er auf der Erde lebt,   315
So lange ſei dir's nicht verboten.
Es irrt der Menſch ſo lang er ſtrebt.

Mephiſtopheles.

Da dank' ich euch; denn mit den Todten
Hab' ich mich niemals gern befangen.
Am meiſten lieb' ich mir die vollen friſchen Wangen.   320
Für einen Leichnam bin ich nicht zu Haus;
Mir geht es wie der Katze mit der Maus.

Der Herr.

Nun gut, es ſei dir überlaſſen!
Zieh dieſen Geiſt von ſeinem Urquell ab,
Und führ' ihn, kannſt du ihn erfaſſen,   325
Auf deinem Wege mit herab,
Und ſteh beſchämt, wenn du bekennen mußt:
Ein guter Menſch in ſeinem dunklen Drange
Iſt ſich des rechten Weges wohl bewußt.

Mephistopheles.

330 Schon gut! nur dauert es nicht lange.
Mir ist für meine Wette gar nicht bange.
Wenn ich zu meinem Zweck gelange,
Erlaubt ihr mir Triumph aus voller Brust.
Staub soll er fressen, und mit Lust,
335 Wie meine Muhme, die berühmte Schlange.

Der Herr.

Du darfst auch da nur frei erscheinen;
Ich habe Deinesgleichen nie gehaßt.
Von allen Geistern die verneinen
Ist mir der Schalk am wenigsten zur Last.
340 Des Menschen Thätigkeit kann allzuleicht erschlaffen,
Er liebt sich bald die unbedingte Ruh;
Drum geb' ich gern ihm den Gesellen zu,
Der reizt und wirkt und muß als Teufel schaffen.
Doch ihr, die echten Göttersöhne,
345 Erfreut euch der lebendig reichen Schöne!
Das Werdende, das ewig wirkt und lebt,
Umfass' euch mit der Liebe holden Schranken,
Und was in schwankender Erscheinung schwebt,
Befestiget mit dauernden Gedanken.

Der Himmel schließt, die Erzengel vertheilen sich.

Mephistopheles allein.

350 Von Zeit zu Zeit seh' ich den Alten gern,
Und hüte mich mit ihm zu brechen.
Es ist gar hübsch von einem großen Herrn,
So menschlich mit dem Teufel selbst zu sprechen.

———

Der Tragödie — Erster Theil

Nacht.

*In einem hochgewölbten engen gothischen Zimmer Faust unruhig
auf seinem Sessel am Pulte.*

Faust.

Habe nun, ach! Philosophie,
355 Juristerei und Medicin,
Und leider auch Theologie!
Durchaus studirt, mit heißem Bemühn.
Da steh' ich nun, ich armer Thor!
Und bin so klug als wie zuvor;
360 Heiße Magister, heiße Doctor gar,
Und ziehe schon an die zehen Jahr,
Herauf, herab und quer und krumm,
Meine Schüler an der Nase herum —
Und sehe, daß wir nichts wissen können!
365 Das will mir schier das Herz verbrennen.
Zwar bin ich gescheidter als alle die Laffen,
Doctoren, Magister, Schreiber und Pfaffen;
Mich plagen keine Scrupel noch Zweifel,
Fürchte mich weder vor Hölle noch Teufel —
370 Dafür ist mir auch alle Freud' entrissen,
Bilde mir nicht ein was Rechts zu wissen,
Bilde mir nicht ein ich könnte was lehren
Die Menschen zu bessern und zu bekehren.

(21)

Auch hab' ich weder Gut noch Geld,
Noch Ehr' und Herrlichkeit der Welt;   375
Es möchte kein Hund ſo länger leben!
Drum hab' ich mich der Magie ergeben,
Ob mir durch Geiſtes Kraft und Mund
Nicht manch Geheimniß würde kund;
Daß ich nicht mehr, mit ſauerm Schweiß,   380
Zu ſagen brauche was ich nicht weiß;
Daß ich erkenne was die Welt
Im Innerſten zuſammenhält,
Schau' alle Wirkenskraft und Samen,
Und thu' nicht mehr in Worten kramen.   385

O ſähſt du, voller Mondenſchein,
Zum letztenmal auf meine Pein,
Den ich ſo manche Mitternacht
An dieſem Pult herangewacht:
Dann, über Büchern und Papier,   390
Trübſel'ger Freund, erſchienſt du mir!
Ach! könnt' ich doch auf Berges=Höhn
In deinem lieben Lichte gehn,
Um Bergeshöhle mit Geiſtern ſchweben,
Auf Wieſen in deinem Dämmer weben,   395
Von allem Wiſſensqualm entladen
In deinem Thau geſund mich baden!

Weh! ſteck' ich in dem Kerker noch?
Verfluchtes dumpfes Mauerloch,
Wo ſelbſt das liebe Himmelslicht
Trüb durch gemahlte Scheiben bricht!   400
Beſchränkt von dieſem Bücherhauf,
Den Würme nagen, Staub bedeckt,

Den, bis an's hohe Gewölb' hinauf,
405 Ein angeraucht Papier umsteckt;
Mit Gläsern, Büchsen rings umstellt,
Mit Instrumenten vollgepfropft,
Urväter Hausrath drein gestopft —
Das ist deine Welt! das heißt eine Welt!

410 Und fragst du noch, warum dein Herz
Sich bang in deinem Busen klemmt?
Warum ein unerklärter Schmerz
Dir alle Lebensregung hemmt?
Statt der lebendigen Natur,
415 Da Gott die Menschen schuf hinein,
Umgibt in Rauch und Moder nur
Dich Thiergerippʼ und Todtenbein.

Flieh! Auf! Hinaus in's weite Land!
Und dieß geheimnißvolle Buch,
420 Von Nostradamus eigner Hand,
Ist dir es nicht Geleit genug?
Erkennest dann der Sterne Lauf,
Und wenn Natur dich unterweis't,
Dann geht die Seelenkraft dir auf,
425 Wie spricht ein Geist zum andern Geist.
Umsonst, daß trocknes Sinnen hier
Die heil'gen Zeichen dir erklärt.
Ihr schwebt, ihr Geister, neben mir;
Antwortet mir, wenn ihr mich hört!

Er schlägt das Buch auf und erblickt das Zeichen des Makrokosmus.

430 Ha! welche Wonne fließt in diesem Blick
Auf einmal mir durch alle meine Sinnen!

Ich fühle junges heil'ges Lebensglück
Neuglühend mir durch Nerv' und Adern rinnen.
War es ein Gott, der diese Zeichen schrieb,
Die mir das innre Toben stillen,   435
Das arme Herz mit Freude füllen,
Und mit geheimnißvollem Trieb
Die Kräfte der Natur rings um mich her enthüllen?
Bin ich ein Gott?   Mir wird so licht!
Ich schau' in diesen reinen Zügen   440
Die wirkende Natur vor meiner Seele liegen.
Jetzt erst erkenn' ich was der Weise spricht:
„Die Geisterwelt ist nicht verschlossen;
„Dein Sinn ist zu, dein Herz ist todt!
„Auf, bade, Schüler, unverdrossen   445
„Die ird'sche Brust im Morgenroth!"

Er beschaut das Zeichen.

Wie alles sich zum Ganzen webt,
Eins in dem andern wirkt und lebt!
Wie Himmelskräfte auf und nieder steigen
Und sich die goldnen Eimer reichen!   450
Mit segenduftenden Schwingen
Vom Himmel durch die Erde dringen,
Harmonisch all' das All durchklingen!

Welch Schauspiel! aber ach! ein Schauspiel nur!
Wo faß' ich dich, unendliche Natur?   455
Euch Brüste, wo?   Ihr Quellen alles Lebens,
An denen Himmel und Erde hängt,
Dahin die welke Brust sich drängt —
Ihr quellt, ihr tränkt, und schmacht' ich so vergebens?

Er schlägt unwillig das Buch um und erblickt das Zeichen des Erdgeistes.

460 Wie anders wirkt dieß Zeichen auf mich ein!
Du, Geist der Erde, bist mir näher;
Schon fühl' ich meine Kräfte höher,
Schon glüh' ich wie von neuem Wein,
Ich fühle Muth mich in die Welt zu wagen,
465 Der Erde Weh, der Erde Glück zu tragen,
Mit Stürmen mich herumzuschlagen,
Und in des Schiffbruchs Knirschen nicht zu zagen.
Es wölkt sich über mir —
Der Mond verbirgt sein Licht —
470 Die Lampe schwindet!
Es dampft! — Es zucken rothe Strahlen
Mir um das Haupt — Es weht
Ein Schauer vom Gewölb' herab
Und faßt mich an!
475 Ich fühl's, du schwebst um mich, erflehter Geist.
Enthülle dich!
Ha! wie's in meinem Herzen reißt!
Zu neuen Gefühlen
All' meine Sinnen sich erwühlen!
480 Ich fühle ganz mein Herz dir hingegeben!
Du mußt! du mußt! und kostet' es mein Leben!

Er faßt das Buch und spricht das Zeichen des Geistes geheimnißvoll aus.
Es zuckt eine röthliche Flamme, der Geist erscheint in der Flamme.

Geist.

Wer ruft mir?

Faust abgewendet.

Schreckliches Gesicht!

Geist.

Du hast mich mächtig angezogen,
An meiner Sphäre lang gesogen,
485 Und nun —

Faust.
Weh! ich ertrag' dich nicht!

Geist.

Du flehst erathmend mich zu schauen,
Meine Stimme zu hören, mein Antlitz zu sehn;
Mich neigt dein mächtig Seelenflehn,
Da bin ich! — Welch erbärmlich Grauen
Faßt Übermenschen dich! Wo ist der Seele Ruf?   490
Wo ist die Brust, die eine Welt in sich erschuf,
Und trug und hegte, die mit Freudebeben
Erschwoll, sich uns, den Geistern, gleich zu heben?
Wo bist du, Faust, deß Stimme mir erklang,
Der sich an mich mit allen Kräften drang?   495
Bist du es, der, von meinem Hauch umwittert,
In allen Lebenstiefen zittert,
Ein furchtsam weggekrümmter Wurm?

Faust.

Soll ich dir, Flammenbildung, weichen?
Ich bin's, bin Faust, bin Deinesgleichen!   500

Geist.

In Lebensfluthen, im Thatensturm
Wall' ich auf und ab,
Wehe hin und her!
Geburt und Grab,
Ein ewiges Meer,   505
Ein wechselnd Weben,
Ein glühend Leben,
So schaff' ich am sausenden Webstuhl der Zeit,
Und wirke der Gottheit lebendiges Kleid.

Faust.

510 Der du die weite Welt umschweifst,
Geschäftiger Geist, wie nah fühl' ich mich dir!

Geist.

Du gleichst dem Geist den du begreifst,
Nicht mir!

Verschwindet.

Faust zusammenstürzend.

Nicht dir?
515 Wem denn?
Ich Ebenbild der Gottheit!
Und nicht einmal dir!

Es klopft.

O Tod! ich kenn's — das ist mein Famulus —
Es wird mein schönstes Glück zu nichte!
520 Daß diese Fülle der Gesichte
Der trockne Schleicher stören muß!

Wagner im Schlafrocke und der Nachtmütze, eine Lampe in der Hand.
Faust wendet sich unwillig.

Wagner.

Verzeiht! ich hör' euch declamiren;
Ihr las't gewiß ein griechisch Trauerspiel?
In dieser Kunst möcht' ich was profitiren,
525 Denn heut zu Tage wirkt das viel.
Ich hab' es öfters rühmen hören,
Ein Komödiant könnt' einen Pfarrer lehren.

Faust.

Ja, wenn der Pfarrer ein Komödiant ist;
Wie das denn wohl zu Zeiten kommen mag.

Wagner.

Ach! wenn man so in sein Museum gebannt ist,   530
Und sieht die Welt kaum einen Feiertag,
Kaum durch ein Fernglas, nur von weiten,
Wie soll man sie durch Überredung leiten?

Faust.

Wenn ihr's nicht fühlt, ihr werdet's nicht erjagen,
Wenn es nicht aus der Seele dringt,   535
Und mit urkräftigem Behagen
Die Herzen aller Hörer zwingt.
Sitzt ihr nur immer! Leimt zusammen,
Braut ein Ragout von andrer Schmaus,
Und blas't die kümmerlichen Flammen   540
Aus eurem Aschenhäufchen h'raus!
Bewundrung von Kindern und Affen,
Wenn euch darnach der Gaumen steht;
Doch werdet ihr nie Herz zu Herzen schaffen,
Wenn es euch nicht von Herzen geht.   545

Wagner.

Allein der Vortrag macht des Redners Glück;
Ich fühl' es wohl noch bin ich weit zurück.

Faust.

Such' Er den redlichen Gewinn!
Sei Er kein schellenlauter Thor!
Es trägt Verstand und rechter Sinn   550
Mit wenig Kunst sich selber vor;
Und wenn's euch Ernst ist was zu sagen,
Ist's nöthig Worten nachzujagen?
Ja, eure Reden, die so blinkend sind, —

555 In denen ihr der Menschheit Schnitzel kräuselt,
Sind unerquicklich wie der Nebelwind,
Der herbstlich durch die dürren Blätter säuselt!

Wagner.

Ach Gott! die Kunst ist lang!
Und kurz ist unser Leben.
560 Mir wird, bei meinem kritischen Bestreben,
Doch oft um Kopf und Busen bang.
Wie schwer sind nicht die Mittel zu erwerben,
Durch die man zu den Quellen steigt!
Und eh' man nur den halben Weg erreicht,
565 Muß wohl ein armer Teufel sterben.

Faust.

Das Pergament ist das der heil'ge Bronnen,
Woraus ein Trunk den Durst auf ewig stillt?
Erquickung hast du nicht gewonnen,
Wenn sie dir nicht aus eigner Seele quillt.

Wagner.

570 Verzeiht! es ist ein groß Ergetzen,
Sich in den Geist der Zeiten zu versetzen,
Zu schauen wie vor uns ein weiser Mann gedacht,
Und wie wir's dann zuletzt so herrlich weit gebracht.

Faust.

O ja, bis an die Sterne weit!
575 Mein Freund, die Zeiten der Vergangenheit
Sind uns ein Buch mit sieben Siegeln;
Was ihr den Geist der Zeiten heißt,
Das ist im Grund der Herren eigner Geist,
In dem die Zeiten sich bespiegeln.

Da ist's denn wahrlich oft ein Jammer!   580
Man läuft euch bei dem ersten Blick davon.
Ein Kehrichtfaß und eine Rumpelkammer,
Und höchstens eine Haupt= und Staatsaction
Mit trefflichen pragmatischen Maximen,
Wie sie den Puppen wohl im Munde ziemen!   585

Wagner.

Allein die Welt! des Menschen Herz und Geist!
Möcht' jeglicher doch was davon erkennen.

Faust.

Ja was man so erkennen heißt!
Wer darf das Kind bei'm rechten Namen nennen?
Die wenigen, die was davon erkannt,   590
Die thöricht g'nug ihr volles Herz nicht wahrten,
Dem Pöbel ihr Gefühl, ihr Schauen offenbarten,
Hat man von je gekreuzigt und verbrannt.
Ich bitt' euch, Freund, es ist tief in der Nacht,
Wir müssen's dießmal unterbrechen.   595

Wagner.

Ich hätte gern nur immer fortgewacht,
Um so gelehrt mit euch mich zu besprechen.
Doch morgen, als am ersten Ostertage,
Erlaubt mir ein' und andre Frage.
Mit Eifer hab' ich mich der Studien befliffen;   600
Zwar weiß ich viel, doch möcht' ich alles wissen.
Ab.
Faust allein.

Wie nur dem Kopf nicht alle Hoffnung schwindet,
Der immerfort an schalem Zeuge klebt,

Mit gier'ger Hand nach Schätzen gräbt,
605 Und froh ist wenn er Regenwürmer findet!

Darf eine solche Menschenstimme hier,
Wo Geisterfülle mich umgab, ertönen?
Doch ach! für dießmal dank' ich dir,
Dem ärmlichsten von allen Erdensöhnen.
610 Du rissest mich von der Verzweiflung los,
Die mir die Sinne schon zerstören wollte.
Ach! die Erscheinung war so riesengroß,
Daß ich mich recht als Zwerg empfinden sollte.

Ich, Ebenbild der Gottheit, das sich schon
615 Ganz nah gedünkt dem Spiegel ew'ger Wahrheit,
Sein selbst genoß in Himmelsglanz und Klarheit,
Und abgestreift den Erdensohn;
Ich, mehr als Cherub, dessen freie Kraft
Schon durch die Adern der Natur zu fließen
620 Und, schaffend, Götterleben zu genießen
Sich ahnungsvoll vermaß, wie muß ich's büßen!
Ein Donnerwort hat mich hinweggerafft.

Nicht darf ich dir zu gleichen mich vermessen!
Hab' ich die Kraft dich anzuziehn besessen,
625 So hatt' ich dich zu halten keine Kraft.
In jenem sel'gen Augenblicke
Ich fühlte mich so klein, so groß;
Du stießest grausam mich zurücke,
In's ungewisse Menschenloos.
630 Wer lehret mich? was soll ich meiden?
Soll ich gehorchen jenem Drang?
Ach! unsre Thaten selbst, so gut als unsre Leiden,
Sie hemmen unsres Lebens Gang.

Dem Herrlichsten, was auch der Geist empfangen,
Drängt immer fremd und fremder Stoff sich an;   635
Wenn wir zum Guten dieser Welt gelangen,
Dann heißt das Beß're Trug und Wahn.
Die uns das Leben gaben, herrliche Gefühle,
Erstarren in dem irdischen Gewühle.

Wenn Phantasie sich sonst mit kühnem Flug   640
Und hoffnungsvoll zum Ewigen erweitert,
So ist ein kleiner Raum ihr nun genug,
Wenn Glück auf Glück im Zeitenstrudel scheitert.
Die Sorge nistet gleich im tiefen Herzen,
Dort wirket sie geheime Schmerzen,   645
Unruhig wiegt sie sich und störet Lust und Ruh;
Sie deckt sich stets mit neuen Masken zu,
Sie mag als Haus und Hof, als Weib und Kind erscheinen,
Als Feuer, Wasser, Dolch und Gift;
Du bebst vor allem was nicht trifft,   650
Und was du nie verlierst das mußt du stets beweinen.

Den Göttern gleich' ich nicht!   Zu tief ist es gefühlt;
Dem Wurme gleich' ich, der den Staub durchwühlt;
Den, wie er sich im Staube nährend lebt,
Des Wandrers Tritt vernichtet und begräbt.   655

Ist es nicht Staub was diese hohe Wand,
Aus hundert Fächern, mir verenget;
Der Trödel, der mit tausendfachem Tand
In dieser Mottenwelt mich dränget?
Hier soll ich finden was mir fehlt?
Soll ich vielleicht in tausend Büchern lesen,   660

Daß überall die Menschen sich gequält,
Daß hie und da ein Glücklicher gewesen? —
Was grinsest du mir hohler Schädel her?
665 Als daß dein Hirn wie meines einst verwirret
Den leichten Tag gesucht und in der Dämmrung schwer,
Mit Lust nach Wahrheit, jämmerlich geirret.
Ihr Instrumente freilich spottet mein,
Mit Rad und Kämmen, Walz' und Bügel:
670 Ich stand am Thor, ihr solltet Schlüssel sein;
Zwar euer Bart ist kraus, doch hebt ihr nicht die Riegel.
Geheimnißvoll am lichten Tag
Läßt sich Natur des Schleiers nicht berauben,
Und was sie deinem Geist nicht offenbaren mag,
675 Das zwingst du ihr nicht ab mit Hebeln und mit Schrauben.
Du alt Geräthe das ich nicht gebraucht,
Du stehst nur hier, weil dich mein Vater brauchte.
Du alte Rolle, du wirst angeraucht,
So lang an diesem Pult die trübe Lampe schmauchte.
680 Weit besser hätt' ich doch mein Weniges verpraßt,
Als mit dem Wenigen belastet hier zu schwitzen!
Was du ererbt von deinen Vätern hast,
Erwirb es um es zu besitzen.
Was man nicht nützt ist eine schwere Last;
685 Nur was der Augenblick erschafft das kann er nützen.

Doch warum heftet sich mein Blick auf jene Stelle?
Ist jenes Fläschchen dort den Augen ein Magnet?
Warum wird mir auf einmal lieblich helle,
Als wenn im nächt'gen Wald uns Mondenglanz umweht?

690 Ich grüße dich, du einzige Phiole!
Die ich mit Andacht nun herunterhole,

In dir verehr' ich Menſchenwitz und Kunſt.
Du Inbegriff der holden Schlummerſäfte,
Du Auszug aller tödtlich feinen Kräfte,
Erweiſe deinem Meiſter deine Gunſt!   695
Ich ſehe dich, es wird der Schmerz gelindert,
Ich faſſe dich, das Streben wird gemindert,
Des Geiſtes Fluthſtrom ebbet nach und nach.
In's hohe Meer werd' ich hinausgewieſen,
Die Spiegelfluth erglänzt zu meinen Füßen,   700
Zu neuen Ufern lockt ein neuer Tag.

Ein Feuerwagen ſchwebt, auf leichten Schwingen,
An mich heran!   Ich fühle mich bereit
Auf neuer Bahn den Äther zu durchdringen,
Zu neuen Sphären reiner Thätigkeit.   705
Dieß hohe Leben, dieſe Götterwonne!
Du, erſt noch Wurm, und die verdieneſt du?
Ja, kehre nur der holden Erdenſonne
Entſchloſſen deinen Rücken zu!
Vermeſſe dich die Pforten aufzureißen,   710
Vor denen jeder gern vorüber ſchleicht!
Hier iſt es Zeit durch Thaten zu beweiſen,
Daß Manneswürde nicht der Götterhöhe weicht,
Vor jener dunkeln Höhle nicht zu beben,
In der ſich Phantaſie zu eigner Qual verdammt,   715
Nach jenem Durchgang hinzuſtreben,
Um deſſen engen Mund die ganze Hölle flammt;
Zu dieſem Schritt ſich heiter zu entſchließen
Und, wär' es mit Gefahr, in's Nichts dahin zu fließen.

Nun komm herab, kryſtallne reine Schale!   720
Hervor aus deinem alten Futterale,

An die ich viele Jahre nicht gedacht!
Du glänztest bei der Väter Freudenfeste,
Erheitertest die ernsten Gäste,
725 Wenn einer dich dem andern zugebracht.
Der vielen Bilder künstlich reiche Pracht,
Des Trinkers Pflicht, sie reimweis zu erklären,
Auf Einen Zug die Höhlung auszuleeren,
Erinnert mich an manche Jugend=Nacht;
730 Ich werde jetzt dich keinem Nachbar reichen,
Ich werde meinen Witz an deiner Kunst nicht zeigen;
Hier ist ein Saft, der eilig trunken macht.
Mit brauner Fluth erfüllt er deine Höhle.
Den ich bereitet, den ich wähle,
735 Der letzte Trunk sei nun, mit ganzer Seele,
Als festlich hoher Gruß, dem Morgen zugebracht!

           Er setzt die Schale an den Mund.

Glockenklang und Chorgesang.

Chor der Engel.

    Christ ist erstanden!
    Freude dem Sterblichen,
    Den die verderblichen,
    Schleichenden, erblichen
740   Mängel umwanden.

Faust.

Welch tiefes Summen, welch ein heller Ton,
Zieht mit Gewalt das Glas von meinem Munde?
Verkündiget ihr dumpfen Glocken schon
745 Des Osterfestes erste Feierstunde?

Ihr Chöre ſingt ihr ſchon den tröſtlichen Geſang,
Der einſt, um Grabes Nacht, von Engelslippen klang,
Gewißheit einem neuen Bunde?

Chor der Weiber.

Mit Specereien
Hatten wir ihn gepflegt,   750
Wir ſeine Treuen
Hatten ihn hingelegt;
Tücher und Binden
Reinlich umwanden wir,
Ach! und wir finden   755
Chriſt nicht mehr hier.

Chor der Engel.

Chriſt iſt erſtanden!
Selig der Liebende,
Der die betrübende,
Heilſam' und übende   760
Prüfung beſtanden!

Fauſt.

Was ſucht ihr mächtig und gelind,
Ihr Himmelstöne, mich am Staube?
Klingt dort umher, wo weiche Menſchen ſind.
Die Botſchaft hör' ich wohl, allein mir fehlt der Glaube; 765
Das Wunder iſt des Glaubens liebſtes Kind.
Zu jenen Sphären wag' ich nicht zu ſtreben,
Woher die holde Nachricht tönt;
Und doch, an dieſen Klang von Jugend auf gewöhnt,
Ruft er auch jetzt zurück mich in das Leben.   770
Sonſt ſtürzte ſich der Himmels-Liebe Kuß

Auf mich herab, in ernster Sabbathstille;
Da klang so ahnungsvoll des Glockentones Fülle,
Und ein Gebet war brünstiger Genuß;
775 Ein unbegreiflich holdes Sehnen
Trieb mich durch Wald und Wiesen hinzugehn,
Und unter tausend heißen Thränen
Fühlt' ich mir eine Welt entstehn.
Dieß Lied verkündete der Jugend muntre Spiele,
780 Der Frühlingsfeier freies Glück;
Erinnrung hält mich nun mit kindlichem Gefühle
Vom letzten ernsten Schritt zurück.
O tönet fort ihr süßen Himmelslieder!
Die Thräne quillt, die Erde hat mich wieder!

Chor der Jünger.

785 Hat der Begrabene
Schon sich nach oben,
Lebend Erhabene,
Herrlich erhoben;
Ist er in Werdelust
790 Schaffender Freude nah;
Ach! an der Erde Brust
Sind wir zum Leide da.
Ließ er die Seinen
Schmachtend uns hier zurück;
795 Ach! wir beweinen,
Meister dein Glück!

Chor der Engel.

Christ ist erstanden,
Aus der Verwesung Schoos;
Reißet von Banden
800 Freudig euch los!

Thätig ihn preiſenden,
Liebe beweiſenden,
Brüderlich ſpeiſenden,
Predigend reiſenden,
Wonne verheißenden   805
Euch iſt der Meiſter nah,
Euch iſt er da!

Vor dem Thor.

Spaziergänger aller Art ziehen hinaus.

Einige Handwerksbursche.
Warum denn dort hinaus?

Andre.
Wir gehn hinaus auf's Jägerhaus.

Die ersten.
810 Wir aber wollen nach der Mühle wandern.

Ein Handwerksbursch.
Ich rath' euch nach dem Wasserhof zu gehn.

Zweiter.
Der Weg dahin ist gar nicht schön.

Die zweiten.
Was thust denn du?

Ein dritter.
Ich gehe mit den andern.

Vierter.
Nach Burgdorf kommt herauf, gewiß dort findet ihr
815 Die schönsten Mädchen und das beste Bier,
Und Händel von der ersten Sorte.

Fünfter.

Du überlustiger Gesell,
Juckt dich zum drittenmal das Fell?
Ich mag nicht hin, mir graut es vor dem Orte.

Dienstmädchen.

Nein, nein! ich gehe nach der Stadt zurück.   820

Andre.

Wir finden ihn gewiß bei jenen Pappeln stehen.

Erste.

Das ist für mich kein großes Glück;
Er wird an deiner Seite gehen,
Mit dir nur tanzt er auf dem Plan.
Was gehn mich deine Freuden an!   825

Andre.

Heut ist er sicher nicht allein,
Der Krauskopf, sagt er, würde bei ihm sein.

Schüler.

Blitz, wie die wackern Dirnen schreiten!
Herr Bruder, komm! wir müssen sie begleiten.
Ein starkes Bier, ein beizender Toback,   830
Und eine Magd im Putz das ist nun mein Geschmack.

Bürgermädchen.

Da sieh mir nur die schönen Knaben!
Es ist wahrhaftig eine Schmach;
Gesellschaft könnten sie die allerbeste haben,
Und laufen diesen Mägden nach!   835

Zweiter Schüler zum ersten.

Nicht so geschwind! dort hinten kommen zwei,
Sie sind gar niedlich angezogen,
's ist meine Nachbarin dabei;
Ich bin dem Mädchen sehr gewogen.
840 Sie gehen ihren stillen Schritt
Und nehmen uns doch auch am Ende mit.

Erster.

Herr Bruder, nein!   Ich bin nicht gern genirt.
Geschwind! daß wir das Wildpret nicht verlieren.
Die Hand, die Samstags ihren Besen führt,
845 Wird Sonntags dich am besten caressiren.

Bürger.

Nein, er gefällt mir nicht der neue Burgemeister!
Nun, da er's ist, wird er nur täglich dreister.
Und für die Stadt was thut denn er?
Wird es nicht alle Tage schlimmer?
850 Gehorchen soll man mehr als immer,
Und zahlen mehr als je vorher.

Bettler singt.

Ihr guten Herrn, ihr schönen Frauen,
So wohlgeputzt und backenroth,
Belieb' es euch mich anzuschauen,
855 Und seht und mildert meine Noth!
Laßt hier mich nicht vergebens leiern!
Nur der ist froh, der geben mag.
Ein Tag den alle Menschen feiern,
Er sei für mich ein Erntetag.

Andrer Bürger.

Nichts Beſſers weiß ich mir an Sonn= und Feiertagen,   860
Als ein Geſpräch von Krieg und Kriegsgeſchrei,
Wenn hinten, weit, in der Türkei,
Die Völker auf einander ſchlagen.
Man ſteht am Fenſter, trinkt ſein Gläschen aus
Und ſieht den Fluß hinab die bunten Schiffe gleiten;   865
Dann kehrt man Abends froh nach Haus,
Und ſegnet Fried' und Friedenszeiten.

Dritter Bürger.

Herr Nachbar, ja! ſo laß ich's auch geſchehn,
Sie mögen ſich die Köpfe ſpalten,
Mag alles durcheinandergehn;   870
Doch nur zu Hauſe bleib's bei'm Alten.

Alte zu den Bürgermädchen.

Ei! wie gepußt! das ſchöne junge Blut!
Wer ſoll ſich nicht in euch vergaffen? —
Nur nicht ſo ſtolz!   Es iſt ſchon gut!
Und was ihr wünſcht das wüßt' ich wohl zu ſchaffen.   875

Bürgermädchen.

Agathe fort! ich nehme mich in Acht
Mit ſolchen Hexen öffentlich zu gehen;
Sie ließ mich zwar, in Sanct Andreas Nacht,
Den künft'gen Liebſten leiblich ſehen —

Die Andre.

Mir zeigte ſie ihn im Kryſtall,   880
Soldatenhaft, mit mehreren Verwegnen;
Ich ſeh' mich um, ich ſuch' ihn überall,
Allein mir will er nicht begegnen.

Soldaten.

Burgen mit hohen
885 Mauern und Zinnen,
Mädchen mit stolzen
Höhnenden Sinnen
Möcht' ich gewinnen!
Kühn ist das Mühen,
890 Herrlich der Lohn!

Und die Trompete
Lassen wir werben,
Wie zu der Freude,
So zum Verderben.
895 Das ist ein Stürmen!
Das ist ein Leben!
Mädchen und Burgen
Müssen sich geben.
Kühn ist das Mühen,
900 Herrlich der Lohn!
Und die Soldaten
Ziehen davon.

Faust und Wagner.

Faust.

Vom Eise befreit sind Strom und Bäche
Durch des Frühlings holden belebenden Blick;
905 Im Thale grünet Hoffnungs-Glück;
Der alte Winter, in seiner Schwäche,
Zog sich in rauhe Berge zurück.
Von dorther sendet er, fliehend, nur

Ohnmächtige Schauer körnigen Eiſes
In Streifen über die grünende Flur ;   910
Aber die Sonne duldet kein Weißes,
Überall regt sich Bildung und Streben,
Alles will sie mit Farben beleben ;
Doch an Blumen fehlt's im Revier,
Sie nimmt geputzte Menschen dafür.   915
Kehre dich um, von diesen Höhen
Nach der Stadt zurück zu sehen.
Aus dem hohlen finstern Thor
Dringt ein buntes Gewimmel hervor.
Jeder sonnt sich heute so gern.   920
Sie feiern die Auferstehung des Herrn,
Denn sie sind selber auferstanden,
Aus niedriger Häuser dumpfen Gemächern,
Aus Handwerks= und Gewerbes=Banden,
Aus dem Druck von Giebeln und Dächern,   925
Aus der Straßen quetschender Enge,
Aus der Kirchen ehrwürdiger Nacht
Sind sie alle an's Licht gebracht.
Sieh nur, sieh! wie behend sich die Menge
Durch die Gärten und Felder zerschlägt,   930
Wie der Fluß, in Breit' und Länge,
So manchen lustigen Nachen bewegt,
Und bis zum Sinken überladen
Entfernt sich dieser letzte Kahn.
Selbst von des Berges fernen Pfaden   935
Blinken uns farbige Kleider an.
Ich höre schon des Dorfs Getümmel,
Hier ist des Volkes wahrer Himmel,
Zufrieden jauchzet Groß und Klein :
Hier bin ich Mensch, hier darf ich's sein!   940

Wagner.

Mit euch, Herr Doctor, zu spazieren
Ist ehrenvoll und ist Gewinn;
Doch würd' ich nicht allein mich her verlieren,
Weil ich ein Feind von allem Rohen bin.
945 Das Fiedeln, Schreien, Kegelschieben,
Ist mir ein gar verhaßter Klang;
Sie toben wie vom bösen Geist getrieben
Und nennen's Freude, nennen's Gesang.

Bauern unter der Linde.

Tanz und Gesang.

Der Schäfer putzte sich zum Tanz,
950 Mit bunter Jacke, Band und Kranz,
Schmuck war er angezogen.
Schon um die Linde war es voll;
Und alles tanzte schon wie toll.
Juchhe! Juchhe!
955 Juchheisa! Heisa! He!
So ging der Fiedelbogen.

Er drückte hastig sich heran,
Da stieß er an ein Mädchen an
Mit seinem Ellenbogen;
960 Die frische Dirne kehrt' sich um
Und sagte: nun das find' ich dumm!
Juchhe! Juchhe!
Juchheisa! Heisa! He!
Seid nicht so ungezogen.

Doch hurtig in dem Kreiſe ging's,   965
Sie tanzten rechts, ſie tanzten links,
Und alle Röcke flogen.
Sie wurden roth, ſie wurden warm
Und ruhten athmend Arm in Arm,
Juchhe! Juchhe!   970
Juchheiſa! Heiſa! He!
Und Hüft' an Ellenbogen.

Und thu' mir doch nicht ſo vertraut!
Wie mancher hat nicht ſeine Braut
Belogen und betrogen!   975
Er ſchmeichelte ſie doch bei Seit'
Und von der Linde ſcholl es weit:
Juchhe! Juchhe!
Juchheiſa! Heiſa! He!
Geſchrei und Fiedelbogen.   980

Alter Bauer.

Herr Doctor, das iſt ſchön von euch,
Daß ihr uns heute nicht verſchmäht,
Und unter dieſes Volksgedräng',
Als ein ſo Hochgelahrter, geht.
So nehmet auch den ſchönſten Krug,   985
Den wir mit friſchem Trunk gefüllt,
Ich bring' ihn zu und wünſche laut,
Daß er nicht nur den Durſt euch ſtillt;
Die Zahl der Tropfen, die er hegt,
Sei euren Tagen zugelegt.   990

Fauſt.

Ich nehme den Erquickungs=Trank,
Erwidr' euch allen Heil und Dank.

Das Volk ſammelt ſich im Kreis umher.

Alter Bauer.

Fürwahr es iſt ſehr wohl gethan,
Daß ihr am frohen Tag erſcheint;
995 Habt ihr es vormals doch mit uns
An böſen Tagen gut gemeint!
Gar mancher ſteht lebendig hier,
Den euer Vater noch zuletzt
Der heißen Fieberwuth entriß,
1000 Als er der Seuche Ziel geſetzt.
Auch damals ihr, ein junger Mann,
Ihr gingt in jedes Krankenhaus,
Gar manche Leiche trug man fort,
Ihr aber kamt geſund heraus;
1005 Beſtandet manche harte Proben;
Dem Helfer half der Helfer droben.

Alle.

Gesundheit dem bewährten Mann,
Daß er noch lange helfen kann!

Fauſt.

Vor jenem droben ſteht gebückt,
1010 Der helfen lehrt und Hülfe ſchickt!

Er geht mit Wagnern weiter.

Wagner.

Welch ein Gefühl mußt du, o großer Mann,
Bei der Verehrung dieser Menge haben!

O glücklich, wer von ſeinen Gaben
Solch einen Vortheil ziehen kann!
Der Vater zeigt dich ſeinem Knaben,   1015
Ein jeder fragt und drängt und eilt,
Die Fiedel ſtockt, der Tänzer weilt.
Du gehſt, in Reihen ſtehen ſie,
Die Mützen fliegen in die Höh':
Und wenig fehlt, ſo beugten ſich die Knie,   1020
Als käm' das Venerabile.

Fauſt.

Nur wenig Schritte noch hinauf zu jenem Stein,
Hier wollen wir von unſrer Wandrung raſten.
Hier ſaß ich oft gedankenvoll allein
Und quälte mich mit Beten und mit Faſten.   1025
An Hoffnung reich, im Glauben feſt,
Mit Thränen, Seufzen, Händeringen
Dacht' ich das Ende jener Peſt
Vom Herrn des Himmels zu erzwingen.
Der Menge Beifall tönt mir nun wie Hohn.   1030
O könnteſt du in meinem Innern leſen,
Wie wenig Vater und Sohn
Solch eines Ruhmes werth geweſen!
Mein Vater war ein dunkler Ehrenmann,
Der über die Natur und ihre heil'gen Kreiſe,   1035
In Redlichkeit, jedoch auf ſeine Weiſe,
Mit grillenhafter Mühe ſann.
Der, in Geſellſchaft von Adepten,
Sich in die ſchwarze Küche ſchloß,
Und, nach unendlichen Recepten,   1040
Das Widrige zuſammengoß.

Da ward ein rother Leu, ein kühner Freier,
Im lauen Bad der Lilie vermählt
Und beide dann mit offnem Flammenfeuer
1045 Aus einem Brautgemach in's andere gequält.
Erschien darauf mit bunten Farben
Die junge Königin im Glas,
Hier war die Arzenei, die Patienten starben,
Und niemand fragte: wer genas?
1050 So haben wir mit höllischen Latwergen
In diesen Thälern, diesen Bergen,
Weit schlimmer als die Pest getobt.
Ich habe selbst den Gift an Tausende gegeben,
Sie welkten hin, ich muß erleben
1055 Daß man die frechen Mörder lobt.

Wagner.

Wie könnt ihr euch darum betrüben!
Thut nicht ein braver Mann genug,
Die Kunst, die man ihm übertrug,
Gewissenhaft und pünctlich auszuüben?
1060 Wenn du, als Jüngling, deinen Vater ehrst,
So wirst du gern von ihm empfangen;
Wenn du, als Mann, die Wissenschaft vermehrst,
So kann dein Sohn zu höhrem Ziel gelangen.

Faust.

O glücklich, wer noch hoffen kann
1065 Aus diesem Meer des Irrthums aufzutauchen!
Was man nicht weiß das eben brauchte man,
Und was man weiß kann man nicht brauchen.
Doch laß uns dieser Stunde schönes Gut

Durch solchen Trübsinn nicht verkümmern!
Betrachte wie in Abendsonne=Gluth   1070
Die grünumgebnen Hütten schimmern.
Sie rückt und weicht, der Tag ist überlebt,
Dort eilt sie hin und fördert neues Leben.
O daß kein Flügel mich vom Boden hebt,
Ihr nach und immer nach zu streben!   1075
Ich säh' im ewigen Abendstrahl
Die stille Welt zu meinen Füßen,
Entzündet alle Höhn, beruhigt jedes Thal,
Den Silberbach in goldne Ströme fließen.
Nicht hemmte dann den göttergleichen Lauf   1080
Der wilde Berg mit allen seinen Schluchten;
Schon thut das Meer sich mit erwärmten Buchten
Vor den erstaunten Augen auf.
Doch scheint die Göttin endlich wegzusinken;
Allein der neue Trieb erwacht,   1085
Ich eile fort ihr ew'ges Licht zu trinken,
Vor mir den Tag und hinter mir die Nacht,
Den Himmel über mir und unter mir die Wellen.
Ein schöner Traum, indessen sie entweicht.
Ach! zu des Geistes Flügeln wird so leicht   1090
Kein körperlicher Flügel sich gesellen.
Doch ist es jedem eingeboren,
Daß sein Gefühl hinauf und vorwärts dringt,
Wenn über uns im blauen Raum verloren,
Ihr schmetternd Lied die Lerche singt;   1095
Wenn über schroffen Fichtenhöhen
Der Adler ausgebreitet schwebt,
Und über Flächen, über Seen,
Der Kranich nach der Heimath strebt.

Wagner.

1100 Ich hatte selbst oft grillenhafte Stunden,
Doch solchen Trieb hab' ich noch nie empfunden.
Man sieht sich leicht an Wald und Feldern satt,
Des Vogels Fittich werd' ich nie beneiden.
Wie anders trägen uns die Geistesfreuden,
1105 Von Buch zu Buch, von Blatt zu Blatt!
Da werden Winternächte hold und schön,
Ein selig Leben wärmet alle Glieder,
Und ach! entrollst du gar ein würdig Pergamen,
So steigt der ganze Himmel zu dir nieder.

Faust.

1110 Du bist dir nur des einen Triebs bewußt;
O lerne nie den andern kennen!
Zwei Seelen wohnen, ach! in meiner Brust,
Die eine will sich von der andern trennen;
Die eine hält, in derber Liebeslust,
1115 Sich an die Welt mit klammernden Organen;
Die andre hebt gewaltsam sich vom Dust
Zu den Gefilden hoher Ahnen.
O gibt es Geister in der Luft,
Die zwischen Erd' und Himmel herrschend weben,
1120 So steiget nieder aus dem goldnen Dust
Und führt mich weg, zu neuem buntem Leben!
Ja, wäre nur ein Zaubermantel mein!
Und trüg' er mich in fremde Länder,
Mir sollt' er um die köstlichsten Gewänder,
1125 Nicht feil um einen Königsmantel sein.

Wagner.

Berufe nicht die wohlbekannte Schaar,
Die strömend sich im Dunstkreis überbreitet,

Dem Menſchen tauſendfältige Gefahr,
Von allen Enden her, bereitet.
Vom Norden dringt der ſcharfe Geiſterzahn　　　　　1130
Auf dich herbei, mit pfeilgeſpitzten Zungen;
Von Morgen ziehn, vertrocknend, ſie heran,
Und nähren ſich von deinen Lungen;
Wenn ſie der Mittag aus der Wüſte ſchickt,
Die Gluth auf Gluth um deinen Scheitel häufen,　　　1135
So bringt der Weſt den Schwarm, der erſt erquickt,
Um dich und Feld und Aue zu erſäufen.
Sie hören gern, zum Schaden froh gewandt,
Gehorchen gern, weil ſie uns gern betrügen,
Sie ſtellen wie vom Himmel ſich geſandt,　　　　　1140
Und liſpeln engliſch, wenn ſie lügen.
Doch gehen wir! Ergraut iſt ſchon die Welt,
Die Luft gekühlt, der Nebel fällt!
Am Abend ſchätzt man erſt das Haus. —
Was ſtehſt du ſo und blickſt erſtaunt hinaus?　　　　1145
Was kann dich in der Dämmrung ſo ergreifen?

Fauſt.

Siehſt du den ſchwarzen Hund durch Saat und Stoppel ſtreifen?

Wagner.

Ich ſah ihn lange ſchon, nicht wichtig ſchien er mir.

Fauſt.

Betracht' ihn recht! Für was hältſt du das Thier?

Wagner.

Für einen Pudel, der auf ſeine Weiſe　　　　　　　1150
Sich auf der Spur des Herren plagt.

Faust.

Bemerkst du, wie in weitem Schneckenkreise
Er um uns her und immer näher jagt?
Und irr' ich nicht, so zieht ein Feuerstrudel
1155   Auf seinen Pfaden hinterdrein.

Wagner.

Ich sehe nichts als einen schwarzen Pudel;
Es mag bei euch wohl Augentäuschung sein.

Faust.

Mir scheint es, daß er magisch leise Schlingen
Zu künft'gem Band um unsre Füße zieht.

Wagner.

1160   Ich seh' ihn ungewiß und furchtsam uns umspringen,
Weil er, statt seines Herrn, zwei Unbekannte sieht.

Faust.

Der Kreis wird eng, schon ist er nah!

Wagner.

Du siehst! ein Hund, und kein Gespenst ist da.
Er knurrt und zweifelt, legt sich auf den Bauch,
1165   Er wedelt. Alles Hunde Brauch.

Faust.

Geselle dich zu uns!   Komm hier!

Wagner.

Es ist ein pudelnärrisch Thier.
Du stehest still, er wartet auf;
Du sprichst ihn an, er strebt an dir hinauf;

Verliere was, er wird es bringen,　　　　　　1170
Nach deinem Stock in's Waſſer ſpringen.

Fauſt.

Du haſt wohl Recht; ich finde nicht die Spur
Von einem Geiſt, und alles iſt Dreſſur.

Wagner.

Dem Hunde, wenn er gut gezogen,
Wird ſelbſt ein weiſer Mann gewogen.　　　　1175
Ja, deine Gunſt verdient er ganz und gar,
Er der Studenten trefflicher Scolar.

Sie gehen in das Stadt=Thor

Studirzimmer.

Faust mit dem Pudel hereintretend.

Faust.

Verlassen hab' ich Feld und Auen,
Die eine tiefe Nacht bedeckt,
1180   Mit ahnungsvollem heil'gem Grauen
In uns die beß're Seele weckt.
Entschlafen sind nun wilde Triebe,
Mit jedem ungestümen Thun;
Es regt sich die Menschenliebe,
1185   Die Liebe Gottes regt sich nun.

Sei ruhig Pudel! renne nicht hin und wieder!
An der Schwelle was schnoperst du hier?
Lege dich hinter den Ofen nieder,
Mein bestes Kissen geb' ich dir.
1190   Wie du draußen auf dem bergigen Wege
Durch Rennen und Springen ergetzt uns hast,
So nimm nun auch von mir die Pflege,
Als ein willkommner stiller Gast.

Ach wenn in unsrer engen Zelle
1195   Die Lampe freundlich wieder brennt,
Dann wird's in unserm Busen helle,
Im Herzen, das sich selber kennt.

Vernunft fängt wieder an zu ſprechen,
Und Hoffnung wieder an zu blühn;
Man ſehnt ſich nach des Lebens Bächen,　　　1200
Ach! nach des Lebens Quelle hin.

Knurre nicht Pudel!　Zu den heiligen Tönen,
Die jetzt meine ganze Seel' umfaſſen,
Will der thieriſche Laut nicht paſſen.
Wir ſind gewohnt, daß die Menſchen verhöhnen　　　1205
Was ſie nicht verſtehn,
Daß ſie vor dem Guten und Schönen,
Das ihnen oft beſchwerlich iſt, murren;
Will es der Hund, wie ſie, beknurren?

Aber ach! ſchon fühl' ich bei dem beſten Willen,　　　1210
Befriedigung nicht mehr aus dem Buſen quillen.
Aber warum muß der Strom ſo bald verſiegen,
Und wir wieder im Durſte liegen?
Davon hab' ich ſo viel Erfahrung.
Doch dieſer Mangel läßt ſich erſetzen,　　　1215
Wir lernen das Überirdiſche ſchätzen,
Wir ſehnen uns nach Offenbarung,
Die nirgends würd'ger und ſchöner brennt,
Als in dem neuen Teſtament.
Mich drängt's den Grundtext aufzuſchlagen,　　　1220
Mit redlichem Gefühl einmal
Das heilige Original
In mein geliebtes Deutſch zu übertragen.

　　　Er ſchlägt ein Volum auf und ſchickt ſich an.

Geſchrieben ſteht: „im Anfang war das W o r t!“
Hier ſtock' ich ſchon!　Wer hilft mir weiter fort?　　　1225

Ich kann das Wort so hoch unmöglich schätzen,
Ich muß es anders übersetzen,
Wenn ich vom Geiste recht erleuchtet bin.
Geschrieben steht: im Anfang war der Sinn.
1230 Bedenke wohl die erste Zeile,
Daß deine Feder sich nicht übereile!
Ist es der Sinn, der alles wirkt und schafft?
Es sollte stehn: im Anfang war die Kraft!
Doch, auch indem ich dieses niederschreibe,
1235 Schon warnt mich was, daß ich dabei nicht bleibe.
Mir hilft der Geist! Auf einmal seh' ich Rath
Und schreibe getrost: im Anfang war die That!

Soll ich mit dir das Zimmer theilen,
Pudel, so laß das Heulen,
1240 So laß das Bellen!
Solch einen störenden Gesellen
Mag ich nicht in der Nähe leiden.
Einer von uns beiden
Muß die Zelle meiden.
1245 Ungern heb' ich das Gastrecht auf,
Die Thür ist offen, hast freien Lauf.
Aber was muß ich sehen!
Kann das natürlich geschehen?
Ist es Schatten? ist's Wirklichkeit?
1250 Wie wird mein Pudel lang und breit!
Er hebt sich mit Gewalt,
Das ist nicht eines Hundes Gestalt!
Welch ein Gespenst bracht' ich in's Haus!
Schon sieht er wie ein Nilpferd aus,
1255 Mit feurigen Augen, schrecklichem Gebiß.

O! du biſt mir gewiß!
Für ſolche halbe Höllenbrut
Iſt Salomonis Schlüſſel gut.

G e i ſt e r auf dem Gange.

Drinnen gefangen iſt einer!
Bleibet haußen, folg' ihm keiner!   1260
Wie im Eiſen der Fuchs
Zagt ein alter Höllenluchs.
Aber gebt Acht!
Schwebet hin, ſchwebet wieder,
Auf und nieder,   1265
Und er hat ſich losgemacht.
Könnt ihr ihm nützen,
Laßt ihn nicht ſitzen!
Denn er that uns allen
Schon viel zu Gefallen.   1270

F a u ſt.

Erſt zu begegnen dem Thiere,
Brauch' ich den Spruch der Viere:

Salamander ſoll glühen,
Undene ſich winden,
Sylphe verſchwinden,   1275
Kobold ſich mühen.

Wer ſie nicht kennte
Die Elemente,
Ihre Kraft
Und Eigenſchaft,   1280
Wäre kein Meiſter
Über die Geiſter.

Verschwind' in Flammen
Salamander!
1285 Rauschend fließe zusammen
Undene!
Leucht' in Meteoren=Schöne
Sylphe!
Bring'häusliche Hülfe
1290 Incubus! incubus!
Tritt hervor und mache den Schluß.

Keines der Viere
Steckt in dem Thiere.
Es liegt ganz ruhig und grins't mich an;
1295 Ich hab' ihm noch nicht weh gethan.
Du sollst mich hören
Stärker beschwören.

Bist du Geselle
Ein Flüchtling der Hölle?
1300 So sieh dieß Zeichen!
Dem sie sich beugen
Die schwarzen Schaaren.

Schon schwillt es auf mit borstigen Haaren.

Verworfnes Wesen!
1305 Kannst du ihn lesen?
Den nie Entsproß'nen,
Unausgesprochnen,
Durch alle Himmel Gegoß'nen
Freventlich Durchstochnen?

Hinter den Ofen gebannt   1310
Schwillt es wie ein Elephant,
Den ganzen Raum füllt es an,
Es will zum Nebel zerfließen.
Steige nicht zur Decke hinan!
Lege dich zu des Meiſters Füßen!   1315
Du ſiehſt daß ich nicht vergebens drohe.
Ich verſenge dich mit heiliger Lohe!
Erwarte nicht
Das dreimal glühende Licht!
Erwarte nicht   1320
Die ſtärkſte von meinen Künſten!

Mephiſtopheles tritt, indem der Nebel fällt, gekleidet wie ein fah-
renber Scholaſticus, hinter dem Ofen hervor.

Mephiſtopheles.

Wozu der Lärm? was ſteht dem Herrn zu Dienſten?

Fauſt.

Das alſo war des Pudels Kern!
Ein fahrender Scolaſt? Der Caſus macht mich lachen.

Mephiſtopheles.

Ich ſalutire den gelehrten Herrn!   1325
Ihr habt mich weidlich ſchwitzen machen.

Fauſt.

Wie nennſt du dich?

Mephiſtopheles.

Die Frage ſcheint mir klein
Für einen der das Wort ſo ſehr verachtet,
Der, weit entfernt von allem Schein,
Nur in der Weſen Tiefe trachtet.   1330

Faust.

Bei euch, ihr Herrn, kann man das Wesen
Gewöhnlich aus dem Namen lesen,
Wo es sich allzudeutlich weis't,
Wenn man euch Fliegengott, Verderber, Lügner heißt.
1335 Nun gut, wer bist du denn?

Mephistopheles.

                Ein Theil von jener Kraft,
Die stets das Böse will und stets das Gute schafft.

Faust.

Was ist mit diesem Räthselwort gemeint?

Mephistopheles.

Ich bin der Geist der stets verneint!
Und das mit Recht; denn alles was entsteht
1340 Ist werth daß es zu Grunde geht;
Drum besser wär's daß nichts entstünde.
So ist denn alles was ihr Sünde,
Zerstörung, kurz das Böse nennt,
Mein eigentliches Element.

Faust.

1345 Du nennst dich einen Theil, und stehst doch ganz vor mir.

Mephistopheles.

Bescheidne Wahrheit sprech' ich dir.
Wenn sich der Mensch, die kleine Narrenwelt,
Gewöhnlich für ein Ganzes hält;
Ich bin ein Theil des Theils, der Anfangs alles war,
1350 Ein Theil der Finsterniß, die sich das Licht gebar,

Das stolze Licht, das nun der Mutter Nacht
Den alten Rang, den Raum ihr streitig macht,
Und doch gelingt's ihm nicht, da es, so viel es strebt,
Verhaftet an den Körpern klebt.
Von Körpern strömt's, die Körper macht es schön,				1355
Ein Körper hemmt's auf seinem Gange,
So, hoff' ich, dauert es nicht lange
Und mit den Körpern wird's zu Grunde gehn.

Faust.

Nun kenn' ich deine würd'gen Pflichten!
Du kannst im Großen nichts vernichten,				1360
Und fängst es nun im Kleinen an.

Mephistopheles.

Und freilich ist nicht viel damit gethan.
Was sich dem Nichts entgegenstellt,
Das Etwas, diese plumpe Welt,
So viel als ich schon unternommen,				1365
Ich wußte nicht ihr beizukommen,
Mit Wellen, Stürmen, Schütteln, Brand,
Geruhig bleibt am Ende Meer und Land!
Und dem verdammten Zeug, der Thier= und Menschenbrut,
Dem ist nun gar nichts anzuhaben.				1370
Wie viele hab' ich schon begraben!
Und immer circulirt ein neues frisches Blut.
So geht es fort, man möchte rasend werden!
Der Luft, dem Wasser, wie der Erden
Entwinden tausend Keime sich,				1375
Im Trocknen, Feuchten, Warmen, Kalten!
Hätt' ich mir nicht die Flamme vorbehalten,
Ich hätte nichts Aparts für mich.

Faust.

So setzest du der ewig regen,
1380 Der heilsam schaffenden Gewalt
Die kalte Teufelsfaust entgegen,
Die sich vergebens tückisch ballt!
Was Anders suche zu beginnen
Des Chaos wunderlicher Sohn!

Mephistopheles.

1385 Wir wollen wirklich uns besinnen,
Die nächstenmale mehr davon!
Dürft' ich wohl dießmal mich entfernen?

Faust.

Ich sehe nicht warum du fragst.
Ich habe jetzt dich kennen lernen,
1390 Besuche nun mich wie du magst.
Hier ist das Fenster, hier die Thüre,
Ein Rauchfang ist dir auch gewiß.

Mephistopheles.

Gesteh' ich's nur! Daß ich hinausspaziere
Verbietet mir ein kleines Hinderniß,
1395 Der Drudenfuß auf eurer Schwelle —

Faust.

Das Pentagramma macht dir Pein?
Ei sage mir, du Sohn der Hölle,
Wenn das dich bannt, wie kamst du denn herein?
Wie ward ein solcher Geist betrogen?

Mephistopheles.

1400 Beschaut es recht! es ist nicht gut gezogen;

Der eine Winkel, der nach außen zu,
Iſt, wie du ſiehſt, ein wenig offen.

F a u ſt.

Das hat der Zufall gut getroffen!
Und mein Gefangner wärſt denn du?
Das iſt von ungefähr gelungen!   1405

M e p h i ſt o p h e l e s.

Der Pudel merkte nichts als er hereingeſprungen,
Die Sache ſieht jetzt anders aus;
Der Teufel kann nicht aus dem Haus.

F a u ſt.

Doch warum gehſt du nicht durch's Fenſter?

M e p h i ſt o p h e l e s.

's iſt ein Geſetz der Teufel und Geſpenſter: 1410
Wo ſie hereingeſchlüpft, da müſſen ſie hinaus.
Das Erſte ſteht uns frei, bei'm Zweiten ſind wir Knechte.

F a u ſt.

Die Hölle ſelbſt hat ihre Rechte?
Das find' ich gut, da ließe ſich ein Pact,
Und ſicher wohl, mit euch ihr Herren ſchließen?   1415

M e p h i ſt o p h e l e s.

Was man verſpricht, das ſollſt du rein genießen,
Dir wird davon nichts abgezwackt.
Doch das iſt nicht ſo kurz zu faſſen,
Und wir beſprechen das zunächſt;
Doch jetzo bitt' ich, hoch und höchſt,   1420
Für dieſesmal mich zu entlaſſen.

Fauft.

So bleibe doch noch einen Augenblick,
Um mir erst gute Mähr' zu sagen.

Mephistopheles.

Jetzt laß mich los! ich komme bald zurück;
1425   Dann magst du nach Belieben fragen.

Fauft.

Ich habe dir nicht nachgestellt,
Bist du doch selbst in's Garn gegangen.
Den Teufel halte wer ihn hält!
Er wird ihn nicht sobald zum zweitenmale fangen.

Mephistopheles.

1430   Wenn dir's beliebt, so bin ich auch bereit
Dir zur Gesellschaft hier zu bleiben;
Doch mit Bedingniß, dir die Zeit,
Durch meine Künste, würdig zu vertreiben.

Fauft.

Ich seh' es gern, das steht dir frei;
1435   Nur daß die Kunst gefällig sei!

Mephistopheles.

Du wirst, mein Freund, für deine Sinnen,
In dieser Stunde mehr gewinnen,
Als in des Jahres Einerlei.
Was dir die zarten Geister singen,
1440   Die schönen Bilder, die sie bringen,
Sind nicht ein leeres Zauberspiel.
Auch dein Geruch wird sich ergetzen,

Dann wirst du deinen Gaumen letzen,
Und dann entzückt sich dein Gefühl.
Bereitung braucht es nicht voran,   1445
Beisammen sind wir, fanget an!

            Geister.
        Schwindet, ihr dunkeln
        Wölbungen droben!
        Reizender schaue
        Freundlich der blaue   1450
        Äther herein!
        Wären die dunkeln
        Wolken zerronnen!
        Sternelein funkeln,
        Mildere Sonnen   1455
        Scheinen darein.
        Himmlischer Söhne
        Geistige Schöne,
        Schwankende Beugung
        Schwebet vorüber.   1460
        Sehnende Neigung
        Folget hinüber;
        Und der Gewänder
        Flatternde Bänder
        Decken die Länder,   1465
        Decken die Laube,
        Wo sich für's Leben,
        Tief in Gedanken,
        Liebende geben.
        Laube bei Laube!   1470
        Sprossende Ranken!
        Lastende Traube

Stürzt in's Behälter
Drängender Kelter,
1475 Stürzen in Bächen
Schäumende Weine,
Rieseln durch reine
Edle Gesteine,
Lassen die Höhen
1480 Hinter sich liegen,
Breiten zu Seen
Sich um's Genügen
Grünender Hügel.
Und das Geflügel
1485 Schlürfet sich Wonne,
Flieget der Sonne,
Flieget den hellen
Inseln entgegen,
Die sich auf Wellen
1490 Gauklend bewegen;
Wo wir in Chören
Jauchzende hören,
Über den Auen
Tanzende schauen,
1495 Die sich im Freien
Alle zerstreuen.
Einige klimmen
Über die Höhen,
Andere schwimmen
1500 Über die Seen,
Andere schweben;
Alle zum Leben,
Alle zur Ferne

Liebender Sterne,
Seliger Huld.   1505

Mephiſtopheles.

Er ſchläft! So recht, ihr luſt'gen, zarten Jungen!
Ihr habt ihn treulich eingeſungen!
Für dieß Concert bin ich in eurer Schuld.
Du biſt noch nicht der Mann den Teufel feſt zu halten!
Umgaukelt ihn mit ſüßen Traumgeſtalten,   1510
Verſenkt ihn in ein Meer des Wahns;
Doch dieſer Schwelle Zauber zu zerſpalten
Bedarf ich eines Rattenzahns.
Nicht lange brauch' ich zu beſchwören,
Schon raſchelt eine hier und wird ſogleich mich hören. 1515

Der Herr der Ratten und der Mäuſe,
Der Fliegen, Fröſche, Wanzen, Läuſe,
Befiehlt dir dich hervor zu wagen
Und dieſe Schwelle zu benagen,
Sowie er ſie mit Öl betupft —   1520
Da kommſt du ſchon hervorgehupft.
Nur friſch an's Werk! Die Spitze, die mich bannte,
Sie ſitzt ganz vornen an der Kante.
Noch einen Biß, ſo iſt's geſchehn. —

Nun, Fauſte, träume fort, bis wir uns wiederſehn.   1525

Fauſt erwachend.

Bin ich denn abermals betrogen?
Verſchwindet ſo der geiſterreiche Drang,
Daß mir ein Traum den Teufel vorgelogen,
Und daß ein Pudel mir entſprang?

———

Studirzimmer.

Fauſt. Mephiſtopheles.

Fauſt.

1530   Es klopft? Herein! Wer will mich wieder plagen?

Mephiſtopheles.

Ich bin's.

Fauſt.

Herein!

Mephiſtopheles.

Du mußt es dreimal ſagen.

Fauſt.

Herein denn!

Mephiſtopheles.

So gefällſt du mir.
Wir werden, hoff' ich, uns vertragen!
Denn dir die Grillen zu verjagen
1535   Bin ich, als edler Junker, hier,
In rothem goldverbrämtem Kleide,
Das Mäntelchen von ſtarrer Seide,
Die Hahnenfeder auf dem Hut,
Mit einem langen ſpitzen Degen,
1540   Und rathe nun dir, kurz und gut,
Dergleichen gleichfalls anzulegen;

Damit du, losgebunden, frei,
Erfahreſt was das Leben ſei.

F a u ſt.

In jedem Kleide werd' ich wohl die Pein
Des engen Erdelebens fühlen.   1545
Ich bin zu alt, um nur zu ſpielen,
Zu jung, um ohne Wunſch zu ſein.
Was kann die Welt mir wohl gewähren?
Entbehren ſollſt du! ſollſt entbehren!
Das iſt der ewige Geſang,   1550
Der jedem an die Ohren klingt,
Den, unſer ganzes Leben lang,
Uns heiſer jede Stunde ſingt.
Nur mit Entſetzen wach' ich Morgens auf,
Ich möchte bittre Thränen weinen,   1555
Den Tag zu ſehn, der mir in ſeinem Lauf
Nicht Einen Wunſch erfüllen wird, nicht Einen,
Der ſelbſt die Ahnung jeder Luſt
Mit eigenſinnigem Krittel mindert,
Die Schöpfung meiner regen Bruſt   1560
Mit tauſend Lebensfratzen hindert.
Auch muß ich, wenn die Nacht ſich niederſenkt,
Mich ängſtlich auf das Lager ſtrecken;
Auch da wird keine Raſt geſchenkt,
Mich werden wilde Träume ſchrecken.   1565
Der Gott, der mir im Buſen wohnt,
Kann tief mein Innerſtes erregen;
Der über allen meinen Kräften thront,
Er kann nach außen nichts bewegen;
Und ſo iſt mir das Daſein eine Laſt,   1570
Der Tod erwünſcht, das Leben mir verhaßt.

Mephistopheles.

Und doch ist nie der Tod ein ganz willkommner Gast.

Faust.

O selig der, dem er im Siegesglanze
Die blut'gen Lorbeern um die Schläfe windet,
1575 Den er, nach rasch durchras'tem Tanze,
In eines Mädchens Armen findet!
O wär' ich vor des hohen Geistes Kraft
Entzückt, entseelt dahin gesunken!

Mephistopheles.

Und doch hat jemand einen braunen Saft,
1580 In jener Nacht, nicht ausgetrunken.

Faust.

Das Spioniren, scheint's, ist deine Lust.

Mephistopheles.

Allwissend bin ich nicht; doch viel ist mir bewußt.

Faust.

Wenn aus dem schrecklichen Gewühle
Ein süß bekannter Ton mich zog,
1585 Den Rest von kindlichem Gefühle
Mit Anklang froher Zeit betrog;
So fluch' ich allem was die Seele
Mit Lock= und Gaukelwerk umspannt,
Und sie in diese Trauerhöhle
1590 Mit Blend= und Schmeichelkräften bannt!
Verflucht voraus die hohe Meinung,
Womit der Geist sich selbst umfängt!
Verflucht das Blenden der Erscheinung,
Die sich an unsre Sinne drängt!

Verflucht was uns in Träumen heuchelt,   1595
Des Ruhms, der Namensdauer Trug!
Verflucht was als Beſitz uns ſchmeichelt,
Als Weib und Kind, als Knecht und Pflug!
Verflucht ſei Mammon, wenn mit Schätzen
Er uns zu kühnen Thaten regt,   1600
Wenn er zu müßigem Ergetzen
Die Polſter uns zurechte legt!
Fluch ſei dem Balſamſaft der Trauben!
Fluch jener höchſten Liebeshuld!
Fluch ſei der Hoffnung! Fluch dem Glauben,   1605
Und Fluch vor allen der Geduld!

        G e i ſ t e r = C h o r unſichtbar.
        Weh! weh!
        Du haſt ſie zerſtört,
        Die ſchöne Welt,
        Mit mächtiger Fauſt;   1610
        Sie ſtürzt, ſie zerfällt!
        Ein Halbgott hat ſie zerſchlagen!
        Wir tragen
        Die Trümmern in's Nichts hinüber,
        Und klagen   1615
        Über die verlorne Schöne.
        Mächtiger
        Der Erdenſöhne,
        Prächtiger
        Baue ſie wieder,   1620
        In deinem Buſen baue ſie auf!
        Neuen Lebenslauf
        Beginne,
        Mit hellem Sinne,

1625
    Und neue Lieder
    Tönen darauf!

Mephistopheles.

    Dieß sind die kleinen
    Von den Meinen.
    Höre, wie zu Lust und Thaten

1630
    Altklug sie rathen!
    In die Welt weit,
    Aus der Einsamkeit,
    Wo Sinnen und Säfte stocken,
    Wollen sie dich locken.

1635
Hör' auf mit deinem Gram zu spielen,
Der, wie ein Geier, dir am Leben frißt;
Die schlechteste Gesellschaft läßt dich fühlen,
Daß du ein Mensch mit Menschen bist.
Doch so ist's nicht gemeint

1640
Dich unter das Pack zu stoßen.
Ich bin keiner von den Großen;
Doch willst du, mit mir vereint,
Deine Schritte durch's Leben nehmen,
So will ich mich gern bequemen

1645
Dein zu sein, auf der Stelle.
Ich bin dein Geselle
Und, mach' ich dir's recht,
Bin ich dein Diener, bin dein Knecht!

Faust.

Und was soll ich dagegen dir erfüllen?

Mephistopheles.

1650
Dazu hast du noch eine lange Frist.

Fauſt.

Nein, nein! der Teufel iſt ein Egoiſt
Und thut nicht leicht um Gottes Willen
Was einem andern nützlich iſt.
Sprich die Bedingung deutlich aus;
Ein ſolcher Diener bringt Gefahr in's Haus.   1655

Mephiſtopheles.

Ich will mich h i e r zu deinem Dienſt verbinden,
Auf deinen Wink nicht räſten und nicht ruhn;
Wenn wir uns d r ü b e n wieder finden,
So ſollſt du mir das Gleiche thun.

Fauſt.

Das Drüben kann mich wenig kümmern;   1660
Schlägſt du erſt dieſe Welt zu Trümmern,
Die andre mag darnach entſtehn.
Aus dieſer Erde quillen meine Freuden,
Und dieſe Sonne ſcheinet meinen Leiden;
Kann ich mich erſt von ihnen ſcheiden,   1665
Dann mag was will und kann geſchehn.
Davon will ich nichts weiter hören,
Ob man auch künftig haßt und liebt,
Und ob es auch in jenen Sphären
Ein Oben oder Unten gibt.   1670

Mephiſtopheles.

In dieſem Sinne kannſt du's wagen.
Verbinde dich; du ſollſt, in dieſen Tagen,
Mit Freuden meine Künſte ſehn,
Ich gebe dir was noch kein Menſch geſehn.

Faust.

1675 Was willst du armer Teufel geben?
Ward eines Menschen Geist, in seinem hohen Streben,
Von Deinesgleichen je gefaßt?
Doch hast du Speise die nicht sättigt, hast
Du rothes Gold, das ohne Rast,
1680 Quecksilber gleich, dir in der Hand zerrinnt,
Ein Spiel, bei dem man nie gewinnt,
Ein Mädchen, das an meiner Brust
Mit Augeln schon dem Nachbar sich verbindet,
Der Ehre schöne Götterlust,
1685 Die, wie ein Meteor, verschwindet?
Zeig' mir die Frucht die fault, eh' man sie bricht,
Und Bäume die sich täglich neu begrünen!

Mephistopheles.

Ein solcher Auftrag schreckt mich nicht,
Mit solchen Schätzen kann ich dienen.
1690 Doch, guter Freund, die Zeit kommt auch heran
Wo wir was Guts in Ruhe schmausen mögen.

Faust.

Werd' ich beruhigt je mich auf ein Faulbett legen,
So sei es gleich um mich gethan!
Kannst du mich schmeichelnd je belügen
1695 Daß ich mir selbst gefallen mag,
Kannst du mich mit Genuß betrügen;
Das sei für mich der letzte Tag!
Die Wette biet' ich!

Mephistopheles.
Top!

Faust.

Und Schlag auf Schlag!

Werd' ich zum Augenblicke sagen:
Verweile doch! du bist so schön!   1700
Dann magst du mich in Fesseln schlagen,
Dann will ich gern zu Grunde gehn!
Dann mag die Todtenglocke schallen,
Dann bist du deines Dienstes frei,
Die Uhr mag stehn, der Zeiger fallen,   1705
Es sei die Zeit für mich vorbei!

Mephistopheles.

Bedenk' es wohl, wir werden's nicht vergessen.

Faust.

Dazu hast du ein volles Recht,
Ich habe mich nicht freventlich vermessen.
Wie ich beharre bin ich Knecht,   1710
Ob dein, was frag' ich, oder wessen.

Mephistopheles.

Ich werde heute gleich, bei'm Doctorschmaus,
Als Diener, meine Pflicht erfüllen.
Nur eins! — Um Lebens oder Sterbens willen,
Bitt' ich mir ein paar Zeilen aus.   1715

Faust.

Auch was Geschriebnes forderst du Pedant?
Hast du noch keinen Mann, nicht Mannes=Wort gekannt?
Ist's nicht genug, daß mein gesprochnes Wort
Auf ewig soll mit meinen Tagen schalten?
Ras't nicht die Welt in allen Strömen fort,   1720
Und mich soll ein Versprechen halten?

Doch dieser Wahn ist uns in's Herz gelegt,
Wer mag sich gern davon befreien?
Beglückt wer Treue rein im Busen trägt,
1725 Kein Opfer wird ihn je gereuen!
Allein ein Pergament, beschrieben und beprägt,
Ist ein Gespenst, vor dem sich alle scheuen.
Das Wort erstirbt schon in der Feder,
Die Herrschaft führen Wachs und Leder.
1730 Was willst du böser Geist von mir?
Erz, Marmor, Pergament, Papier?
Soll ich mit Griffel, Meißel, Feder schreiben?
Ich gebe jede Wahl dir frei.

Mephistopheles.

Wie magst du deine Rednerei
1735 Nur gleich so hitzig übertreiben?
Ist doch ein jedes Blättchen gut.
Du unterzeichnest dich mit einem Tröpfchen Blut.

Faust.

Wenn dieß dir völlig G'nüge thut,
So mag es bei der Fratze bleiben.

Mephistopheles.

1740 Blut ist ein ganz besondrer Saft.

Faust.

Nur keine Furcht, daß ich dieß Bündniß breche!
Das Streben meiner ganzen Kraft
Ist g'rade das was ich verspreche.
Ich habe mich zu hoch gebläht;
1745 In deinen Rang gehör' ich nur.
Der große Geist hat mich verschmäht,

Vor mir verſchließt ſich die Natur.
Des Denkens Faden iſt zerriſſen,
Mir ekelt lange vor allem Wiſſen.
Laß in den Tiefen der Sinnlichkeit
Uns glühende Leidenſchaften ſtillen!   1750
In undurchdrungnen Zauberhüllen
Sei jedes Wunder gleich bereit!
Stürzen wir uns in das Rauſchen der Zeit,
In's Rollen der Begebenheit!   1755
Da mag denn Schmerz und Genuß,
Gelingen und Verdruß,
Mit einander wechſeln wie es kann;
Nur raſtlos bethätigt ſich der Mann.

Mephiſtopheles.

Euch iſt kein Maß und Ziel geſetzt.   1760
Beliebt's euch überall zu naſchen,
Im Fliehen etwas zu erhaſchen,
Bekomm' euch wohl was euch ergetzt!
Nur greift mir zu und ſeid nicht blöde.

Fauſt.

Du höreſt ja, von Freud' iſt nicht die Rede.   1765
Dem Taumel weih' ich mich, dem ſchmerzlichſten Genuß,
Verliebtem Haß, erquickendem Verdruß.
Mein Buſen, der vom Wiſſensdrang geheilt iſt,
Soll keinen Schmerzen künftig ſich verſchließen,
Und was der ganzen Menſchheit zugetheilt iſt,   1770
Will ich in meinem innern Selbſt genießen,
Mit meinem Geiſt das Höchſt' und Tiefſte greifen,
Ihr Wohl und Weh auf meinen Buſen häufen,
Und ſo mein eigen Selbſt zu ihrem Selbſt erweitern,
Und, wie ſie ſelbſt, am End' auch ich zerſcheitern.   1775

Mephistopheles.

O glaube mir, der manche tausend Jahre
An dieser harten Speise kaut,
Daß von der Wiege bis zur Bahre
Kein Mensch den alten Sauerteig verdaut!
1780 Glaub' unser einem, dieses Ganze
Ist nur für einen Gott gemacht!
Er findet sich in einem ew'gen Glanze,
Uns hat er in die Finsterniß gebracht,
Und euch taugt einzig Tag und Nacht.

Faust.

1785 Allein ich will!

Mephistopheles.

Das läßt sich hören!
Doch nur vor Einem ist mir bang;
Die Zeit ist kurz, die Kunst ist lang.
Ich dächt', ihr ließet euch belehren.
Associirt euch mit einem Poeten,
1790 Laßt den Herrn in Gedanken schweifen,
Und alle edlen Qualitäten
Auf euren Ehren=Scheitel häufen,
Des Löwen Muth,
Des Hirsches Schnelligkeit,
1795 Des Italieners feurig Blut,
Des Nordens Daurbarkeit;
Laßt ihn euch das Geheimniß finden,
Großmuth und Arglist zu verbinden,
Und euch, mit warmen Jugendtrieben,
1800 Nach einem Plane, zu verlieben.
Möchte selbst solch einen Herren kennen,
Würd' ihn Herrn Mikrokosmus nennen.

Faust.

Was bin ich denn, wenn es nicht möglich ist
Der Menschheit Krone zu erringen,
Nach der sich alle Sinne dringen?　　　1805

Mephistopheles.

Du bist am Ende — was du bist.
Setz' dir Perrücken auf von Millionen Locken,
Setz' deinen Fuß auf ellenhohe Socken,
Du bleibst doch immer was du bist.

Faust.

Ich fühl's, vergebens hab' ich alle Schätze　　　1810
Des Menschengeists auf mich herbeigerafft,
Und wenn ich mich am Ende niedersetze,
Quillt innerlich doch keine neue Kraft;
Ich bin nicht um ein Haar breit höher,
Bin dem Unendlichen nicht näher.　　　1815

Mephistopheles.

Mein guter Herr, ihr seht die Sachen,
Wie man die Sachen eben sieht;
Wir müssen das gescheidter machen,
Eh' uns des Lebens Freude flieht.
Was Henker! freilich Händ' und Füße　　　1820
Und Kopf und H —— die sind dein;
Doch alles, was ich frisch genieße,
Ist das drum weniger mein?
Wenn ich sechs Hengste zahlen kann,
Sind ihre Kräfte nicht die meine?　　　1825
Ich renne zu und bin ein rechter Mann,
Als hätt' ich vier und zwanzig Beine.

Drum frisch! Laß alles Sinnen sein,
Und g'rad' mit in die Welt hinein!
1830 Ich sag' es dir: ein Kerl, der speculirt,
Ist wie ein Thier, auf dürrer Heide
Von einem bösen Geist im Kreis herum geführt,
Und rings umher liegt schöne grüne Weide.

Faust.

Wie fangen wir das an?

Mephistopheles.
Wir gehen eben fort.

1835 Was ist das für ein Marterort?
Was heißt das für ein Leben führen,
Sich und die Jungens ennuyiren?
Laß du das dem Herrn Nachbar Wanst!
Was willst du dich das Stroh zu dreschen plagen?
1840 Das Beste, was du wissen kannst,
Darfst du den Buben doch nicht sagen.
Gleich hör' ich einen auf dem Gange!

Faust.
Mir ist's nicht möglich ihn zu sehn.

Mephistopheles.
Der arme Knabe wartet lange,
1845 Der darf nicht ungetröstet gehn.
Komm, gib mir deinen Rock und Mütze;
Die Maske muß mir köstlich stehn.
Er kleidet sich um.
Nun überlaß es meinem Witze!
Ich brauche nur ein Viertelstündchen Zeit;
1850 Indessen mache dich zur schönen Fahrt bereit!
Faust ab.

Mephiſtopheles in Fauſt's langem Kleide.

Verachte nur Vernunft und Wiſſenſchaft,
Des Menſchen allerhöchſte Kraft,
Laß nur in Blend= und Zauberwerken
Dich von dem Lügengeiſt beſtärken,
So hab' ich dich ſchon unbedingt —   1855
Ihm hat das Schickſal einen Geiſt gegeben,
Der ungebändigt immer vorwärts dringt,
Und deſſen übereiltes Streben
Der Erde Freuden überſpringt.
Den ſchlepp' ich durch das wilde Leben,   1860
Durch flache Unbedeutenheit,
Er ſoll mir zappeln, ſtarren, kleben,
Und ſeiner Unerſättlichkeit
Soll Speiſ' und Trank vor gier'gen Lippen ſchweben;
Er wird Erquickung ſich umſonſt erflehn,   1865
Und hätt' er ſich auch nicht dem Teufel übergeben,
Er müßte doch zu Grunde gehn.

                    Ein Schüler tritt auf.

                    Schüler.

Ich bin allhier erſt kurze Zeit,
Und komme voll Ergebenheit,
Einen Mann zu ſprechen und zu kennen,   1870
Den alle mir mit Ehrfurcht nennen.

                    Mephiſtopheles.

Eure Höflichkeit erfreut mich ſehr!
Ihr ſeht einen Mann wie andre mehr.
Habt ihr euch ſonſt ſchon umgethan?

Schüler.

1875 Ich bitt' euch, nehmt euch meiner an!
Ich komme mit allem guten Muth,
Leidlichem Geld und frischem Blut;
Meine Mutter wollte mich kaum entfernen;
Möchte gern was Rechts hieraußen lernen.

Mephistopheles.

1880 Da seid ihr eben recht am Ort.

Schüler.

Aufrichtig, möchte schon wieder fort:
In diesen Mauern, diesen Hallen,
Will es mir keineswegs gefallen.
Es ist ein gar beschränkter Raum,
1885 Man sieht nichts Grünes, keinen Baum,
Und in den Sälen, auf den Bänken,
Vergeht mir Hören, Sehn und Denken.

Mephistopheles.

Das kommt nur auf Gewohnheit an.
So nimmt ein Kind der Mutter Brust
1890 Nicht gleich im Anfang willig an,
Doch bald ernährt es sich mit Lust.
So wird's euch an der Weisheit Brüsten
Mit jedem Tage mehr gelüsten.

Schüler.

An ihrem Hals will ich mit Freuden hangen;
1895 Doch sagt mir nur, wie kann ich hingelangen?

Mephistopheles.

Erklärt euch, eh' ihr weiter geht,
Was wählt ihr für eine Facultät?

Schüler.

Ich wünſchte recht gelehrt zu werden,
Und möchte gern was auf der Erden
Und in dem Himmel iſt erfaſſen,   1900
Die Wiſſenſchaft und die Natur.

Mephiſtopheles.

Da ſeid ihr auf der rechten Spur;
Doch müßt ihr euch nicht zerſtreuen laſſen.

Schüler.

Ich bin dabei mit Seel' und Leib;
Doch freilich würde mir behagen   1905
Ein wenig Freiheit und Zeitvertreib
An ſchönen Sommerfeiertagen.

Mephiſtopheles.

Gebraucht der Zeit, ſie geht ſo ſchnell von hinnen,
Doch Ordnung lehrt euch Zeit gewinnen.
Mein theurer Freund, ich rath' euch drum   1910
Zuerſt Collegium Logicum.
Da wird der Geiſt euch wohl dreſſirt,
In ſpaniſche Stiefeln eingeſchnürt,
Daß er bedächtiger ſo fortan
Hinſchleiche die Gedankenbahn,   1915
Und nicht etwa, die Kreuz und Quer,
Irrlichtelire hin und her.
Dann lehret man euch manchen Tag,
Daß, was ihr ſonſt auf Einen Schlag
Getrieben, wie Eſſen und Trinken frei,   1920
Eins! Zwei! Drei! dazu nöthig ſei.
Zwar iſt's mit der Gedanken-Fabrik

Wie mit einem Weber=Meisterstück,
Wo Ein Tritt tausend Fäden regt,
1925 Die Schifflein herüber hinüber schießen,
Die Fäden ungesehen fließen,
Ein Schlag tausend Verbindungen schlägt:
Der Philosoph der tritt herein,
Und beweis't euch, es müßt' so sein:
1930 Das Erst' wär' so, das Zweite so,
Und drum das Dritt' und Vierte so;
Und wenn das Erst' und Zweit' nicht wär',
Das Dritt' und Viert' wär' nimmermehr.
Das preisen die Schüler aller Orten,
1935 Sind aber keine Weber geworden.
Wer will was Lebendigs erkennen und beschreiben,
Sucht erst den Geist heraus zu treiben,
Dann hat er die Theile in seiner Hand,
Fehlt leider! nur das geistige Band.
1940 Encheiresin naturae nennt's die Chemie,
Spottet ihrer selbst und weiß nicht wie.

Schüler.

Kann euch nicht eben ganz verstehen.

Mephistopheles.

Das wird nächstens schon besser gehen,
Wenn ihr lernt alles reduciren
1945 Und gehörig classificiren.

Schüler.

Mir wird von alle dem so dumm,
Als ging' mir ein Mühlrad im Kopf herum.

Mephiſtopheles.

Nachher, vor allen andern Sachen,
Müßt ihr euch an die Metaphyſik machen!
Da ſeht daß ihr tiefſinnig faßt,   1950
Was in des Menſchen Hirn nicht paßt;
Für was drein geht und nicht drein geht,
Ein prächtig Wort zu Dienſten ſteht.
Doch vorerſt dieſes halbe Jahr
Nehmt ja der beſten Ordnung wahr.   1955
Fünf Stunden habt ihr jeden Tag;
Seid drinnen mit dem Glockenſchlag!
Habt euch vorher wohl präparirt,
Paragraphos wohl einſtudirt,
Damit ihr nachher beſſer ſeht,   1960
Daß er nichts ſagt, als was im Buche ſteht;
Doch euch des Schreibens ja befleißt,
Als dictirt' euch der Heilig' Geiſt!

Schüler.

Das ſollt ihr mir nicht zweimal ſagen!
Ich denke mir wie viel es nützt;   1965
Denn, was man ſchwarz auf weiß beſitzt,
Kann man getroſt nach Hauſe tragen.

Mephiſtopheles.

Doch wählt mir eine Facultät!

Schüler.

Zur Rechtsgelehrſamkeit kann ich mich nicht bequemen.

Mephiſtopheles.

Ich kann es euch ſo ſehr nicht übel nehmen,   1970
Ich weiß wie es um dieſe Lehre ſteht.

Es erben sich Gesetz' und Rechte
Wie eine ew'ge Krankheit fort;
Sie schleppen von Geschlecht sich zum Geschlechte,
1975 Und rücken sacht von Ort zu Ort.
Vernunft wird Unsinn, Wohlthat Plage;
Weh dir, daß du ein Enkel bist!
Vom Rechte, das mit uns geboren ist,
Von dem ist leider! nie die Frage.

Schüler.

1980 Mein Abscheu wird durch euch vermehrt.
O glücklich der! den ihr belehrt.
Fast möcht' ich nun Theologie studiren.

Mephistopheles.

Ich wünschte nicht euch irre zu führen.
Was diese Wissenschaft betrifft,
1985 Es ist so schwer den falschen Weg zu meiden,
Es liegt in ihr so viel verborgnes Gift,
Und von der Arzenei ist's kaum zu unterscheiden.
Am besten ist's auch hier, wenn ihr nur Einen hört,
Und auf des Meisters Worte schwört.
1990 Im Ganzen — haltet euch an Worte!
Dann geht ihr durch die sichre Pforte
Zum Tempel der Gewißheit ein.

Schüler.

Doch ein Begriff muß bei dem Worte sein.

Mephistopheles.

Schon gut! Nur muß man sich nicht allzu ängstlich quälen;
1995 Denn eben wo Begriffe fehlen,
Da stellt ein Wort zur rechten Zeit sich ein.
Mit Worten läßt sich trefflich streiten,

Mit Worten ein System bereiten,
An Worte läßt sich trefflich glauben,
Von einem Wort läßt sich kein Jota rauben.　　　　2000

Schüler.

Verzeiht, ich halt' euch auf mit vielen Fragen,
Allein ich muß euch noch bemühn.
Wollt ihr mir von der Medicin
Nicht auch ein kräftig Wörtchen sagen?
Drei Jahr ist eine kurze Zeit,　　　　2005
Und, Gott! das Feld ist gar zu weit.
Wenn man einen Fingerzeig nur hat,
Läßt sich's schon eher weiter fühlen.

Mephistopheles für sich.

Ich bin des trocknen Tons nun satt,
Muß wieder recht den Teufel spielen.　　　　2010

Laut.

Der Geist der Medicin ist leicht zu fassen;
Ihr durchstudirt die groß' und kleine Welt
Um es am Ende gehn zu lassen,
Wie's Gott gefällt.
Vergebens daß ihr ringsum wissenschaftlich schweift,　　　　2015
Ein jeder lernt nur was er lernen kann;
Doch der den Augenblick ergreift,
Das ist der rechte Mann.
Ihr seid noch ziemlich wohlgebaut,
An Kühnheit wird's euch auch nicht fehlen,　　　　2020
Und wenn ihr euch nur selbst vertraut,
Vertrauen euch die andern Seelen.
Besonders lernt die Weiber führen;

Es ist ihr ewig Weh und Ach
2025 So tausendfach
Aus Einem Punkte zu curiren,
Und wenn ihr halbweg ehrbar thut,
Dann habt ihr sie all' unter'm Hut.
Ein Titel muß sie erst vertraulich machen,
2030 Daß eure Kunst viel Künste übersteigt;
Zum Willkomm' tappt ihr dann nach allen Siebensachen,
Um die ein andrer viele Jahre streicht,
Versteht das Pülslein wohl zu drücken,
Und fasset sie, mit feurig schlauen Blicken,
2035 Wohl um die schlanke Hüfte frei,
Zu sehn, wie fest geschnürt sie sei.

Schüler.

Das sieht schon besser aus!   Man sieht doch wo und wie?

Mephistopheles.

Grau, theurer Freund, ist alle Theorie,
Und grün des Lebens goldner Baum.

Schüler.

2040 Ich schwör' euch zu, mir ist's als wie ein Traum.
Dürft' ich euch wohl ein andermal beschweren,
Von eurer Weisheit auf den Grund zu hören?

Mephistopheles.

Was ich vermag, soll gern geschehn.

Schüler.

Ich kann unmöglich wieder gehn,
2045 Ich muß euch noch mein Stammbuch überreichen.
Gönn' eure Gunst mir dieses Zeichen!

Mephiſtopheles.

Sehr wohl.

Er ſchreibt und gibt's.

Schüler lieſt.

Eritis sicut Deus, scientes bonum et malum.

Macht's ehrerbietig zu und empfiehlt ſich.

Mephiſtopheles.

Folg' nur dem alten Spruch und meiner Muhme der Schlange,
Dir wird gewiß einmal bei deiner Gottähnlichkeit bange!   2050

Fauſt tritt auf.

Fauſt.

Wohin ſoll es nun gehn?

Mephiſtopheles.

Wohin es dir gefällt.

Wir ſehn die kleine, dann die große Welt.
Mit welcher Freude, welchem Nutzen,
Wirſt du den Curſum durchſchmarutzen!

Fauſt.

Allein bei meinem langen Bart   2055
Fehlt mir die leichte Lebensart.
Es wird mir der Verſuch nicht glücken;
Ich wußte nie mich in die Welt zu ſchicken,
Vor andern fühl' ich mich ſo klein;
Ich werde ſtets verlegen ſein.   2060

Mephiſtopheles.

Mein guter Freund, das wird ſich alles geben;
Sobald du dir vertrauſt, ſobald weißt du zu leben.

Faust.

Wie kommen wir denn aus dem Haus?
Wo hast du Pferde, Knecht und Wagen?

Mephistopheles.

2065   Wir breiten nur den Mantel aus,
Der soll uns durch die Lüfte tragen.
Du nimmst bei diesem kühnen Schritt
Nur keinen großen Bündel mit.
Ein bißchen Feuerluft, die ich bereiten werde,
2070   Hebt uns behend von dieser Erde.
Und sind wir leicht, so geht es schnell hinauf;
Ich gratulire dir zum neuen Lebenslauf.

Auerbachs Keller in Leipzig.

Frosch.
Will keiner trinken? keiner lachen?
Ich will euch lehren Gesichter machen!
Ihr seid ja heut wie nasses Stroh, 2075
Und brennt sonst immer lichterloh.

Brander.
Das liegt an dir; du bringst ja nichts herbei,
Nicht eine Dummheit, keine Sauerei.

Frosch.
gießt ihm ein Glas Wein über den Kopf.
Da hast du beides!

Brander.
Doppelt Schwein!

Frosch.
Ihr wollt es ja, man soll es sein! 2080

Siebel.
Zur Thür hinaus wer sich entzweit!
Mit offner Brust singt Runda, sauft und schreit!
Auf! Holla! Ho!

Altmayer.

Weh mir, ich bin verloren!
Baumwolle her! der Kerl sprengt mir die Ohren.

Siebel.

2085 Wenn das Gewölbe widerschallt,
Fühlt man erst recht des Basses Grundgewalt.

Frosch.

So recht, hinaus mit dem der etwas übel nimmt!
A! tara lara da!

Altmayer.

A! tara lara da!

Frosch.

Die Kehlen sind gestimmt.

Singt.

2090 Das liebe heil'ge Röm'sche Reich,
Wie hält's nur noch zusammen?

Brander.

Ein garstig Lied! Pfui! Ein politisch Lied
Ein leidig Lied! Dankt Gott mit jedem Morgen,
Daß ihr nicht braucht für's Röm'sche Reich zu sorgen!
2095 Ich halt' es wenigstens für reichlichen Gewinn,
Daß ich nicht Kaiser oder Kanzler bin.
Doch muß auch uns ein Oberhaupt nicht fehlen;
Wir wollen einen Papst erwählen.
Ihr wißt, welch eine Qualität
2100 Den Ausschlag gibt, den Mann erhöht.

Frosch singt.

Schwing' dich auf, Frau Nachtigall,
Grüß' mir mein Liebchen zehentausendmal.

Siebel.

Dem Liebchen keinen Gruß! ich will davon nichts hören!

Froſch.

Dem Liebchen Gruß und Kuß! du wirſt mir's nicht verwehren!
Singt.

Riegel auf! in ſtiller Nacht.　　　　　2105
Riegel auf! der Liebſte wacht.
Riegel zu! des Morgens früh.

Siebel.

Ja, ſinge, ſinge nur, und lob' und rühme ſie!
Ich will zu meiner Zeit ſchon lachen.
Sie hat mich angeführt, dir wird ſie's auch ſo machen.　2110
Zum Liebſten ſei ein Kobold ihr beſchert!
Der mag mit ihr auf einem Kreuzweg ſchäkern;
Ein alter Bock, wenn er vom Blocksberg kehrt,
Mag im Galopp noch gute Nacht ihr meckern!
Ein braver Kerl von echtem Fleiſch und Blut　　2115
Iſt für die Dirne viel zu gut.
Ich will von keinem Gruße wiſſen,
Als ihr die Fenſter eingeſchmiſſen!

Brander auf den Tiſch ſchlagend.

Paßt auf! paßt auf! Gehorchet mir!
Ihr Herrn geſteht, ich weiß zu leben;　　　　2120
Verliebte Leute ſitzen hier,
Und dieſen muß, nach Standsgebühr,
Zur guten Nacht ich was zum Beſten geben.
Gebt Acht! Ein Lied vom neuſten Schnitt!
Und ſingt den Rundreim kräftig mit!　　　　2125

Er singt.

Es war eine Ratt' im Kellernest,
Lebte nur von Fett und Butter,
Hatte sich ein Ränzlein angemäst't
Als wie der Doctor Luther.
2130 Die Köchin hatt' ihr Gift gestellt;
Da ward's so eng ihr in der Welt,
Als hätte sie Lieb' im Leibe.

Chorus jauchzend.

Als hätte sie Lieb' im Leibe.

Brander.

Sie fuhr herum, sie fuhr heraus,
2135 Und soff aus allen Pfützen,
Zernagt', zerkratzt' das ganze Haus,
Wollte nichts ihr Wüthen nützen;
Sie thät gar manchen Angstesprung,
Bald hatte das arme Thier genung,
2140 Als hätt' es Lieb' im Leibe.

Chorus.

Als hätt' es Lieb' im Leibe.

Brander.

Sie kam vor Angst am hellen Tag
Der Küche zugelaufen,
Fiel an den Herd und zuckt' und lag,
2145 Und thät erbärmlich schnaufen.
Da lachte die Vergifterin noch:
Ha! sie pfeift auf dem letzten Loch,
Als hätte sie Lieb' im Leibe.

Chorus.

Als hätte ſie Lieb' im Leibe.

Siebel.

Wie ſich die platten Burſche freuen!   2150
Es iſt mir eine rechte Kunſt,
Den armen Ratten Gift zu ſtreuen!

Brander.

Sie ſtehn wohl ſehr in deiner Gunſt?

Altmayer.

Der Schmerbauch mit der kahlen Platte!
Das Unglück macht ihn zahm und mild;   2155
Er ſieht in der geſchwollnen Ratte
Sein ganz natürlich Ebenbild.

Fauſt und Mephiſtopheles.

Mephiſtopheles.

Ich muß dich nun vor allen Dingen
In luſtige Geſellſchaft bringen,
Damit du ſiehſt wie leicht ſich's leben läßt.   2160
Dem Volke hier wird jeder Tag ein Feſt.
Mit wenig Witz und viel Behagen
Dreht jeder ſich im engen Zirkeltanz,
Wie junge Katzen mit dem Schwanz.
Wenn ſie nicht über Kopfweh klagen,   2165
So lang der Wirth nur weiter borgt,
Sind ſie vergnügt und unbeſorgt.

Brander.

Die kommen eben von der Reiſe,
Man ſieht's an ihrer wunderlichen Weiſe;
Sie ſind nicht eine Stunde hier.   2170

Frosch.

Wahrhaftig du hast Recht!   Mein Leipzig lob' ich mir!
Es ist ein klein Paris, und bildet seine Leute.

Siebel.

Für was siehst du die Fremden an?

Frosch.

Laßt mich nur gehn!   Bei einem vollen Glase,
2175 Zieh ich, wie einen Kinderzahn,
Den Burschen leicht die Würmer aus der Nase.
Sie scheinen mir aus einem edlen Haus,
Sie sehen stolz und unzufrieden aus.

Brander.

Marktschreier sind's gewiß, ich wette!

Altmayer.

2180 Vielleicht.

Frosch.

Gib Acht, ich schraube sie!

Mephistopheles zu Faust.

Den Teufel spürt das Völkchen nie,
Und wenn er sie bei'm Kragen hätte!

Faust.

Seid uns gegrüßt, ihr Herrn!

Siebel.

Viel Dank zum Gegengruß.

Leise, Mephistopheles von der Seite ansehend.

Was hinkt der Kerl auf Einem Fuß?

Mephistopheles.

Ist es erlaubt, uns auch zu euch zu setzen?   2185
Statt eines guten Trunks, den man nicht haben kann,
Soll die Gesellschaft uns ergetzen.

Altmayer.

Ihr scheint ein sehr verwöhnter Mann.

Frosch.

Ihr seid wohl spät von Rippach aufgebrochen?
Habt ihr mit Herren Hans noch erst zu Nacht gespeis't?   2190

Mephistopheles.

Heut sind wir ihn vorbei gereis't!
Wir haben ihn das letztemal gesprochen.
Von seinen Vettern wußt' er viel zu sagen,
Viel Grüße hat er uns an jeden aufgetragen.

Er neigt sich gegen Frosch.

Altmayer leise.

Da hast du's! der versteht's!   2195

Siebel.

Ein pfiffiger Patron!

Frosch.

Nun, warte nur, ich krieg' ihn schon!

Mephistopheles.

Wenn ich nicht irrte, hörten wir
Geübte Stimmen Chorus singen?
Gewiß, Gesang muß trefflich hier
Von dieser Wölbung widerklingen!   2200

Frosch.
Seid ihr wohl gar ein Virtuos?

Mephistopheles.
O nein! die Kraft ist schwach, allein die Lust ist groß.

Altmayer.
Gebt uns ein Lied!

Mephistopheles.
Wenn ihr begehrt, die Menge.

Siebel.
Nur auch ein nagelneues Stück!

Mephistopheles.
2205 Wir kommen erst aus Spanien zurück,
Dem schönen Land des Weins und der Gesänge.

Singt.
Es war einmal ein König,
Der hatt' einen großen Floh —

Frosch.
Horcht! Einen Floh! Habt ihr das wohl gefaßt?
2210 Ein Floh ist mir ein saubrer Gast.

Mephistopheles singt.
Es war einmal ein König,
Der hatt' einen großen Floh,
Den liebt' er gar nicht wenig,
Als wie seinen eignen Sohn.
2215   Da rief er seinen Schneider,
Der Schneider kam heran:
Da, miß dem Junker Kleider,
Und miß ihm Hosen an!

Brander.

Vergeßt nur nicht dem Schneider einzuschärfen,
Daß er mir auf's genauste mißt,   2220
Und daß, so lieb sein Kopf ihm iſt,
Die Hoſen keine Falten werfen!

Mephiſtopheles.

In Sammet und in Seide
War er nun angethan,
Hatte Bänder auf dem Kleide,   2225
Hatt' auch ein Kreuz daran,
Und war sogleich Miniſter,
Und hatt' einen großen Stern.
Da wurden seine Geschwiſter
Bei Hof auch große Herrn.   2230

Und Herrn und Frauen am Hofe
Die waren sehr geplagt,
Die Königin und die Zofe
Gestochen und genagt,
Und durften sie nicht knicken,   2235
Und weg sie jucken nicht.
Wir knicken und erſticken
Doch gleich wenn einer ſticht.

Chorus jauchzend.

Wir knicken und erſticken
Doch gleich wenn einer ſticht.   2240

Froſch.

Bravo! Bravo! Das war schön!

Siebel.

So soll es jedem Floh ergehn!

Brander.

Spitzt die Finger und packt sie fein!

Altmayer.

Es lebe die Freiheit! Es lebe der Wein!

Mephistopheles.

2245 Ich tränke gern ein Glas, die Freiheit hoch zu ehren,
Wenn eure Weine nur ein bißchen besser wären.

Siebel.

Wir mögen das nicht wieder hören!

Mephistopheles.

Ich fürchte nur der Wirth beschweret sich;
Sonst gäb' ich diesen werthen Gästen
2250 Aus unserm Keller was zum Besten.

Siebel.

Nur immer her! ich nehm's auf mich.

Frosch.

Schafft ihr ein gutes Glas, so wollen wir euch loben.
Nur gebt nicht gar zu kleine Proben;
Denn wenn ich judiciren soll,
2255 Verlang' ich auch das Maul recht voll.

Altmayer leise.

Sie sind vom Rheine, wie ich spüre.

Mephistopheles.

Schafft einen Bohrer an!

Brander.

Was soll mit dem geschehn?

Ihr habt doch nicht die Fässer vor der Thüre?

Altmayer.

Dahinten hat der Wirth ein Körbchen Werkzeug stehn.

Mephistopheles nimmt den Bohrer. Zu Frosch.

Nun sagt, was wünschet ihr zu schmecken?   2260

Frosch.

Wie meint ihr das?   Habt ihr so mancherlei?

Mephistopheles.

Ich stell' es einem jeden frei.

Altmayer zu Frosch.

Aha, du fängst schon an die Lippen abzulecken.

Frosch.

Gut, wenn ich wählen soll, so will ich Rheinwein haben.

Das Vaterland verleiht die allerbesten Gaben.   2265

Mephistopheles

indem er an dem Platz, wo Frosch sitzt, ein Loch in den Tischrand bohrt.

Verschafft ein wenig Wachs, die Pfropfen gleich zu machen!

Altmayer.

Ach das sind Taschenspielersachen.

Mephistopheles zu Brander.

Und ihr?

Brander.

Ich will Champagner Wein,

Und recht mussirend soll er sein!

Mephistopheles bohrt; einer hat indessen die Wachspfropfen gemacht
und verstopft.

Brander.

2270 Man kann nicht stets das Fremde meiden,
Das Gute liegt uns oft so fern.
Ein echter deutscher Mann mag keinen Franzen leiden,
Doch ihre Weine trinkt er gern.

Siebel
indem sich Mephistopheles seinem Platze nähert.

Ich muß gestehn, den sauern mag ich nicht,
2275 Gebt mir ein Glas vom echten süßen!

Mephistopheles bohrt.
Euch soll sogleich Tokayer fließen.

Altmayer.
Nein, Herren, seht mir in's Gesicht!
Ich seh' es ein, ihr habt uns nur zum Besten.

Mephistopheles.

Ei! Ei! Mit solchen edlen Gästen
2280 Wär' es ein bißchen viel gewagt.
Geschwind!   Nur g'rad' heraus gesagt!
Mit welchem Weine kann ich dienen?

Altmayer.
Mit jedem.   Nur nicht lang gefragt.

Nachdem die Löcher alle gebohrt und verstopft sind,

Mephistopheles mit seltsamen Gebärden.
Trauben trägt der Weinstock!
2285 Hörner der Ziegenbock;

Der Wein ist saftig, Holz die Reben,
Der hölzerne Tisch kann Wein auch geben.
Ein tiefer Blick in die Natur!
Hier ist ein Wunder, glaubet nur!
Nun zieht die Pfropfen und genießt!   2290

Alle

indem sie die Pfropfen ziehen, und jedem der verlangte Wein
in's Glas läuft.

O schöner Brunnen, der uns fließt!

Mephistopheles.

Nur hütet euch, daß ihr mir nichts vergießt!

Sie trinken wiederholt.

Alle singen.

Uns ist ganz kannibalisch wohl,
Als wie fünfhundert Säuen!

Mephistopheles.

Das Volk ist frei, seht an, wie wohl's ihm geht!   2295

Faust.

Ich hätte Lust nun abzufahren.

Mephistopheles.

Gib nur erst Acht, die Bestialität
Wird sich gar herrlich offenbaren.

Siebel.

trinkt unvorsichtig, der Wein fließt auf die Erde und wird zur Flamme.

Helft! Feuer! Helft! Die Hölle brennt!

Mephistopheles die Flamme besprechend.

2300 Sei ruhig, freundlich Element!

Zu dem Gesellen.

Für dießmal war es nur ein Tropfen Fegefeuer.

Siebel.

Was soll das sein? Wart'! Ihr bezahlt es theuer!
Es scheinet, daß ihr uns nicht kennt.

Frosch.

Laß Er uns das zum zweitenmale bleiben!

Altmayer.

2305 Ich dächt', wir hießen ihn ganz sachte seitwärts gehn.

Siebel.

Was Herr? Er will sich unterstehn,
Und hier sein Hocuspocus treiben?

Mephistopheles.

Still, altes Weinfaß!

Siebel.

Besenstiel!
Du willst uns gar noch grob begegnen?

Brander.

2310 Wart' nur! Es sollen Schläge regnen!

Altmayer

zieht einen Pfropf aus dem Tisch, es springt ihm Feuer entgegen.

Ich brenne! ich brenne!

Siebel.

Zauberei!
Stoßt zu! der Kerl ist vogelfrei!

Sie ziehen die Messer und gehen auf Mephistopheles los.

M e p h i ſ t o p h e l e s mit ernſthafter Gebärde.

Falſch Gebild und Wort
Verändern Sinn und Ort!
Seid hier und dort!   2315

Sie ſtehn erſtaunt und ſehn einander an.

A l t m a y e r.

Wo bin ich?   Welches ſchöne Land!

F r o ſ ch.

Weinberge! Seh' ich recht?

S i e b e l.

Und Trauben gleich zur Hand!

B r a n d e r.

Hier unter dieſem grünen Laube,
Seht, welch ein Stock! Seht, welche Traube!

Er faßt Siebeln bei der Naſe.   Die andern thun es wechſelſeitig
und heben die Meſſer.

M e p h i ſ t o p h e l e s wie oben.

Irrthum, laß los der Augen Band!   2320
Und merkt euch wie der Teufel ſpaße.

Er verſchwindet mit Fa u ſt, die Geſellen fahren aus einander.

S i e b e l.

Was gibt's?

A l t m a y e r.

Wie?

F r o ſ ch.

War das deine Naſe?

Brander zu Siebel.

Und deine hab' ich in der Hand!

Altmayer.

Es war ein Schlag, der ging durch alle Glieder!
2325　Schafft einen Stuhl, ich sinke nieder!

Frosch.

Nein, sagt mir nur, was ist geschehn?

Siebel.

Wo ist der Kerl? Wenn ich ihn spüre,
Er soll mir nicht lebendig gehn!

Altmayer.

Ich hab' ihn selbst hinaus zur Kellerthüre —
2330　Auf einem Fasse reiten sehn —
Es liegt mir bleischwer in den Füßen.

　　　　　Sich nach dem Tische wendend.

Mein! Sollte wohl der Wein noch fließen?

Siebel.

Betrug war alles, Lug und Schein.

Frosch.

Mir däuchte doch als tränk' ich Wein.

Brander.

2335　Aber wie war es mit den Trauben?

Altmayer.

Nun sag' mir eins, man soll kein Wunder glauben!

———————

Hexenküche.

Auf einem niedrigen Herde steht ein großer Keſſel über dem Feuer. In dem Dampfe, der davon in die Höhe ſteigt, zeigen ſich verſchiedene Geſtalten. Eine Meerkatze ſitzt bei dem Keſſel und ſchäumt ihn, und ſorgt daß er nicht überläuft. Der Meerkater mit den Jungen ſitzt darneben und wärmt ſich. Wände und Decke ſind mit dem ſeltſamſten Hexenhausrath ausgeſchmückt.

Fauſt. Mephiſtopheles.

Fauſt.

Mir widerſteht das tolle Zauberweſen;
Verſprichſt du mir, ich ſoll geneſen,
In dieſem Wuſt von Raſerei?
Verlang' ich Rath von einem alten Weibe? 2340
Und ſchafft die Sudelköcherei
Wohl dreißig Jahre mir vom Leibe?
Weh mir, wenn du nichts Beſſers weißt!
Schon iſt die Hoffnung mir verſchwunden.
Hat die Natur und hat ein edler Geiſt
Nicht irgend einen Balſam ausgefunden? 2345

Mephiſtopheles.

Mein Freund, nun ſprichſt du wieder klug!
Dich zu verjüngen gibt's auch ein natürlich Mittel;
Allein es ſteht in einem andern Buch,
Und iſt ein wunderlich Capitel.
2350

Faust.

Ich will es wissen.

Mephistopheles.

Gut! Ein Mittel, ohne Geld
Und Arzt und Zauberei zu haben:
Begib dich gleich hinaus auf's Feld,
Fang' an zu hacken und zu graben,
2355 Erhalte dich und deinen Sinn
In einem ganz beschränkten Kreise,
Ernähre dich mit ungemischter Speise,
Leb' mit dem Vieh als Vieh, und acht' es nicht für Raub,
Den Acker, den du erntest, selbst zu düngen;
2360 Das ist das beste Mittel, glaub',
Auf achtzig Jahr dich zu verjüngen!

Faust.

Das bin ich nicht gewöhnt, ich kann mich nicht bequemen,
Den Spaten in die Hand zu nehmen.
Das enge Leben steht mir gar nicht an.

Mephistopheles.

2365 So muß denn doch die Hexe dran.

Faust.

Warum denn just das alte Weib!
Kannst du den Trank nicht selber brauen?

Mephistopheles.

Das wär' ein schöner Zeitvertreib!
Ich wollt' indeß wohl tausend Brücken bauen.
2370 Nicht Kunst und Wissenschaft allein,
Geduld will bei dem Werke sein.

Ein stiller Geist ist Jahre lang geschäftig;
Die Zeit nur macht die feine Gährung kräftig.
Und alles was dazu gehört,
Es sind gar wunderbare Sachen!   2375
Der Teufel hat sie's zwar gelehrt;
Allein der Teufel kann's nicht machen.

Die Thiere erblickend.

Sieh, welch ein zierliches Geschlecht!
Das ist die Magd! das ist der Knecht!

Zu den Thieren.

Es scheint, die Frau ist nicht zu Hause?   2380

Die Thiere.

Bei'm Schmause,
Aus dem Haus
Zum Schornstein hinaus!

Mephistopheles.

Wie lange pflegt sie wohl zu schwärmen?

Die Thiere.

So lange wir uns die Pfoten wärmen.   2385

Mephistopheles zu Faust.

Wie findest du die zarten Thiere?

Faust.

So abgeschmackt als ich nur jemand sah!

Mephistopheles.

Nein, ein Discours wie dieser da
Ist g'rade der den ich am liebsten führe!

Zu den Thieren.

2390 So sagt mir doch, verfluchte Puppen,
Was quirlt ihr in dem Brei herum?

Thiere.
Wir kochen breite Bettelsuppen.

Mephistopheles.
Da habt ihr ein groß Publicum.

Der Kater
macht sich herbei und schmeichelt dem Mephistopheles.

O würfle nur gleich,
2395 Und mache mich reich,
Und laß mich gewinnen!
Gar schlecht ist's bestellt,
Und wär' ich bei Geld,
So wär' ich bei Sinnen.

Mephistopheles.
2400 Wie glücklich würde sich der Affe schätzen,
Könnt' er nur auch in's Lotto setzen!
Indessen haben die jungen Meerkätzchen mit einer großen Kugel gespielt
und rollen sie hervor.

Der Kater.
Das ist die Welt;
Sie steigt und fällt
Und rollt beständig;
2405 Sie klingt wie Glas;
Wie bald bricht das!
Ist hohl inwendig.
Hier glänzt sie sehr,
Und hier noch mehr,

Ich bin lebendig!   2410
Mein lieber Sohn,
Halt' dich davon!
Du mußt ſterben!
Sie iſt von Thon,
Es gibt Scherben.   2415

Mephiſtopheles.
Was ſoll das Sieb?

Der Kater holt es herunter.
Wärſt du ein Dieb,
Wollt' ich dich gleich erkennen.
Er läuft zur Kätzin und läßt ſie durchſehen.
Sieh durch das Sieb!
Erkennſt du den Dieb,   2420
Und darfſt ihn nicht nennen?

Mephiſtopheles ſich dem Feuer nähernd.
Und dieſer Topf?

Kater und Kätzin.
Der alberne Tropf!
Er kennt nicht den Topf,
Er kennt nicht den Keſſel!   2425

Mephiſtopheles.
Unhöfliches Thier!

Der Kater.
Den Wedel nimm hier,
Und ſetz' dich in Seſſel!
Er nöthigt den Mephiſtopheles zu ſitzen.

Faust

welcher diese Zeit über vor einem Spiegel gestanden, sich ihm bald
genähert, bald sich von ihm entfernt hat.

Was seh' ich?   Welch ein himmlisch Bild
2430 Zeigt sich in diesem Zauberspiegel!
O Liebe, leihe mir den schnellsten deiner Flügel,
Und führe mich in ihr Gefild!
Ach wenn ich nicht auf dieser Stelle bleibe,
Wenn ich es wage nah zu gehn,
2435 Kann ich sie nur als wie im Nebel sehn!
Das schönste Bild von einem Weibe!
Ist's möglich, ist das Weib so schön?
Muß ich an diesem hingestreckten Leibe
Den Inbegriff von allen Himmeln sehn?
2440 So etwas findet sich auf Erden?

Mephistopheles.

Natürlich, wenn ein Gott sich erst sechs Tage plagt,
Und selbst am Ende bravo sagt,
Da muß es was Gescheidtes werden.
Für dießmal sieh dich immer satt;
2445 Ich weiß dir so ein Schätzchen auszuspüren,
Und selig wer das gute Schicksal hat,
Als Bräutigam sie heim zu führen!

Faust sieht immerfort in den Spiegel. Mephistopheles, sich in dem
Sessel dehnend und mit dem Wedel spielend, fährt fort zu sprechen.

Hier sitz' ich wie der König auf dem Throne,
Den Scepter halt' ich hier, es fehlt nur noch die Krone.

Die Thiere

welche bisher allerlei wunderliche Bewegungen durch einander gemacht
haben, bringen dem Mephistopheles eine Krone mit großem Geschrei.

O ſei doch ſo gut,   2450
Mit Schweiß und mit Blut
Die Krone zu leimen!

*Sie gehn ungeſchickt mit der Krone um und zerbrechen ſie in zwei Stücke
mit welchen ſie herumſpringen.*

Nun iſt es geſchehn!
Wir reden und ſehn,
Wir hören und reimen;   2455

F a u ſt *gegen den Spiegel.*
Weh mir! ich werde ſchier verrückt.

M e p h i ſ t o p h e l e s *auf die Thiere deutend.*
Nun fängt mir an faſt ſelbſt der Kopf zu ſchwanken.

D i e   T h i e r e.
Und wenn es uns glückt,
Und wenn es ſich ſchickt,
So ſind es Gedanken!   2460

F a u ſt *wie oben.*
Mein Buſen fängt mir an zu brennen!
Entfernen wir uns nur geſchwind!

M e p h i ſ t o p h e l e s *in obiger Stellung.*
Nun, wenigſtens muß man bekennen,
Daß es aufrichtige Poeten ſind.

*Der Keſſel, welchen die Kätzin bisher außer Acht gelaſſen, fängt an überzu-
laufen; es entſteht eine große Flamme, welche zum Schornſtein hinaus
ſchlägt. Die Hexe kommt durch die Flamme mit entſetzlichem Geſchrei
herunter gefahren.*

D i e   H e x e.
Au! Au! Au! Au!   2465
Verdammtes Thier! Verfluchte Sau!

Versäumst den Kessel, versengst die Frau!
Verfluchtes Thier!

Faust und Mephistopheles erblickend.

Was ist das hier?
2470 Wer seid ihr hier?
Was wollt ihr da?
Wer schlich sich ein?
Die Feuerpein
Euch in's Gebein!

Sie fährt mit dem Schaumlöffel in den Kessel und spritzt Flammen nach
    Faust, Mephistopheles und den Thieren. Die Thiere winseln.

Mephistopheles

welcher den Wedel, den er in der Hand hält, umkehrt und unter die Gläser
und Töpfe schlägt.

2475 Entzwei! entzwei!
Da liegt der Brei!
Da liegt das Glas!
Es ist nur Spaß,
Der Tact, du Aas,
2480 Zu deiner Melodei.

Indem die Hexe voll Grimm und Entsetzen zurücktritt.

Erkennst du mich? Gerippe! Scheusal du!
Erkennst du deinen Herrn und Meister?
Was hält mich ab, so schlag' ich zu,
Zerschmettre dich und deine Katzen-Geister!
2485 Hast du vor'm rothen Wamms nicht mehr Respect?
Kannst du die Hahnenfeder nicht erkennen?
Hab' ich dieß Angesicht versteckt?
Soll ich mich etwa selber nennen?

Die Hexe.

O Herr, verzeiht den rohen Gruß!
Seh' ich doch keinen Pferdefuß.
Wo sind denn eure beiden Raben?

                                                   2490

Mephistopheles.

Für dießmal kommst du so davon;
Denn freilich ist es eine Weile schon,
Daß wir uns nicht gesehen haben.
Auch die Cultur, die alle Welt beleckt,
Hat auf den Teufel sich erstreckt.
Das nordische Phantom ist nun nicht mehr zu schauen;
Wo siehst du Hörner, Schweif und Klauen?
Und was den Fuß betrifft, den ich nicht missen kann,
Der würde mir bei Leuten schaden;
Darum bedien' ich mich, wie mancher junge Mann,
Seit vielen Jahren falscher Waden.

    2495

    2500

Die Hexe tanzend.

Sinn und Verstand verlier' ich schier,
Seh' ich den Junker Satan wieder hier!

Mephistopheles.

Den Namen, Weib, verbitt' ich mir!

    2505

Die Hexe.

Warum?   Was hat er euch gethan?

Mephistopheles.

Er ist schon lang in's Fabelbuch geschrieben;
Allein die Menschen sind nichts besser dran.
Den Bösen sind sie los, die Bösen sind geblieben.
Du nennst mich Herr Baron, so ist die Sache gut;
Ich bin ein Cavalier, wie andre Cavaliere.

    2510

Du zweifelst nicht an meinem edlen Blut;
Sieh her, das ist das Wappen, das ich führe!
Er macht eine unanständige Gebärde.

Die Hexe lacht unmäßig.

Ha! Ha! Das ist in eurer Art!
2515 Ihr seid ein Schelm, wie ihr nur immer wart.

Mephistopheles zu Faust.

Mein Freund, das lerne wohl verstehn!
Dieß ist die Art mit Hexen umzugehn.

Die Hexe.

Nun sagt, ihr Herren, was ihr schafft.

Mephistopheles.

Ein gutes Glas von dem bekannten Saft,
2520 Doch muß ich euch um's ält'ste bitten;
Die Jahre doppeln seine Kraft.

Die Hexe.

Gar gern! Hier hab' ich eine Flasche,
Aus der ich selbst zuweilen nasche,
Die auch nicht mehr im mind'sten stinkt;
2525 Ich will euch gern ein Gläschen geben.
Leise.

Doch wenn es dieser Mann unvorbereitet trinkt,
So kann er, wißt ihr wohl, nicht eine Stunde leben.

Mephistopheles.

Es ist ein guter Freund, dem es gedeihen soll;
Ich gönn' ihm gern das Beste deiner Küche.
2530 Zieh deinen Kreis, sprich deine Sprüche,
Und gib ihm eine Tasse voll!

Die Hexe, mit ſeltſamen Gebärden, zieht einen Kreis und ſtellt wunderbare Sachen hinein; indeſſen fangen die Gläſer an zu klingen, die Keſſel zu
tönen, und machen Muſik. Zuletzt bringt ſie ein großes Buch, ſtellt die
Meerkatzen in den Kreis, die ihr zum Pult dienen und die Fackel halten
müſſen. Sie winkt Fauſten, zu ihr zu treten.

F a u ſ t zu Mephiſtopheles.

Nein, ſage mir, was ſoll das werden?
Das tolle Zeug, die raſenden Gebärden,
Der abgeſchmackteſte Betrug,
Sind mir bekannt, verhaßt genug.   2535

M e p h i ſ t o p h e l e s.

Ei, Poſſen! Das iſt nur zum Lachen;
Sei nur nicht ein ſo ſtrenger Mann!
Sie muß als Arzt ein Hocuspocus machen,
Damit der Saft dir wohl gedeihen kann.

Er nöthigt Fauſten in den Kreis zu treten.

D i e H e x e

mit großer Emphaſe fängt an aus dem Buche zu declamiren.

Du mußt verſtehn!   2540
Aus Eins mach' Zehn,
Und Zwei laß gehn,
Und Drei mach' gleich,
So biſt du reich.
Verlier' die Vier!   2545
Aus Fünf und Sechs,
So ſagt die Hex',
Mach' Sieben und Acht,
So iſt's vollbracht:
Und neun iſt Eins,   2550
Und Zehn iſt keins.
Das iſt das Hexen-Einmal-Eins!

Fauſt.

Mich dünkt, die Alte ſpricht im Fieber.

Mephiſtopheles.

Das iſt noch lange nicht vorüber,
2555   Ich kenn' es wohl, ſo klingt das ganze Buch;
Ich habe manche Zeit damit verloren,
Denn ein vollkommner Widerſpruch
Bleibt gleich geheimnißvoll für Kluge wie für Thoren.
Mein Freund, die Kunſt iſt alt und neu.
2560   Es war die Art zu allen Zeiten,
Durch Drei und Eins, und Eins und Drei
Irrthum ſtatt Wahrheit zu verbreiten.
So ſchwätzt und lehrt man ungeſtört;
Wer will ſich mit den Narrn befaſſen?
2565   Gewöhnlich glaubt der Menſch, wenn er nur Worte hört,
Es müſſe ſich dabei doch auch was denken laſſen.

Die Hexe fährt fort.

Die hohe Kraft
Der Wiſſenſchaft,
Der ganzen Welt verborgen!
2570   Und wer nicht denkt,
Dem wird ſie geſchenkt,
Er hat ſie ohne Sorgen.

Fauſt.

Was ſagt ſie uns für Unſinn vor?
Es wird mir gleich der Kopf zerbrechen.
2575   Mich dünkt, ich hör' ein ganzes Chor
Von hunderttauſend Narren ſprechen.

Mephiſtopheles.

Genug, genug, o treffliche Sibylle!
Gib deinen Trank herbei, und fülle

Die Schale raſch bis an den Rand hinan;
Denn meinem Freund wird dieſer Trunk nicht ſchaden: 2580
Er iſt ein Mann von vielen Graden,
Der manchen guten Schluck gethan.

Die Hexe mit vielen Ceremonien, ſchenkt den Trank in eine Schale;
wie ſie Fauſt an den Mund bringt, entſteht eine leichte Flamme.

Mephiſtopheles.

Nur friſch hinunter! Immer zu!
Es wird dir gleich das Herz erfreuen.
Biſt mit dem Teufel du und du,   2585
Und willſt dich vor der Flamme ſcheuen?

Die Hexe löſ't den Kreis. Fauſt tritt heraus.

Mephiſtopheles.

Nun friſch hinaus! Du darfſt nicht ruhn.

Die Hexe.

Mög' euch das Schlückchen wohl behagen!

Mephiſtopheles *zur Hexe.*

Und kann ich dir was zu Gefallen thun,
So darfſt du mir's nur auf Walpurgis ſagen.   2590

Die Hexe.

Hier iſt ein Lied! wenn ihr's zuweilen ſingt,
So werdet ihr beſondre Wirkung ſpüren.

Mephiſtopheles *zu Fauſt.*

Komm nur geſchwind und laß dich führen;
Du mußt nothwendig transſpiriren,
Damit die Kraft durch Inn= und Außres dringt.   2595
Den edlen Müßiggang lehr' ich hernach dich ſchätzen,
Und bald empfindeſt du mit innigem Ergetzen,
Wie ſich Cupido regt und hin und wieder ſpringt.

Faust.

Laß mich nur schnell noch in den Spiegel schauen!
2600 Das Frauenbild war gar zu schön!

Mephistopheles.

Nein! Nein! Du sollst das Muster aller Frauen
Nun bald leibhaftig vor dir sehn.

Leise.

Du siehst, mit diesem Trank im Leibe,
Bald Helenen in jedem Weibe.

————————

Straße.

Faust. Margarete vorüber gehend.

Faust.
Mein schönes Fräulein, darf ich wagen,   2605
Meinen Arm und Geleit Ihr anzutragen?

Margarete.
Bin weder Fräulein, weder schön,
Kann ungeleitet nach Hause gehn.

Sie macht sich los und ab.

Faust.
Bei'm Himmel, dieses Kind ist schön!
So etwas hab' ich nie gesehn.   2610
Sie ist so sitt= und tugendreich,
Und etwas schnippisch doch zugleich.
Der Lippe Roth, der Wange Licht,
Die Tage der Welt vergeß' ich's nicht!
Wie sie die Augen niederschlägt,   2615
Hat tief sich in mein Herz geprägt!
Wie sie kurz angebunden war,
Das ist nun zum Entzücken gar!

Mephistopheles tritt auf.

Faust.
Hör', du mußt mir die Dirne schaffen!

Mephistopheles.

2620 Nun, welche?

Faust.
Sie ging just vorbei.

Mephistopheles.

Da die?   Sie kam von ihrem Pfaffen,
Der sprach sie aller Sünden frei;
Ich schlich mich hart am Stuhl vorbei,
Es ist ein gar unschuldig Ding,
2625 Das eben für nichts zur Beichte ging;
Über die hab' ich keine Gewalt.

Faust.

Ist über vierzehn Jahr doch alt.

Mephistopheles.

Du sprichst ja wie Hans Liederlich,
Der begehrt jede liebe Blum' für sich,
2630 Und dünkelt ihm es wär' kein' Ehr'
Und Gunst die nicht zu pflücken wär';
Geht aber doch nicht immer an.

Faust.

Mein Herr Magister Lobesan,
Laß Er mich mit dem Gesetz in Frieden!
2635 Und das sag' ich Ihm kurz und gut,
Wenn nicht das süße junge Blut
Heut Nacht in meinen Armen ruht,
So sind wir um Mitternacht geschieden.

Mephistopheles.

Bedenkt was gehn und stehen mag!

Ich brauche wenigstens vierzehn Tag,   2640
Nur die Gelegenheit auszuspüren.

Faust.

Hätt' ich nur sieben Stunden Ruh,
Brauchte den Teufel nicht dazu,
So ein Geschöpfchen zu verführen.

Mephistopheles.

Ihr sprecht schon fast wie ein Franzos;   2645
Doch bitt ich', laßt's euch nicht verdrießen:
Was hilft's nur grade zu genießen?
Die Freud' ist lange nicht so groß,
Als wenn ihr erst herauf, herum,
Durch allerei Brimborium,   2650
Das Püppchen geknetet und zugericht't,
Wie's lehret manche wälsche Geschicht'.

Faust.

Hab' Appetit auch ohne das.

Mephistopheles.

Jetzt ohne Schimpf und ohne Spaß.
Ich sag' euch, mit dem schönen Kind   2655
Geht's ein= für allemal nicht geschwind.
Mit Sturm ist da nichts einzunehmen;
Wir müssen uns zur List bequemen.

Faust.

Schaff' mir etwas vom Engelsschatz!
Führ' mich an ihren Ruheplatz!   2660
Schaff' mir ein Halstuch von ihrer Brust,
Ein Strumpfband meiner Liebeslust!

Mephistopheles.

Damit ihr seht, daß ich eurer Pein
Will förderlich und dienstlich sein;
2665   Wollen wir keinen Augenblick verlieren,
Will euch noch heut in ihr Zimmer führen.

Faust.

Und soll sie sehn? sie haben?

Mephistopheles.

        Nein!

Sie wird bei einer Nachbarin sein.
Indessen könnt ihr ganz allein
2670   An aller Hoffnung künft'ger Freuden
In ihrem Dunstkreis satt euch weiden.

Faust.

Können wir hin?

Mephistopheles.

     Es ist noch zu früh.

Faust.

Sorg' du mir für ein Geschenk für sie!
Ab.

Mephistopheles.

Gleich schenken? Das ist brav! Da wird er reüssiren!
2675   Ich kenne manchen schönen Platz
Und manchen alt vergrabnen Schatz;
Ich muß ein bißchen revidiren.
Ab.

Abend.

Ein kleines reinliches Zimmer.

Margarete ihre Zöpfe flechtend und aufbindend.

Margarete.

Ich gäb' was drum, wenn ich nur wüßt'
Wer heut der Herr gewesen ist!
Er sah gewiß recht wacker aus,   2680
Und ist aus einem edlen Haus;
Das konnt' ich ihm an der Stirne lesen —
Er wär' auch sonst nicht so keck gewesen.

Ab.

Mephistopheles. Faust.

Mephistopheles.

Herein, ganz leise, nur herein!

Faust nach einigem Stillschweigen.

Ich bitte dich, laß mich allein!   2685

Mephistopheles herumspürend.

Nicht jedes Mädchen hält so rein.

Ab.

Faust rings aufschauend.

Willkommen süßer Dämmerschein!
Der du dies Heiligthum durchwebst:
Ergreif' mein Herz, du süße Liebespein!

2690 Die du vom Thau der Hoffnung schmachtend lebst.
Wie athmet rings Gefühl der Stille,
Der Ordnung, der Zufriedenheit!
In dieser Armuth welche Fülle!
In diesem Kerker welche Seligkeit!

Er wirft sich auf den ledernen Sessel am Bette.

2695 O nimm mich auf! der du die Vorwelt schon
Bei Freud' und Schmerz im offnen Arm empfangen!
Wie oft, ach! hat an diesem Väter=Thron
Schon eine Schaar von Kindern rings gehangen!
Vielleicht hat, dankbar für den heil'gen Christ,
2700 Mein Liebchen hier, mit vollen Kinderwangen,
Dem Ahnherrn fromm die welke Hand geküßt.
Ich fühl', o Mädchen, deinen Geist
Der Füll' und Ordnung um mich säuseln,
Der mütterlich dich täglich unterweis't,
2705 Den Teppich auf den Tisch dich reinlich breiten heißt,
Sogar den Sand zu deinen Füßen kräuseln.
O liebe Hand! so göttergleich!
Die Hütte wird durch dich ein Himmelreich.
Und hier!

Er hebt einen Bettvorhang auf.

Was faßt mich für ein Wonnegraus!
2710 Hier möcht' ich volle Stunden säumen.
Natur! Hier bildetest in leichten Träumen
Den eingebornen Engel aus;
Hier lag das Kind! mit warmem Leben
Den zarten Busen angefüllt,
2715 Und hier mit heilig reinem Weben
Entwirkte sich das Götterbild!

Und du!   Was hat dich hergeführt?
Wie innig fühl' ich mich gerührt!
Was willſt du hier?   Was wird das Herz dir ſchwer?
Armſel'ger Fauſt! ich kenne dich nicht mehr.   2720

Umgibt mich hier ein Zauberduft?
Mich drang's ſo g'rade zu genießen,
Und fühle mich in Liebestraum zerfließen!
Sind wir ein Spiel von jedem Druck der Luft?

Und träte ſie den Augenblick herein,   2725
Wie würdeſt du für deinen Frevel büßen!
Der große Hans, ach wie ſo klein!
Läg', hingeſchmolzen, ihr zu Füßen.

Mephiſtopheles kommt.

Mephiſtopheles.

Geſchwind!   Ich ſeh' ſie unten kommen.

Fauſt.

Fort! Fort! Ich kehre nimmermehr!   2730

Mephiſtopheles.

Hier iſt ein Käſtchen leidlich ſchwer,
Ich hab's wo anders hergenommen.
Stellt's hier nur immer in den Schrein,
Ich ſchwör' euch, ihr vergehn die Sinnen;
Ich that euch Sächelchen hinein,   2735
Um eine andre zu gewinnen.
Zwar Kind iſt Kind und Spiel iſt Spiel.

Fauſt.

Ich weiß nicht ſoll ich?

Mephistopheles.

Fragt ihr viel?
Meint ihr vielleicht den Schatz zu wahren?
2740 Dann rath' ich eurer Lüsternheit,
Die liebe schöne Tageszeit
Und mir die weitre Müh zu sparen.
Ich hoff' nicht daß ihr geizig seid!
Ich kratz' den Kopf, reib' an den Händen —

Er stellt das Kästchen in den Schrein und drückt das Schloß wieder zu.

2745 Nur fort! geschwind! —
Um euch das süße junge Kind
Nach Herzens Wunsch und Will' zu wenden;
Und ihr seht drein,
Als solltet ihr in den Hörsaal hinein,
2750 Als stünden grau leibhaftig vor euch da
Physik und Metaphysica!
Nur fort!

Ab.

Margarete mit einer Lampe.

Margarete.

Es ist so schwül, so dumpfig hie

Sie macht das Fenster auf.

Und ist doch eben so warm nicht drauß'.
2755 Es wird mir so, ich weiß nicht wie —
Ich wollt', die Mutter käm' nach Haus.
Mir läuft ein Schauer über'n ganzen Leib —
Bin doch ein thöricht furchtsam Weib!

Sie fängt an zu singen, indem sie sich auszieht.

Es war ein König in Thule
2760 Gar treu bis an das Grab,

Dem sterbend seine Buhle
Einen goldnen Becher gab.

Es ging ihm nichts darüber,
Er leert' ihn jeden Schmaus;
Die Augen gingen ihm über,   2765
So oft er trank daraus.

Und als er kam zu sterben,
Zählt' er seine Städt' im Reich,
Gönnt' alles seinem Erben,
Den Becher nicht zugleich.   2770

Er saß bei'm Königsmahle,
Die Ritter um ihn her,
Auf hohem Väter=Saale,
Dort auf dem Schloß am Meer.

Dort stand der alte Zecher,   2775
Trank letzte Lebensgluth,
Und warf den heiligen Becher
Hinunter in die Fluth.

Er sah ihn stürzen, trinken
Und sinken tief in's Meer,   2780
Die Augen thäten ihm sinken,
Trank nie einen Tropfen mehr.

Sie eröffnet den Schrein, ihre Kleider einzuräumen, und erblickt das
Schmuckkästchen.

Wie kommt das schöne Kästchen hier herein?
Ich schloß doch ganz gewiß den Schrein.

2785 Es ist doch wunderbar!   Was mag wohl drinne sein?
    Vielleicht bracht's jemand als ein Pfand,
    Und meine Mutter lieh darauf.
    Da hängt ein Schlüsselchen am Band,
    Ich denke wohl ich mach' es auf!
2790 Was ist das?   Gott im Himmel!   Schau',
    So was hab' ich mein' Tage nicht gesehn!
    Ein Schmuck!   Mit dem könnt' eine Edelfrau
    Am höchsten Feiertage gehn.
    Wie sollte mir die Kette stehn?
2795 Wem mag die Herrlichkeit gehören?

       Sie putzt sich damit auf und tritt vor den Spiegel.

    Wenn nur die Ohrring' meine wären!
    Man sieht doch gleich ganz anders drein.
    Was hilft euch Schönheit, junges Blut?
    Das ist wohl alles schön und gut,
2800 Allein man läßt's auch alles sein;
    Man lobt euch halb mit Erbarmen.
    Nach Golde drängt,
    Am Golde hängt
    Doch alles.   Ach wir Armen!

Spaziergang.

Fauft in Gedanken auf und ab gehend. Zu ihm Mephiftopheles.

Mephiftopheles.

Bei aller verſchmähten Liebe! Bei'm höllischen Elemente! 2805
Ich wollt' ich wüßte was Ärgers, daß ich's fluchen könnte!

Fauft.

Was haſt? was kneipt dich denn ſo ſehr?
So kein Geſicht ſah ich in meinem Leben!

Mephiftopheles.

Ich möcht' mich gleich dem Teufel übergeben,
Wenn ich nur ſelbſt kein Teufel wär'! 2810

Fauft.

Hat ſich dir was im Kopf verſchoben?
Dich kleidet's, wie ein Raſender zu toben!

Mephiftopheles.

Denkt nur, den Schmuck für Gretchen angeſchafft,
Den hat ein Pfaff hinweggerafft! —
Die Mutter kriegt das Ding zu ſchauen, 2815
Gleich fängt's ihr heimlich an zu grauen:
Die Frau hat gar einen feinen Geruch,
Schnuffelt immer im Gebetbuch,

Und riecht's einem jeden Möbel an,
2820 Ob das Ding heilig ist oder profan;
Und an dem Schmuck da spürt sie's klar,
Daß dabei nicht viel Segen war.
Mein Kind, rief sie, ungerechtes Gut
Befängt die Seele, zehrt auf das Blut;
2825 Wollen's der Mutter Gottes weihen,
Wird uns mit Himmels=Manna erfreuen!
Margretlein zog ein schiefes Maul,
Ist halt, dacht' sie, ein geschenkter Gaul,
Und wahrlich! gottlos ist nicht der,
2830 Der ihn so fein gebracht hierher.
Die Mutter ließ einen Pfaffen kommen;
Der hatte kaum den Spaß vernommen,
Ließ sich den Anblick wohl behagen.
Er sprach: So ist man recht gesinnt!
2835 Wer überwindet der gewinnt.
Die Kirche hat einen guten Magen,
Hat ganze Länder aufgefressen,
Und doch noch nie sich übergessen;
Die Kirch' allein, meine lieben Frauen,
2840 Kann ungerechtes Gut verdauen.

Faust.

Das ist ein allgemeiner Brauch,
Ein Jud' und König kann es auch.

Mephistopheles.

Strich drauf ein Spange, Kett' und Ring',
Als wären's eben Pfifferling',
2845 Dankt' nicht weniger und nicht mehr,
Als ob's ein Korb voll Nüsse wär',

Verſprach ihnen allen himmliſchen Lohn —
Und ſie waren ſehr erbaut davon.

Fauſt.
Und Gretchen?

Mephiſtopheles.
Sitzt nun unruhvoll,
Weiß weder was ſie will noch ſoll,   2850
Denkt an's Geſchmeide Tag und Nacht,
Noch mehr an den der's ihr gebracht.

Fauſt.
Des Liebchens Kummer thut mir leid.
Schaff' du ihr gleich ein neu Geſchmeid'!
Am erſten war ja ſo nicht viel.   2855

Mephiſtopheles.
O ja, dem Herrn iſt alles Kinderſpiel!

Fauſt.
Und mach', und richt's nach meinem Sinn,
Häng' dich an ihre Nachbarin!
Sei Teufel doch nur nicht wie Brei,
Und ſchaff' einen neuen Schmuck herbei!   2860

Mephiſtopheles.
Ja, gnäd'ger Herr, von Herzen gerne.
Fauſt ab.

Mephiſtopheles.
So ein verliebter Thor verpufft
Euch Sonne, Mond und alle Sterne
Zum Zeitvertreib dem Liebchen in die Luft.
Ab.

Der Nachbarin Haus.

Marthe allein.

Marthe.

2865 Gott verzeih's meinem lieben Mann,
Er hat an mir nicht wohl gethan!
Geht da stracks in die Welt hinein,
Und läßt mich auf dem Stroh allein.
Thät ihn doch wahrlich nicht betrüben,
2870 Thät ihn, weiß Gott, recht herzlich lieben.

Sie weint.

Vielleicht ist er gar todt! — O Pein!
Hätt' ich nur einen Todtenschein!

Margarete kommt.

Margarete.

Frau Marthe!

Marthe.

Gretelchen, was soll's?

Margarete.

Fast sinken mir die Kniee nieder!
2875 Da find' ich so ein Kästchen wieder
In meinem Schrein, von Ebenholz,
Und Sachen herrlich ganz und gar,
Weit reicher als das erste war.

Marthe.

Das muß Sie nicht der Mutter ſagen;
Thät's wieder gleich zur Beichte tragen.　　　2880

Margarete.

Ach ſeh' Sie nur! ach ſchau' Sie nur!

Marthe putzt ſie auf.

O du glückſel'ge Creatur!

Margarete.

Darf mich, leider, nicht auf der Gaſſen,
Noch in der Kirche mit ſehen laſſen.

Marthe.

Komm du nur oft zu mir herüber,　　　2885
Und leg' den Schmuck hier heimlich an;
Spazier' ein Stündchen lang dem Spiegelglas vorüber,
Wir haben unſre Freude dran;
Und dann gibt's einen Anlaß, gibt's ein Feſt,
Wo man's ſo nach und nach den Leuten ſehen läßt.　　　2890
Ein Kettchen erſt, die Perle dann in's Ohr;
Die Mutter ſieht's wohl nicht, man macht ihr auch was vor.

Margarete.

Wer konnte nur die beiden Kästchen bringen?
Es geht nicht zu mit rechten Dingen!
Es klopft.

Margarete.

Ach Gott! mag das meine Mutter ſein?　　　2895

Marthe durch's Vorhängel guckend.

Es iſt ein fremder Herr — Herein!
Mephiſtopheles tritt auf.

Mephistopheles.

Bin so frei g'rad' herein zu treten,
Muß bei den Frauen Verzeihn erbeten.

Tritt ehrerbietig vor Margareten zurück.

Wollte nach Frau Marthe Schwerdtlein fragen!

Marthe.

2900 Ich bin's, was hat der Herr zu sagen?

Mephistopheles *leise zu ihr.*

Ich kenne Sie jetzt, mir ist das genug;
Sie hat da gar vornehmen Besuch.
Verzeiht die Freiheit die ich genommen!
Will Nachmittage wieder kommen.

Marthe *laut.*

2905 Denk', Kind, um alles in der Welt!
Der Herr dich für ein Fräulein hält.

Margarete.

Ich bin ein armes junges Blut;
Ach Gott! der Herr ist gar zu gut:
Schmuck und Geschmeide sind nicht mein.

Mephistopheles.

2910 Ach, es ist nicht der Schmuck allein;
Sie hat ein Wesen, einen Blick so scharf!
Wie freut mich's daß ich bleiben darf.

Marthe.

Was bringt Er denn? Verlange sehr —

Mephistopheles.

Ich wollt' ich hätt' eine frohere Mähr'!

Ich hoffe Sie läßt mich's drum nicht büßen:　　2915
Ihr Mann ist todt und läßt Sie grüßen.

Marthe.

Ist todt? das treue Herz!　O weh!
Mein Mann ist todt!　Ach ich vergeh'!

Margarete.

Ach! liebe Frau, verzweifelt nicht!

Mephistopheles.

So hört die traurige Geschicht'!　　　　　　2920

Margarete.

Ich möchte drum mein' Tag' nicht lieben;
Würde mich Verlust zu Tode betrüben.

Mephistopheles.

Freud' muß Leid, Leid muß Freude haben.

Marthe.

Erzählt mir seines Lebens Schluß!

Mephistopheles.

Er liegt in Padua begraben　　　　　　　　2925
Bei'm heiligen Antonius,
An einer wohlgeweihten Stätte
Zum ewig kühlen Ruhebette.

Marthe.

Habt ihr sonst nichts an mich zu bringen?

Mephistopheles.

Ja, eine Bitte, groß und schwer;　　　　　　2930
Laß' Sie doch ja für ihn dreihundert Messen singen!
Im übrigen sind meine Taschen leer.

Marthe.

Was! Nicht ein Schaustück? Kein Geschmeid'?
Was jeder Handwerksbursch im Grund des Säckels spart,
2935 Zum Angedenken aufbewahrt,
Und lieber hungert, lieber bettelt!

Mephistopheles.

Madam, es thut mir herzlich leid;
Allein er hat sein Geld wahrhaftig nicht verzettelt.
Auch er bereute seine Fehler sehr,
2940 Ja, und bejammerte sein Unglück noch viel mehr.

Margarete.

Ach! daß die Menschen so unglücklich sind!
Gewiß ich will für ihn manch Requiem noch beten.

Mephistopheles.

Ihr wäret werth, gleich in die Eh zu treten:
Ihr seid ein liebenswürdig Kind.

Margarete.

2945 Ach nein, das geht jetzt noch nicht an.

Mephistopheles.

Ist's nicht ein Mann, sei's derweil' ein Galan.
's ist eine der größten Himmelsgaben,
So ein lieb Ding im Arm zu haben.

Margarete.

Das ist des Landes nicht der Brauch.

Mephistopheles.

2950 Brauch oder nicht! Es gibt sich auch.

Marthe.

Erzählt mir doch!

Mephiſtopheles.

       Ich ſtand an ſeinem Sterbebette,
Es war was beſſer als von Miſt,
Von halbgefaultem Stroh; allein er ſtarb als Chriſt,
Und fand daß er weit mehr noch auf der Zeche hätte.
Wie, rief er, muß ich mich von Grund aus haſſen,   2955
So mein Gewerb, mein Weib ſo zu verlaſſen!
Ach! die Erinnrung tödtet mich.
Vergäb' ſie mir nur noch in dieſem Leben! —

Marthe weinend.

Der gute Mann! ich hab' ihm längſt vergeben.

Mephiſtopheles.

Allein, weiß Gott! ſie war mehr Schuld als ich.   2960

Marthe.

Das lügt er!   Was! am Rand des Grabs zu lügen!

Mephiſtopheles.

Er fabelte gewiß in letzten Zügen,
Wenn ich nur halb ein Kenner bin.
Ich hatte, ſprach er, nicht zum Zeitvertreib zu gaffen,
Erſt Kinder, und dann Brot für ſie zu ſchaffen,   2965
Und Brot im allerweit'ſten Sinn,
Und konnte nicht einmal mein Theil in Frieden eſſen.

Marthe.

Hat er ſo aller Treu', ſo aller Lieb' vergeſſen,
Der Plackerei bei Tag und Nacht!

Mephistopheles.

2970 Nicht doch, er hat euch herzlich dran gedacht.
Er sprach: Als ich nun weg von Malta ging,
Da betet' ich für Frau und Kinder brünstig;
Uns war denn auch der Himmel günstig,
Daß unser Schiff ein türkisch Fahrzeug fing,
2975 Das einen Schatz des großen Sultans führte.
Da ward der Tapferkeit ihr Lohn,
Und ich empfing denn auch, wie sich gebührte,
Mein wohlgemess'nes Theil davon.

Marthe.

Ei wie? Ei wo? Hat er's vielleicht vergraben?

Mephistopheles.

2980 Wer weiß, wo nun es die vier Winde haben.
Ein schönes Fräulein nahm sich seiner an,
Als er in Napel fremd umherspazierte;
Sie hat an ihm viel Liebs und Treus gethan,
Daß er's bis an sein selig Ende spürte.

Marthe.

2985 Der Schelm! der Dieb an seinen Kindern!
Auch alles Elend, alle Noth
Konnt' nicht sein schändlich Leben hindern!

Mephistopheles.

Ja seht! dafür ist er nun todt.
Wär' ich nun jetzt an eurem Platze,
2990 Betraurt' ich ihn ein züchtig Jahr,
Visirte dann unterweil' nach einem neuen Schatze.

Marthe.

Ach Gott! wie doch mein erſter war,
Find’ ich nicht leicht auf dieſer Welt den andern!
Es konnte kaum ein herziger Närrchen ſein.
Er liebte nur das allzuviele Wandern, 2995
Und fremde Weiber, und fremden Wein,
Und das verfluchte Würfelſpiel.

Mephiſtopheles.

Nun, nun, ſo konnt’ es gehn und ſtehen,
Wenn er euch ungefähr ſo viel
Von ſeiner Seite nachgeſehen. 3000
Ich ſchwör’ euch zu, mit dem Beding
Wechſelt’ ich ſelbſt mit euch den Ring!

Marthe.

O es beliebt dem Herrn zu ſcherzen!

Mephiſtopheles für ſich.

Nun mach’ ich mich bei Zeiten fort!
Die hielte wohl den Teufel ſelbſt bei’m Wort. 3005
Zu Gretchen.
Wie ſteht es denn mit Ihrem Herzen?

Margarete.

Was meint der Herr damit?

Mephiſtopheles für ſich.

Du guts unſchuldigs Kind!
Laut.
Lebt wohl ihr Fraun!

Margarete.

Lebt wohl!

Marthe.

O sagt mir doch geschwind!

Ich möchte gern ein Zeugniß haben,

3010 Wo, wie und wann mein Schatz gestorben und begraben.

Ich bin von je der Ordnung Freund gewesen,

Möcht' ihn auch todt im Wochenblättchen lesen.

Mephistopheles.

Ja, gute Frau, durch zweier Zeugen Mund

Wird allerwegs die Wahrheit kund;

3015 Habe noch gar einen feinen Gesellen,

Den will ich euch vor den Richter stellen.

Ich bring' ihn her.

Marthe.

O thut das ja!

Mephistopheles.

Und hier die Jungfrau ist auch da? —

Ein braver Knab'! ist viel gereis't,

3020 Fräuleins alle Höflichkeit erweis't.

Margarete.

Müßte vor dem Herren schamroth werden.

Mephistopheles.

Vor keinem Könige der Erden.

Marthe.

Da hinter'm Haus in meinem Garten

Wollen wir der Herrn heut Abend warten.

Straße.

Faust. Mephistopheles.

Faust.

Wie ist's? Will's fördern? Will's bald gehn?   3025

Mephistopheles.

Ah bravo! Find' ich euch in Feuer?
In kurzer Zeit ist Gretchen euer.
Heut Abend sollt ihr sie bei Nachbar' Marthen sehn:
Das ist ein Weib wie auserlesen
Zum Kuppler= und Zigeunerwesen!   3030

Faust.

So recht!

Mephistopheles,

Doch wird auch was von uns begehrt.

Faust.

Ein Dienst ist wohl des andern werth.

Mephistopheles.

Wir legen nur ein gültig Zeugniß nieder,
Daß ihres Eheherrn ausgereckte Glieder
In Padua an heil'ger Stätte ruhn.   3035

Faust.

Sehr klug! Wir werden erst die Reise machen müssen!

Mephistopheles.

Sancta Simplicitas! darum ist's nicht zu thun;
Bezeugt nur ohne viel zu wissen.

Faust.

Wenn Er nichts Bessers hat, so ist der Plan zerrissen.

Mephistopheles.

3040 O heil'ger Mann! Da wärt ihr's nun!
Ist es das erstemal in eurem Leben,
Daß ihr falsch Zeugniß abgelegt?
Habt ihr von Gott, der Welt und was sich drin bewegt,
Vom Menschen, was sich ihm in Kopf und Herzen regt,
3045 Definitionen nicht mit großer Kraft gegeben?
Mit frecher Stirne, kühner Brust?
Und wollt ihr recht in's Innre gehen,
Habt ihr davon, ihr müßt es g'rad' gestehen,
So viel als von Herrn Schwerdtleins Tod gewußt!

Faust.

3050 Du bist und bleibst ein Lügner, ein Sophiste.

Mephistopheles.

Ja, wenn man's nicht ein bißchen tiefer wüßte.
Denn morgen wirst, in allen Ehren,
Das arme Gretchen nicht bethören,
Und alle Seelenlieb' ihr schwören?

Faust.

3055 Und zwar von Herzen.

Mephistopheles.

Gut und schön!
Dann wird von ewiger Treu' und Liebe,

Von einzig überallmächt'gem Triebe —
Wird das auch so von Herzen gehn?

Faust.

Laß das! Es wird! — Wenn ich empfinde,
Für das Gefühl, für das Gewühl   3060
Nach Namen suche, keinen finde,
Dann durch die Welt mit allen Sinnen schweife,
Nach allen höchsten Worten greife,
Und diese Gluth, von der ich brenne,
Unendlich, ewig, ewig nenne,   3065
Ist das ein teuflisch Lügenspiel?

Mephistopheles.

Ich hab' doch Recht!

Faust.

       Hör'! merk' dir dieß —
Ich bitte dich, und schone meine Lunge —
Wer Recht behalten will und hat nur eine Zunge,
Behält's gewiß.   3070
Und komm, ich hab' des Schwätzens Überdruß,
Denn du hast Recht, vorzüglich weil ich muß.

Garten.

Margarete an Faustens Arm, Marthe mit Mephistopheles auf und ab spazierend.

Margarete.

Ich fühl' es wohl, daß mich der Herr nur schont,
Herab sich läßt, mich zu beschämen.
3075 Ein Reisender ist so gewohnt
Aus Gütigkeit fürlieb zu nehmen;
Ich weiß zu gut, daß solch erfahrnen Mann
Mein arm Gespräch nicht unterhalten kann.

Faust.

Ein Blick von dir, Ein Wort mehr unterhält,
3080 Als alle Weisheit dieser Welt.

Er küßt ihre Hand.

Margarete.

Incommodirt euch nicht! Wie könnt ihr sie nur küssen?
Sie ist so garstig, ist so rauh!
Was hab' ich nicht schon alles schaffen müssen!
Die Mutter ist gar zu genau.

Gehn vorüber.

Marthe.

3085 Und ihr, mein Herr, ihr reis't so immer fort?

Mephiſtopheles.

Ach, daß Gewerb' und Pflicht uns dazu treiben!
Mit wie viel Schmerz verläßt man manchen Ort,
Und darf doch nun einmal nicht bleiben!

Marthe.

In raſchen Jahren geht's wohl an,
So um und um frei durch die Welt zu ſtreifen;   3090
Doch kömmt die böſe Zeit heran,
Und ſich als Hageſtolz allein zum Grab zu ſchleifen,
Das hat noch keinem wohl gethan.

Mephiſtopheles.

Mit Grauſen ſeh' ich das von weiten.

Marthe.

Drum, werther Herr, berathet euch in Zeiten.   3095

Gehn vorüber.

Margarete.

Ja, aus den Augen, aus dem Sinn!
Die Höflichkeit iſt euch geläufig;
Allein ihr habt der Freunde häufig,
Sie ſind verſtändiger als ich bin.

Fauſt.

O Beſte! glaube, was man ſo verſtändig nennt,   3100
Iſt oft mehr Eitelkeit und Kurzſinn.

Margarete.

Wie?

Faust.

Ach, daß die Einfalt, daß die Unschuld nie
Sich selbst und ihren heil'gen Werth erkennt!
Daß Demuth, Niedrigkeit, die höchsten Gaben
3105 Der liebevoll austheilenden Natur —

Margarete.

Denkt ihr an mich ein Augenblickchen nur,
Ich werde Zeit genug an euch zu denken haben.

Faust.

Ihr seid wohl viel allein?

Margarete.

Ja, unsre Wirthschaft ist nur klein,
3110 Und doch will sie versehen sein.
Wir haben keine Magd; muß kochen, fegen, stricken
Und nähn, und laufen früh und spat;
Und meine Mutter ist in allen Stücken
So accurat!
3115 Nicht daß sie just so sehr sich einzuschränken hat;
Wir könnten uns weit eh'r als andre regen:
Mein Vater hinterließ ein hübsch Vermögen,
Ein Häuschen und ein Gärtchen vor der Stadt.
Doch hab' ich jetzt so ziemlich stille Tage;
3120 Mein Bruder ist Soldat,
Mein Schwesterchen ist todt.
Ich hatte mit dem Kind wohl meine liebe Noth;
Doch übernähm' ich gern noch einmal alle Plage,
So lieb war mir das Kind.

Faust.
Ein Engel, wenn dir's glich.

Margarete.

Ich zog es auf, und herzlich liebt' es mich.   3125
Es war nach meines Vaters Tod geboren.
Die Mutter gaben wir verloren,
So elend wie sie damals lag,
Und sie erholte sich sehr langsam, nach und nach.
Da konnte sie nun nicht dran denken   3130
Das arme Würmchen selbst zu tränken,
Und so erzog ich's ganz allein,
Mit Milch und Wasser; so ward's mein.
Auf meinem Arm, in meinem Schoos
War's freundlich, zappelte, ward groß.   3135

Fauſt.

Du haſt gewiß das reinſte Glück empfunden.

Margarete.

Doch auch gewiß gar manche ſchwere Stunden.
Des Kleinen Wiege ſtand zu Nacht
An meinem Bett, es durfte kaum ſich regen,
War ich erwacht;   3140
Bald mußt' ich's tränken, bald es zu mir legen,
Bald, wenn's nicht ſchwieg, vom Bett aufſtehn,
Und tänzelnd in der Kammer auf und nieder gehn,
Und früh am Tage ſchon am Waſchtrog ſtehn;
Dann auf dem Markt und an dem Herde ſorgen,   3145
Und immer fort wie heut ſo morgen.
Da geht's, mein Herr, nicht immer muthig zu;
Doch ſchmeckt dafür das Eſſen, ſchmeckt die Ruh.

Gehn vorüber.

Marthe.

Die armen Weiber sind doch übel dran:
3150 Ein Hagestolz ist schwerlich zu bekehren.

Mephistopheles.

Es käme nur auf Euresgleichen an,
Mich eines Bessern zu belehren.

Marthe.

Sagt g'rad', mein Herr, habt ihr noch nichts gefunden?
Hat sich das Herz nicht irgendwo gebunden?

Mephistopheles.

3155 Das Sprichwort sagt: Ein eigner Herd,
Ein braves Weib, sind Gold und Perlen werth.

Marthe.

Ich meine, ob ihr niemals Lust bekommen?

Mephistopheles.

Man hat mich überall recht höflich aufgenommen.

Marthe.

Ich wollte sagen: ward's nie Ernst in eurem Herzen?

Mephistopheles.

3160 Mit Frauen soll man sich nie unterstehn zu scherzen.

Marthe.

Ach, ihr versteht mich nicht!

Mephistopheles.

     Das thut mir herzlich leid!
Doch ich versteh' — daß ihr sehr gütig seid.

    Gehn vorüber.

Faust.

Du kanntest mich, o kleiner Engel, wieder,
Gleich als ich in den Garten kam?

Margarete.

Saht ihr es nicht? ich schlug die Augen nieder. 3165

Faust.

Und du verzeihst die Freiheit, die ich nahm,
Was sich die Frechheit unterfangen,
Als du jüngst aus dem Dom gegangen?

Margarete.

Ich war bestürzt, mir war das nie geschehn;
Es konnte niemand von mir Übels sagen. 3170
Ach, dacht' ich, hat er in deinem Betragen
Was Freches, Unanständiges gesehn?
Es schien ihn gleich nur anzuwandeln,
Mit dieser Dirne g'rade hin zu handeln.
Gesteh' ich's doch! Ich wußte nicht was sich 3175
Zu eurem Vortheil hier zu regen gleich begonnte;
Allein gewiß, ich war recht bös' auf mich,
Daß ich auf euch nicht böser werden konnte.

Faust.

Süß Liebchen!

Margarete.

Laßt einmal!
Sie pflückt eine Sternblume und zupft die Blätter ab, eins nach dem andern.

Faust.

Was soll das? Einen Strauß?

Margarete.

3180 Nein, es soll nur ein Spiel.

Faust.
                         Wie?

Margarete.
                              Geht, ihr lacht mich aus.
Sie rupft und murmelt.

Faust.

Was murmelst du?

Margarete halb laut.
              Er liebt mich — liebt mich nicht.

Faust.

Du holdes Himmels=Angesicht!

Margarete fährt fort.

Liebt mich — Nicht — Liebt mich — Nicht —
Das letzte Blatt ausrupfend, mit holder Freude.

Er liebt mich!

Faust

              Ja, mein Kind! Laß dieses Blumenwort
3185 Dir Götterausspruch sein. Er liebt dich!
Verstehst du, was das heißt? Er liebt dich!
Er faßt ihre beiden Hände.

Margarete.

Mich überläuft's!

Faust.

O schaudre nicht! Laß diesen Blick,
Laß diesen Händedruck dir sagen,

Was unausſprechlich iſt: 3190
Sich hinzugeben ganz und eine Wonne
Zu fühlen, die ewig ſein muß!
Ewig! — Ihr Ende würde Verzweiflung ſein.
Nein, kein Ende!   Kein Ende!

Margarete drückt ihm die Hände, macht ſich los und läuft weg.
Er ſteht einen Augenblick in Gedanken, dann folgt er ihr.

Marthe kommend.

Die Nacht bricht an.

Mephiſtopheles.
                    Ja, und wir wollen fort.   3195

Marthe.

Ich bät' euch länger hier zu bleiben,
Allein es iſt ein gar zu böſer Ort.
Es iſt als hätte niemand nichts zu treiben
Und nichts zu ſchaffen,
Als auf des Nachbarn Schritt und Tritt zu gaffen,   3200
Und man kommt in's Gered', wie man ſich immer ſtellt.
Und unſer Pärchen?

Mephiſtopheles.
                    Iſt den Gang dort aufgeflogen.
Muthwill'ge Sommervögel!

Marthe.
                    Er ſcheint ihr gewogen.

Mephiſtopheles.

Und ſie ihm auch.   Das iſt der Lauf der Welt.

Ein Gartenhäuschen.

Margarete springt herein, steckt sich hinter die Thür, hält die Fingerspitze an die Lippen und guckt durch die Ritze.

Margarete.

3205 Er kommt!

Faust kommt.

Faust.

Ach, Schelm, so neckst du mich!
Treff' ich dich!

Er küßt sie.

Margarete ihn fassend und den Kuß zurückgebend.

Bester Mann! von Herzen lieb' ich dich!

Mephistopheles klopft an.

Faust stampfend.

Wer da?

Mephistopheles.

Gut Freund!

Faust.

Ein Thier!

Mephistopheles.

Es ist wohl Zeit zu scheiden.

Marthe kommt.

Marthe.

Ja, es iſt ſpät, mein Herr.

Fauſt.

            Darf ich euch nicht geleiten?

Margarete.

Die Mutter würde mich — Lebt wohl!

Fauſt.

            Muß ich denn gehn?

Lebt wohl!

Marthe.

     Ade!

Margarete.

       Auf baldig Wiederſehn!   3210

Fauſt und Mephiſtopheles ab.

Margarete.

Du lieber Gott! was ſo ein Mann
Nicht alles, alles denken kann!
Beſchämt nur ſteh' ich vor ihm da,
Und ſag' zu allen Sachen ja.
Bin doch ein arm unwiſſend Kind,   3215
Begreife nicht was er an mir find't.

       Ab.

Wald und Höhle.

Faust.

Erhabner Geist, du gabst mir, gabst mir alles,
Warum ich bat.   Du hast mir nicht umsonst
Dein Angesicht im Feuer zugewendet.
3220 Gabst mir die herrliche Natur zum Königreich,
Kraft, sie zu fühlen, zu genießen.   Nicht
Kalt staunenden Besuch erlaubst du nur,
Vergönnest mir in ihre tiefe Brust
Wie in den Busen eines Freunds zu schauen.
3225 Du führst die Reihe der Lebendigen
Vor mir vorbei, und lehrst mich meine Brüder
Im stillen Busch, in Luft und Wasser kennen.
Und wenn der Sturm im Walde braus't und knarrt,
Die Riesenfichte stürzend Nachbaräste
3230 Und Nachbarstämme quetschend nieder streift,
Und ihrem Fall dumpf hohl der Hügel donnert;
Dann führst du mich zur sichern Höhle, zeigst
Mich dann mir selbst, und meiner eignen Brust
Geheime tiefe Wunder öffnen sich.
3235 Und steigt vor meinem Blick der reine Mond
Besänftigend herüber: schweben mir
Von Felsenwänden, aus dem feuchten Busch,

Der Vorwelt silberne Gestalten auf,
Und lindern der Betrachtung strenge Lust.

O daß dem Menschen nichts Vollkommnes wird,   3240
Empfind' ich nun.   Du gabst zu dieser Wonne,
Die mich den Göttern nah und näher bringt,
Mir den Gefährten, den ich schon nicht mehr
Entbehren kann, wenn er gleich, kalt und frech,
Mich vor mir selbst erniedrigt, und zu nichts,   3245
Mit einem Worthauch, deine Gaben wandelt.
Er facht in meiner Brust ein wildes Feuer
Nach jenem schönen Bild geschäftig an.
So tauml' ich von Begierde zu Genuß,
Und im Genuß verschmacht' ich nach Begierde.   3250

       Mephistopheles tritt auf.

Mephistopheles.

Habt ihr nun bald das Leben g'nug geführt?
Wie kann's euch in die Länge freuen?
Es ist wohl gut, daß man's einmal probirt;
Dann aber wieder zu was Neuen!

Faust.

Ich wollt', du hättest mehr zu thun,   3255
Als mich am guten Tag zu plagen.

Mephistopheles.

Nun nun! ich laß' dich gerne ruhn,
Du darfst mir's nicht im Ernste sagen.
An dir Gesellen unhold, barsch und toll,
Ist wahrlich wenig zu verlieren.   3260
Den ganzen Tag hat man die Hände voll!

Was ihm gefällt und was man lassen soll,
Kann man dem Herrn nie an der Nase spüren.

Faust.

Das ist so just der rechte Ton!
3265 Er will noch Dank, daß er mich ennuyirt.

Mephistopheles.

Wie hätt'st du, armer Erdensohn,
Dein Leben ohne mich geführt?
Vom Kribskrabs der Imagination
Hab' ich dich doch auf Zeiten lang curirt;
3270 Und wär' ich nicht, so wärst du schon
Von diesem Erdball abspaziert.
Was hast du da in Höhlen, Felsenritzen
Dich wie ein Schuhu zu versitzen?
Was schlurfst aus dumpfem Moos und triefendem Gestein,
3275 Wie eine Kröte Nahrung ein?
Ein schöner süßer Zeitvertreib!
Dir steckt der Doctor noch im Leib.

Faust.

Verstehst du, was für neue Lebenskraft
Mir dieser Wandel in der Öde schafft?
3280 Ja, würdest du es ahnen können,
Du wärest Teufel g'nug mein Glück mir nicht zu gönnen.

Mephistopheles.

Ein überirdisches Vergnügen!
In Nacht und Thau auf den Gebirgen liegen,
Und Erd' und Himmel wonniglich umfassen,
3285 Zu einer Gottheit sich aufschwellen lassen,
Der Erde Mark mit Ahnungsdrang durchwühlen,

Alle sechs Tagewerk' im Busen fühlen,
In stolzer Kraft ich weiß nicht was genießen,
Bald liebewonniglich in alles überfließen,
Verschwunden ganz der Erdensohn,
Und dann die hohe Intuition —   3290

           Mit einer Gebärde.

Ich darf nicht sagen wie — zu schließen!

              F a u st.

Pfui über dich!

         M e p h i s t o p h e l e s.

        Das will euch nicht behagen;
Ihr habt das Recht gesittet pfui zu sagen.
Man darf das nicht vor keuschen Ohren nennen,   3295
Was keusche Herzen nicht entbehren können.
Und kurz und gut, ich gönn' Ihm das Vergnügen,
Gelegentlich sich etwas vorzulügen;
Doch lange hält Er das nicht aus.
Du bist schon wieder abgetrieben,   3300
Und, währt es länger, aufgerieben
In Tollheit oder Angst und Graus.
Genug damit! Dein Liebchen sitzt dadrinne
Und alles wird ihr eng und trüb.
Du kommst ihr gar nicht aus dem Sinne,   3305
Sie hat dich übermächtig lieb.
Erst kam deine Liebeswuth übergeflossen,
Wie vom geschmolznen Schnee ein Bächlein übersteigt;
Du hast sie ihr in's Herz gegossen;
Nun ist dein Bächlein wieder seicht.   3310
Mich dünkt, anstatt in Wäldern zu thronen,
Ließ' es dem großen Herren gut,

Das arme affenjunge Blut
Für seine Liebe zu belohnen.
3315 Die Zeit wird ihr erbärmlich lang;
Sie steht am Fenster, sieht die Wolken ziehn
Über die alte Stadtmauer hin.
Wenn ich ein Vöglein wär'! so geht ihr Gesang
Tagelang, halbe Nächte lang.
3320 Einmal ist sie munter, meist betrübt,
Einmal recht ausgeweint,
Dann wieder ruhig, wie's scheint,
Und immer verliebt.

Faust.

Schlange! Schlange!

Mephistopheles für sich.

3325 Gelt! daß ich dich fange!

Faust.

Verruchter! hebe dich von hinnen,
Und nenne nicht das schöne Weib!
Bring' die Begier zu ihrem süßen Leib
Nicht wieder vor die halbverrückten Sinnen!

Mephistopheles.

3330 Was soll es denn? Sie meint, du seist entflohn,
Und halb und halb bist du es schon.

Faust.

Ich bin ihr nah, und wär' ich noch so fern,
Ich kann sie nie vergessen, nie verlieren;
Ja ich beneide schon den Leib des Herrn,
3335 Wenn ihre Lippen ihn indeß berühren.

Mephiſtopheles.

Gar wohl, mein Freund!   Ich hab' euch oft beneidet
Um's Zwillingspaar, das unter Roſen weidet.

Fauſt.

Entfliehe, Kuppler!

Mephiſtopheles.

   Schön!   Ihr ſchimpft und ich muß lachen.
Der Gott, der Bub= und Mädchen ſchuf,
Erkannte gleich den edelſten Beruf,   3340
Auch ſelbſt Gelegenheit zu machen.
Nur fort, es iſt ein großer Jammer!
Ihr ſollt in eures Liebchens Kammer,
Nicht etwa in den Tod!

Fauſt.

Was iſt die Himmelsfreud' in ihren Armen?   3345
Laß mich an ihrer Bruſt erwarmen!
Fühl' ich nicht immer ihre Noth?
Bin ich der Flüchtling nicht? der Unbehauſ'te?
Der Unmenſch ohne Zweck und Ruh,
Der wie ein Waſſerſturz von Fels zu Felſen brauſ'te, 3350
Begierig wüthend nach dem Abgrund zu?
Und ſeitwärts ſie, mit kindlich dumpfen Sinnen,
Im Hüttchen auf dem kleinen Alpenfeld,
Und all ihr häusliches Beginnen
Umfangen in der kleinen Welt.   3355
Und ich, der Gottverhaßte,
Hatte nicht genug,
Daß ich die Felſen faßte
Und ſie zu Trümmern ſchlug!
Sie, ihren Frieden mußt' ich untergraben!   3360

Du, Hölle, mußtest dieses Opfer haben!
Hilf, Teufel, mir die Zeit der Angst verkürzen!
Was muß geschehn, mag's gleich geschehn!
Mag ihr Geschick auf mich zusammenstürzen
3365 Und sie mit mir zu Grunde gehn.

Mephistopheles.

Wie's wieder siedet, wieder glüht!
Geh ein und tröste sie, du Thor!
Wo so ein Köpfchen keinen Ausgang sieht,
Stellt er sich gleich das Ende vor.
3370 Es lebe wer sich tapfer hält!
Du bist doch sonst so ziemlich eingeteufelt,
Nichts Abgeschmackters find' ich auf der Welt,
Als einen Teufel der verzweifelt.

Gretchens Stube.

Gretchen am Spinnrade allein.

Gretchen.

Meine Ruh ist hin,
Mein Herz ist schwer;
Ich finde sie nimmer   3375
Und nimmermehr.

Wo ich ihn nicht hab'
Ist mir das Grab,
Die ganze Welt   3380
Ist mir vergällt.

Mein armer Kopf
Ist mir verrückt,
Mein armer Sinn
Ist mir zerstückt.   3385

Meine Ruh ist hin,
Mein Herz ist schwer;
Ich finde sie nimmer
Und nimmermehr.

Nach ihm nur schau' ich   3390
Zum Fenster hinaus,

Nach ihm nur geh' ich
Aus dem Haus.

Sein hoher Gang,
3395   Sein' edle Gestalt,
Seines Mundes Lächeln,
Seiner Augen Gewalt,

Und seiner Rede
Zauberfluß,
3400   Sein Händedruck,
Und ach sein Kuß!

Meine Ruh ist hin,
Mein Herz ist schwer;
Ich finde sie nimmer
3405   Und nimmermehr.

Mein Busen drängt
Sich nach ihm hin.
Ach dürft' ich fassen
Und halten ihn,

3410   Und küssen ihn
So wie ich wollt',
An seinen Küssen
Vergehen sollt'!

Marthens Garten.

Margarete. Faust.

Margarete.
Versprich mir, Heinrich!

Faust.
   Was ich kann!

Margarete.
Nun sag', wie hast du's mit der Religion?   3415
Du bist ein herzlich guter Mann,
Allein ich glaub', du hält'st nicht viel davon.

Faust.
Laß das, mein Kind! Du fühlst ich bin dir gut;
Für meine Lieben ließ' ich Leib und Blut,
Will niemand sein Gefühl und seine Kirche rauben.   3420

Margarete.
Das ist nicht recht, man muß dran glauben!

Faust.
Muß man?

Margarete.
   Ach! wenn ich etwas auf dich könnte!
Du ehrst auch nicht die heil'gen Sacramente.

Faust.

Ich ehre sie.

Margarete.

Doch ohne Verlangen.
3425 Zur Messe, zur Beichte bist du lange nicht gegangen.
Glaubst du an Gott?

Faust.

Mein Liebchen, wer darf sagen:
Ich glaub' an Gott?
Magst Priester oder Weise fragen,
Und ihre Antwort scheint nur Spott
3430 Über den Frager zu sein.

Margarete.

So glaubst du nicht?

Faust.

Mißhör' mich nicht, du holdes Angesicht!
Wer darf ihn nennen?
Und wer bekennen:
Ich glaub' ihn?
3435 Wer empfinden
Und sich unterwinden
Zu sagen: ich glaub' ihn nicht?
Der Allumfasser,
Der Allerhalter,
3440 Faßt und erhält er nicht
Dich, mich, sich selbst?
Wölbt sich der Himmel nicht dadroben?
Liegt die Erde nicht hierunten fest?

Und ſteigen freundlich blickend
Ewige Sterne nicht herauf?   3445
Schau' ich nicht Aug' in Auge dir,
Und drängt nicht alles
Nach Haupt und Herzen dir,
Und webt in ewigem Geheimniß
Unſichtbar ſichtbar neben dir?   3450
Erfüll' davon dein Herz, ſo groß es iſt,
Und wenn du ganz in dem Gefühle ſelig biſt,
Nenn' es dann wie du willſt,
Nenn's Glück! Herz! Liebe! Gott!
Ich habe keinen Namen   3455
Dafür!   Gefühl iſt alles;
Name iſt Schall und Rauch,
Umnebelnd Himmelsgluth.

Margarete.

Das iſt alles recht ſchön und gut;
Ungefähr ſagt das der Pfarrer auch,   3460
Nur mit ein bißchen andern Worten.

Fauſt.

Es ſagen's aller Orten
Alle Herzen unter dem himmliſchen Tage,
Jedes in ſeiner Sprache;
Warum nicht ich in der meinen?   3465

Margarete.

Wenn man's ſo hört, möcht's leidlich ſcheinen,
Steht aber doch immer ſchief darum;
Denn du haſt kein Chriſtenthum.

Faust.

Liebs Kind!

Margarete.

Es thut mir lang schon weh,

3470 Daß ich dich in der Gesellschaft seh'.

Faust.

Wie so?

Margarete.

Der Mensch, den du da bei dir hast,

Ist mir in tiefer innrer Seele verhaßt;

Es hat mir in meinem Leben

So nichts einen Stich in's Herz gegeben,

3475 Als des Menschen widrig Gesicht.

Faust.

Liebe Puppe, fürcht' ihn nicht!

Margarete.

Seine Gegenwart bewegt mir das Blut.

Ich bin sonst allen Menschen gut;

Aber, wie ich mich sehne dich zu schauen,

3480 Hab' ich vor dem Menschen ein heimlich Grauen,

Und halt' ihn für einen Schelm dazu!

Gott verzeih mir's, wenn ich ihm Unrecht thu'!

Faust.

Es muß auch solche Käuze geben.

Margarete.

Wollte nicht mit Seinesgleichen leben!

3485 Kommt er einmal zur Thür herein,

Sieht er immer so spöttisch drein,

Und halb ergrimmt;
Man ſieht, daß er an nichts keinen Antheil nimmt;
Es ſteht ihm an der Stirn' geſchrieben,
Daß er nicht mag eine Seele lieben.   3490
Mir wird's ſo wohl in deinem Arm,
So frei, ſo hingegeben warm,
Und ſeine Gegenwart ſchnürt mir das Innre zu.

Fauſt.

Du ahnungsvoller Engel du!

Margarete.

Das übermannt mich ſo ſehr,   3495
Daß, wo er nur mag zu uns treten,
Mein' ich ſogar, ich liebte dich nicht mehr.
Auch wenn er da iſt, könnt' ich nimmer beten,
Und das frißt mir in's Herz hinein;
Dir, Heinrich, muß es auch ſo ſein.   3500

Fauſt.

Du haſt nun die Antipathie!

Margarete.

Ich muß nun fort.

Fauſt.

Ach kann ich nie
Ein Stündchen ruhig dir am Buſen hängen,
Und Bruſt an Bruſt und Seel' in Seele drängen?

Margarete.

Ach wenn ich nur alleine ſchlief'!   3505
Ich ließ' dir gern heut Nacht den Riegel offen;

Doch meine Mutter schläft nicht tief:
Und würden wir von ihr betroffen,
Ich wär' gleich auf der Stelle todt!

Faust.

3510 Du Engel, das hat keine Noth.
Hier ist ein Fläschchen! Drei Tropfen nur
In ihren Trank umhüllen
Mit tiefem Schlaf gefällig die Natur.

Margarete.

Was thu' ich nicht um deinetwillen?
3515 Es wird ihr hoffentlich nicht schaden!

Faust.

Würd' ich sonst, Liebchen, dir es rathen?

Margarete.

Seh' ich dich, bester Mann, nur an,
Weiß nicht was mich nach deinem Willen treibt;
Ich habe schon so viel für dich gethan,
3520 Daß mir zu thun fast nichts mehr übrig bleibt.

Ab.

Mephistopheles tritt auf.

Mephistopheles.

Der Grasaff'! ist er weg?

Faust.

Hast wieder spionirt?

Mephistopheles.

Ich hab's ausführlich wohl vernommen,
Herr Doctor wurden da katechisirt;

Hoff' es soll Ihnen wohl bekommen.
Die Mädels sind doch sehr interessirt,   3525
Ob einer fromm und schlicht nach altem Brauch.
Sie denken, duckt er da, folgt er uns eben auch.

Faust.

Du Ungeheuer siehst nicht ein,
Wie diese treue liebe Seele
Von ihrem Glauben voll,   3530
Der ganz allein
Ihr selig machend ist, sich heilig quäle,
Daß sie den liebsten Mann verloren halten soll.

Mephistopheles.

Du übersinnlicher sinnlicher Freier,
Ein Mägdelein nasführet dich.   3535

Faust.

Du Spottgeburt von Dreck und Feuer!

Mephistopheles.

Und die Physiognomie versteht sie meisterlich.
In meiner Gegenwart wird's ihr sie weiß nicht wie,
Mein Mäskchen da weissagt verborgnen Sinn;
Sie fühlt, daß ich ganz sicher ein Genie,   3540
Vielleicht wohl gar der Teufel bin.
Nun heute Nacht —?

Faust.
          Was geht dich's an?

Mephistopheles.

Hab' ich doch meine Freude dran!

Am Brunnen.

Gretchen und Lieschen mit Krügen.

Lieschen.

Hast nichts von Bärbelchen gehört?

Gretchen.

3545   Kein Wort.   Ich komm' gar wenig unter Leute.

Lieschen.

Gewiß, Sibylle sagt' mir's heute!
Die hat sich endlich auch bethört.
Das ist das Vornehmthun!

Gretchen.

           Wie so?

Lieschen.

                 Es stinkt!
Sie füttert zwei, wenn sie nun ißt und trinkt.

Gretchen.

3550   Ach!

Lieschen.

So ist's ihr endlich recht ergangen.
Wie lange hat sie an dem Kerl gehangen!
Das war ein Spazieren,

Auf Dorf und Tanzplatz führen,
Mußt' überall die Erste sein,   3555
Curtesirt' ihr immer mit Pastetchen und Wein;
Bild't' sich was auf ihre Schönheit ein,
War doch so ehrlos sich nicht zu schämen
Geschenke von ihm anzunehmen.
War ein Gekos' und ein Geschleck';   3560
Da ist denn auch das Blümchen weg!

Gretchen.

Das arme Ding!

Lieschen.

Bedauerst sie noch gar!

Wenn unser eins am Spinnen war,
Uns Nachts die Mutter nicht hinunterließ,
Stand sie bei ihrem Buhlen süß,   3565
Auf der Thürbank und im dunkeln Gang
Ward ihnen keine Stunde zu lang.
Da mag sie denn sich ducken nun,
Im Sünderhemdchen Kirchbuß' thun!

Gretchen.

Er nimmt sie gewiß zu seiner Frau.   3570

Lieschen.

Er wär' ein Narr! Ein flinker Jung'
Hat anderwärts noch Luft genung.
Er ist auch fort.

Gretchen.

Das ist nicht schön!

Lieschen.

Kriegt sie ihn, soll's ihr übel gehn.

3575 Das Kränzel reißen die Buben ihr,
Und Häckerling streuen wir vor die Thür!
Ab.

G r e t c h e n nach Hause gehend.

Wie konnt' ich sonst so tapfer schmählen,
Wenn thät ein armes Mägdlein fehlen!
Wie konnt' ich über andrer Sünden
3580 Nicht Worte g'nug der Zunge finden!
Wie schien mir's schwarz, und schwärzt's noch gar,
Mir's immer doch nicht schwarz g'nug war,
Und segnet' mich und that so groß,
Und bin nun selbst der Sünde bloß!
3585 Doch — alles was dazu mich trieb,
Gott! war so gut! ach war so lieb!

Zwinger.

In der Mauerhöhle ein Andachtsbild der Mater dolorosa, Blumenkrüge davor. Gretchen steckt frische Blumen in die Krüge.

Gretchen.

Ach neige,
Du Schmerzenreiche,
Dein Antlitz gnädig meiner Noth!

Das Schwert im Herzen,   3590
Mit tausend Schmerzen
Blickst auf zu deines Sohnes Tod.

Zum Vater blickst du,
Und Seufzer schickst du
Hinauf um sein' und deine Noth.   3595

Wer fühlet,
Wie wühlet
Der Schmerz mir im Gebein?
Was mein armes Herz hier banget,
Was es zittert, was verlanget,   3600
Weißt nur du, nur du allein!

Wohin ich immer gehe,
Wie weh, wie weh, wie wehe

Wird mir im Busen hier!
3605   Ich bin ach kaum alleine,
Ich wein', ich wein', ich weine,
Das Herz zerbricht in mir.

Die Scherben vor meinem Fenster
Bethaut' ich mit Thränen, ach!
3610   Als ich am frühen Morgen
Dir diese Blumen brach.

Schien hell in meine Kammer
Die Sonne früh herauf,
Saß ich in allem Jammer
3615   In meinem Bett schon auf.

Hilf! rette mich von Schmach und Tod!
Ach neige,
Du Schmerzenreiche,
Dein Antlitz gnädig meiner Noth!

Nacht.

Straße vor Gretchens Thüre.

Valentin Soldat, Gretchens Bruder.

Valentin.

Wenn ich so saß bei einem Gelag,   3620
Wo mancher sich berühmen mag,
Und die Gesellen mir den Flor
Der Mägdlein laut gepriesen vor,
Mit vollem Glas das Lob verschwemmt,
Den Ellenbogen aufgestemmt   3625
Saß ich in meiner sichern Ruh,
Hört' all dem Schwadroniren zu,
Und streiche lächelnd meinen Bart,
Und kriege das volle Glas zur Hand
Und sage: alles nach seiner Art!   3630
Aber ist Eine im ganzen Land,
Die meiner trauten Gretel gleicht,
Die meiner Schwester das Wasser reicht?
Top! Top! Kling! Klang! das ging herum;
Die einen schrieen: er hat Recht,   3635
Sie ist die Zier vom ganzen Geschlecht!
Da saßen alle die Lober stumm.
Und nun! — um 's Haar sich auszuraufen
Und an den Wänden hinauf zu laufen! —
Mit Stichelreden, Naserümpfen   3640
Soll jeder Schurke mich beschimpfen!

Soll wie ein böser Schuldner sitzen,
Bei jedem Zufallswörtchen schwitzen!
Und möcht' ich sie zusammenschmeißen;
3645 Könnt' ich sie doch nicht Lügner heißen.

Was kommt heran! Was schleicht herbei?
Irr' ich nicht, es sind ihrer zwei.
Ist er's, gleich pack' ich ihn bei'm Felle!
Soll nicht lebendig von der Stelle!

Faust. Mephistopheles.

Faust.

3650 Wie von dem Fenster dort der Sacristei
Aufwärts der Schein des ew'gen Lämpchens flämmert
Und schwach und schwächer seitwärts dämmert,
Und Finsterniß drängt ringsum bei!
So sieht's in meinem Busen nächtig.

Mephistopheles.

3655 Und mir ist's wie dem Kätzlein schmächtig,
Das an den Feuerleitern schleicht,
Sich leis' dann um die Mauern streicht;
Mir ist's ganz tugendlich dabei,
Ein bißchen Diebsgelüst, ein bißchen Rammelei.
3660 So spukt mir schon durch alle Glieder
Die herrliche Walpurgisnacht.
Die kommt uns übermorgen wieder,
Da weiß man doch warum man wacht.

Faust.

Rückt wohl der Schatz indessen in die Höh',
3665 Den ich dorthinten flimmern seh'?

Mephiſtopheles.

Du kannſt die Freude bald erleben,
Das Keſſelchen herauszuheben.
Ich ſchielte neulich ſo hinein,
Sind herrliche Löwenthaler drein.

Fauſt.

Nicht ein Geſchmeide, nicht ein Ring,   3670
Meine liebe Buhle damit zu zieren?

Mephiſtopheles.

Ich ſah dabei wohl ſo ein Ding
Als wie eine Art von Perlenſchnüren.

Fauſt.

So iſt es recht! Mir thut es weh,
Wenn ich ohne Geſchenke zu ihr geh'.   3675

Mephiſtopheles.

Es ſollt' euch eben nicht verdrießen
Umſonſt auch etwas zu genießen.
Jetzt da der Himmel voller Sterne glüht,
Sollt ihr ein wahres Kunſtſtück hören:
Ich ſing' ihr ein moraliſch Lied,   3680
Um ſie gewiſſer zu bethören.

Singt zur Cither.

Was machſt du mir
Vor Liebchens Thür,
Kathrinchen, hier
Bei frühem Tagesblicke?   3685
Laß, laß es ſein!
Er läßt dich ein

Als Mädchen ein,
Als Mädchen nicht zurücke.

3690   Nehmt euch in Acht!
Ist es vollbracht,
Dann gute Nacht
Ihr armen, armen Dinger!
Habt ihr euch lieb,
3695   Thut keinem Dieb
Nur nichts zu Lieb',
Als mit dem Ring am Finger.

Valentin tritt vor.

Wen lockst du hier? bei'm Element!
Vermaledeiter Rattenfänger!
3700   Zum Teufel erst das Instrument!
Zum Teufel hinterdrein den Sänger!

Mephistopheles.

Die Cither ist entzwei! an der ist nichts zu halten.

Valentin.

Nun soll es an ein Schädelspalten!

Mephistopheles zu Faust.

Herr Doctor nicht gewichen!   Frisch!
3705   Hart an mich an, wie ich euch führe.
Heraus mit eurem Flederwisch!
Nur zugestoßen!   Ich parire.

Valentin.

Parire den!

Mephistopheles.

Warum denn nicht?

Valentin.

Auch den!

Mephistopheles.

Gewiß!

Valentin.

Ich glaub', der Teufel ficht!

Was ist denn das?   Schon wird die Hand mir lahm.   3710

Mephistopheles zu Faust.

Stoß' zu!

Valentin fällt.

O weh!

Mephistopheles.

Nun ist der Lümmel zahm!

Nun aber fort!   Wir müssen gleich verschwinden:

Denn schon entsteht ein mörderlich Geschrei.

Ich weiß mich trefflich mit der Policei,

Doch mit dem Blutbann schlecht mich abzufinden.   3715

Marthe am Fenster.

Heraus!   Heraus!

Gretchen am Fenster.

Herbei ein Licht!

Marthe wie oben.

Man schilt und rauft, man schreit und ficht.

Volk.

Da liegt schon einer todt!

Marthe heraustretend.

Die Mörder sind sie denn entflohn?

Gretchen heraustretend.

3720 Wer liegt hier?

Volk.

Deiner Mutter Sohn.

Gretchen.

Allmächtiger! welche Noth!

Valentin.

Ich sterbe! das ist bald gesagt
Und bälder noch gethan.
Was steht ihr Weiber, heult und klagt?
3725 Kommt her und hört mich an!

Alle treten um ihn.

Mein Gretchen sieh! du bist noch jung,
Bist gar noch nicht gescheidt genung,
Machst deine Sachen schlecht.
Ich sag' dir's im Vertrauen nur:
3730 Du bist doch nun einmal eine Hur';
So sei's auch eben recht.

Gretchen.

Mein Bruder! Gott! Was soll mir das?

Valentin.

Laß unsern Herr Gott aus dem Spaß.
Geschehn ist leider nun geschehn,
3735 Und wie es gehn kann, so wird's gehn.
Du fingst mit Einem heimlich an,

Bald kommen ihrer mehre dran,
Und wenn dich erſt ein Dutzend hat,
So hat dich auch die ganze Stadt.

Wenn erſt die Schande wird geboren,　　　　　　3740
Wird ſie heimlich zur Welt gebracht,
Und man zieht den Schleier der Nacht
Ihr über Kopf und Ohren;
Ja, man möchte ſie gern ermorden.
Wäch'ſt ſie aber und macht ſich groß,　　　　　　3745
Dann geht ſie auch bei Tage bloß,
Und iſt doch nicht ſchöner geworden.
Je häßlicher wird ihr Geſicht,
Je mehr ſucht ſie des Tages Licht.

Ich ſeh' wahrhaftig ſchon die Zeit,　　　　　　3750
Daß alle brave Bürgersleut',
Wie von einer angeſteckten Leichen,
Von dir, du Metze! ſeitab weichen.
Dir ſoll das Herz im Leib verzagen,
Wenn ſie dir in die Augen ſehn!　　　　　　3755
Sollſt keine goldne Kette mehr tragen!
In der Kirche nicht mehr am Altar ſtehn!
In einem ſchönen Spitzenkragen
Dich nicht bei'm Tanze wohlbehagen!
In eine finſtre Jammerecken　　　　　　3760
Unter Bettler und Krüppel dich verſtecken,
Und wenn dir denn auch Gott verzeiht,
Auf Erden ſein vermaledeit!

Marthe.
Befehlt eure Seele Gott zu Gnaden!
Wollt ihr noch Läſtrung auf euch laden?　　　　　　3765

Valentin.

Könnt' ich dir nur an den dürren Leib,
Du schändlich kupplerisches Weib!
Da hofft' ich aller meiner Sünden
Vergebung reiche Maß zu finden.

Gretchen.

3770 Mein Bruder! Welche Höllenpein!

Valentin.

Ich sage, laß die Thränen sein!
Da du dich sprachst der Ehre los,
Gabst mir den schwersten Herzensstoß.
Ich gehe durch den Todesschlaf
3775 Zu Gott ein als Soldat und brav.
Stirbt.

————

Dom.

Amt, Orgel und Gesang.

Gretchen unter vielem Volke. Böser Geist hinter Gretchen.

Böser Geist.

Wie anders, Gretchen, war dir's,
Als du noch voll Unschuld
Hier zum Altar trat'st,
Aus dem vergriffnen Büchelchen
Gebete lalltest,   3780
Halb Kinderspiele,
Halb Gott im Herzen!
Gretchen!
Wo steht dein Kopf?
In deinem Herzen   3785
Welche Missethat?
Bet'st du für deiner Mutter Seele, die
Durch dich zur langen, langen Pein hinüberschlief?
Auf deiner Schwelle wessen Blut?
— Und unter deinem Herzen   3790
Regt sich's nicht quillend schon,
Und ängstet dich und sich
Mit ahnungsvoller Gegenwart?

(186)

Gretchen.

Weh! Weh!
Wär' ich der Gedanken los,
Die mir herüber und hinüber gehen
Wider mich!

3795

Chor.

Dies irae, dies illa
Solvet saeclum in favilla.

Orgelton.

Böser Geist.

Grimm faßt dich!
Die Posaune tönt!
Die Gräber beben!
Und dein Herz,
Aus Aschenruh
Zu Flammenqualen
Wieder aufgeschaffen,
Bebt auf!

3800

3805

Gretchen.

Wär' ich hier weg!
Mir ist als ob die Orgel mir
Den Athem versetzte,
Gesang mein Herz
Im Tiefsten löf'te.

3810

Chor.

Judex ergo cum sedebit,
Quidquid latet adparebit,
Nil inultum remanebit.

3815

Gretchen.

Mir wird ſo eng!
Die Mauern=Pfeiler
Befangen mich!
Das Gewölbe
Drängt mich! — Luft!   3820

Böſer Geiſt.

Verbirg dich!   Sünd' und Schande
Bleibt nicht verborgen.
Luft?   Licht?
Weh dir!

Chor.

Quid sum miser tunc dicturus?   3825
Quem patronum rogaturus?
Cum vix justus sit securus.

Böſer Geiſt.

Ihr Antlitz wenden
Verklärte von dir ab.
Die Hände dir zu reichen,   3830
Schauert's den Reinen.
Weh!

Chor.

Quid sum miser tunc dicturus?

Gretchen.

Nachbarin! Euer Fläſchchen! —
     Sie fällt in Ohnmacht.

Walpurgisnacht.

Harzgebirg. Gegend von Schierke und Elend.

Faust. Mephistopheles.

Mephistopheles.

3835 Verlangst du nicht nach einem Besenstiele?
Ich wünschte mir den allerderbsten Bock.
Auf diesem Weg sind wir noch weit vom Ziele.

Faust.

So lang ich mich noch frisch auf meinen Beinen fühle,
Genügt mir dieser Knotenstock.
3840 Was hilft's daß man den Weg verkürzt! —
Im Labyrinth der Thäler hinzuschleichen,
Dann diesen Felsen zu ersteigen,
Von dem der Quell sich ewig sprudelnd stürzt,
Das ist die Lust, die solche Pfade würzt!
3845 Der Frühling webt schon in den Birken
Und selbst die Fichte fühlt ihn schon;
Sollt' er nicht auch auf unsre Glieder wirken?

Mephistopheles.

Fürwahr ich spüre nichts davon!
Mir ist es winterlich im Leibe;

Ich wünſchte Schnee und Froſt auf meiner Bahn.   3850
Wie traurig ſteigt die unvollkommne Scheibe
Des rothen Monds mit ſpäter Gluth heran,
Und leuchtet ſchlecht, daß man bei jedem Schritte,
Vor einen Baum, vor einen Felſen rennt!
Erlaub' daß ich ein Irrlicht bitte!   3855
Dort ſeh' ich eins, das eben luſtig brennt.
He da! mein Freund! Darf ich dich zu uns fodern?
Was willſt du ſo vergebens lodern?
Sei doch ſo gut und leucht' uns da hinauf!

Irrlicht.

Aus Ehrfurcht, hoff' ich, ſoll es mir gelingen,   3860
Mein leichtes Naturell zu zwingen;
Nur zickzack geht gewöhnlich unſer Lauf.

Mephiſtopheles.

Ei! Ei!   Er denkt's den Menſchen nachzuahmen.
Geh' Er nur g'rad', in's Teufels Namen!
Sonſt blaſ' ich Ihm Sein Flacker=Leben aus.   3865

Irrlicht.

Ich merke wohl, ihr ſeid der Herr vom Haus,
Und will mich gern nach euch bequemen.
Allein bedenkt! der Berg iſt heute zaubertoll,
Und wenn ein Irrlicht euch die Wege weiſen ſoll,
So müßt ihr's ſo genau nicht nehmen.   3870

Fauſt, Mephiſtopheles, Irrlicht im Wechſelgeſang.

In die Traum= und Zauberſphäre
Sind wir, ſcheint es, eingegangen.
Führ' uns gut und mach' dir Ehre!

Daß wir vorwärts bald gelangen,
3875   In den weiten öden Räumen.

Seh' die Bäume hinter Bäumen,
Wie sie schnell vorüber rücken,
Und die Klippen, die sich bücken,
Und die langen Felsennasen,
3880   Wie sie schnarchen, wie sie blasen!

Durch die Steine, durch den Rasen
Eilet Bach und Bächlein nieder.
Hör' ich Rauschen? hör' ich Lieder?
Hör' ich holde Liebesklage,
3885   Stimmen jener Himmelstage?
Was wir hoffen, was wir lieben!
Und das Echo, wie die Sage
Alter Zeiten, hallet wider.

Uhu! Schuhu! tönt es näher,
3890   Kauz und Kibitz und der Häher,
Sind sie alle wach geblieben?
Sind das Molche durch's Gesträuche?
Lange Beine, dicke Bäuche!
Und die Wurzeln, wie die Schlangen,
3895   Winden sich aus Fels und Sande,
Strecken wunderliche Bande,
Uns zu schrecken, uns zu fangen;
Aus belebten derben Masern
Strecken sie Polypenfasern
3900   Nach dem Wandrer.   Und die Mäuse

Tauſendfärbig, ſchaarenweiſe,
Durch das Moos und durch die Heide!
Und die Funkenwürmer fliegen,
Mit gedrängten Schwärme=Zügen,
Zum verwirrenden Geleite.   3905

Aber ſag' mir ob wir ſtehen,
Oder ob wir weiter gehen?
Alles, alles ſcheint zu drehen,
Fels und Bäume, die Geſichter
Schneiden, und die irren Lichter,   3910
Die ſich mehren, die ſich blähen.

Mephiſtopheles.

Faſſe wacker meinen Zipfel!
Hier iſt ſo ein Mittelgipfel,
Wo man mit Erſtaunen ſieht,
Wie im Berg der Mammon glüht.   3915

Fauſt.

Wie ſeltſam glimmert durch die Gründe
Ein morgenröthlich trüber Schein!
Und ſelbſt bis in die tiefen Schlünde
Des Abgrunds wittert er hinein.
Da ſteigt ein Dampf, dort ziehen Schwaden,   3920
Hier leuchtet Gluth aus Dunſt und Flor,
Dann ſchleicht ſie wie ein zarter Faden,
Dann bricht ſie wie ein Quell hervor.
Hier ſchlingt ſie eine ganze Strecke,
Mit hundert Adern, ſich durch's Thal,   3925
Und hier in der gedrängten Ecke

Vereinzelt sie sich auf einmal.
Da sprühen Funken in der Nähe,
Wie ausgestreuter goldner Sand.
3930 Doch schau'! in ihrer ganzen Höhe
Entzündet sich die Felsenwand.

Mephistopheles.

Erleuchtet nicht zu diesem Feste
Herr Mammon prächtig den Palast?
Ein Glück daß du's gesehen hast;
3935 Ich spüre schon die ungestümen Gäste.

Faust.

Wie rast die Windsbraut durch die Luft!
Mit welchen Schlägen trifft sie meinen Nacken!

Mephistopheles.

Du mußt des Felsens alte Rippen packen,
Sonst stürzt sie dich hinab in dieser Schlünde Gruft.
3940 Ein Nebel verdichtet die Nacht.
Höre wie's durch die Wälder kracht!
Aufgescheucht fliegen die Eulen.
Hör', es splittern die Säulen
Ewig grüner Paläste.
3945 Girren und Brechen der Äste!
Der Stämme mächtiges Dröhnen!
Der Wurzeln Knarren und Gähnen!
Im fürchterlich verworrenen Falle
Über einander krachen sie alle,
3950 Und durch die übertrümmerten Klüfte
Zischen und heulen die Lüfte.

Hörſt du Stimmen in der Höhe?
In der Ferne, in der Nähe?
Ja, den ganzen Berg entlang
Strömt ein wüthender Zaubergeſang!   3955

Hexen im Chor.

Die Hexen zu dem Brocken ziehn,
Die Stoppel iſt gelb, die Saat iſt grün.
Dort ſammelt ſich der große Hauf,
Herr Urian ſitzt oben auf.
So geht es über Stein und Stock,   3960
Es f—t die Hexe, es ſt—t der Bock.

Stimme.

Die alte Baubo kommt allein;
Sie reitet auf einem Mutterſchwein.

Chor.

So Ehre denn, wem Ehre gebührt!
Frau Baubo vor! und angeführt!   3965
Ein tüchtig Schwein und Mutter drauf,
Da folgt der ganze Hexenhauf.

Stimme.

Welchen Weg kommſt du her?

Stimme.

Über'n Ilſenſtein!
Da guckt' ich der Eule in's Neſt hinein.
Die macht' ein Paar Augen!

Stimme.

O fahre zur Hölle.   3970
Was reit'ſt du ſo ſchnelle!

Stimme.

Mich hat sie geschunden,
Da sieh nur die Wunden!

Hexen. Chor.

Der Weg ist breit, der Weg ist lang,
3975   Was ist das für ein toller Drang?
Die Gabel sticht, der Besen kratzt,
Das Kind erstickt, die Mutter platzt.

Hexenmeister. Halbes Chor.

Wir schleichen wie die Schneck' im Haus,
Die Weiber alle sind voraus.
3980   Denn, geht es zu des Bösen Haus,
Das Weib hat tausend Schritt voraus.

Andre Hälfte.

Wir nehmen das nicht so genau,
Mit tausend Schritten macht's die Frau;
Doch, wie sie auch sich eilen kann,
3985   Mit Einem Sprunge macht's der Mann.

Stimme oben.

Kommt mit, kommt mit, vom Felsensee!

Stimmen von unten.

Wir möchten gern mit in die Höh.
Wir waschen und blank sind wir ganz und gar;
Aber auch ewig unfruchtbar.

Beide Chöre.

3990   Es schweigt der Wind, es flieht der Stern,
Der trübe Mond verbirgt sich gern.

Im Sauſen ſprüht das Zauber=Chor
Viel tauſend Feuerfunken hervor.

Stimme von unten.

Halte! Halte!

Stimme von oben.

Wer ruft da aus der Felſenſpalte?   3995

Stimme unten.

Nehmt mich mit! Nehmt mich mit!
Ich ſteige ſchon dreihundert Jahr,
Und kann den Gipfel nicht erreichen.
Ich wäre gern bei Meinesgleichen.

Beide Chöre.

Es trägt der Beſen, trägt der Stock,   4000
Die Gabel trägt, es trägt der Bock;
Wer heute ſich nicht heben kann,
Iſt ewig ein verlorner Mann.

Halbhexe unten.

Ich tripple nach, ſo lange Zeit;
Wie ſind die andern ſchon ſo weit!   4005
Ich hab' zu Hauſe keine Ruh,
Und komme hier doch nicht dazu.

Chor der Hexen.

Die Salbe gibt den Hexen Muth,
Ein Lumpen iſt zum Segel gut,
Ein gutes Schiff iſt jeder Trog;   4010
Der flieget nie, der heut nicht flog.

Beide Chöre.

Und wenn wir um den Gipfel ziehn,
So streichet an dem Boden hin,
Und deckt die Heide weit und breit
4015 Mit eurem Schwarm der Hexenheit.
Sie lassen sich nieder.

Mephistopheles.

Das drängt und stößt, das ruscht und klappert!
Das zischt und quirlt, das zieht und plappert!
Das leuchtet, sprüht und stinkt und brennt!
Ein wahres Hexenelement!
4020 Nur fest an mir! sonst sind wir gleich getrennt.
Wo bist du?

Faust in der Ferne.
Hier!

Mephistopheles.

Was! dort schon hingerissen?
Da werd' ich Hausrecht brauchen müssen.
Platz! Junker Voland kommt. Platz! süßer Pöbel, Platz!
Hier, Doctor, fasse mich! und nun, in Einem Satz,
4025 Laß uns aus dem Gedräng' entweichen;
Es ist zu toll, sogar für Meinesgleichen.
Dort neben leuchtet was mit ganz besondrem Schein,
Es zieht mich was nach jenen Sträuchen.
Komm, komm! wir schlupfen da hinein.

Faust.

4030 Du Geist des Widerspruchs! Nur zu! du magst mich führen.
Ich denke doch, das war recht klug gemacht;

Zum Brocken wandeln wir in der Walpurgisnacht,
Um uns beliebig nun hieſelbſt zu iſoliren.

Mephiſtopheles.

Da ſieh nur welche bunten Flammen!
Es iſt ein muntrer Club beiſammen.　　　　　　　　4035
Im Kleinen iſt man nicht allein.

Fauſt.

Doch droben möcht' ich lieber ſein!
Schon ſeh' ich Gluth und Wirbelrauch.
Dort ſtrömt die Menge zu dem Böſen;
Da muß ſich manches Räthſel löſen.　　　　　　　　4040

Mephiſtopheles.

Doch manches Räthſel knüpft ſich auch.
Laß du die große Welt nur ſauſen,
Wir wollen hier im Stillen hauſen.
Es iſt doch lange hergebracht,
Daß in der großen Welt man kleine Welten macht.　　4045
Da ſeh' ich junge Hexchen nackt und bloß,
Und alte die ſich klug verhüllen.
Seid freundlich, nur um meinetwillen;
Die Müh iſt klein, der Spaß iſt groß.
Ich höre was von Inſtrumenten tönen!　　　　　　　4050
Verflucht Geſchnarr! Man muß ſich dran gewöhnen.
Komm mit! Komm mit! Es kann nicht anders ſein,
Ich tret' heran und führe dich herein,
Und ich verbinde dich auf's neue.
Was ſagſt du, Freund? das iſt kein kleiner Raum.　　4055
Da ſieh nur hin! du ſiehſt das Ende kaum.
Ein Hundert Feuer brennen in der Reihe;

Man tanzt, man schwatzt, man kocht, man trinkt, man liebt;
Nun sage mir, wo es was Bessers gibt?

Faust.

4060 Willst du dich nun, um uns hier einzuführen,
Als Zaubrer oder Teufel produciren?

Mephistopheles.

Zwar bin ich sehr gewohnt incognito zu gehn,
Doch läßt am Galatag man seinen Orden sehn.
Ein Knieband zeichnet mich nicht aus,
4065 Doch ist der Pferdefuß hier ehrenvoll zu Haus.
Siehst du die Schnecke da?   Sie kommt herangekrochen;
Mit ihrem tastenden Gesicht
Hat sie mir schon was abgerochen.
Wenn ich auch will, verläugn' ich hier mich nicht.
4070 Komm nur! von Feuer gehen wir zu Feuer,
Ich bin der Werber und du bist der Freier.

Zu einigen, die um verglimmende Kohlen sitzen.

Ihr alten Herrn, was macht ihr hier am Ende?
Ich lobt' euch, wenn ich euch hübsch in der Mitte fände,
Von Saus umzirkt und Jugendbraus;
4075 Genug allein ist jeder ja zu Haus.

General.

Wer mag auf Nationen trauen!
Man habe noch so viel für sie gethan;
Denn bei dem Volk, wie bei den Frauen,
Steht immerfort die Jugend oben an.

Minister.

4080 Jetzt ist man von dem Rechten allzuweit,
Ich lobe mir die guten Alten;

Denn freilich, da wir alles galten,
Da war die rechte goldne Zeit.

Parvenu.

Wir waren wahrlich auch nicht dumm,
Und thaten oft was wir nicht ſollten;   4085
Doch jetzo kehrt ſich alles um und um,
Und eben da wir's feſt erhalten wollten.

Autor.

Wer mag wohl überhaupt jetzt eine Schrift
Von mäßig klugem Inhalt leſen!
Und was das liebe junge Volk betrifft,   4090
Das iſt noch nie ſo naſeweis geweſen.

Mephiſtopheles der auf einmal ſehr alt erſcheint.

Zum jüngſten Tag fühl' ich das Volk gereift,
Da ich zum letztenmal den Hexenberg erſteige,
Und, weil mein Fäßchen trübe läuft,
So iſt die Welt auch auf der Neige.   4095

Trödelhexe.

Ihr Herren geht nicht ſo vorbei!
Laßt die Gelegenheit nicht fahren!
Aufmerkſam blickt nach meinen Waaren;
Es ſteht dahier gar mancherlei.
Und doch iſt nichts in meinem Laden,   4100
Dem keiner auf der Erde gleicht,
Das nicht einmal zum tücht'gen Schaden
Der Menſchen und der Welt gereicht.
Kein Dolch iſt hier, von dem nicht Blut gefloſſen,
Kein Kelch, aus dem ſich nicht, in ganz geſunden Leib, 4105

Verzehrend heißes Gift ergossen,
Kein Schmuck, der nicht ein liebenswürdig Weib
Verführt, kein Schwert, das nicht den Bund gebrochen,
Nicht etwa hinterrücks den Gegenmann durchstochen.

Mephistopheles.

4110 Frau Muhme! Sie versteht mir schlecht die Zeiten,
Gethan geschehn! Geschehn gethan!
Verleg' Sie sich auf Neuigkeiten!
Nur Neuigkeiten ziehn uns an.

Faust.

Daß ich mich nur nicht selbst vergesse!
4115 Heiß' ich mir das doch eine Messe!

Mephistopheles.

Der ganze Strudel strebt nach oben;
Du glaubst zu schieben und du wirst geschoben.

Faust.

Wer ist denn das?

Mephistopheles.

Betrachte sie genau!
Lilith ist das.

Faust.

Wer?

Mephistopheles.

Adam's erste Frau.

4120 Nimm dich in Acht vor ihren schönen Haaren,
Vor diesem Schmuck, mit dem sie einzig prangt.
Wenn sie damit den jungen Mann erlangt,
So läßt sie ihn sobald nicht wieder fahren.

Fauſt.

Da ſitzen zwei, die Alte mit der Jungen;
Die haben ſchon was Rechts geſprungen!　　　　4125

Mephiſtopheles.

Das hat nun heute keine Ruh.
Es geht zum neuen Tanz; nun komm! wir greifen zu.

Fauſt mit der Jungen tanzend.

Einſt hatt’ ich einen ſchönen Traum;
Da ſah ich einen Apfelbaum,
Zwei ſchöne Äpfel glänzten dran,　　　　4130
Sie reizten mich, ich ſtieg hinan.

Die Schöne.

Der Äpfelchen begehrt ihr ſehr
Und ſchon vom Paradieſe her.
Von Freuden fühl’ ich mich bewegt,
Daß auch mein Garten ſolche trägt.　　　　4135

Mephiſtopheles mit der Alten.

Einſt hatt’ ich einen wüſten Traum;
Da ſah ich einen geſpaltnen Baum,
Der hatt’ ein — — —;
So — es war, gefiel mir’s doch.

Die Alte.

Ich biete meinen beſten Gruß　　　　4140
Dem Ritter mit dem Pferdefuß!
Halt’ Er einen — — bereit,
Wenn Er — — — nicht ſcheut.

Proktophantasmiſt.

Verfluchtes Volk! was unterſteht ihr euch?

4145 Hat man euch lange nicht bewiesen,
Ein Geist steht nie auf ordentlichen Füßen?
Nun tanzt ihr gar, uns andern Menschen gleich!

Die Schöne tanzend.
Was will denn der auf unserm Ball?

Faust tanzend.
Ei! der ist eben überall.
4150 Was andre tanzen muß er schätzen.
Kann er nicht jeden Schritt beschwätzen,
So ist der Schritt so gut als nicht geschehn.
Am meisten ärgert ihn, sobald wir vorwärts gehn.
Wenn ihr euch so im Kreise drehen wolltet,
4155 Wie er's in seiner alten Mühle thut,
Das hieß' er allenfalls noch gut;
Besonders wenn ihr ihn darum begrüßen solltet.

Proktophantasmist.
Ihr seid noch immer da! Nein das ist unerhört.
Verschwindet doch! Wir haben ja aufgeklärt!
4160 Das Teufelspack es fragt nach keiner Regel.
Wir sind so klug und dennoch spukt's in Tegel.
Wie lange hab' ich nicht am Wahn hinausgekehrt
Und nie wird's rein, das ist doch unerhört!

Die Schöne.
So hört doch auf uns hier zu ennuyiren!

Proktophantasmist.
4165 Ich sag's euch Geistern in's Gesicht,
Den Geistesdespotismus leid' ich nicht;
Mein Geist kann ihn nicht exerciren.
Es wird fortgetanzt.

Heut, ſeh' ich, will mir nichts gelingen;
Doch eine Reiſe nehm' ich immer mit
Und hoffe noch, vor meinem letzten Schritt,   4170
Die Teufel und die Dichter zu bezwingen.

          Mephiſtopheles.

Er wird ſich gleich in eine Pfütze ſetzen,
Das iſt die Art wie er ſich ſoulagirt,
Und wenn Blutegel ſich an ſeinem Steiß ergetzen,
Iſt er von Geiſtern und von Geiſt curirt.   4175

          Zu Fauſt, der aus dem Tanz getreten iſt.

Was läſſeſt du das ſchöne Mädchen fahren,
Das dir zum Tanz ſo lieblich ſang?

          Fauſt.

Ach! mitten im Geſange ſprang
Ein rothes Mäuschen ihr aus dem Munde.

          Mephiſtopheles.

Das iſt was Rechts!   Das nimmt man nicht genau; 4180
Genug die Maus war doch nicht grau.
Wer fragt danach in einer Schäferſtunde?

          Fauſt.

Dann ſah ich —

          Mephiſtopheles.
          Was?

          Fauſt.
               Mephiſto, ſiehſt du dort
Ein blaſſes ſchönes Kind allein und ferne ſtehen?
Sie ſchiebt ſich langſam nur vom Ort,   4185
Sie ſcheint mit geſchloſſ'nen Füßen zu gehen.

Ich muß bekennen, daß mir däucht,
Daß sie dem guten Gretchen gleicht.

Mephistopheles.

Laß das nur stehn! Dabei wird's niemand wohl.
4190 Es ist ein Zauberbild, ist leblos, ein Idol.
Ihm zu begegnen ist nicht gut;
Vom starren Blick erstarrt des Menschen Blut,
Und er wird fast in Stein verkehrt,
Von der Meduse hast du ja gehört.

Faust.

4195 Fürwahr es sind die Augen einer Todten,
Die eine liebende Hand nicht schloß.
Das ist die Brust, die Gretchen mir geboten,
Das ist der süße Leib, den ich genoß.

Mephistopheles.

Das ist die Zauberei, du leicht verführter Thor!
4200 Denn jedem kommt sie wie sein Liebchen vor.

Faust.

Welch eine Wonne! welch ein Leiden!
Ich kann von diesem Blick nicht scheiden.
Wie sonderbar muß diesen schönen Hals
Ein einzig rothes Schnürchen schmücken,
4205 Nicht breiter als ein Messerrücken!

Mephistopheles.

Ganz recht! ich seh' es ebenfalls.
Sie kann das Haupt auch unter'm Arme tragen;
Denn Perseus hat's ihr abgeschlagen. —
Nur immer diese Lust zum Wahn!

Komm doch das Hügelchen heran, 4210
Hier iſt's ſo luſtig wie im Prater;
Und hat man mir's nicht angethan,
So ſeh' ich wahrlich ein Theater.
Was gibt's denn da?

Servibilis.

Gleich fängt man wieder an.
Ein neues Stück, das letzte Stück von ſieben; 4215
Soviel zu geben iſt allhier der Brauch.
Ein Dilettant hat es geſchrieben,
Und Dilettanten ſpielen's auch.
Verzeiht ihr Herrn, wenn ich verſchwinde;
Mich dilettirt's den Vorhang aufzuziehn. 4220

Mephiſtopheles.

Wenn ich euch auf dem Blocksberg finde,
Das find' ich gut; denn da gehört ihr hin.

Walpurgisnachtstraum

oder

Oberons und Titanias Goldne Hochzeit.

Intermezzo.

Theatermeister.

Heute ruhen wir einmal
Miedings wackre Söhne.
4225 Alter Berg und feuchtes Thal,
Das ist die ganze Scene!

Herold.

Daß die Hochzeit golden sei
Soll'n funfzig Jahr sein vorüber;
Aber ist der Streit vorbei,
4230 Das golden ist mir lieber.

Oberon.

Seid ihr Geister wo ich bin,
So zeigt's in diesen Stunden;
König und die Königin,
Sie sind auf's neu verbunden.

Puck.

4235 Kommt der Puck und dreht sich quer
Und schleift den Fuß im Reihen;

Hundert kommen hinterher
Sich auch mit ihm zu freuen.

Ariel.

Ariel bewegt den Sang
In himmliſch reinen Tönen;　　　　　　4240
Viele Fratzen lockt ſein Klang,
Doch lockt er auch die Schönen.

Oberon.

Gatten, die ſich vertragen wollen,
Lernen's von uns beiden!
Wenn ſich zweie lieben ſollen,　　　　　4245
Braucht man ſie nur zu ſcheiden.

Titania.

Schmollt der Mann und grillt die Frau,
So faßt ſie nur behende,
Führt mir nach dem Mittag Sie,
Und Ihn an Nordens Ende.　　　　　　4250

Orcheſter Tutti.

Fortissimo.

Fliegenſchnauz' und Mückennaſ'
Mit ihren Anverwandten,
Froſch im Laub und Grill' im Gras
Das ſind die Muſikanten!

Solo.

Seht da kommt der Dudelſack!　　　　　4255
Es iſt die Seifenblaſe.
Hört den Schneckeſchnickeſchnack
Durch ſeine ſtumpfe Naſe.

Geist der sich erst bildet.

Spinnenfuß und Krötenbauch
Und Flügelchen dem Wichtchen!
Zwar ein Thierchen gibt es nicht,
Doch gibt es ein Gedichtchen.

Ein Pärchen.

Kleiner Schritt und hoher Sprung
Durch Honigthau und Düfte;
Zwar du trippelst mir genung,
Doch geht's nicht in die Lüfte.

Neugieriger Reisender.

Ist das nicht Maskeraden=Spott?
Soll ich den Augen trauen,
Oberon den schönen Gott
Auch heute hier zu schauen?

Orthodox.

Keine Klauen, keinen Schwanz!
Doch bleibt es außer Zweifel,
So wie die Götter Griechenlands,
So ist auch er ein Teufel.

Nordischer Künstler.

Was ich ergreife das ist heut
Fürwahr nur skizzenweise;
Doch ich bereite mich bei Zeit
Zur italiän'schen Reise.

Purist.

Ach! mein Unglück führt mich her:
Wie wird nicht hier geludert!

Und von dem ganzen Hexenheer
Sind zweie nur gepudert!

Junge Hexe.

Der Puder iſt ſowie der Rock
Für alt' und graue Weibchen;
Drum ſitz' ich nackt auf meinem Bock   4285
Und zeig' ein derbes Leibchen.

Matrone.

Wir haben zu viel Lebensart,
Um hier mit euch zu maulen;
Doch hoff' ich, ſollt ihr jung und zart,
So wie ihr ſeid, verfaulen.   4290

Capellmeiſter.

Fliegenſchnauz' und Mückennaſ'
Umſchwärmt mir nicht die Nackte!
Froſch im Laub und Grill' im Gras,
So bleibt doch auch im Tacte!

Windfahne nach der einen Seite.

Geſellſchaft wie man wünſchen kann.   4295
Wahrhaftig lauter Bräute!
Und Junggeſellen, Mann für Mann!
Die hoffnungsvollſten Leute.

Windfahne nach der andern Seite.

Und thut ſich nicht der Boden auf
Sie alle zu verſchlingen,
So will ich mit behendem Lauf   4300
Gleich in die Hölle ſpringen.

Xenien.

Als Insecten sind wir da,
Mit kleinen scharfen Scheren,
4305   Satan, unsern Herrn Papa,
Nach Würden zu verehren.

Hennings.

Seht! wie sie in gedrängter Schaar
Naiv zusammen scherzen.
Am Ende sagen sie noch gar,
4310   Sie hätten gute Herzen.

Musaget.

Ich mag in diesem Hexenheer
Mich gar zu gern verlieren;
Denn freilich diese wüßt' ich eh'r,
Als Musen anzuführen.

Ci-devant Genius der Zeit.

4315   Mit rechten Leuten wird man was.
Komm, fasse meinen Zipfel!
Der Blocksberg, wie der deutsche Parnaß,
Hat gar einen breiten Gipfel.

Neugieriger Reisender.

Sagt wie heißt der steife Mann?
4320   Er geht mit stolzen Schritten.
Er schnopert was er schnopern kann.
„Er spürt nach Jesuiten."

Kranich.

In dem Klaren mag ich gern
Und auch im Trüben fischen;

Darum ſeht ihr den frommen Herrn   4325
Sich auch mit Teufeln miſchen.

Weltkind.

Ja für die Frommen, glaubet mir,
Iſt alles ein Vehikel;
Sie bilden auf dem Blocksberg hier
Gar manches Conventikel.   4330

Tänzer.

Da kommt ja wohl ein neues Chor?
Ich höre ferne Trommeln.
Nur ungeſtört! es ſind im Rohr
Die uniſonen Dommeln.

Tanzmeiſter.

Wie jeder doch die Beine lupft!   4335
Sich wie er kann herauszieht!
Der Krumme ſpringt, der Plumpe hupft
Und fragt nicht wie es ausſieht.

Fiedeler.

Das haßt ſich ſchwer das Lumpenpack
Und gäb’ ſich gern das Neſtchen;
Es eint ſie hier der Dudelſack,   4340
Wie Orpheus Leier die Beſtjen.

Dogmatiker.

Ich laſſe mich nicht irre ſchrein,
Nicht durch Kritik noch Zweifel.
Der Teufel muß doch etwas ſein;   4345
Wie gäb’s denn ſonſt auch Teufel?

Idealift.

Die Phantasie in meinem Sinn
Ist dießmal gar zu herrisch.
Fürwahr, wenn ich das alles bin,
4350 So bin ich heute närrisch.

Realift.

Das Wesen ist mir recht zur Qual
Und muß mich baß verdrießen;
Ich stehe hier zum erstenmal
Nicht fest auf meinen Füßen.

Supernaturalift.

4355 Mit viel Vergnügen bin ich da
Und freue mich mit diesen;
Denn von den Teufeln kann ich ja
Auf gute Geister schließen.

Skeptiker.

Sie gehn den Flämmchen auf der Spur,
4360 Und glaub'n sich nah dem Schatze.
Auf Teufel reimt der Zweifel nur;
Da bin ich recht am Platze.

Capellmeiſter.

Frosch im Laub und Grill' im Gras
Verfluchte Dilettanten!
4365 Fliegenschnauz' und Mückennas'
Ihr seid doch Musikanten!

Die Gewandten.

Sanssouci so heißt das Heer
Von luſtigen Geſchöpfen,

Auf den Füßen geht's nicht mehr,
Drum gehn wir auf den Köpfen.

4370

Die Unbehülflichen.

Sonſt haben wir manchen Biſſen erſchranzt,
Nun aber Gott befohlen!
Unſere Schuhe ſind durchgetanzt,
Wir laufen auf nackten Sohlen.

Irrlichter.

Von dem Sumpfe kommen wir,

4375

Woraus wir erſt entſtanden;
Doch ſind wir gleich im Reihen hier
Die glänzenden Galanten.

Sternſchnuppe.

Aus der Höhe ſchoß ich her
Im Stern= und Feuerſcheine,

4380

Liege nun im Graſe quer,
Wer hilft mir auf die Beine?

Die Maſſiven.

Platz und Platz! und ringsherum!
So gehn die Gräschen nieder,
Geiſter kommen, Geiſter auch

4385

Sie haben plumpe Glieder.

Puck.

Tretet nicht ſo maſtig auf
Wie Elephantenkälber,
Und der plumpſt' an dieſem Tag
Sei Puck der derbe ſelber.

4390

Ariel.

Gab die liebende Natur
Gab der Geist euch Flügel,
Folget meiner leichten Spur,
Auf zum Rosenhügel!

Orchester.

Pianissimo.

4395 Wolkenzug und Nebelflor
Erhellen sich von oben.
Luft im Laub und Wind im Rohr
Und alles ist zerstoben.

———

Trüber Tag.

Feld.

Fauſt. Mephiſtopheles.

Fauſt.

Im Elend! Verzweifelnd! Erbärmlich auf der Erde lange
verirrt und nun gefangen! Als Miſſethäterin im Kerker zu
entſetzlichen Qualen eingeſperrt das holde unſelige Geſchöpf!
Bis dahin! dahin! — Verrätheriſcher nichtswürdiger Geiſt, und
das haſt du mir verheimlicht! — Steh nur, ſteh! Wälze die 5
teufliſchen Augen ingrimmend im Kopf herum! Steh und
trutze mir durch deine unerträgliche Gegenwart! Gefangen!
Im unwiederbringlichen Elend! Böſen Geiſtern übergeben
und der richtenden gefühlloſen Menſchheit! Und mich wiegſt
du indeß in abgeſchmackten Zerſtreuungen, verbirgſt mir ihren 10
wachſenden Jammer und läſſeſt ſie hülflos verderben!

Mephiſtopheles.

Sie iſt die Erſte nicht.

Fauſt.

Hund! abſcheuliches Unthier! — Wandle ihn, du unend=
licher Geiſt! wandle den Wurm wieder in ſeine Hundsgeſtalt,
wie er ſich oft nächtlicher Weile gefiel vor mir herzutrotten, dem 15
harmloſen Wandrer vor die Füße zu kollern und ſich dem nie=
derſtürzenden auf die Schultern zu hängen. Wandl' ihn wieder
in ſeine Lieblingsbildung, daß er vor mir im Sand auf dem

(216)

Bauch krieche, ich ihn mit Füßen trete, den verworfnen! —
20 Die Erste nicht! — Jammer! Jammer! von keiner Menschen-
seele zu fassen, daß mehr als ein Geschöpf in die Tiefe dieses
Elendes versank, daß nicht das erste genug that für die Schuld
aller übrigen in seiner windenden Todesnoth vor den Augen
des ewig Verzeihenden! Mir wühlt es Mark und Leben durch,
25 das Elend dieser Einzigen; du grinsest gelassen über das Schicksal von Tausenden hin!

Mephistopheles.

Nun sind wir schon wieder an der Grenze unseres Witzes, da
wo euch Menschen der Sinn überschnappt. Warum machst du
Gemeinschaft mit uns, wenn du sie nicht durchführen kannst?
30 Willst fliegen und bist vor'm Schwindel nicht sicher? Drangen
wir uns dir auf, oder du dich uns?

Faust.

Fletsche deine gefräßigen Zähne mir nicht so entgegen! Mir
ekelt's! — Großer herrlicher Geist, der du mir zu erscheinen
würdigtest, der du mein Herz kennest und meine Seele, warum
35 an den Schandgesellen mich schmieden, der sich am Schaden
weidet und am Verderben sich letzt?

Mephistopheles.

Endigst du?

Faust.

Rette sie! oder weh dir! Den gräßlichsten Fluch über dich
auf Jahrtausende!

Mephistopheles.

40 Ich kann die Bande des Rächers nicht lösen, seine Riegel
nicht öffnen. — Rette sie! — Wer war's, der sie in's Verderben
stürzte? Ich oder du?

Faust blickt wild umher.

Mephistopheles.

Greifst du nach dem Donner? Wohl, daß er euch elenden
Sterblichen nicht gegeben ward! Den unschuldig Entgegnenden
zu zerschmettern, das ist so Tyrannen=Art sich in Verlegen= 45
heiten Luft zu machen.

Faust.

Bringe mich hin! Sie soll frei sein!

Mephistopheles.

Und die Gefahr der du dich aussetzest? Wisse, noch liegt
auf der Stadt Blutschuld von deiner Hand. Über des Er=
schlagenen Stätte schweben rächende Geister und lauern auf 50
den wiederkehrenden Mörder.

Faust.

Noch das von dir? Mord und Tod einer Welt über dich
Ungeheuer! Führe mich hin, sag' ich, und befrei' sie!

Mephistopheles.

Ich führe dich und was ich thun kann, höre! Habe ich alle
Macht im Himmel und auf Erden? Des Thürners Sinne will 55
ich umnebeln, bemächtige dich der Schlüssel und führe sie her=
aus mit Menschenhand. Ich wache! die Zauberpferde sind
bereit, ich entführe euch. Das vermag ich.

Faust.

Auf und davon!

———

Nacht.

Offen Feld.

Fauft Mephiftopheles, auf schwarzen Pferden daher braufend.

Fauft.
Was weben die dort um den Rabenftein?

Mephiftopheles.
4400 Weiß nicht was fie kochen und fchaffen.

Fauft.
Schweben auf, fchweben ab, neigen fich, beugen fich.

Mephiftopheles.
Eine Hexenzunft.

Fauft.
Sie ftreuen und weihen.

Mephiftopheles.
Vorbei! Vorbei!

———

Kerker.

Faust mit einem Bund Schlüssel und einer Lampe, vor einem eisernen Thürchen.

Faust.

Mich faßt ein längst entwohnter Schauer,   4405
Der Menschheit ganzer Jammer faßt mich an.
Hier wohnt sie hinter dieser feuchten Mauer,
Und ihr Verbrechen war ein guter Wahn!
Du zauderst zu ihr zu gehen!
Du fürchtest sie wieder zu sehen!   4410
Fort!   Dein Zagen zögert den Tod heran.

Er ergreift das Schloß. Es singt inwendig.

Meine Mutter, die Hur',
Die mich umgebracht hat!
Mein Vater, der Schelm,
Der mich geſſen hat!   4415
Mein Schwesterlein klein
Hub auf die Bein',
An einem kühlen Ort;
Da ward ich ein schönes Waldvögelein;
Fliege fort, fliege fort!   4420

Faust *aufschließend.*

Sie ahnet nicht, daß der Geliebte lauscht,
Die Ketten klirren hört, das Stroh, das rauscht.

Er tritt ein.

M a r g a r e t e sich auf dem Lager verbergend.

Weh! Weh! Sie kommen. Bittrer Tod!

F a u s t leise.

Still! Still! Ich komme dich zu befreien.

M a r g a r e t e sich vor ihn hinwälzend.

4425 Bist du ein Mensch, so fühle meine Noth!

F a u s t.

Du wirst die Wächter aus dem Schlafe schreien!
Er faßt die Ketten, sie aufzuschließen.

M a r g a r e t e auf den Knieen.

Wer hat dir Henker diese Macht
Über mich gegeben!
Du holst mich schon um Mitternacht.
4430 Erbarme dich und laß mich leben!
Ist's morgen früh nicht zeitig genung?
Sie steht auf.
Bin ich doch noch so jung, so jung!
Und soll schon sterben!
Schön war ich auch, und das war mein Verderben.
4435 Nah war der Freund, nun ist er weit;
Zerrissen liegt der Kranz, die Blumen zerstreut.
Fasse mich nicht so gewaltsam an!
Schone mich! Was hab' ich dir gethan?
Laß mich nicht vergebens flehen,
4440 Hab' ich dich doch mein' Tage nicht gesehen!

F a u s t.

Werd' ich den Jammer überstehen!

Margarete.

Ich bin nun ganz in deiner Macht.
Laß mich nur erſt das Kind noch tränken.
Ich herzt’ es dieſe ganze Nacht;
Sie nahmen mir’s, um mich zu kränken   4445
Und ſagen nun, ich hätt’ es umgebracht.
Und niemals werb’ ich wieder froh.
Sie ſingen Lieder auf mich! Es iſt bös von den Leuten!
Ein altes Mährchen endigt ſo,
Wer heißt ſie’s deuten?   4450

Fauſt wirft ſich nieder.

Ein Liebender liegt dir zu Füßen
Die Jammerknechtſchaft aufzuſchließen.

Margarete wirft ſich zu ihm.

O laß uns knien die Heil’gen anzurufen!
Sieh! unter dieſen Stufen,
Unter der Schwelle   4455
Siedet die Hölle!
Der Böſe,
Mit furchtbarem Grimme,
Macht ein Getöſe!

Fauſt laut.

Gretchen! Gretchen!   4460

Margarete aufmerkſam.

Das war des Freundes Stimme!

Sie ſpringt auf. Die Ketten fallen ab.

Wo iſt er? Ich hab’ ihn rufen hören.
Ich bin frei! Mir ſoll niemand wehren.

An seinen Hals will ich fliegen,
4465 An seinem Busen liegen!
Er rief Gretchen! Er stand auf der Schwelle.
Mitten durch's Heulen und Klappen der Hölle,
Durch den grimmigen teuflischen Hohn,
Erkannt' ich den süßen, den liebenden Ton.

Faust.

4470 Ich bin's!

Margarete.

Du bist's! O sag' es noch einmal!
Ihn fassend.
Er ist's! Er ist's! Wohin ist alle Qual?
Wohin die Angst des Kerkers? der Ketten?
Du bist's! Kommst mich zu retten!
Ich bin gerettet! —
4475 Schon ist die Straße wieder da,
Auf der ich dich zum erstenmale sah,
Und der heitere Garten,
Wo ich und Marthe deiner warten.

Faust *fortstrebend.*

Komm mit! Komm mit!

Margarete.

O weile!
4480 Weil' ich doch so gern wo du weilest!
Liebkosend.

Faust.

Eile!
Wenn du nicht eilest,
Werden wir's theuer büßen müssen.

Margarete.

Wie? du kannſt nicht mehr küſſen?
Mein Freund, ſo kurz von mir entfernt,   4485
Und haſt 's Küſſen verlernt?
Warum wird mir an deinem Halſe ſo bang?
Wenn ſonſt von deinen Worten, deinen Blicken
Ein ganzer Himmel mich überdrang,
Und du mich küßteſt als wollteſt du mich erſticken.   4490
Küſſe mich!
Sonſt küſſ' ich dich!

Sie umfaßt ihn.

O weh! deine Lippen ſind kalt,
Sind ſtumm.
Wo iſt dein Lieben   4495
Geblieben?
Wer brachte mich drum?

Sie wendet ſich von ihm.

Fauſt.

Komm! Folge mir! Liebchen, faſſe Muth!
Ich herze dich mit tauſendfacher Gluth;
Nur folge mir! Ich bitte dich nur dieß!   4500

Margarete zu ihm gewendet.

Und biſt du's denn?   Und biſt du's auch gewiß?

Fauſt.

Ich bin's! Komm mit!

Margarete.

Du machſt die Feſſeln los,
Nimmſt wieder mich in deinen Schoos.

Wie kommt es, daß du dich vor mir nicht scheust? —
4505 Und weißt du denn, mein Freund, wen du befreist?

Faust.

Komm! komm! Schon weicht die tiefe Nacht.

Margarete.

Meine Mutter hab' ich umgebracht,
Mein Kind hab' ich ertränkt.
War es nicht dir und mir geschenkt?
4510 Dir auch. — Du bist's! ich glaub' es kaum.
Gib deine Hand! Es ist kein Traum!
Deine liebe Hand! — Ach aber sie ist feucht!
Wische sie ab! Wie mich däucht
Ist Blut dran.
4515 Ach Gott! Was hast du gethan!
Stecke den Degen ein;
Ich bitte dich drum!

Faust.

Laß das Vergangne vergangen sein,
Du bringst mich um.

Margarete.

4520 Nein, du mußt übrig bleiben!
Ich will dir die Gräber beschreiben.
Für die mußt du sorgen
Gleich morgen;
Der Mutter den besten Platz geben,
4525 Meinen Bruder sogleich darneben,
Mich ein wenig bei Seit',
Nur nicht gar zu weit!

Und das Kleine mir an die rechte Bruſt.
Niemand wird ſonſt bei mir liegen! —
Mich an deine Seite zu ſchmiegen   4530
Das war ein ſüßes, ein holdes Glück!
Aber es will mir nicht mehr gelingen;
Mir iſt's als müßt' ich mich zu dir zwingen,
Als ſtießeſt du mich von dir zurück;
Und doch biſt du's und blickſt ſo gut, ſo fromm.   4535

                    Fauſt.
Fühlſt du daß ich es bin, ſo komm!

                  Margarete.
Dahinaus?
                    Fauſt.
In's Freie.
                  Margarete.
          Iſt das Grab drauß',
Lauert der Tod, ſo komm!
Von hier in's ewige Ruhebett   4540
Und weiter keinen Schritt —
Du gehſt nun fort?   O Heinrich, könnt' ich mit!

                    Fauſt.
Du kannſt! So wolle nur! Die Thür ſteht offen.

                  Margarete.
Ich darf nicht fort; für mich iſt nichts zu hoffen.
Was hilft es fliehn?   Sie lauern doch mir auf.   4545
Es iſt ſo elend betteln zu müſſen,
Und noch dazu mit böſem Gewiſſen!
Es iſt ſo elend in der Fremde ſchweifen,
Und ſie werden mich doch ergreifen!

Fauſt.

4550 Ich bleibe bei dir.

Margarete.

Geſchwind! Geſchwind!
Rette dein armes Kind.
Fort! Immer den Weg
Am Bach hinauf,
4555 Über den Steg,
In den Wald hinein,
Links wo die Planke ſteht,
Im Teich.
Faß' es nur gleich!
4560 Es will ſich heben,
Es zappelt noch!
Rette! Rette!

Fauſt.

Beſinne dich doch!
Nur Einen Schritt, ſo biſt du frei!

Margarete.

4565 Wären wir nur den Berg vorbei!
Da ſitzt meine Mutter auf einem Stein,
Es faßt mich kalt bei'm Schopfe!
Da ſitzt meine Mutter auf einem Stein
Und wackelt mit dem Kopfe;
4570 Sie winkt nicht, ſie nickt nicht, der Kopf iſt ihr ſchwer,
Sie ſchlief ſo lange, ſie wacht nicht mehr.
Sie ſchlief, damit wir uns freuten,
Es waren glückliche Zeiten!

Fauſt.

Hilft hier kein Flehen, hilft kein Sagen;
So wag' ich's dich hinweg zu tragen.   4575

Margarete.

Laß mich! Nein, ich leide keine Gewalt!
Faſſe mich nicht ſo mörderiſch an!
Sonſt hab' ich dir ja alles zu Lieb' gethan.

Fauſt.

Der Tag graut! Liebchen! Liebchen!

Margarete.

Tag! Ja es wird Tag! der letzte Tag dringt herein;   4580
Mein Hochzeittag ſollt' es ſein!
Sag' niemand daß du ſchon bei Gretchen warſt.
Weh meinem Kranze!
Es iſt eben geſchehn!
Wir werden uns wiederſehn;   4585
Aber nicht bei'm Tanze.
Die Menge drängt ſich, man hört ſie nicht.
Der Platz, die Gaſſen
Können ſie nicht faſſen.
Die Glocke ruft, das Stäbchen bricht. —   4590
Wie ſie mich binden und packen!
Zum Blutſtuhl bin ich ſchon entrückt.
Schon zuckt nach jedem Nacken
Die Schärfe die nach meinem zückt.
Stumm liegt die Welt wie das Grab!   4595

Fauſt.

O wär' ich nie geboren!

Mephistopheles erscheint draußen.

Auf! oder ihr seid verloren.
Unnützes Zagen! Zaudern und Plaudern!
Meine Pferde schaudern,
4600 Der Morgen dämmert auf.

Margarete.

Was steigt aus dem Boden herauf?
Der! der! Schick' ihn fort!
Was will der an dem heiligen Ort?
Er will mich!

Faust.
Du sollst leben!

Margarete.

4605 Gericht Gottes! Dir hab' ich mich übergeben!

Mephistopheles zu Faust.
Komm! komm! Ich lasse dich mit ihr im Stich.

Margarete.

Dein bin ich, Vater! Rette mich!
Ihr Engel! Ihr heiligen Schaaren,
Lagert euch umher, mich zu bewahren!
4610 Heinrich! Mir graut's vor dir.

Mephistopheles.

Sie ist gerichtet!

Stimme von oben.
Ist gerettet!

M e p h i ſ t o p h e l e s zu Fauſt.

Her zu mir!

Verſchwindet mit Fa u ſt.

S t i m m e von innen, verhallend.

Heinrich! Heinrich!

———

NOTES.

ABBREVIATIONS.

Cf.	Compare, see.
C.M.	Christlich Meynenden Faust-book (Intr. p. xvii).
D.M.	Deutsche Mythologie (see under Grimm, Appendix I).
Fgm.	Fragment of 1790 (Intr. p. xliv).
G.-J.	Goethe-Jahrbuch.
Intr.	Introduction.
l.	line.
p.	page.
Par.	Paralipomena (see under Strenlke, Appendix I).
U.	Urfaust, Göchhausen Faust (Intr. pp. xxxix, xl).
V. L.	Vierteljahrschrift für Litteraturgeschichte.
Wb.	Wörterbuch.
Werke.	Goethe's Works, Weimar Edition (Intr. p. x, foot-note).
Werke H.	" " Hempel " " " "
=	equivalent to.
>	passing into, becoming.
+	ensuing stage-direction.

Other common abbreviations, including those of familiar grammatical and philological terms, books of the Bible, etc., do not require explanations. Where a work is referred to by the author's name only, consult the bibliographical list in Appendix I.

Zueignung.

THESE fine stanzas, written, as we now know from Goethe's diary, on the 24th of June, 1797, are in no sense a part of the drama of *Faust*, but simply an 'occasional' lyric. The poet, now in middle life, has determined to resume work upon *Faust*. In 'dedicating' himself to the task he gives expression to the feelings that come to him as he thinks of his youth when the work was begun. Cf. Intr. p. lix. The meter, a regular eight-line stanza with feminine rimes *a*, *c*, and masculine rimes *b*, combining according to the system *ababcc*, was a favorite one with Goethe in pensive, elegiac moods.

1. **ſchwankende Geſtalten,** 'wavering forms'; Faust, Mephistopheles, Gretchen, etc., conceived as air-phantoms. Goethe often alludes to his poetic musings under the image of communing with spirits. Cf. his *Tasso*, l. 562. In a letter to Schiller of July 1, 1797, he speaks of the 'air-phantoms of *Faust*.' — **Wieder,** 'again,' with allusion to their first approach in the poet's youth.

2. **trüben,** 'dim'; his early vision was not yet clear.

4. **Wahn;** not exactly 'illusion,' nor 'delusion,' but 'fantastic idea,' viz., the early project of dramatizing the Faust-legend. To the Goethe of 1797 this project, as he had long ago conceived it, appears quixotic, based on illusion. Cf. Intr. p. lix.

5. **mögt ihr walten,** 'you may have your way.'

6. **Wie ihr . . . . ſteigt.** At the noontide of his life the poet has reached a clear height, from which the youthful *Faust* and its mental associations present themselves as a region of 'foggy mist.' Cf. the letter to Schiller of June 22, 1797, where, as here, **Dunſt und Nebel** is a hendiadys for **Nebeldunſt.** From out this dim medium the 'forms' rise about him and mutely insist upon a renewal of the earlier comradeship. He resolves to yield to their importunity.

8. umwittert. The verb means 'to encompass' in the form of an atmospheric influence. The 'forms' are surrounded by a magic aura, at the touch of which the poet is thrilled with the old youthful agitation.

10. Schatten ; visions of youthful friends now dead, or otherwise lost to view.

12. erſte Lieb' und Freundſchaft. If we attempt to think of any one in particular, which is not at all necessary, it should probably be of Friederike Brion and the friendships of 1772–1775. There had been earlier loves and friendships, but these were the 'first' of the awakened, liberated Goethe, the Goethe of *Faust*. Still, Schröer sees here an allusion to the Frankfurt Gretchen of *Werke*, XXVI., 266 ff. Cf. Intr. p. lxxxi. — The bad rime auf : herauf was probably deliberate. Rimes to auf are scarce in German. Vischer, G.-J., IV., 9, calls the apparent negligence unverbeſſerlich ſchön.

13. Klage, 'mourner's plaint.'

18. Die Seelen . . . . ſang. The friends from far and near to whom, in Frankfurt and later in Weimar, Goethe was wont to read his *Faust*. Cf. Intr. p. xxxviii.

21. Leid. The early *Faust* is conceived as a record of 'suffering,' a common image with Goethe for his poetic 'confessions.' Cf. Thomas's *Goethe's Tasso*, Intr. p. xlix ff. On the reading Lied cf. Appendix II. — **unbekannten Menge ;** the general public, the 'unknown multitude,' who have read the printed Fragment of 1790, and will read the new scenes that are to be added. They may praise the art of the poem, but they will not feel for the 'suffering' that underlies it.

22. macht . . . . bang, 'makes my heart misgive me.' To an English ear the dat. sounds unnatural, but it is the historically correct construction — es iſt mir, thut mir, macht mir bang, just like es thut mir wohl. Ich bin bang, es macht mein Herz bang, are comparatively modern.

23. was, 'they who'; here, like the es in l. 24, of persons. This is a common use of the neut. sing. pronoun to refer to 'several persons in a general way' (Hart). Cf. Schiller's *Tell*, I, 3 : Das ſchlendert wie die Schnecken, 'those fellows dawdle like snails.' — **Lied** refers to the early *Faust*, or perhaps to Goethe's youthful singing generally. With erfreuet supply hat, rather than hätte, taking ſonſt in the sense of 'formerly' rather than in that of 'else.'

26. 𝕲𝖊𝖎𝖘𝖙𝖊𝖗𝖗𝖊𝖎𝖈𝖍 ; the 'spirit-realm' of departed friends.

28. 𝖑𝖎𝖘𝖕𝖊𝖑𝖓𝖉 𝕷𝖎𝖊𝖉 ; of this Dedication. As the poet surrenders him-self to the memories of his youth, the rush of feeling overcomes him and the hitherto clear notes of his lyre die away in 'plaintive' (𝖑𝖎𝖘𝖕𝖊𝖑𝖓𝖉), 'un-certain' tones like those of an Æolian harp.

29. 𝕾𝖈𝖍𝖆𝖚𝖊𝖗, 'feeling of awe.' — 𝕿𝖍𝖗ä𝖓𝖊 𝖋𝖔𝖑𝖌𝖙 𝖉𝖊𝖓 𝕿𝖍𝖗ä𝖓𝖊𝖓; *metri gratia* for 𝕿𝖍𝖗ä𝖓𝖊 𝖋𝖔𝖑𝖌𝖙 𝖉𝖊𝖗 𝕿𝖍𝖗ä𝖓𝖊. So in l. 4658 we find 𝖂𝖚𝖓𝖘𝖈𝖍 𝖚𝖒 𝖂ü𝖓𝖘𝖈𝖍𝖊, for 𝖂𝖚𝖓𝖘𝖈𝖍 𝖚𝖒 𝖂𝖚𝖓𝖘𝖈𝖍, 'wish after wish.'

𝖁𝖔𝖗𝖘𝖕𝖎𝖊𝖑 𝖆𝖚𝖋 𝖉𝖊𝖒 𝕿𝖍𝖊𝖆𝖙𝖊𝖗.

The Prelude is a dialogue in which the function of the playwright is considered from three different points of view: that of the Manager, who wishes to draw the crowd and make money; that of the Comedian, who wishes to provide amusement for the young; and that of the Poet with his ideal notions of art for art's sake. The fiction, which makes no claim to naturalness, is this: A company of players have arrived in a German city, set up their temporary theater of boards, and announced a play. But, though the audience has already gathered, the play has not yet been com-posed; even its general character is quite undetermined. So the Manager and the 'Merry-Andrew,' the actor who takes the part of the funny man, advise the Poet how to go to work. At the end of the conference we must imagine the Poet to improvise the play of *Faust*. Of course the Poet is Goethe, but — so is the Manager and the Comedian. As director of the Weimar theater Goethe was quite familiar with the manager's point of view, while in his youth he had written several farces and satirical plays the chief aim of which was amusement 'for the present.' The Prelude is not meant to imply that *Faust* embodies only the austere views of the Poet, that he follows his own bent and pays no attention to the advice of the other two; the humorous point of the whole is that all three get their demands complied with. *Faust* is as full of action, as motley, as spectacu-lar, as free-and-easy in its technique, as the Manager could wish; it con-tains enough humor and hocus-pocus to satisfy the Comedian, while it is after all a work of art, made not for the crowd or for the moment, but for the best and for the ages. It has been thought that the Prelude was suggested by the Hindu drama *Çakuntala*, a translation of which by Forster appeared in 1791 and greatly interested Goethe. The *Çakuntala* has a prelude in which the Director converses with an actress about the play that is to be given.

The meter of the Prelude is irregular (*vers irréguliers*, cf. Bartsch in G.-J., I., 131). It consists of rimed iambic lines of four or five feet, with occasional alexandrines. The rimes are either crossed or consecutive, and masculine rimes alternate with feminine. Consecutive pairs of the same gender do not occur. Alexandrines are lines 55, 104, 117, 119, 126, 129, 140, 148, 165, 180, 181 and 225. No special significance attaches to their use; that is, they are not employed deliberately for any specific effect.

The Prelude was probably written in 1798.

35. in deutſchen Landen. The words seem to imply that the players, who are Germans (cf. unſern in l. 231), have lately returned from a tour in some foreign land. Perhaps, however, there is no such implication, but only an allusion to well-known German conditions.

39. Pfoſten ; the 'posts' supporting the stage. — Aufgeſchlagen, 'thrown up'; implying hasty or temporary construction.

41. Augenbrannen. The original and now usual form is Augenbrauen, which Goethe also uses.

43. verſöhnt, 'conciliates.'

48. mit Bedeutung, 'while having some significance,' 'while not trivial.'

51. Wehen, 'throes.' The spasmodic surgings of the crowd are likened to birth-pains. So at least Sanders Wb., *sub voce* Weh.

52. enge Gnadenpforte ; in allusion to the 'strait (i. e. narrow) gate,' στενὴ πύλη, of Matt. vii, 13.

53. vor Vieren, 'before four o'clock.' The declined plu. Viere occurs only in certain set phrases, e. g., mit Vieren, 'with four horses'; auf allen Vieren, 'on all fours'; um Viere, 'at four o'clock.' The plays at Weimar usually began at six or half-past-five p. m.

55. The simile was suggested, no doubt, by what had lately been going on in Paris. See Carlyle's *French Revolution*, bk. 6, chapter "In Queue."

59–74. The Poet speaks at first in the stanza of the Zueignung. With the sentiment expressed cf. Goethe's *Tasso*, l. 454:

Die Menge macht den Künstler irr' und scheu.

60. uns . . . , entflieht, 'our wit forsakes us.'

62. Strudel, 'vortex' of vulgarity.

63. stillen Himmelsenge, 'quiet, celestial nook' of personal affection and sympathy. The thought is that the best incentive to good work is the desire to please the friends whom one loves. Cf. Thomas's Goethe's *Tasso*, ll. 447–8, and the editor's note.

64. Wo nur, 'where alone,' the nur being *metri gratia* for allein. The phrase wo nur commonly means 'wherever.' Of course nur can not be taken with Dichter.

66. Götterhand. In compounds, Götter= is often used without polytheistic tinge in the sense of divine. — Erpflegen is a rare verb quoted in Grimm Wb. for this passage only and defined *curare*. The er= gives the force 'to nurse effectively,' 'nurse into health and vigor.'

68. schüchtern vorgelallt, 'timidly stammered out.' The poetic artist is thought of as 'timid' about entrusting the child of his love to the wild waves of contemporary opinion; his work is 'stammered forth' because he feels that it is an imperfect utterance of his thought.

69. Mißrathen . . . . gelungen, 'miscarrying now, and now perhaps succeeding,' according as the poet is more or less lucky in his attempt at utterance. On the force of the participles see Brandt, § 295.

70. des . . . . Gewalt. By the 'power of the wild moment' is meant the distracting interests of the time. These 'engulf' the poem, i. e., cause it to be overlooked or ignored for a season.

71–2. The thought is that a poet's work may be before the world for years before it is recognized for what it really is. No reference to the long incubation of the subject in the poet's mind.

79. Gegenwart, 'present,' i. e., the now and the here, the Jetztwelt, as contrasted with Nachwelt. Taylor's 'presence' is wrong. — Braven Knaben, 'fine young fellow.'

80. ist immer . . . . was, 'counts anyway for *something* also.' Immer is here a strengthening particle used to enforce an assertion in view of opposition. Cf. Goethe's immer ein schön Stück Arbeit, 'undeniably a handsome piece of work'; immer ein hübscher Bursche, 'a pretty fellow certainly.' Schon was, means 'at least something,' i. e., *something*, with emphasis.

81–4. Directed against the words of the Poet in ll. 59 ff. The thought is that a poet who knows how to please will not feel bitter toward 'the people.' On the contrary, he will prefer a large public that he may be more sure of producing a great effect.

83–4. Er wünscht .... erschüttern; less briefly expressed: Er wünscht sich einen großen viel mehr als einen kleinen Kreis, um seinen Kreis gewisser zu erschüttern. The argument is not that among many there will be more to feel the poet's power, but rather that the small circle of intimate friends who know the poet in his daily walk are less likely to be thrilled through and through by his work.

85. brav, 'accommodating.' — Musterhaft, 'exemplary' (from the speaker's point of view).

90. Man kommt zu schaun. Cf. the quotation from Lessing, Intr. p. xx.

93. Habt .... gewonnen, 'you have forthwith won in the world-at-large,' i. e., you are the idol of a great public. So Goethe speaks of persons zerstreut in der Breite der Welt. Cf. Grimm Wb. *sub voce* Breite. Taylor's 'by sheer diffuseness' is wrong; that would require durch die Breite.

99. gleich in Stücken, 'right in pieces,' i. e., straightaway, without bothering about the harmony of the 'piece.'

100. Ragout, 'stew.'

102. ein Ganzes, 'an artistic whole.'

103. zerpflücken, 'pick to pieces'; not however in the sense of 'find fault with.' Each spectator will pick out, without regard to the poetic harmony of the whole, the separate parts that suit him best.

104. sei. The subjunctive of indirect question, not now usual after a present tense, is common in Goethe. Cf. ll. 272, 1543, 2321, 3532.

106. Der .... Pfuscherei, 'the botchwork of those nice fellows.' Die sauberen Herren (sauber of course sarcastic) are the popular playwrights who make sensational spectacular dramas of the kind just commended by the Manager. Perhaps Goethe may have thought of Kotzebue.

107. Maxime, 'sovereign rule' (Lat. *maxima regula*).

112. seht .... hin; i. e., at the assembled audience.

114. übertiſchten Mahle, 'overloaded table.' Tiſch comes from Lat. *discus* and meant at first 'dish,' whence tiſchen (but usually auftiſchen), 'to serve, or set out dishes' for a meal, and übertiſchen, 'to supply dishes in excess.' An übertiſchtes Mahl is thus 'a feast over-supplied with dishes.'

115–6. The play-goer who has just been reading the papers is pre-occupied with the news of the day.

119. zum Beſten geben, 'contribute.' On this line the commentators quote Ovid's *Ars Amatoria*, I., 99:

> Spectatum veniunt, veniunt spectentur ut ipsae,

which may well have been in Goethe's mind in view of his early fondness for Ovid.

120. ſpielen .... mit, 'join in the play without wages.' Fine toilets in the audience, as well as the acting upon the stage, draw the crowd and swell the profits.

122. Was macht .... froh? 'Why does a full house make you glad?' That is, do you proudly imagine that the crowd is here out of regard for high art?

131. verwirren, 'bewilder.'

132. At the end of this line the Poet makes a sign of impatience.

136. Menſchenrecht. The poet's 'natural right,' as appears from what follows, is his right to follow his artistic instinct for harmony.

139. jedes Element, 'every element'; not of society, but of nature, as in l. 1278. The poet is a magician.

140–9. The ideal poet is here conceived as one who takes up into his own being the unharmonious facts of nature (zurückſchlingen, 'absorb,' as in l. 8665), and gives them forth again in harmonious form. The whole passage will appear clearer from a comparison of *Tasso*, ll. 160 ff.

> Sein Ohr vernimmt den Einklang der Natur;
> Was die Geſchichte reicht, das Leben gibt,
> Sein Buſen nimmt es gleich und willig auf:
> Das weit Zerſtreute ſammelt ſein Gemüth
> Und ſein Gefühl belebt das Unbelebte.

The doings of nature are 'monotonous'; she winds her endless thread upon the spindle, indifferent to the steady, unvarying hum. Or, her work is 'discordant'; the totality of her creations make a universal ugly jangle. It is the Poet who measures off (theilt ab) this monotonous round, gives life to that which without him were lifeless (belebend; cf. the belebt das Unbelebte of *Tasso*), and imparts to the whole a rhythmic movement.

146. die fließend immer gleiche Reihe = die immer gleich fließende Reihe.

148. Wer ruft . . . . Weihe, 'who summons the isolated fact to the general solemnization?' Nature becomes through the poet a grand, solemn symphony, in which each single, separate fact is duly related to the whole and so made a note in the universal harmony.

150. Wer läßt . . . . wüthen? 'Who causes the tempest to rage to (the accompaniment of human) passions?' The poet leads us to see our own moods in the aspects of nature — passion in the storm and pensive calm in the sunset.

154. Blätter; the laurel wreath.

156. Wer sichert . . . . Götter? 'Who assures Olympus and shows gods assembled?' The climax culminates here in the thought that we owe heaven itself to the poet. Goethe uses the terms of Greek polytheism, but his thought is of wider application. Not only has the poet a noble office in dealing with the highest interests of this world, being the interpreter of nature (ll. 146–51), the singer of love (ll. 152–3), and the herald of all meritorious achievement (ll. 154–55), but as seer, *vates*, he gives us a vision of divine things beyond. — **Sichert den Olymp** is to be taken in the sense of 'gives the assurance of heaven.' By the 'uniting' of the gods is not meant the reconciling of their discords, but more simply the poetic revelation of them as a divine assemblage, or **Götterverein** — such a revelation as Homer gives us.

158–83. The speaker will have the Poet take the evolution of an ordinary love-affair as a model in the conduct of his 'poetical business.' The love-affair begins accidentally, proceeds of itself, with little need of planning or artistic motivation, and consists of a rapid succession of interesting situations that appeal to the general sympathy — particularly of the young.

163. wird es angefochten, 'it is touched by adversity.'

167. Greift . . . . hinein; lit. 'thrust in your hand.' Changing the figure, one might say: Just plunge into the full current of human life.

168–69. The thought is: Every one lives 'the life of man,' but few have thought about it so as to know it objectively as it is. Hence, when real life is presented on the stage, it seems at once familiar and novel, and so is always interesting. — **Interessant** here with secondary accent on the antepenultima. Fr. *intéressant.*

170. wenig ; apparently = ein wenig, rather than nur wenig.

180. Noch, 'as yet'; i. e., they are not too old.

181. Schwung, 'soaring flight' of feeling or imagination. — **Schein,** 'illusion.'

182. Wer fertig ist, 'one who has done with growing'; in antithesis to the following ein Werdender.

184–97. In these lines the Poet is very evidently the middle-aged Goethe recalling his own youth.

188. Cf. dem trüben Blick in l. 2.

193. Den Drang .... Trug, 'the bent for truth and the fondness for illusion.' The contradiction is only apparent. 'Truth' is here used in the sense of 'fidelity to nature,' while 'illusion' refers especially to the counterfeit presentments of 'the boards that signify the world.'

206–13. The logic of the passage is this : Though youth may be necessary for the soldier, the lover, the athlete, the reveller (ll. 198–205), still (doch) it is not so for the poet as such. Even in riper years, when his harp has become an old story, he can yet by dint of resolution strike the familiar strings with spirit and sweetness. The flood of song may no longer well up spontaneously as in his youth (cf. ll. 186–7), but he can still set himself a poetic goal and move toward it, though slowly, perhaps, and with much digression. Nor will the world think less of him for his slow, meandering pace, or ascribe it to the weakness of age ; since what people call the childishness of age is only a survival of real childhood. — The speaker here ignores the fiction that the audience is waiting. There is really no time for 'sauntering.' The lines may be taken as a quiet *pro domo* of Goethe in defence of his own leisurely gait in the composition of *Faust.*

209. mit holdem Irren, 'with winsome deviation.'

218. Stimmung, 'mood.' There has really been no talk of 'mood' in the Prelude, but one acquainted with Goethe will understand the question here asked. He knew very well what it was to make resolution do duty for the favor of the Muses. What the Manager says in ll. 218–30 is not mere Philistinism, and not altogether satire upon those who 'expect a poet to furnish verses to order' (Hart). There is, of course, a touch of humorous *brutalité* in the idea of 'commanding one's poetry' as if it were a body of soldiers; but underneath the humor there is a true and serious side to what the Manager says. For, after all, a great poem is a matter of high resolve and long-continued, strenuous toil; and the poet has no better right than any other brain-worker to be the bond-slave of his mood.

224. braut unverzüglich dran, 'go at the brew without delay.'

228. beim Schopfe fassen, 'seize by the forelock.' Cf. our 'take time by the forelock,' for 'go at a thing at once.'

229–30. The mere fact that one has begun is a strong incentive to continue.

231–2. The thought is: There are with us Germans no rigid dramatic standards to prevent one from experimenting *ad libitum.*

234. Prospecte, 'scenery.'

235. das groß' und kleine Himmelslicht; the sun and moon.

238. An Thier und Bögeln; for an Thieren und Bögeln. The omission of the ending in the first of two words having the same ending and connected by und is a frequent license with Goethe.

242. Vom Himmel .... Hölle. This phrase merely explains what the Manager means by 'traversing the whole circle of creation.' He has a choice collection of stage properties for the representation of scenes earthly, celestial and infernal, and he wants to have them used for a grand spectacular variety-show. He does not mean to prescribe that the action shall begin in heaven and end in hell, but only that heaven and hell as well as earth shall be included in the spectacle. He has in mind the scope rather than the termini of the action. — Many years after the Prelude was written, namely, May 6, 1827, Goethe said to Eckermann: "People come and ask what idea I have embodied in my *Faust.* As if I knew myself and could express it! 'From heaven through the world to hell,' — that might answer if need were, only that is not an idea, but rather the course of the action." But here, too, the phrase Gang der Handlung can refer only to the scope, not to the goal, of the action; for the First Part, which alone existed in 1827, does not end in hell, nor does the Second Part as afterwards completed. Nor was there ever any thought of having it so end. Hell is however represented toward the end of the Second Part, and since the whole begins and ends in heaven, we see that the Manager's prescription is exactly complied with. — Loeper is hardly right in thinking that there is here an allusion to the old mystery-stage with its (fictitious) three stories representing heaven, earth and hell.

Prolog im Himmel.

This portion of the drama was also written, probably, in the year 1798. For a brief discussion of the Prologue in its relation to the general plan of *Faust*, see Intr. p. lxviii. Some of the extant puppet-plays begin with a prologue in hell, and if this was the case with the one, or ones, which Goethe saw in his youth, he may have got from that source the hint for a scene defining the relation of Faust's career to the supernatural world, though *his* plan clearly called for a prologue in heaven rather than in hell. There is, however, no positive evidence that the idea of the Prologue antedates the year 1797. On resuming *Faust* at that time, Goethe saw the need of foreshadowing the general character of his work in its ethical and theological aspect. The subject was a familiar one connected in the mind of the public with certain definite traditionary associations, but he proposed, while following the tradition in many details, to depart from it radically in the conception of Faust's character and final destiny. He had not indicated this purpose in the Fragment of 1790, nor would it appear at all clearly from the action of the First Part. Hence the need of a prologue which should serve to put the reader or spectator on the right track at the outset.

The chief interest of the Prologue, apart from the matchless poetry of the opening chants, centers in the mild Pelagian theology that is put into the mouth of the Lord. Cf. Intr. p. xxxvi. Faust is not looked on as at variance with his Maker; he is no doomed sinner needing to be saved by a miracle of grace, but a being who is passing through a natural course of development, like a young tree for whose flowers and fruit the gardener is willing to wait. In other words, he is a 'servant of the Lord'; and if his service is now somewhat 'confused,' he is going to see more clearly soon. This, taken in connection with what we subsequently learn of Faust's character, with the compact in ll. 1692–1706, and with the saying of the angels in ll. 11936–7:

> „Wer immer strebend sich bemüht,
>
> Den können wir erlösen,"

can only mean that all 'striving,' i. e., all idealism that looks beyond the egoistic pleasure of the moment, is at bottom 'service of the Lord'; service which may be more or less 'clear' and so may occasion less or more of error, but will not fail of divine approval at the last. To accord with this conception, the devil must be an enemy of idealism. Mephistopheles is accordingly introduced in the Prologue as one of the spirits of negation, a humorous 'wag' whose divinely appointed office it is to spur men to activity for their own good, and thus unwittingly work out the Lord's purposes. His incentive is not greed for the souls of dead men, but the pleasure of leading men 'in his way' while they are alive. Hence he professes not to care for Faust's soul after death, though later, as legendary devil, he does manifest an interest in it.

The dramatic setting of the scene was suggested by the book of Job, in which we read (i. 6), that 'there was a day when the sons of God came to present themselves before the Lord, and Satan came also among them.' In the Hebrew poem the Lord calls attention to his 'servant Job, an upright man,' but Satan thinks that Job's uprightness is due to his prosperity. To test the matter, Satan is given permission to try to turn Job from the service of the Lord by means of affliction. Mephistopheles is to try the same experiment upon Faust by means of pleasure. In both poems the devil fails and the word of the Lord is verified. Cf. the address of J. Landsberger, *Das Buch Hiob und Goethe's Faust*, Darmstadt, 1882.

242+. **Die himmlischen Heerschaaren.** The Eng. 'heavenly host' of Luke ii. 13, cf. Acts vii. 42, translates the Gr. στρατιά 'army.' — **Mephistopheles.** The origin of the name is still a moot question. Most plausible, perhaps, is Seydel's derivation (G.-J., V., 353) from Hebrew *mefiztofel*, 'destroyer-liar,' or, perhaps, 'forger of lies' (G.-J., VII., 310). That the word was originally a Greek compound μη-φαυστο-φιλης 'no friend of Faust,' or μη-φωτο-φιλης 'no friend of light,' is not probable: one who knew enough to write such Greek would know too much to write it. Little is to be said, too, for the derivation proposed by A. Rudolf (G.-J., I., 385), namely, Hephaistophiles, 'Hephaestus' friend,' 'devil's friend,' as antithesis to Theophilus, 'God's friend.' For yet other guesses see G.-J., III., 340, and IV., 432; also an article by Roscher in the *Abhandlungen der sächsischen Gesellschaft der Wissenschaften*, XX., 1–133. A recent speculation makes the name a corruption of Megist-Ophiel, as applied to Hermes Trismegistus; see *Trans. Amer. Phil. Ass.*, XXXV., 148 ff. Goethe discusses the word in a letter to Zelter of Nov. 20, 1829, giving it a 'fantastic origin contemporary with that of the Faust-legend.' In this letter he encloses an extract from *Faust's Höllenzwang* of 1612, in which are found some scores of spirit-names like Osphadiel, Dirachiel, Kirotiel, Mephistophiel. Unless these names are also capable of being explained as compounds, it would seem possible that Goethe is exactly right in ascribing to the word a 'fantastic origin.' As to the form of the name, the earlier Faust-books and Pfitzer have Mephostophiles, though Marlowe changed it to Mephostophilis, with a vocative Mephosto, and Shakespeare made it Mephistophilus. The form Mephistopheles was used in the Christlich Meynenden Faust-book and became then the usual one with writers of the eighteenth century. — **Die drei Erzengel.** Raphael is not mentioned in the Bible, but appears in the apocrypha (Tobit xii. 15) as 'one of the seven holy angels which go in and out before the glory of the Holy One.' Gabriel is mentioned in Daniel and also in Luke i. 19 ('I am Gabriel that stand in the presence of God'). Michael is mentioned in Daniel, Jude and Revelations, and he only is called an 'archangel' in the Bible (Jude 9). In the book of Enoch we hear of 'four great archangels,' viz., Gabriel, Michael, Uriel, and Suriel or Raphael. **Die drei treten vor** need not be taken as implying that there are just three archangels in heaven, but only that *the* three most illustrious ones, the three who are to take part in the scene, present themselves before the Lord.

243. tönt, 'makes music.' Cf. Job xxxviii. 7, 'The morning stars sang together,' and Isaiah xliv. 23, 'Sing, O ye heavens.' The Pfitzer Faust-book, which Goethe is known to have used, says (p. 185) that the planets 'roar' (toben) so violently that the sound is like that of thunder. Cf. also the quotation from Goethe's *Satyros*, n. to ll. 447-53.

244. Brudersphären; presumably the planets, rather than the fixed stars. The syntax is as if we had the compound **Brudersphären-Wett-gesang.**

246. Donnergang, 'thunder-march.' The course of the sun through space is conceived as swift, majestic, and attended by a roar like that of thunder. Klopstock describes God as moving,

Wenn er dem Ziele sich naht, mit dem Donnergang der Entscheidung.

248. Wenn keiner . . . . mag, 'though no one can fathom it.' By 'fathoming the sun,' is meant the comprehension of it as a phenomenon; **mag** in its original meaning of 'can.'

255. **Flüssen;** not the waves nor the tides, but seething 'floods' into which the waves break and recoil as they are driven up against the rocks.

261–2. **bilden . . . . Wirkung,** 'form in their fury a chain of deepest effect.' The seaward and landward winds produce far-reaching consequences. Fichte shows in one of his lectures that if a grain of sand on the beach were to lie a few inches from where it does lie, the whole antecedent history of the world must have been different. So Emerson calls all Nature 'a subtle chain of countless rings.'

263–4. **flammt . . . . vor.** Aside from the exigencies of meter there is a subtle, untranslatable difference between es flammt dem Pfade vor and es flammt vor dem Pfade. The compound gives a finer poetical effect.

265. **Doch.** The logic is this: Grand as are the phenomena of storm, thunder and lightning on earth, still it is the *gentle* movement of the day that most excites the reverence of the angels. **Boten** = ἄγγελοι, 'angels.'

268. **Da,** 'since.' Some good commentators, e.g., Schröer, Witkowski, think it concessive, like the corresponding wenn (= wenn auch) in l. 248. Strehlke Wb. gives it the meaning da wo, E. Schmidt that of da doch, während. But the common meaning of da gives a good sense, namely, that *since* the Lord's nature is unfathomable, the contemplation of his works affords the angels an ever fresh source of strength. What one understands perfectly becomes in time an old story.

271. **naht.** Mephisto's buffoon humor expresses itself in the conceit that the Lord is a genial householder who appears now and then in the servants' quarters to inquire how things are going. Or, perhaps the Lord is to be thought of as a benevolent monarch holding a sort of medieval Heerschau. In that case Gesinde would mean his 'retainers.' In fact, the Lord does not 'approach,' but only permits an approach. For in view of the words der Himmel schließt,'l. 349+, we must think of the Lord as occupying a 'most holy place' which is veiled from the celestial host, the veil being however drawn aside to admit the favored ones into the divine presence.

275. **hohe Worte machen,** 'make fine phrases,' like the archangels.

277. **Mein Pathos,** 'pathos from me;' 'pathos' in the sense of serious feeling earnestly expressed.

280. **fid),** 'themselves,' not 'one another.'

282. **Wunderlid),** 'singular.' Notice that l. 282 parodies ll. 250 and 270. — **Als wie** is a frequent pleonasm with Goethe. Cf. ll. 359, 2129, 2214, 2294.

285. **Vernunft,** 'reason.' When used in its philosophical sense, as here, or expressly contrasted with **Verstand,** 'understanding,' 'sense,' **Vernunft** means the faculty by which we apprehend the 'connection of truths' (Wolff, as quoted by Sanders Wb.). In other words, it is the faculty with which we grasp general and abstract ideas. Thus **Vernunft** is, or was held by German philosophers to be, the attribute that distinguishes man from the lower animals, these having at best only **Verstand.** (But when **Vernunft** is used popularly, or without thought of **Verstand,** it may be ascribed to brutes. Cf. Schiller's *Tell,* I., 1: **Das Thier hat auch Vernunft.**) — In **nennt's,** the **es = das scheinbar himmlische Licht.**

286. **Nur** merely strengthens **allein,** giving the sense of 'to no other end than.' But the collocation is very unusual. — The devil's theory is this: Man's 'reason' does nothing for him but give him an absurd conceit of himself, which leads him to plume himself on his superiority to the brutes that perish. When, therefore, he *does* act like the brutes, his conduct is worse than theirs, because they make no fine pretensions. They never talk of truth, beauty, righteousness, immortality, etc.

287. **mit Verlaub .... Gnaden,** 'with your Grace's permission.' **Ew.** is for **Euer,** historically a gen. plu. **Euer Gnaden** is a stereotyped form constant for all cases.

288. **Cicaden,** 'grasshoppers,' not 'cicadae.' On the point of the comparison, see Intr. p. lxxvi.

290. **gleich,** 'straightway.' The attempt to fly fails forthwith.

292. The meaning is: Not only can man not fly very high or very long, but when he sinks back to earth, he is not even content with the cleaner media of an animal existence.

298. **selbst;** to be taken with **ich,** not with **die armen.**

300. **euch.** Ordinarily the change from **du** to **Ihr** is in the direction of greater respectfulness; here, since the Lord is addressed, it has the exactly opposite effect.

302. **Die Gährung,** 'the ferment' of his soul.

308. verworren, 'confusedly'; like one wandering in the dark or in 'misty fog.'

310. grünt, 'shows signs of life.'

314. meine Straße; acc. of the way. Mephisto's 'way' is that of egoistic pleasure.

315-6. The implication clearly is, that when Faust's life on earth is over, Mephistopheles is to have no further right to trouble him.

318. Da, 'there,' i. e., so far as that restriction is concerned.

319. Hab' ich .... befangen, 'I have never cared to concern myself.' For the use of befangen as = befassen, Grimm Wb. quotes only this case from Goethe, but several from Richter. As to Mephisto's professed indifference to dead men, cf. Intr. p. lxxi–ii.

320. lieb' ich mir. Lieben with reflexive dat. is much used by Goethe. It means 'to like,' 'to have a fancy for.'

325. erfassen, 'get hold of.'

327. Another intimation that Mephistopheles is to be baffled. He is to 'stand abashed' and 'confess.'

328-9. Ein guter .... bewußt, 'a good man in his vague striving is quite conscious of the right way.' An important, difficult, and famous passage. Obviously ein guter Mensch can not mean 'a good man' in the ordinary sense. Of course a good man is 'conscious of the right way' and tries to follow it; that is the very nature of 'goodness.' Goethe uses guter in about the sense of tüchtiger or hochstrebender, meaning one who is 'good' — for something; one who has ideals and tries to realize them; or, in different words, one who possesses that 'good will' which Goethe calls the 'foundation in matters of right conduct.' (Das Hauptfunda= ment des Sittlichen ist der gute Wille; *Werke*, H., XIX., 77.) For an exactly similar use of the phrase cf. *Werke*, H., VIII., 198:

> Denn was ein guter Mensch erreichen kann
> Ist nicht im engen Raum des Lebens zu erreichen,

where it is applied to an artist and can, therefore, have nothing to do with conventional 'goodness.' — The phrase in seinem dunklen Drange is not easily translatable. Grimm Wb., defines Drang for this passage as An= reizung, innerer Trieb, *impetus, impulsus*. Dunklen means 'not fully understood,' hence 'vague.'—The point involved is, at bottom, the old issue between the Augustinian and the Pelagian theology: the question whether a man, if he follows his natural bent, will surely and finally go wrong or not; whether he is of himself a helpless wanderer in the dark, requiring to be *put* upon the right way by a miracle of divine intervention, or whether he has that in him which will enable him to *find* the right way and follow it. Goethe takes the Pelagian view, but only on the supposition that the man is ein guter Mensch from the first. For Faust is by no means a representative of humanity, as he is sometimes called, but only of that portion of it who strive, whose will is good. — It may be noted, finally, that no formal confession of discomfiture, like that here foreshadowed, ever comes from Mephistopheles. He is, however, discomfited, for Faust's idealism proves invincible.

334-5. The allusion is to Genesis iii. 14, where God says to the serpent, 'dust shalt thou eat all the days of thy life.' By 'eating dust with delight' the devil means being satisfied with egoistic pleasure.

336. Du darfst .... erscheinen, 'there too thou mayest act thy part quite unhindered'; auch da, in boasting over the Lord as well as in trying to lead Faust astray; nur with frei in the sense of 'not otherwise than,' 'quite.' Observe that erscheinen does not mean 'to appear' = *videri*, which would call for scheinen, but 'to show one's self,' 'play one's part.'

339. Schalk, 'wag.' Mephistopheles is given this name as a being who acts in a spirit of cynical humor, — for the fun of the thing, so to speak. The Lord's work is to him a field for practical joking. Those other unnamed spirits which are more troublesome to the Lord would doubtless be such as carry on the work of negation, opposition and destruction in a spirit of bitter, malignant earnest. That Mephistopheles is here *a* spirit, but later (l. 1338) *the* spirit of negation, or (l. 2181) *the* devil, need occasion no surprise. *The* devil is a theological abstraction. What history gives us first is many devils of different national characters and different names, which names and characters were then blended in the conception of *the* devil. Cf. Intr. p. lxxv. Thus Goethe treats his Mephistopheles at pleasure either as one in a kindred hierarchy of devils, making e. g. the tempter of Genesis his 'cousin' (l. 335), or as a personification of a *part* of the negative principle of darkness that is at war with light (l. 1335), or again as *the* spirit of negation, *the* devil. The witch calls him Junker Satan (l. 2504). On the Brocken he calls himself Junker Voland (l. 4023), while the devil on the throne is Herr Urian (l. 3959). In

the puppet-plays *the* devil is sometimes called Pluto. In the original legend Mephistopheles is an envoy of Lucifer.

340–3. The doctrine is that men thrive by opposition. Cynical criticism and obstruction bring out our best qualities and incite us to work for the realization of our ideals.

341. 𝔈𝔯 𝔩𝔦𝔢𝔟𝔱 𝔣𝔦𝔠𝔥. Cf. l. 320, note.

343. 𝔇𝔢𝔯 𝔯𝔢𝔦𝔷𝔱 .... 𝔣𝔠𝔥𝔞𝔣𝔣𝔢𝔫, 'who stimulates, exerts influence and must, as devil (i. e., by virtue of his devilish nature), be doing.' But some take the last clause to mean 'must, though devil, produce'; i. e., though his work is destruction, by stimulating man to productive activity, he becomes in spite of himself a producer.

344 𝔊ö𝔱𝔱𝔢𝔯𝔣ö𝔥𝔫𝔢, 'sons of God,' as in Genesis vi. 2, and Job i. 6. The reference is of course to the archangels. Cf. l. 66, note.

345–9. This passage defies translation and resists close logical analysis, but the general import is this: Mephistopheles is to go to earth to carry on his opposition to the Lord's purposes, but the angels are to remain at the center of creative power, beholding with joy and love the beautiful creation that is ever realizing itself about them, and seeing in every transient phenomenon a manifestation of the eternal thought of God. 𝔇𝔞𝔰 𝔚𝔢𝔯𝔡𝔢𝔫𝔡𝔢, 'the evolving world,' is creation considered not as a fact, but as a living process, the ever progressing realization of the divine plan. 𝔚𝔞𝔰 𝔦𝔫 𝔣𝔠𝔥𝔴𝔞𝔫𝔨𝔢𝔫𝔡𝔢𝔯 𝔈𝔯𝔣𝔠𝔥𝔢𝔦𝔫𝔲𝔫𝔤 𝔣𝔠𝔥𝔴𝔢𝔟𝔱, 'what floats in unsteady phenomenal manifestation,' e. g., suns, planets, storms, man's earthly life — all things that come and go as parts of the phenomenal world. 𝔅𝔢𝔣𝔢𝔣𝔱𝔦𝔤𝔢𝔱 𝔪𝔦𝔱 𝔡𝔞𝔲𝔢𝔯𝔫𝔡𝔢𝔫 𝔊𝔢𝔡𝔞𝔫𝔨𝔢𝔫, 'fix, i. e., hold steadfast, with enduring thoughts.' But Strehlke Wb. gives 𝔟𝔢𝔣𝔢𝔣𝔱𝔦𝔤𝔢𝔫 as = 𝔣𝔱ä𝔯𝔨𝔢𝔫, 𝔣𝔦𝔠𝔥𝔢𝔯𝔫. All that 'appears' is a manifestation of the Eternal Thought. The angels are invited to participate in this thought, or, in Spinozan phrase, to view the world *sub specie æternitatis.*

349+. 𝔇𝔢𝔯 𝔥𝔦𝔪𝔪𝔢𝔩, the 'most holy place.' Cf l. 270, note.

350. 𝔇𝔢𝔫 𝔄𝔩𝔱𝔢𝔫, 'the old man,' 'the governor.'

𝔑 𝔞 𝔠𝔥 𝔱.

This scene, up to Wagner's exit, belongs to the oldest stratum of *Faust*. On its subjective side it is rooted in Goethe's youthful disgust with academic learning and in the fantastic feeling for 'nature' to which he had been led by his study of the alchemists and mystics, and by the influence of Herder. See Intr. pp. xxiii–xxxv. In beginning with a soliloquy of Faust, Goethe follows the puppet-plays (but see above, the general note upon the Prologue), which in turn follow Marlowe. In the puppet-plays, Faust's success in conjuring is always dependent on a certain book which is brought him by two or more students. In Goethe, Faust has the book of Nostradamus from the first, and nothing is said of its provenience. This book is conceived as possessing occult properties such that the mere contemplation of its symbols produces wonderful effects upon the beholder's mental state, while the appropriate 'utterance' of one of the symbols causes the corresponding spirit to appear in visible form.

In the year 1885 Wilhelm Scherer published an article (G.-J., vi., 231) in which he drew attention to and tried to account for certain seeming incongruities in ll. 354–521. As the result of a close analysis of the logical connection and the 'inner form' of the passage Scherer was led to conjecture that Goethe wrote ll. 354–85 having in mind a Faust who *has decided* to resort to magic and has actually tried to evoke a spirit, but has failed for lack of the right book ; and that it was the poet's intention to write a scene which should put Faust in possession of the book (as in the puppet-plays) the opening of which was to be followed by the magic effects of ll. 430–67. After this was to come a renewed and successful attempt to evoke the Earth-Spirit, with the dialogue as in ll. 468–521. As for ll. 386–427, Scherer supposes them to have been written as a substitute for ll. 354–85; i.e., as a new beginning on the presupposition that Faust already has the book but can do nothing with it in his study, its magic being effective only in the open air. Lastly Scherer supposes that, having decided after all to retain the original beginning, Goethe did not reject the second beginning, but

inserted it after the other and bridged the awkward transition by
inserting the lines

> Ihr schwebt, ihr Geister, neben mir ;
> Antwortet mir, wenn ihr mich hört !

This series of hypotheses has provoked much discussion of which no
account can be given here; cf. E. Schmidt, introduction to *Göchhausen
Faust*, 7th ed., p. xxvii, and the same scholar's commentary in the Jubilee Edition of Goethe, XIII., 275; also Collin, *Faust in seiner ältesten
Gestalt*, p. 18 ff.; Niejahr, *Euphorion*, IV., 273; Minor, Goethe's *Faust*, I.,
35 ff. The discussion shows that Scherer's difficulties are to some extent real, since different scholars of the highest competence have different ways of meeting them. This much, however, has become clear:
We are not required to assume that Goethe began the play twice, or
that he ever planned to write, and then failed to write, any passage necessary to the understanding of his thought.

The first crux is the transition at l. 386. It certainly does seem a little
strange that Faust, having just spoken hopefully of his interest in
magic and led us to expect some kind of magic procedure, should
suddenly apostrophize the moon and wish that he were a discar-
nate spirit, i.e., that he were dead. But Goethe's purpose is not
merely to motivate the resort to magic as due to unsatisfied intellectual curiosity. His Faust is not a mere *Teufelsbeschwörer* who hopes
to get what he wants by calling up a demon and asking questions, as in
the legend. *Our* Faust is a profoundly miserable man, oppressed by a
sense of the narrowness and futility of the life he has been leading. The
magic on which he has set his hopes is the higher, the so-called 'natural'
magic, which is to free him from the trammels of human nature, and
make him such as he imagines the spirits to be, i.e., free, joyous, active,
knowing by direct intuition. It was thus very necessary that Goethe's
exposition should not only motivate the resort to magic, as in the puppet-plays, but also indicate the *kind of magic* that Faust has in view, and
the superhuman nature of his longings. Hence the apostrophe to the
moon, which at once reminds him of futile studies in the past and suggests the higher possibilities of a spirit-life in nature.

The second crux is the meaning of das weite Land in l. 418. Scherer took it to mean 'out-of-doors' in the literal sense; as if Faust for a moment entertained the thought of seizing his book and rushing out into the night. There is some ground for this interpretation in the fact that in the legend, if not in the puppet-plays, Faust does his first conjuring in the woods at night. It seems more probable, however, that das weite Land does not refer to a place of conjuring at all, but is used figuratively for the sphere of natural magic as contrasted with Faust's previous studies. In other words, when he opens the book and proceeds to use it, he does actually betake himself ins weite Land, albeit he remains physically in his study.

Another question of interest in connection with this opening scene relates to the literary sources of Goethe's spirit-lore. Whence came his ideas of natural magic, of ecstatic intercourse with spirits, and of wonderful exaltation and illumination of the soul by their aid? The sources that Goethe himself mentions by name (Intr. p. xxvii. and Werke, XXVII., 204) are Welling, Paracelsus, Van Helmont, and the Aurea Catena Homeri. But he says that there were 'others,' and makes this general observation: 'The basis [of my lore] was Neoplatonism. Hermetism, mysticism, and cabbalism contributed their parts, and so I built me a world that looked strange enough.'

With a view to throwing light on the Earth-Spirit Graffunder made a careful examination of these sources in 1892. Two years later E. Schmidt suggested a possible indebtedness of Goethe to Swedenborg. Following up this hint Morris (Goethe-Studien, 2d series, 1899) brought together a number of passages suggestive of Swedenborgian influence and making it appear that the mysterious 'wise man' of l. 442 was no other than the Swedish spiritist. More recently an American editor, Goebel, has drawn attention to what he believes to be an important source not hitherto noted, namely Jamblichus, whose treatise De Mysteriis does in fact contain passages that have a suggestive resemblance to lines in Faust. But the case is not made out for the predominant influence of any one source (cf. Hohlfeld's review in Mod. Lang. Review, III., 379). The truth is that the cabbalists, to call the whole tribe by that one name, have a strong family resemblance; and since the ideas in question are rather vague and elusive it is possible to cite parallels from any or all of them, but hard to determine which one if any was Goethe's particular *vade mecum.* Nor is the matter of vital importance for the understanding of *Faust.* It is enough to know that Goethe got from his mystics, in whom for a little while he was very deeply interested, the idea of a natural magic, higher and nobler than the ordinary black art, whereby the magician could not only enter into communion with superior spirits, but become like them in knowledge and power.

354. **Habe.** Supply ich. The omission of the subject is colloquial and characteristic of the free-and-easy Hans Sachs style. In the older portions of *Faust* it is common in the sing., somewhat less so in the plu. — **Philosophie,** 'philosophy,' but not in the strict technical sense. It is, rather, a broad term for the studies belonging to the 'philosophical faculty' of a university.

355. **Juristerei;** contemptuous for Jurisprudenz.

356. **leider auch.** Faust is primarily a theologian (cf. l. 372-3), and in making him especially dissatisfied with theology, Goethe follows the legend. The 'science of God' is the study from which a seeker after ultimate truth would naturally expect the most; whereas Faust has been led by it only to doubts that have destroyed his peace of mind. Cf. l. 370.

357. **Durchaus;** here = durch und durch, i. e., 'thoroughly.'

360. **Magister,** 'Master' of Arts; the second degree in the sequence bachelor, master, doctor. U. has here : Heiße Docktor und Professor gar. The reason for the change is not quite obvious, since Faust is very certainly to be thought of as a professor. Was it because C. M. states expressly that Faust received the degree of 'Master' at Ingolstadt, or because the magician was popularly known as 'Doctor' Faust?

361. **schon.** As to Faust's age, cf. Intr. p. xlvii. — **An** is unaccented, i. e., does not go with ziehe, but with die zehen Jahr, to denote approximation; 'well-nigh these ten years.' — The older **zehen,** M. H. G. *zëhen* > *zén,* is often used by Goethe in his youth, even where no metrical considerations require it, e. g., *Briefe,* I., 133, 187. — **Jahr ;** plu. with –e omitted, as it was very often omitted, in all sorts of words, in the South-German dialect of the youthful Goethe.

365. **Das .... verbrennen,** 'that (insight) is just about consuming my heart as with fire.' On will, cf. Brandt, § 267, 6. — **Schier** = 'all but,' 'just about'; not the Eng. 'sheer,' nor the schier of Luther's Bible, meaning 'soon.'

366. Laffen, 'ninnies'; used collectively of the classes mentioned in l. 367.

367. Schreiber, 'scribes,' or 'notaries,' learned in the law; not 'ecclesiastics,' nor 'students of theology.'

370. Dafür, 'as an offset to that,' 'on the other hand.' The thought is that Faust has won liberty at the expense of peace. This sense of dafür is not noted in Grimm or Strehlke, but is common in Goethe's early writings. Cf., e. g., *Briefe*, I., 181 (letter to Oeser): Die Cabinette hier sind zwar klein, dafür sind sie häufig und ausgesucht. Cf. also l. 2988.

371. was Rechts, 'anything worth while.' Cf. ll. 1879 and 4125.

374–5. This vulgar motive for Faust's study of magic does not appear in the oldest Faust-book, but is as old as Widman, who says (Cap. 13, Scheible, II., 359): Dieweil er weder geldt, kost noch speiß und andres habe, so hab er auch sich fürnehmlich dem Teufel ergeben.

376. möchte, 'could'; mögen in the old sense of können.

378. Geistes .... Mund; seemingly a hendiadys for durch den kräftigen Mund eines Geistes, 'through some mighty spirit-voice.'

379. manch Geheimnis, 'many a mystery.' But Faust is not thinking of definite answers to definite questions. What he hopes for is a wonderful transformation of his own nature, so that he will comprehend the whole world-riddle by direct intuition. See App. III.

380–1. Not that Faust now thinks to give up teaching if he succeeds as magician. He wishes to teach with better insight.

382–4. Faust wishes to comprehend the central power that sustains the order of nature, to gaze upon the formative energy that pervades the world, and to behold the primordial substances (Samen) out of which all things have grown. Take Samen as a plu. with alle repeated. The word is common in Welling (see Intr. p. xxvii). Believing the various forms of existence to be more or less interconvertible, the alchemists reached the conception of certain fundamental substances which are the basis of all things that are. These they called 'seeds.'

385. thu' .... kramen, 'do business.' The use of thun as a periphrastic auxiliary, like Eng. 'do,' is a South-German provincialism which is frequent in *Faust*; cf. ll. 2145, 2781, 2869 etc.; also Brandt, § 274, 6.

386. Mondenschein; now usually Mondschein or Mondesschein, but the old weak decl., especially in composition, is common in the classics.

389. herangewacht; an intransitive used transitively. Sanders Wb. gives the meaning as fo lange wachen, bis das Objekt erfcheint. But does it not rather mean 'to watch mounting' the sky? Cf. ſteigt heran in l. 3851–2, and ſteigt herüber in l. 3235–6.

390. Büchern. U. and Fgm. have Bücher. The change was made, seemingly, to bring out more clearly the thought intended, viz.: 'Thy beams have found me sitting here over my (magic) books and papers.' Kögel, V. L., I., 55, thinks the books and papers on the shelves are meant, and that the acc. is required. But in that case one can not realize the picture. The books and paper are not those of ll. 402, 405, but the tools with which Faust has been engaged in a futile study of magic (the 'paper' for drawing). Cf. the 'night-brooding magus' letter of Goethe, *Briefe*, I., 200, in which he speaks of himself as eingeſperrt, allein, Circkel, Papier, Feder und Dinte, und zwei Bücher, mein ganzes Rüſtzeug.

392–95. The language is here reminiscent of Ossian. See App. III.

396. Wiſſensqualm, 'choke-damp of learning.'

397. geſund . . . . baden, 'bathe to health '; factitive predicate.

402. Beſchränkt von, 'bound by'; pple. with Mauerloch.

403. Würme; the regular M. H. G. plu., familiar to Goethe from Luther's Bible. But he also uses the modern Würmer. Cf. l. 605.

405. Ein . . . . umſteckt, 'with smoke-begrimed paper stuck around in it' (the Bücherhauf). U. has mit angeraucht Papier beſteckt (the participle going with Mauerloch). The change leaves the picture less clear. Papier refers probably to manuscripts stuck here and there between the books; not to labels or dust-guards (cf. *Euphorion*, III., 476).

408. drein geſtopft; acc. abs. with Hausrath. The three preceding pples., on the other hand, go with Mauerloch.

411. Sich bang . . . . klemmt, 'falters oppressed' (Taylor).

415. Da Gott . . . . hinein, 'whereinto God created men'; colloquial for in welche Gott die Menſchen hineinſchuf (Hart). For a similar 'whither' construction after a 'where' verb, cf. l. 943.

420. Noſtradamus; the Latin name of Michel de Notredame, a noted French astrologer and physician, born in 1503. His most famous work was a collection of rimed prophecies published in 1555 under the title of *Centuries*. He wrote no book of the kind here ascribed to him. Goethe uses his name as that of a representative astrologist contemporary with Faust, who *might* thus have a manuscript of his. See note to l. 993 ff.

422. Erkenneſt, 'thou shalt understand'; erkennen here = begreifen. — **der Sterne Lauf,** 'the course of the stars'; astrology with its doctrine of spiritistic influence. See App. III.

424-5. geht auf .... Wie, 'will dawn on thee (revealing) how,' etc.; i.e., he will acquire a new spiritual faculty.

426-9. On the logical connection, cf. the introductory note above.

429+. Zeichen des Makrokosmus. Macrocosm, from post-classical Gr. μακρόκοσμος, 'great world,' (lit. 'long world'), was a name given by medieval astrologers and philosophers to the universe-at-large, conceived as an ordered whole consisting of variously interrelated parts. The Gk.-Lat. *cosmus* is opposed to *chaos* and means 'order,' whence *macrocosmus* = 'great order,' or 'great harmony.' By the 'sign' of the macrocosm we are to understand a geometrical figure possessing the magic power to give Faust a beatific vision of the 'grand harmony.' It is not likely that Goethe was thinking of any particular figure, but pictures more or less like what he had in mind are found in Welling, pp. 9, 97, 171 etc. Cf. Intr. p. xxviii.

431. Sinnen; old weak plu. of Sinn, as in ll. 479, 1436, 1633; the usual strong plu. Sinne, in l. 611.

437. Trieb; here in about the sense of 'potency.'

442-6. On the various identifications of the 'wise man' see App. III., and the introductory note above. Probably Goethe was not thinking of any one in particular, and quite certainly he does not put into Faust's mouth a verbatim quotation. Faust has begun to get proof of the reality of spirits and of the possibility of communicating with them. This seems to him to confirm what he has read on the subject in some philosopher whom he refers to vaguely as the 'wise man,' just as we sometimes ascribe a saying to 'the poet' or the 'man of science' without intending to quote literally from a particular person. The thought is that the spirit-world is not closed against man; if it seems so that is because of the inertness of his faculties. But his faculties can be quickened — Faust feels that his own are actually being quickened — by natural magic. He can 'arise' from the bondage of human limitation and 'bathe his earthly breast' in the 'morning-light' of divine intuitive knowledge.

445. Unverdroſſen, 'undismayed,' i.e., undisturbed by any doubts or misgivings as to the reality of the revelation.

447–53. On Faust's mystical vision of the macrocosm, cf. Intr. p. xxviii.; also the quotations from Van Helmont and Faber in App. III. Faust sees the world as a manifestation of energy, unity, spirituality, and harmony. The parts of the macrocosm weave themselves into a whole. Nothing is isolated: one component lives and works in every other. This All is animated by 'celestial powers that ascend and descend, handing to one another the golden vessels.' These powers are conceived as angels with 'wings that exhale blessings'; at the same time, however, they are impersonal essences for they *permeate* the earth and fill it with an all-pervading music. The passage must not be taken too seriously, or its imagery scrutinized too closely, in the hope of getting out of it a clear, coherent mental picture. Still less should we, as do some of the commentators, think to find in this mystical jargon an adumbration of Goethe's maturer views respecting the evolution and interconnection of organic forms. It has, however, some striking resemblances to a jocose cosmogony found in Goethe's farce *Satyros*, act iv. The passage is as follows:

> Wie sich Haß und Lieb' gebar,
> Und das All nun ein Ganzes war,
> Und das Ganze klang
> In lebend wirkendem Ebengesang;
> Sich thäte Kraft in Kraft verzehren,
> Sich thäte Kraft in Kraft vermehren,
> Und auf und ab sich rollend ging,
> Das all und ein' und ewig Ding,
> Immer verändert, immer beständig.

450. Eimer. Düntzer is reminded of the Manichaean doctrine that angels transport the souls of the dead in golden vessels; but see App. III. Possibly Goethe had in mind some picture as yet unidentified.

454 ff. Faust, who has just been likening himself to a god, turns impatiently from the object of his enthusiasm, because it is 'only a spectacle,' whereas he desires food for his soul, nourishment from the breasts of mother Nature. The imagery in ll. 455–9 is biblical; cf. Is. lxvi., 11–12. A hungry man is not to be satisfied by a 'spectacle,' however wonderful. So Faust makes no attempt to evoke the Weltgeist, or Spirit of the Macrocosm, but turns over the leaves of his book impatiently for the sign of a spirit that is 'nearer' to him.

458. welke Brust, 'pining breast.'

459. i̇ḧr trän̈ft, 'ye give to drink,' i. e., ye have nourishment to offer.

459+. Črḋgeiſtes. On the sources of the conception see Intr., pp. xxviii., xxix., xxxv.; also App. III., where the relation of the Earth-Spirit to Goethe's early plan is discussed at some length. The Spirit takes the place of the 'prince of hell' in the Faust books, but is not for that reason a diabolical or malign being. He is rather the personification of terrestrial nature on the side of that awfulness and sublimity which seems to tell of a being that is too great to sympathize with man or be comprehended by him, but is nevertheless the giver of all things that come to him. Cf. Intr. pp. xli. and xlv. In truth, this being is neither cruel nor benignant, but only seems the one or the other, according to the mood of the man, or the degree of his culture. Faust longs for a sympathetic mother, but the spirit that comes at his call is the one of whom Tennyson sings :

> Thou makest thine appeal to me.
> I bring to life, I bring to death.

Later, in 3217 ff., the same Spirit is invoked by Faust as the beneficent giver of all good gifts. In Par. p. 3, Goethe characterizes the spirit as Welt= und Thatengenius.

463. neuem ; equivalent to friſchem.

464–7. The magic effect of the symbol of Nature's energy is a sudden increase of energy, of the will to do and dare, on the part of Faust.

468–74. These lines are rhythmic prose with no trace of meter, save that ll. 468 and 469 would go together as an alexandrine. There are several such passages imbedded in the verse of *Faust* (ll. 514-7, 3183-94, 3437-58), all of them expressive of intense excitement. Scherer, *Goethe's Frühzeit*, p. 76 ff., regarded them as remnants left standing from an original prose version; but U. gives no hint that its verse is translated prose. It is more likely that the verse which appears in U. was verse from the beginning, and that the prose passages were due to a feeling, more or less conscious, that prose was better adapted than rime to the expression of extreme emotion. Here the lines in rhythmic prose take the place of stage-directions and motivate Faust's growing excitement. Without them the spectator would only see a man reading a book.

473. Schauer, 'horror.' Faust experiences a sudden dread which

seems to him to descend, like an invisible spirit, from the vaulted ceiling
and lay hold of him.

475. erflehter Geiſt, 'spirit implored,' 'spirit that I earnestly entreat.'
Cf. Seelenflehen in l. 488.

477. wie's . . . . reißt, 'what a rending there is.'

479. ſich erwühlen, 'burst forth.' The verb means to 'burst open'
as the result (er-) of an inner commotion (wühlen). Cf. the lines from
Goethe's ballad *Der untreue Knabe:*

> Und wie er tappt und wie er fühlt,
> Sich unter ihm die Erd' erwühlt.

481+. After Flamme U. has the phrase in widerlicher Geſtallt, ' in repellent form;' widerlich in the sense of feindlich, abweiſend, cf. E. Schmidt U[7].,
XLI., and Pniower, G.-J. XIX., 244. The sense 'repellent' is quite in harmony with Goethe's original conception. Later, when the Spirit had taken
on the character of the beneficent giver of all things (ll. 3217 ff.), he
erased the phrase, which he could do with good reason, since a spirit
appearing ' in the flame ' must needs be ' repellent.' — The ' flame ' is found
in all the Faust-books, where it pertains naturally to the devil. For the
stage, Goethe directed that the Earth-Spirit should be 'a gigantic face
emerging from behind cloud and filling the entire background.'

482. Geſicht, 'sight,' 'apparition,' rather than 'face.'

484. lang . . . . geſogen, 'long been trying to draw nourishment.' Cf.
the citations in App. III., ll. 442–6.

486. erathmend, 'panting.'

490. Übermenſchen, 'superhuman being'; in sarcastic allusion to
Faust's presumption. — **Der Seele Ruf,** 'thy soul's summons.' The
sense is : What has become of thy grand courage?

495. ſich drang; common in Goethe for the now more usual ſich
drängte. Cf. l. 2722 and ' Dismal Day,' l. 30.

496. umwittert. Cf. l. 8, note.

498. ein . . . . Wurm, 'a worm that wriggles away in fear.' Weggekrümmter is reflexive, in the sense of der ſich weggekrümmt hat; in allusion to Faust's cowering posture.

501–9. The conception is not of a spirit moving up and down, in the
form in which he appears to Faust, *amid* the ' floods of life and the storm
of deeds,' but the Spirit *is* the floods and the storm. The rise and fall of

the waters (auf unb ab), the driving hither and thither of the storm (hin unb her), are manifestations of his activity. That is, the in and im of l. 501 mean 'in the form of,' 'under the aspect of,' and the nouns Geburt, Grab, etc., are in apposition with ich.

509. Kleid. The 'garment' of the Deity consists of the visible forms of nature.

512. Geift. One would expect a more definite promise to send Mephistopheles. Cf. ll. 3241 ff. and the scene 'Dismal Day,' ll. 33–6; also the note in App. III., l. 459+.

518. Famulus; a professor's assistant; in earlier days, a student who lived in his teacher's house and performed various duties, more or less menial, in return for free tuition.

519. Instead of this incongruous line, U. has the perfectly natural

Nun werd ich tiefer tief zu nichte.

Rational grounds for the change are hard to discover. It seems most likely that Goethe, in revising, wished to get rid of the expression tiefer tief and rewrote the line without thinking of the *immediate* connection. He meant to say, that is, that any intercourse with spirits was bliss as compared to a dialogue with the commonplace Wagner, but he forgot that Faust has just 'sunk down' in mortal despair and ought not, in the next breath, to be speaking of the results of his conjuring as his 'fairest happiness.'

520. Fülle. The 'plenitude' must refer to the 'celestial powers' of l. 449 *and* the Earth-Spirit.

521. Der trockne Schleicher, 'the humdrum poke.' U. has Der trockne Schwärmer, which is fatal to the common conception of Wagner as a soulless pedant. Cf. Intr. p. lxxix. The change was made, probably, to avoid the strange collocation 'humdrum enthusiast.'

522–69. The dialogue turns first on public speaking and then, after l. 558, on the study of the past. Wagner stands for the conventional academic ideals of the 18th century, as represented by Gottsched and the other rationalists, while Faust gives expression to the radicalism of the 'storm and stress' revolt, as voiced by Herder. See G. Jacoby, *Herder als Faust*, Leipzig, 1911, for a full treatment of the kinship between the ideas of Herder and those of the youthful Goethe as voiced by Faust.

522. declamiren. Wagner has heard the sonorous, measured speech, or chant, of the Earth-Spirit.

525. das; i. e., das gute Declamiren.

528. The preacher is a comedian if he mouths over words without having his heart in what he says.

530. Museum; = Studirzimmer. At an earlier date the word was common in this sense, but it is now archaic or humorous, as is the term Musensohn, applied to a student. The abode of a Musensohn is naturally a Museum, or 'home of the muses.'

531. Feiertag. The acc. of time is here not quite natural; cf. Brandt, § 208, and 208, 1. The gen. was forbidden by the rime.

532. von weiten, 'from afar'; weiten being the old dat. plu., M. H. G. witen.

534–5. The thought is : If you do not *feel* what you are saying, you will not gain your object by chasing after fine phrases. The 'its' are employed somewhat vaguely. Ihr werdet's nicht erjagen should be taken as apodosis to both the clauses with wenn.

536. urkräftigem Behagen, 'the spell of native vigor.'

538–41. The speaker who is not in earnest, who has nothing of his own to say, but depends upon art and borrowing, is held up to contempt under three distinct images : that of one pasting together scraps of quotation, that of a cook preparing a stew from the remnants of a banquet, and that of a person trying to blow a flame out of a heap of ashes. The point of the last metaphor is that, the speaker's heart being cold and having in it no fuel, he tries to produce the semblance of flame by 'blowing.'

542. Bewundrung; in loose apposition to what precedes.

543. darnach . . . . steht, 'inclines that way.'

546. Allein, 'but,' rather than 'alone.' See, however, G.-J., V., 388.

548. Er. Er is often used in *Faust*, as pronoun of address, where Ihr would be too formal or polite and Du too familiar. In Goethe's youth it was still freely used by parent to child, teacher to pupil, and between gossips; it being regarded as somewhat more respectful than Du. Thus Marthe and Gretchen use both Du and Sie (3d. sing.) to each other, and Faust uses, on occasion, all three pronouns in addressing Wagner. If the speaker has been using Ihr, the change to Er conveys, as here, a touch of frigidity and temper; if he has been using Er, the change to Du is familiar and *gemüthlich* (cf. l. 2882). — **redlichen Gewinn,** 'honest gain.' Some, e. g., Schröer, suppose that Faust actually means to advise Wagner to learn a trade; but in that case why does he go on advising him about oratory? The meaning is rather: Be honest with your hearers; do not seek to gain glory (**des Redners Glück**) through shams.

549. schellenlauter, 'bell-tinkling'; in allusion to the bells worn by court-fools, or, as some think, to St. Paul's 'tinkling cymbals' (see 1 Corinthians, xiii. 7).

555. Schnitzel kräuselt, 'curl gewgaws for men' (**Menschheit** being a dat.); in allusion to the crimping of bits of paper into flowers, or 'cuffs' for candles, or the like. The result is an artificial prettiness without solid foundation. Cf. G.-J., VI., 309, also the **gefärbten Schnitzeln** of *Faust,* l. 5100. There are those, however, who take **Menschheit** as gen. — 'to prink up humanity's leavings.' The idea would then be that the preacher's rhetorical flourishes, decked out with stale quotations, are like artificial flowers made of refuse-paper from humanity's waste-basket.

556. Nebelwind; ornate rhetoric is likened to the wet autumn wind which chills and repels — instead of warming and persuading, like the spring sun of artless eloquence born of honest feeling.

558-9. The saying 'life is short, but the art is long'—ὁ βίος βραχύς, ἡ δὲ τέχνη μακρή, — begins the *Aphorisms* of Hippocrates, who had reference to the healing art. The adage was a favorite one with Goethe. In a letter of Nov. 15, 1774, he writes: **Die Tage sind Kurz und die Kunst lang.** Cf. l. 1787.

560. kritischem Bestreben, 'critical (i. e., philological) pursuits'; the study of ancient documents in order to determine questions of authorship, date, priority, etc., in theology.

561. um, 'in the region of,' 'in,' rather than 'concerning,' though the latter is the common meaning of **um** with **bang.**

562. nicht; pleonastic, as often in exclamations. Thus Goethe writes: **Wie seid ihr nicht so gut,** 'how good you are'; **wie erschrak sie nicht,** 'how frightened she was.' — **Mittel** means rare or expensive books, containing original sources (**Quellen**) of information.

564. den halben Weg, 'half the way' toward becoming a great scholar.

570-85. This dialogue needs to be read in the light of Herder's revolutionary pamphlet, *Auch eine Philosophie* etc., of the year 1774. Herder there pours his scorn upon the fashionable practice of looking at the past *de haut en bas* and treating it as a text for self-complacent reflections on the wonderful progress of the 'age of enlightenment.' Goethe puts Herder's views into the mouth of Faust, and makes Wagner represent the conceited *Aufklärungsphilosophen* (vaguely referred to in l. 578 as ber Herren, cf. ber saubern Herren in l. 106), whom Herder attacks. Cf. Suphan in V. L., I., 527.

576. **Buch** .... **Siegeln**; cf. Rev. v. 1.

580. **ist's.** The es refers to the literary work of the 'gentlemen' — their fine historical 'portraits,' that make allowance for the darkness of the past and show how '*we* in our day' have grown so much wiser and better.

581. **euch**; ethical dat.

582. **Kehrichtfaß .... Rumpelkammer,** 'refuse-tub and lumber-attic.' The historical 'portraits' with their commonplace moral reflections are likened to a household receptacle for worthless odds and ends.

583. **Haupt= und Staatsaction;** a name given to a kind of dramatic performance that became popular in the seventeenth century. The plays dealt with 'state' affairs (bloody tyranny, revolution, political intrigue, etc.), and so were called Staatsactionen. Such a play was called a Hauptaction, 'principal performance,' to distinguish it from the farce given on the same evening. The two titles were then combined. In time the plays became notorious for their spectacular extravagance, their bombast and their crude, obtrusive moralizing. It is this last quality of them which furnishes the point of the comparison in the text.

584. **pragmatischen,** 'didactic.' The puppet-plays were also somewhat given to moralizing comment.

588. **was .... heißt,** 'what is popularly called knowing.' The logic of the reply is: How little do they really know of the human heart who talk thus glibly of 'understanding' it! And if one does attain to some real insight, he had better be silent, lest he be put to death. Cf. Intr. pp. xxx, xxxi. Schröer cites appositely the following passage from a letter of Goethe to Sophie von Laroche, written Dec. 23, 1774: 'To-day I have got back a copy of *Werther* that I had loaned. On the fly-leaf was written: *Tais-toi, Jean-Jacques, ils ne te comprendront point.* This affected

me very strangely, since the passage in *Émile* had always seemed remarkable.'

589. **das Kind;** the truth, as discovered by men of exceptional insight.

596. **hätte .... fortgewacht,** 'should have liked to keep right on sitting up.' U. and Fgm. have the more importunate **hätte gern bis morgen früh gewacht.**

598. **als,** 'as being,' 'since it is.' The lines 598–601 are not found in U. or Fgm. They were evidently added to forecast the Easter walk and to give more point to the following words of Faust.

605. With this line U. and Fgm. break off abruptly. What follows, written after 1797, is a mournful arraignment of life on several counts that have little to do with what precedes: the waning of enthusiasm, the oppressiveness of care, the disappointments of the investigator, the uselessness of old furniture. One feels all along that the speaker, like the poet who wrote the lines, has aged considerably. For a guess as to how the plot would have developed, if Goethe had finished this part of the play in his youth, see App. III., n. to 459+.

607. **Geisterfülle.** Cf. note on **Fülle,** l. 520.

613. **sollte,** 'was fated,' 'could but'; almost = **mußte.**

614–22. Faust here describes the **neue Gefühle** of l. 478.

615. **dem Spiegel.** Divinity is thought of as a dazzling mirror reflecting back a celestial radiance upon the beholder. The conception may owe somewhat to the account of Moses and the Lord in Ex. xxxiii, xxxiv.

616. **Sein selbst,** 'himself;' **sein** the genitive with **genießen.**

617. **abgestreift den Erdensohn,** 'had stripped off mortality.' Supply **hatte.**

618. **mehr als Cherub.** The cherub is a passive servant of divinity; Faust had dreamed of a free, godlike *activity* (**schaffend,** l. 620).

621. **Sich .... vermaß,** 'presumptuously dreamed.' **Ahnungsvoll** means 'bodeful,' usually of ill, here of good.

622. **Donnerwort;** the rebuff in ll. 512–13. — **Mich hinweggerafft,** 'swept me away,' viz., from the place of my high dreams.

631. **jenem Drang;** the impulse to seek help from the spirit-world.

632–3. Our 'deeds' interfere with the course of our life when their effects leave us no longer free to pursue a given line. Faust has evoked the Spirit, thus performing a bold and in one sense successful 'deed,' but the sequel was such that he feels debarred from trying again.

634-5. Dem Herrlichsten .... an, 'foreign and ever more foreign matter crowds itself upon the noblest conceptions of the mind'; i. e., we are not faithful to the thoughts of our supreme moments; lower ideals, compromises, doubts, anxieties crowd in. From this point Faust's soliloquy becomes a series of mournful reflections on the weakness of human nature and the *misère* of life.

635. fremd und fremder; the construction is to be regarded as adverbial, though the subject is fremder Stoff, not Stoff alone. Cf. nah und näher, l. 3242, and fern und ferner, *Tasso*, l. 917. The meaning is, obviously, that the 'noblest conceptions of the mind,' i.e. the 'glorious feelings' experienced in some moment of supreme enthusiasm or insight, are presently invaded by foreign matter in the form of lower ideals, troubles, anxieties, etc.; which foreign matter then becomes ever more foreign with the lapse of time. A somewhat similar thought is expressed in ll. 1210 ff.

639. Erstarren, 'grow torpid.'

644. Sorge, 'anxiety,' 'worry.' In l. 11384 die Sorge is introduced as a gray old hag who makes man a prey to morbid solicitudes. — **Gleich = sogleich,** 'forthwith,' 'straightway.'

647-51. A man worries about his property, his wife, and children; he dreads death from fire, dagger or poison, and is thus continually trembling at the blow that *may* fall, but probably never does fall.

656. Ist es .... verenget, 'is it not dust, that which narrows in this high wall with its hundred compartments (aus = bestehend aus) about me?' With verenget cf. beschränkt in l. 402.

658. Tand, 'frippery.'

664. Was; not = warum. The sense is: 'What means thy grin?'

666. leichten, 'light' in the sense of 'buoyant,' 'making flight easy,' in contrast with the following schwer.

668. freilich; here used, apparently, in the earlier sense of 'certainly,' 'surely', as if there might be some doubt about the skull's mocking. The modern concessive meaning 'to be sure,' 'forsooth,' gives no sense here.

669. Walz und Bügel, 'roller and (stirrup-shaped) handle.'

671. euer .... kraus, 'your web is intricate.' The Bart of a key is the part on which the bits and wards are cut or cast, the part that revolves in the lock; Eng. 'web.'

672. **Geheimnißvoll;** adj. with **Natur.** As scientific thinker, Goethe held that the secrets of nature must be divined from contemplation of objects as they are; that scientific progress must come always in the form of an *aperçu*, or intuition, the mind in nature speaking directly to the mind of man. To seek help from instruments seemed to him like doing violence to nature. So he says of his early botanical studies: 'Cutting up and counting were not in my nature.' On this unscientific prejudice of Goethe and its bearing upon his scientific work, cf. Du Bois-Reymond, *Goethe und kein Ende*, p. 22 ff.

676. **Geräthe;** the **Urväter Hausrath** of l. 408.

678. **Rolle;** some roll of parchment. Düntzer refers it to the lamp-pulley, but that would hardly show smoke enough to attract attention.

682-3. **Was du .... besitzen,** 'what thou hast, as an inheritance from thy fathers, earn it in order to possess it.' This sounds like nonsense, but the meaning depends largely on a Goethean distinction between **haben** and **besitzen. Haben** means 'to have,' **besitzen** 'to own and feel the worth of.' Thus in Goethe's *Künstlers Erdewallen* the artist apostrophizes the picture he is painting, which he loves as his very own, and says of the pro-spective rich purchaser: **er besitzt dich nicht, er hat dich nur,** 'he will merely have thee, not possess thee.' Cf. *Tasso*, l. 114 and the editor's note.— **Erwirb es** means 'pay for it by effort'; cf. Cooper's note in G.-J., XXXII., 182. The sense is then: Use thy inheritance if thou wouldst feel it to be thy very own.— **Haft** is not an auxiliary.

685. **Nur was .... nützen,** 'only what the moment creates can the moment use.' The meaning of this oracular saying is that one can turn to account at any time only that which is the fresh result of one's own pro-ductive activity. The proposition hardly holds good of old furniture, but it does apply to the intellectual legacies of the past, and this is what the poet really has in mind. I can turn to account the wisdom of Solomon or Shakespeare only when I have personally traveled Solomon's or Shake-speare's ground, and so made his creation mine.

690. **Phiole,** 'phial,' in the sense of ' long-necked glass bottle.'

692. **Menschenwitz und Kunst.** Faust is proud of the knowledge and skill which have enabled him to make the deadly opiate.

698. Des Geistes Fluthstrom. The 'flood-tide of the spirit' is the intense excitement under which he has been laboring. The sight of the poison suddenly brings a calmer mood.

699. werd' ich hinausgewiesen, 'I am beckoned out'; more accurately, 'I am shown the way,' 'directed.' — The fateful transition is conceived not as a voyage upon the 'high sea' which separates this life from the other, but as a translation through space out over it.

702. Feuerwagen; in allusion, no doubt, to Elijah's chariot of fire, 2 Kings ii. 11.

705. reiner, 'pure,' i. e., undisturbed by any galling sense of limitation.

707. erst noch, 'but lately.' Cf. l. 653.

710. vermesse; *metri gratia* for **vermiß.** But Goethe uses the weak imperative occasionally, even when meter does not require it.

712 ff. Suicide is here thought of as an act of supreme courage, the assertion of man's independence. The very gods can not compel him to live if he will not. The moral aspect of self-destruction was a question much debated in the eighteenth century. Cf. *Werther's Leiden,* letter of Dec. 20, and E. Schmidt, *Richardson, Rousseau und Goethe,* p. 228. Hell is imagined, after the early Christian artists, as a place of horrible torment, situated underground or in a mountain and approached by a passage (Durchgang) from the mouth of which smoke and flames belch forth. Hinzustreben, l. 716, does not imply that Faust courts damnation, but only that he is in a mood to go boldly and confront these imagined horrors. In reality he thinks them old wives' tales (l. 369).

719. in's Nichts. Du Bois-Reymond, p. 16 ff., objects that Faust, who has just seen a spirit, has no right to be skeptical about the reality of the life beyond. But there are many passages in the poem in which the modern skeptic peeps out from under the legendary mask of Faust. It may be observed, too, that the existence of spirits does not of itself prove man's immortality; and also, finally, that the Faust-books, puppet-plays and Marlowe all make Faust doubt the reality of heaven and hell. Cf. Intr. p. xiii.

720. Schale. We have to think of a costly goblet decorated with pictures. The game alluded to below was like this: One person, filling the beaker, would pledge his neighbor, calling on him for an impromptu rime in explanation of the pictures. In case of failure, the person pledged had to drain the glass at one draught.

723. Freudenfeste; the sing. *metri gratia* for the plu., since no *particular* festival seems to be referred to.

725. zugebracht; in the technical sense of 'pledging' a health, as in l. 736.

736+. Chor der Engel. The choruses in this scene are to be thought of as part of an Easter celebration taking place in a neighboring church. Singers personate the angels of the resurrection, the mourning women and the disciples. Such a service, held in the night before Easter, was once common in the Catholic church. Cf. *Euphorion,* III, 391.

737. Christ ist erstanden; the beginning of an old medieval Easter-song, whence the archaic Christ for Christus.

739–41. Den .... umwanden, 'whom baneful, insidious, hereditary shortcomings (those of human nature) entwined.'

742. tiefes Summen, the bells ringing here and there in the city; **heller Ton,** the chorus close by.

747. um Grabes Nacht, 'about the darkness of the tomb.' Um's Grabes Nacht would be more natural; but cf. Berges-Höhle in l. 394. The line refers to the words 'he is not here, but has arisen,' spoken by the 'two men in shining garments' whom Mary Magdalene and her companion found at the sepulcher. See Luke xxiv. 1 ff. According to John xx. 1, Mary Magdalene came to the tomb very early in the morning, 'when it was yet dark.'

748. Gewißheit .... Bunde, '(giving) confirmation to a new covenant.' Gewißheit is best explained as a kind of 'cognate' acc. with Klang. Cf. Brandt, § 202. The 'new covenant' is the διαθήκη νέα, of Hebrews xii, 24.

749–56. Chor der Weiber. None of the evangelists states that the body of Christ was wrapped, anointed, and laid in the tomb by women;— the office is uniformly represented as performed by Joseph, or by Joseph and Nicodemus, the women watching from a distance. Matthew makes the two Marys come on the morning of the third day, simply 'to see the sepulcher.' According to Mark and Luke, they come with spices, *intending* to anoint the body, but they do not find it. Goethe adapts the details of the gospel narrative to his own purposes.

762–3. Was sucht .... Staube, 'why seek ye me in the dust, ye potent and soothing heavenly tones'? Am Staube differs from im Staube (l.

654) in that it means 'cleaving to the dust.' In some verses of the year
1766 (*Briefe*, I., 46) Goethe writes:

> Da sah ich erst, daß mein erhabner Flug,
> Wie er mir schien, nichts war als das Bemühn
> Des Wurms im Staube, der den Adler sieht
> Zur Sonn' sich schwingen und wie der hinauf
> Sich sehnt. Er sträubt empor und windet sich,
> Und ängstlich spannt er alle Nerven an
> Und bleibt am Staub.

So here, Faust ' cleaves to the dust,' feeling that the lofty flight of religious
feeling is not for him.

764. weiche ; not 'weak' in a contemptuous sense, but 'susceptible,'
' soft-hearted.'

766. The more common and orthodox theory is that faith is the child
of miracle.

771–8. In these reminiscences of Faust we hear Goethe describing the
religious experiences of his own youth.   Cf. Intr. pp. xxvi, xxvii.

771. Kuß ; here of the mystic kiss, the benediction, of divine love.

780. Freies Glück. This 'free happiness ' of the spring festival
(Easter) is described in ll. 903 ff.

785–96. Chor der Jünger. The general sense is : While the risen
Lord is happy in heaven, we here on earth can but mourn our loss, though
our loss is his gain. The first six lines are protasis and concessive, the
last six apodosis, the ließ er of l. 793 simply continuing the inversion sind
wir in l. 792.

787. Lebend Erhabene ; = der auf der Erde lebend Erhabene, i. e.,
der schon auf Erden ein erhabenes Leben führte.

789. Werdelust, 'joy of transition,' i. e., the joy of entering upon a
new existence.

799. Banden; the ' bonds ' of sorrow and depression.

801–5. The participles go with euch in l. 806, and denote condition.
'If you live praising him by your actions (thätig) etc., he is near you.'

𝔙𝔬𝔯 𝔡𝔢𝔪 𝔗𝔥𝔬𝔯.

This scene is not found in U. or Fgm., and there are no external data which show when any part of it was written. It is quite certain that, except ll. 949–80, the text was given its present form in 1797–1801. But was it all gebichtet, as well as geschrieben, at that time? In other words: To what extent did Goethe, in filling in the 'great gap' (cf. Intr. p. lvii.) make use of matter that already existed in his imagination if not on paper? On this question there is much difference of opinion; cf. Kögel, V. L., II., 558.; Pniower, G.-J., XVI., 149; Niejahr, G.-J., XX., 155; and E. Schmidt, *Urfaust*, p. lxiv. The case stands thus : On the one hand, (1) the heart of the whole matter is plainly the introduction of Mephisto in the form of a dog, and such a scene was indisputably a part of the early plan. (2) The setting is reminiscent of Frankfurt down to minute details. (3) There is fairly good evidence of the former existence of a letter by Boie, written in 1774 or 1775, in which the writer told of hearing Goethe read from his *Faust* a scene which introduced Faust, Wagner, a bevy of students, and a dog doing tricks. (See E. Schmidt, *Urfaust*, p. lxv.) On the other hand, the style and the art are unquestionably those of 1797–1801. The characters are types, not individuals. They do not speak the natural language of their kind (cf. ll. 830–31, 844–45, 881). They talk in concert sometimes. Everything is ordered for the *reader*, with reference to picturesqueness. Above all, Faust is a different man, — older, saner, more genial, no longer an obscure and poverty-stricken failure (ll. 374–75), but an elderly man highly venerated by the community. His pessimism has a far more human basis.

Another moot question relates to the time of year. Nominally it is Easter Sunday. The ice has lately melted, there are showers of sleet in the air, vegetation is just starting. At the same time there are peasants dancing under a linden, which would have to be leafless, and there are 'green-girt huts' in the landscape, which must refer either to vintagers' huts or to vine-clad cottages. In a large view of the Faust-drama such little dissonances are of little moment, but they are there. In the case of a very accurate observer, like Goethe, they indicate that the scene was not composed aus einem Gusse. There are older and newer elements.

One may conjecture that Goethe began the play and wrote ll. 354–597 without thinking of any definite time of the year. In U. there is no seasonal suggestion whatever. After Wagner's exit Faust was somehow to make the acquaintance of Mephisto in canine form, but the poodle-devil was quite unmanageable in a serious connection. A canine inter-locutor, or the lower magic necessary for his anthropomorphization, would have made comedy of the suicide scene. In considering how to introduce the dog Goethe thought of letting Faust take a walk with Wagner on a summer day and come upon the beast diverting a bevy of students. The scene shaped itself in his mind with summery touches here and there. In the course of time, however, the happy thought came to him of letting Faust be diverted from suicide, not by the devil, but by a rush of Easter memories. This led to a definite fixation of the time of year, with a cor-responding working over of earlier conceptions. The result is poetically admirable, though the traces of inharmonious visualization are still visible with a philological microscope. Exact chronology is no part of Goethe's scheme in the completed *Faust*. The Second Part opens on a midsummer eve, and the next scene, which must follow it pretty closely, comes at Shrovetide. At the end Faust is a hundred years old, but we do not learn just how the time has passed.

807+. **Vor dem Thor.** The scene as identified in great detail by the late Friedrich Zarncke, V. L., II., 556, is just outside the Sachsenhausen Gate (Affenthor) south of and across the Main from Frankfurt. Here in Goethe's time there was a convergence of the highways leading east to Offenbach, south to Darmstadt and southwest to Mainz. At this point, presumably, the beggar of l. 852 sits with his hand-organ. Here also the 'prentices separate. Some of them wish to go to the 'Forsthaus' (in Goethe Jägerhaus) some two miles southwest, others to the 'Gerbermühle,' lying a mile or more up the river to the east. The 'river inn' is a short distance southeast of the 'mill,' but the way to it lies through low, treeless ground (l. 812). 'Burgdorf' means the village of Oberrad, about a mile southeast, and back from the river, whence the 'up' of l. 814. The name is changed because Goethe did not wish to make his topography explicit: university students and Faust and Wagner would be out of place in Frank-furt. Faust and Wagner walk southeast up toward Oberrad and pause on a height where they can hear the tumult of the 'village' ahead (l. 937) and also have a good retrospect of the city, with the people emerging from the Affenthor, and of the boats on the river. The 'mountain' of l. 935 refers to the heights of the Taunus in the far northwest across the river.

816. **Händel,** 'rows.'

818. **zum drittenmal.** 'Prentice no. 3 has lately been in two fights at Burgdorf.

821+. **Erste ;** i. e., **erstes Dienstmädchen,** the natural gender being followed instead of the grammatical.

824. **Plan,** 'platform' for dancing ; a South German usage of the word.

827+. **Schüler ;** in the sense of the modern **Student. Student** is the word regularly used in U., but in Fgm. it appears uniformly changed to **Schüler.**

830. **beizender Toback. Beizen** is a weak factitive of **beißen** and meant originally 'to make bite,' now usually 'to macerate' or 'pickle.' But **beizend** often means, as here, 'pungent.' **Toback** is the older form, from Sp. *tobacco,* through the Eng. The now usual **Tabak** has the vowel of the Fr. *tabac.* Goethe uses both forms.

831+. **Bürgermädchen ;** girls of the citizen class, intermediate between 'servant-girls' and 'young ladies.' But the latter will do for a translation.

841. **nehmen .... mit,** 'will take us with them too, though, after all.'

842. **Ich .... genirt,** 'I don't like to be under constraint.' The company is too high-toned for him.

844. **Samstags;** South German for **Sonnabends.**

846. **Burgemeister ;** a dialectic survival of M. H. G. *burgemeister.* Goethe seems to have preferred it both early and late to the now more usual **Bürgermeister.**

853. **backenroth,** 'with flushed cheeks'; **rothbackig** = 'ruddy-cheeked' (Schröer).

856. **leiern,** 'grind.' The 'lyre' is here a guitar-like instrument, the strings of which are moved by a wheel turned by a crank, the so-called **Bauernleier** or **deutsche Leier ;** cf. Grimm Wb., VI., 682.

863. **hinten, weit,** 'away off.' There was a Russo-Turkish war in Goethe's youth (1767–74).

872. **das . . . . Blut,** 'the handsome young creatures.' **Junges Blut,** for 'girl,' is a favorite expression with Goethe. Cf. ll. 2636, 2907, 3313, and Grimm, *sub voce* **Blut.** It is here applied to both the girls.

874. **Es ist schon gut,** 'it's all right,' i. e.: *I* know what kind of thoughts are hidden under that proud coquettish air. The 'young ladies' had been last year's customers of the old fortune-teller.

876. **Agathe;** the name of one of the girls.

878. **Sanct Andreas Nacht.** On this night, Nov. 29, German girls were wont to consult the oracles and the fortune-tellers with regard to their future lovers or husbands. For the folk-lore on the subject, see Grimm, D. M., II., 936, and III., 454, 470.

880. **Krystall;** in allusion to the practice of **Krystallsehen;** cf. Grimm Wb., V., 2482, and D. M., III., 431. The fortune-tellers had their customers look at a crystal, a poor mirror, a sword-blade, or other object reflecting the light dimly or confusedly, and imagine that they saw there what they wanted to see. The operator professed to do his wonders by conjuring the indwelling spirit of the crystal.

883–902. **Soldaten.** A company of soldiers march by, singing a song expressive of the soldier-ideal.

892. **Werben;** supply **uns** as object. 'We let the trumpet woo us,' 'we follow the trumpet-call.'

895–6. The thought is: See how we go storming through the world! This is life.

905. **Hoffnungs-Glück.** Cf. Goethe's *Götz*, V., 14: **Die Bäume treiben Knospen und alle Welt hofft.**

909. **Ohnmächtige . . . . Eises,** 'impotent gusts of sleet.'

912. **Bildung und Streben,** 'formation and growth'; vegetation is everywhere starting up and taking shape.

913. **will,** 'is trying.' The sun is personified as a landscape-painter.

914. **Revier,** 'landscape'; originally, 'district along a river-bank,' It. *riviera.* The scene being on the banks of the Main, Goethe may use the word in its original sense.

929. **behend,** 'speedily'; **behe'nd** from M. H. G. *bi hende,* 'by hand.'

940. **Hier . . . . sein.** It is not meant that the people use these words, but that their shouts are so interpreted by Faust, for whom a 'human being' is a person enjoying life in free contact with nature.

941-8. Wagner feels edified by Faust's *talk*, but not by the scene that has inspired it.

943. mich her verlieren = hierher kommen und mich verlieren.

945. Kegelschieben, 'nine-pin bowling.' Instead of balls for bowling, it was formerly the custom to use disks which were *shoved;* hence the term Kegelschieben.

949-80. This song is mentioned in *Meister's Lehrjahre*, II., 11, as a 'song which we can not present to our readers because they might find it absurd or even improper.' The part of *Meister* containing the allusion was finished before Nov. 12, 1783; but see Pniower, p. 39.

973. thu' mir. Thut mir would correspond to the seid nicht of l. 964. The girl's dignity has melted somewhat.

984. Hochgelahrter. From the Middle Ages down into the 18th century, Gelahrter existed side by side with Gelehrter without appreciable difference of meaning. Since then, Gelahrter has been provincial or slightly humorous, like Eng. 'larned.'

987. bring ihn zu. Cf. l. 725, note.

988. nicht nur. The natural correlative sondern auch is omitted.

993 ff. The legend makes Faust's father a peasant. But the father of Paracelsus was a physician, and Nostradamus (cf. l. 420, note) acquired great distinction for his services during the plague. We have here a blending of data derived from different sources. Cf. Intr. p. xxxi.

1001. Auch damals ihr ; = auch ihr damals.

1020. wenig . . . . beugten, 'it lacks little of their bending.' The syntactical logic is: Sie brauchten dich nur ein wenig mehr zu verehren, so beugten sie u. s. w.

1021. das Venerabile ; the holy host, or sacred wafer symbolizing the body of Christ. In Catholic countries the host is borne before solemn processions, and the devout are expected to prostrate themselves before it. Cf. Schiller's *Tell*, l. 1751.

1034. dunkler Ehrenmann, 'obscure gentleman.'

1035. Kreise ; in the sense of Kreisläufe, 'circuits,' or very nearly what we now call 'processes.' So Goethe speaks of Unseres Daseins Kreise, 'the circuits of our existence.'

1037. mit grillenhafter Mühe, 'with cranky zeal'; i. e., without intelligent method.

1038. **Adepten,** 'adepts,' in the earlier sense of one expert in alchemy; lit., 'one who has found' the panacea, Lat. *adipiscor.*

1039. **schwarze Küche,** 'laboratory.' Out of Gr. νεκρομαντεία, i. e., the art of divining by calling up the ghosts of the dead, medieval popular etymology made *nigromantia,* 'black-divining,' as a general term for the 'dark,' 'occult' arts. Whence 'black art,' and 'black kitchen' for the place where it was carried on.

1040. **Recepten,** 'recipes.'

1041. **das Widrige** seems to mean 'the incompatible,' i. e. substances chemically 'opposed' to one another, or perhaps 'the repulsive.'

1042–7. The technical jargon of these lines seems to be partly Goethe's invention; at least nothing just like it has been found in the books of alchemy, though much of the imagery can be pretty closely parallelled from Welling and Paracelsus. Cf. Intr. pp. xxvii, xxviii. The theory was that the panacea would be produced, in the form of a bright-colored precipitate, by mixing two substances in a tepid medium and then treating the mixture in heated retorts. But the fantastic brains of the alchemists conceived the chemical union as a marriage and the precipitation as a birth or offspring; hence they gave to the 'parents' symbolical names of living organisms. In this case the father is 'the red lion' and the mother 'the lily,' but sometimes the mother was called 'the white eagle,' and the name 'lily' was given to the offspring, i. e., the panacea itself, which is here called 'the young queen.' It is not likely that Goethe, who knew nothing of chemistry, was thinking here of any particular chemical bodies; but inasmuch as mercury was, with the alchemists, a favorite substance for these experiments, it is easy to imagine that the 'panacea' would in very fact often turn out to be a deadly poison.

1044. **mit offnem Flammenfeuer;** i. e., the retort was heated in a free flame.

1053. **den Gift;** usually **das Gift,** but now and then **der Gift** in Goethe. Schiller also makes it masc. in *Kabale u. Liebe* V., 7 : **Noch spür' ich den Gift nicht.** The word is hardly, as Schröer thinks, used in the specific sense of 'dose,' though that was the original sense of the word.

1055. **lobt;** in allusion to ll. 995 ff.

1056–63. Here, as in ll. 570 ff., Wagner represents the self-complacent *Aufklärungsphilosoph,* whose watchword is 'the progress of the race.'

1064–7. The logic is: Alas for these fine hopes of yours, that by adding ignorance to ignorance through successive generations, men will ever get their heads above the waters of uncertainty, when we have no foundation of positive, *useful* knowledge on which to build.

1072. **Sie rückt und weicht,** 'it moves and recedes,' i. e., it is gradually disappearing.

1076–88. Faust dreams of flying away after the sun, and enjoying from the upper air a prolonged sunset view.

1078. **beruhigt,** 'hushed' in the evening shadows.

1079. **Silberbach in goldne Ströme.** The great rivers (**Ströme**) would appear 'golden' in the floods of sunlight, the brooks reflecting less light, 'silvery.'

1082. **mit erwärmten Buchten.** The heat of the spring sun would already have 'warmed' the shallow 'bays' of the sea.

1084. **Göttin;** the sun. Faust imagines his flight slackening at the sea-shore and the sun as about to sink from his view after all. Then a 'fresh impulse' comes and sends him out after it over the ocean.

1092–9. This dream of flying like a bird meets us often in Goethe's youthful writings; e. g., in *Werther* (*Werke,* H., XIV., 59) : 'Oh, at those times how often have I longed for the wings of a crane that was flying over me, to soar away to the shore of the boundless sea,' etc. Again, in the *Briefe aus der Schweiz* (*Werke,* H., XVI., 226), flying is spoken of as one of those 'bodily powers which we are not permitted to develop in this life.' The floating clouds inspire him with a 'desire to plunge into infinite space,' and the soaring eagle makes him 'draw deeper and deeper breaths' in his longing to fly.

1095. **schmetternd,** 'shrill-warbling.'

1108. **Pergamen;** the same as **Pergament,** in l. 566. It comes from Gr. (χάρτη) περγαμηνή through Lat. (*charta*) *pergamena,* 'paper of Pergamos'; but the form with *t,* as if from Lat. **pergamentum,* is the prevailing one even in M. H. G. (*permint, permit, perment,* etc.).

1112. **Zwei Seelen ;** see App. III.

1114. **derber Liebeslust,** 'gross amorous desire.'

1116. **Duft,** 'dust'; a little-used Low German loan-word. It occurs again in l. 6758.

1117. **Gefilden hoher Ahnen,** 'abodes of high ancestors.' The Greek imagination, and not the Greek only, gave a home in the sky to the ancestral heroes of eld.

1118. **Geiſter in der Luft**; see App. III.

1127. **ſich überbreitet**; = ſich überall ausbreitet.

1130. **der ſcharfe Geiſterzahn.** The 'bite' of the north wind is attrib-
uted by Wagner to the sharp tooth of one class of weather-spirits.

1133. **nähren ſich .... Lungen.** In Germany the east wind is pre-
vailingly dry, and a dry wind seems to make breathing difficult.

1134. **Wüſte,** 'desert'; the Sahara presumably.

1136. **erſt erquickt.** The 'refreshing' coolness that precedes a shower
is viewed by Wagner as a malicious trick of the spirits to usher in pleas-
antly the subsequent disagreeable 'drenching.'

1147. **Saat und Stoppel**; Saat, the freshly starting grain; Stoppel,
the 'stubble' of last year's crop.

1154. **Feuerſtrudel,** 'fiery whorl.' When this was written, Goethe
probably intended nothing more by his 'fiery whorl' than to intimate (for
the benefit of the reader or spectator) that the dog was no ordinary dog.
We learn further on (l. 1377) that fire is the devil's own element. Later,
however, the poet tried to fit the passage into an optical theory of his to
the effect that dark and light are so related that when a dark or bright
object comes quickly before the eyes in a dim light, there is an instantane-
ous after-sensation of the opposite color. He himself claims to have seen
a trail of light following a poodle that ran by his window at dusk. See the
Nachträge zur Farbenlehre, Werke, H., XXXVI., 517, where ll. 1147–57
are quoted and said to have been written down aus dichteriſcher Ahnung
and in 'semi-consciousness' of a scientific truth which he was able in due
time to verify.

1166. **hier**; = hierher, the converse of the license in l. 943.

1167. **pudelnärriſch,** 'poodle - silly'; i. e., having the characteristic
silliness of poodles. So the German has pudeltreu, 'faithful as a dog,'
pudelnackt, 'stark naked,' pudelnaß, 'wet as a drowned rat' (wet as a dog
coming out of the water), etc.

1173. **Geiſt;** in the double sense of 'spirit'= 'supernatural being,'
and 'spirit' = 'intelligence.'

1177. **der Studenten .... Scolar.** Wagner supposes that they have
found the trained trick-dog of some student. — Scolar, from Lat. *scolaris,*
'scholar,' 'pupil,' is pedantic (but here also *metri gratia*) for Schüler.

Studirzimmer (1).

THERE is little room for doubt that this scene also combines old matter with new, though no portion of it is found in U. or Fgm. The lines that relate to Faust's flood-tide of religious emotion, to the closely following ebb and the consequent resort to written revelation, suggest the youthful Goethe and correspond to phases of his early religious feeling. They presuppose a Faust who is not yet prepared for an utterance like that in l. 765. On the other hand, the interjected remonstrances with the poodle, the conjuring, and very certainly the dialogue, are of late origin, dating probably from the year 1801. Cf. Intr. p. lvii.

The hocus-pocus of the scene is partly invented, partly based on the legend. C. M., after telling how Faust had evoked a spirit in the woods at midnight and secured the promise of a visit at his house next day, proceeds as follows (Scheible, II., 79) : 'Which promise likewise the spirit kept, coming to the house at noon, after long and anxious waiting on the part of Faust, and posting himself in different positions behind the stove; until after another conjuration by Faust, he exhibited a human head and made a deep bow, refusing, however, to come further, on the ground that he was near enough already. Whereat Faust is said to have become wroth and to have threatened a stronger conjuration; which appeared to displease the accursed spirit, seeing that he at once became obedient, save that he caused him (Faust) fresh anxiety when he beheld the room full of fire and the spirit with the aforesaid human head, but with a body shaggy like that of a bear, so that Faust was constrained to ask him once more to retreat behind the stove.'

1180. ahnungsvollem .... Grauen, 'bodeful, solemn sense of awe.'

1181. weckt. The subject is tiefe Nacht. After bedeckt supply und — a somewhat harsh asyndeton, since the object die is not repeated.

1182. wilde Triebe, 'wild impulses,' e. g., the desire to fly.

1187. schnoperst. Schnop(p)ern is the same as schnob(b)ern, and akin to schnüffeln, 'sniff,' 'snuffle.' The occasion of the poodle's snuffling at the threshold is explained further on, ll. 1395 ff.

1200–1. The language is that of strong religious feeling, and the im-

agery is biblical.   Cf. Ps. xxxvi. 9, 'For with thee is the fountain of life';
Jer. xvii. 13, 'The Lord the fountain of living waters';   Rev. xxi. 6, 'the
fountain of the water of life.'   God being thus the fountain-head, the
'brooks of life' are the outflowing streams of divine peace.

1212. der Strom; the stream of religious peace that 'wells forth' from
his own soul. Cf. ll. 568–9.

1215. dieſer Mangel . . . . erſetzen, 'this failure can be made good.'
The thought is, that when the spontaneous inner spring of religious feeling
begins to run low, then we turn for compensation to the supernatural, to
formal written revelation.

1220. Grundtext, 'the fundamental text,' i. e., the Greek original.

1224–37. The question here turns upon the proper rendering of the
word λόγος in John i. 1 (ἐν ἀρχῇ ἦν ὁ λόγος), as that which 'was in the beginning' and 'by which all things were made.' Faust argues that a 'word'
can not have been 'in the beginning,' because a word is the expression of
a 'thought,' which, therefore, must have come first.   But thought can not
have made the world, there must have been 'power,' and yet power is
nothing unless it is put forth in a 'deed.'   He is thus brought around to
the position of Gen. i. 1, which puts a 'deed' of creation at the beginning.
Strictly he should reject this also, for a 'deed' implies a doer.

1244. die Zelle meiden, 'leave the room.'

1249. Schatten, 'phantom,' 'unreal apparition.'

1256. Du biſt mir gewiß, 'I'm sure of you,' 'I can manage you,'
'you're my game.'

1257. halbe Höllenbrut, 'semi-infernal progeny.'   Faust assumes that
the being before him is of a mixed order, partaking somewhat of the infernal nature, but without being a full-fledged spirit of hell.   He decides
therefore to try first a spell of minor potency.

1258. Salomonis Schlüſſel. 'Key of Solomon,' *Clavicula Salomonis*, is the name of a conjurer's book containing spells and directions for
the evocation and exorcism of spirits.   Saga makes the wise Solomon a
magician.

1258+. Geiſter. A supernatural chorus of spirits, minions of Mephistopheles, who have come to help their imprisoned master, if opportunity offers.

1260. hauſſen = hie auſſen.

1262. **zagt,** 'lingers in dismay.'

1271. **begegnen,** 'to meet,' i. e., 'to deal with.'

1272. **Spruch der Viere,** 'formula of the four' elements, earth, air, fire, and water; i. e., a formula intended for dealing with an elemental spirit.

1273–6. Faust here reads or recites from the 'Key.' Salamanders are spirits of fire, undines, or undenes, of water, sylphs of air, and kobolds of earth. The meaning is that a salamander should manifest his true nature by glowing like fire, an undine by making a sinuous motion of swimming, like a fish or a mermaid, a sylph by vanishing in air, a kobold by making a show of being at work. (The kobolds are subterraneous busy-bodies, Eng. 'gnomes.')'

1277–82. Faust soliloquizes, congratulating himself upon his knowledge of elemental spirits.

1283–91. The first having had no effect, Faust recites a second 'formula of the four,' differing somewhat from the other and presumably more potent as being in more mandatory form.

1285. **Rauschend,** 'with a gurgling sound,' like that of flowing water.

1289–90. If the spirit is one whose character it is to 'be busy,' he is to make the motions of helping about the house-work. The Romans gave the name *incubus,* or *incubo,* both to the nightmare and to the malicious sprite supposed to cause it by resting upon (*incumbere*) his sleeping victim. Later, the name was applied to house-spirits without regard to this malicious propensity, and in that sense came near to the German kobold, which might also be a house-spirit. Whence the substitution of Incubus for the **Kobold** of the first formula.

1291. **Schluß,** 'end'; viz., of the disguise.

1295. **Weh.** Since the spirit does not wish to come out of his disguise, any thing that compels him to do so may be said to 'hurt' him.

1300. **dies Zeichen;** a conjurer's diagram (cf. l. 429+, note) containing a symbol of Christ.

1306. **nie Entsproß'nen,** 'never-born'; i. e., eternal.

1307. **Unausgesprochnen,** 'ineffable.'

1308. **Durch .... Gegoss'nen,** 'diffused through all space'; i. e., omnipresent.

1309. **Freventlich Durchstochnen,** 'wantonly pierced' (John xix, 34).

1319. Das .... Licht. The 'trebly glowing light' is a sign of the Trinity; perhaps a triangle with divergent rays symbolizing the 'holy flame' of divine love, which will 'burn' the devil, as do the roses of divine love in ll. 11710 ff.

1321+. fahrender Scholasticus, 'traveling scholar'; i. e., *scholasticus vagans,* a name given in the Middle Ages to the vagabond students who traveled from one university to another and lived by their wits.

1322. Was steht .... Diensten, 'what does the gentleman want'? **Dem Herrn** is a polite circumlocution for **euch,** a use of **Herr** which was common in the 17th century, as it still is in Swedish. See Grimm, Wb., under **Herr.**

1326. weidlich, 'vigorously.' The sense is: You've made it lively for me.

1328. Der .... verachtet; in allusion to l. 1226.

1330. Tiefe .... trachtet, 'delves into the depths'; **Tiefe** being acc. Strehlke Wb., gives the meaning of **trachtet** more exactly as **sich bemüht, dort hinein zu gelangen.**

1331. Bei .... Herrn, 'in case of you (infernal) gentlemen.' Faust knows that he has to do with a devil, since it was the holy symbols that brought him to terms.

1334. Fliegengott, Verderber, Lügner. The first translates Beelzebub, the name of a Philistine god worshiped at Ekron. The name means 'lord of the fly,' the god having been probably at first an averter of insect-pests, like the Greek Ζεὺς ἀπόμυιος. In some MSS. of the New Testament the name is given to Satan, the prince of devils. **Verderber** translates Apollyon (Ἀπολλύων), the 'Destroyer' of Rev. ix. 11, where it is Greek for the Hebrew Abaddon. **Lügner** is not a translation of any devil's name, but in John viii. 44, we read that 'the devil is a liar (ψευστής) and the father of it ' (i. e., of lying).

1336. Mephistopheles means that in doing what *men* call 'the bad ' (cf. ll. 1342-3) he is doing what is, in his own opinion, a good and rational work. He must by no means be understood as admitting that his mischief-making is overruled for good by a higher power.

1347. die kleine Narrenwelt, 'the little fool-world'; a humorous transposition of **die närrische Kleinwelt,** 'the foolish little-world,' 'the silly microcosm,' i. e. man. See App. III.

1349–52. Mephistopheles here speaks as Prince of Darkness, a quality which he derives from the Persian Angra-Mainyus, or Ahriman. Cf. Intr. p. lxxv.

1353–8. The argument is: Light has no original independent existence of its own, being a mere parasite of 'bodies.' (Light is manifested only in connection with bodies that emit or receive it.) But bodies are destined to dissolution. The final result must be, therefore, that light will perish, leaving primeval darkness in possession of the field.

1354. Verhaftet klebt, 'cleaves fast.'

1360. im Großen, 'on a grand scale.'

1364. plumpe, 'clumsy.' Mephistopheles has no eye for the world as a cosmos.

1365. so viel .... unternommen, 'much as I have already undertaken,' i. e., in spite of all my past exertions.

1366. ihr beizukommen, 'to affect it,' 'to do it any harm.' Ihr resumes the antecedent part of was in l. 1363, but takes the gender of Welt.

1368. Geruhig ; = ruhig.

1370. dem .... anzuhaben, 'there's no getting the better of it.'

1374. Der Luft; dat. of separation with sich entwinden, 'start forth.'

1377. Flamme. Only in the fire does no life exist. Mephistopheles can ignore salamanders, for they are of his household.

1378. Aparts; adj. from Fr. à part, 'apart,' 'private.'

1382. vergebens .... ballt, 'clenches with vain malignity.'

1386. Die nächstenmale, 'on future occasions.' Mephistopheles assumes already that they are to see more of each other, but 'this time,' for some unexplained reason, he wishes to be excused. Cf. the introductory note to the next scene.

1392. Ein .... gewiß, 'a chimney is also a sure reliance for you.'

1393. Gesteh' ich's nur, 'just let me confess'; imperative subjunctive. Cf. Brandt, § 284, 1.

1395. Drudenfuß, 'drude's foot'; a magical symbol in the shape of a five-point star (pentagram, pentalpha), designed to keep away evil spirits. The drude of German mythology was a female incubus or nightmare that injured people, especially children, in their sleep. (Later, the name became = Hexe or Unhold.) To keep her off, the magic pentagram was carved or painted on the cradle, bedstead or threshold. As the drude had swan's feet, the pentagram was called 'drude's foot,' from the resemblance to her footprints. Cf. Grimm Wb., II., 1454–5. The Pythagorean pentagram, says E. B. Tylor, is a 'magic symbol still to be seen in every country from Ireland to China.'

1404. wärſt denn du, 'can it be then that you are?' Dubitative subjunctive.— The efficacy of the pentagram depends on the perfect closure of the angle that is presented to the spirit.

1405. das iſt .... gelungen, 'that's a lucky accident.' The thought is the same as in l. 1403, but that refers to the imperfection in the pentagram, this to its effect in imprisoning the devil.

1413. Rechte, 'laws.'

1416. rein, 'undiminished,' 'in full.'

1417. abgezwackt, 'nipped off,' 'subtracted.'

1418. das iſt .... zu faſſen, 'that (i. e., such an inviolable agreement) is not to be dispatched so quickly.' For the use of faſſen, cf.: Ich werde mich kurz faſſen, 'I shall be brief'; der Brief iſt kurz zu faſſen, 'the letter is to be made short.'

1420. bitt' ich .... höchſt, 'I really do entreat you.' The adverb hoch und höchſt has the force of a superlative to ſehr in ich bitte ſehr. It is of very rare occurrence.

1423. mir .... ſagen, 'to tell me the news.' Gute Mähr', M. H. G. guotiu mær, lit., 'good tidings,' is a stereotyped phrase for the entertaining 'news' a visitor may have to relate.

1438. Einerlei, 'monotonous round.'

1441. leeres Zauberſpiel, 'empty trick of magic.' The meaning is that Faust will not only hear the music of the spirits, but will see the pictures they describe, smell the grapes, taste the wine, and experience a sensuous ecstasy.

1445. voran, 'in advance'; here = vorher.

1446+. Geiſter; the same spirits as in l. 1258+. The opportunity they have been waiting for (ll. 1264 ff.) has now come. Their song is an Einſchläferungslied, or 'lullaby.' They put Faust asleep with their music, and at the same time conjure before his vision a series of entrancing pictures that melt together like the visions of a dream. What they sing he sees while sinking into a dreamy trance. As the magic takes effect, the walls of the dingy study seem to vanish and he is under an open sky of supernatural loveliness. The air fills with hovering angels, and the land-scape becomes a great vineyard, with pensive vintagers exchanging love-vows among the vines. From numberless wine-presses rivulets of wine fall, broaden to rivers and flow away toward the 'isles of the blest,' whence come sights and sounds suggestive of boundless happiness.

1448. **Wölbungen;** the vaulted ceiling of Faust's Gothic study (cf. l. 353+).

1449. **Reizender;** not 'more charming' than the 'arches,' for they are not charming at all (cf. ll. 6928 ff.). The comparison is between the be-clouded sky, as it appears at first, and the blue ether.

1455. **Mildere,** 'milder,' i. e., shining with a softer light than the natural sun. These suns do not hide the stars.

1456. **darein;** 'in' upon the scene; not here = darin.

1459. **Beugung;** a loose appositive to Schöne. The angels, as they float past, seem to bend over the dreamer as they hover above him, exciting in him a longing to follow them.

1482. **Genügen,** 'satisfaction,' 'delight.' 'About the delight of ver-dant hills' = about the delightful verdant hills. So Grimm Wb., IV., 3512. Strehlke's um die genügend vorhandenen Hügel is too tame.

1483. **Geflügel;** the birds in the air. A sip of the wonderful wine sends them away in an ecstatic flight toward the source of all blessedness.

1487-8. **hellen Inseln,** 'the bright isles'; i. e., the isles of the blest.

1490. **Gauklend,** 'moving up and down,' in rhythmic spell.

1505. **Huld;** gen. dependent on Ferne. As Faust's vision ends in dreamless sleep, and the figures pass from his view, they seem to be moving off, in their several ways, toward the far-away stars, which are for them sources of life, love and gracious protection.

1516-7. Folk-lore associates the devil with pestiferous, ugly and uncanny animals, especially those of nocturnal habits.

1522. **bannte.** The tense refers back to l. 1393. The 'point' really 'confines' him still, until the rat has done its work. Cf. note to l. 1404.

1525. **Fauste;** the Lat. vocative, used, as in the puppet-plays, with a touch of humor.

1526. **abermals,** 'again'; his first disappointment was with the Earth-Spirit.

1527. **der geisterreiche Drang** = das reiche (zahlreiche) Gedränge der

𝔊𝔢𝔦𝔰𝔱𝔢𝔯; viz., those he has just seen in his vision. The meaning of the somewhat obscurely phrased thought in ll. 1527–9 seems to be: Was there no reality behind all this except a dream and the actual escape of a poodle-dog?

𝔖𝔱𝔲𝔡𝔦𝔯𝔷𝔦𝔪𝔪𝔢𝔯 (²).

This scene, taken in connection with the preceding, suggests certain dramaturgical questions. The main object of the preceding scene is of course to pave the way to the compact. Why, then, when Mephistopheles has come on purpose to find an opportunity to lead Faust 'in his way' (l. 314), should he suddenly assume (l. 1387) the rôle of reluctant prisoner and in the same breath (l. 1386) take it for granted that he and Faust are to meet frequently, when he has not yet been invited to come again? And when the subject of a compact is brought up, why should *he* be eager to postpone it (l. 1420) and beg to be excused for this time without giving any reason for his desire? Why should he resort to a trick to effect his release and then voluntarily return? And since Faust is perfectly willing that he should go (ll. 1390–3), why the elaborate hocus-pocus of the pentagram, the lullaby and the rat?

Add to this the fact that 'Study' (2) assumes all along that Faust and Mephistopheles are old acquaintances. Mephistopheles knocks like any ordinary visitor and assumes a familiar hectoring tone (l. 1531). Faust recognizes the knock and concludes that he is to be 'plagued again,' though we have heard of no plaguing before. He submits to the teasing like one accustomed to such nonsense, and is not in the least surprised to see his visitor. Nothing is said about the trick that had so strangely ended their recent interview. Mephistopheles knows that Faust is subject to the 'blues' (l. 1534), and has come, dressed as a gay young squire, to drive them away. But in the preceding dialogue Faust's characteristic 𝔊𝔯𝔦𝔩𝔩𝔢𝔫, as *we* know them, do not appear; his talk is sober and sensible. Mephistopheles knows of Faust's having meditated suicide (l. 1580). Each has definite and particular knowledge of the other's character and ways. Faust knows what kind of diversions the devil will have to offer (ll. 1678 ff.). It is assumed (l. 1746) that Mephistopheles knows about the Earth-Spirit as a being of rank superior to his own. The devil is perfectly familiar (ll. 1835 ff.) with Faust's professional life. — In short, one can hardly read the scene without feeling that the author of it must have had in view a Faust and a Mephistopheles who have had much more to do with each other than is now provided for in the text.

The explanation is, no doubt, that the substance of 'Study' (2) took shape before 'Study' (1) was written. We have seen already that the early plan contemplated a number of pictures occupying the interval between the poodle's first appearance and Faust's abandonment of his professorship. 'Study' (2), but without the compact as we now have it, was conceived on the presupposition that a friendly relationship between Faust and Mephistopheles has been for some time established. It assumed that the devil has the *entrée* of Faust's house, has become familiar with his master's life, character and pursuits, and has had an opportunity to exhibit his 'arts.' Then, one day, he comes as gay young squire and persuades Faust to give up the scholar's life and 'see the world.'

Again: In the early plan Faust was thought of as constraining the reluctant devil to his service by the power of magic, and the devil was a tormentor; while in the revised plan of 1797 Mephistopheles was to come to Faust of his own accord and be a seducer. Cf. Intr. p. lx.

Now what we have in the latter part of 'Study' (1) is an attempt to blend, as well as might be, these contradictory conceptions and to provide the necessary presuppositions. The poet cuts the Gordian knot by simply letting both parties assume (ll. 1385–92), without obvious grounds on either side, that they are to be familiar friends, and then imputing to Mephistopheles a capricious desire to be 'excused for this time,' in order that an occasion may be provided for an exhibition of his 'arts.'

In making this adjustment, Goethe doubtless calculated that people would not scrutinize too closely the motives of the devil, or wonder much at his knowing things that a common mortal in his position would not know. Moreover, his sudden desire to be excused might be construed as due to a feeling on his part that Faust's religious mood was unfavorable to the tempter's purposes. Then, too, the lullaby might be taken as a diabolical lure pointing to the pleasures of time and sense.

1535. edler Junker, 'noble squire.' In introducing the devil as a gay cavalier, Goethe follows the popular Faust-drama. Creizenach, p. 143, conjectures that the practice began in Catholic Vienna, where the devil as monk, in accordance with the original legend, would not have been acceptable. But Junker Teufel, Junker Satan, etc., are found even in Luther and his contemporaries.

1536. Kleide, 'coat.'

1546-7. The thought is: I am too old to enter upon a frivolous world-tour as man of fashion, and too young to have reached the apathy of age; I have desires which I know that the 'world' can not gratify.

1549. Entbehren sollst du, 'thou shalt do without.' When Faust's 'confusion' is cleared up, he will learn to meet this 'eternal song' with a voluntary renunciation of the things one must 'do without.' Cf. ll. 11441 ff.

1559. eigensinnigem Krittel, 'peevish caviling.' Grimm, Wb., V., 2338, states that the word occurs here for the first time in German literature. Schröer thinks that Goethe may have got the term from Fräulein von Klettenberg, who is known to have used it in the form Krüttel.

1561. Lebensfratzen, 'goblins of life'; the petty cares and annoyances of daily existence, that disturb and irritate one, destroying the serenity of the mind, and rendering productive work impossible. These trials are conceived as tormenting goblins. That this is the meaning of the word appears from Eckermann, III., 162: 'On the Second Part of my *Faust* I can work only in the early hours of the day .... when the goblins of daily life (die Fratzen des täglichen Lebens) have not yet confused me.'

1562-5. Seemingly a reminiscence of Job vii. 13-14.

1569. nach außen, 'outwardly,' 'in the outer world.'

1573-8. The theme is: Happy he who dies in some moment of supreme excitement.

1583. Gewühle, 'frenzy.'

1584. süß bekannter Ton; the Easter music.

1588. Lock- und Gaukelwerk, 'alluring jugglery.' The ideals that men pursue appear to Faust in his bitterness like pleasing phantasms that 'confine' the soul in this 'cave of gloom' because, were it not for them, we should voluntarily leave it.

1591. hohe Meinung; man's high opinion of his own worth and destiny.

1595. **was .... heuchelt,** 'what cheats us in dreams.'

1604. **jener;** in the sense of Lat. *ille,* 'that well known.'

1607–26. A difficult and much disputed passage, the question being whether the spirits are good or bad. If they are bad, why do they 'mourn over lost beauty'? If good, why does Mephistopheles claim them in l. 1628? Probably the dilemma is best met in this way: Goethe imagines an order of spirits whose function it is, when there is an act of destruction, to bear the remains of that which was over into the realm of that which is not. As attendants upon the work of destruction, they are in one sense minions of the destroyer; at the same time they are not in sympathy with destruction, but are rather nature's pall-bearers and mourners at the funeral of beauty. They do their work while deploring the occasion of it. So Faust's curse, involving as it does a complete break with the moral order, is construed as a destruction of the world of beauty. The little sprites bewail the act and pray him to make good the damage by rebuilding the beautiful world in his own breast. This he can do by recovering his faith in life and in ideals of life.

1612. **Halbgott,** 'demigod.' To the 'little ones' the deed of Faust is like that of a Hercules with his club.

1614. **Trümmern;** usually **Trümmer** as *plurale tantum* from **das Trum.** But the fem. sing., **die Trümmer,** is very common, and the weak plu. **Trümmern** not rare.

1619. **Prächtiger;** factitive predicate with **sie.** 'Mighty son of earth, rebuild it more splendid.'

1625. **Lieder;** i. e., songs of congratulation on the part of the spirits.

1629–34. Mephistopheles deliberately perverts the counsel of the spirits in ll. 1622–3. The 'new course of life' they would have Faust 'begin' is a change of heart, of moral attitude. But Mephistopheles distorts their meaning into: Give up the professor's life and try the world.

1633. **Wo .... stocken,** 'where senses and juices stagnate'; i. e., where the senses and the blood become torpid.

1640. **Pack,** 'rabble.'

1641. **keiner von den Großen,** 'none of the great ones,' i. e., only a subordinate. Such was in fact Goethe's early conception of Mephistopheles.

1647. **mach' ich dir's recht,** 'if I suit you.'

1652. um Gotteswillen, 'gratuitously.'

1661. Schlägst du .... Trümmern, 'when you first demolish this world,' i. e., the present earthly life. The end of life is conceived as an act of world-demolition; cf. ll. 1608 ff.

1665. Kann. The verb has a strange sound, since it seems to imply that Faust is anxious to end his earthly life, joys, sorrows and all (for ihnen can not well refer to Leiden exclusively), whereas the connection requires the line to mean simply: 'When I have done with this world.' Unless we resort to Düntzer's too easy solution, that kann is a misprint for muß, soll or werd', we shall have to regard kann ich erst as used loosely for bin ich im Stande, 'when I am in a position,' 'when the time comes.'

1667–70. Logically Faust's indifference to the life beyond is out of place in a dialogue with the devil. What we really hear in these lines, however, is the youthful Goethe arguing in the tone of his time against the religious *Jenseitigkeit,* which busies itself with curious speculations about the life to come. It is noteworthy, however, that the Faust of the legend is at the same time intensely curious about hell and its denizens, and a skeptic with regard to the existence of hell. Cf. Intr. pp. xiii, xiv.

1678. Doch hast du, 'but you have, haven't you?' With the question-mark after l. 1685, ll. 1678–85 must be read with a sarcastic rising inflec-tion. Faust rehearses ironically the stock-in-trade of jugglers' tricks with which he assumes that Mephistopheles will try to amuse him: sham food, illusory liquid gold, sleight-of-hand gambling games, and phantasms of love and glory. It is worth noting that Mephistopheles does actually pur-vey the most of these pleasures. Thus we have sham wine in l. 2291, sham gold in ll. 5711 ff.; while Faust as husband of Helena and transient king of Arcadia gives us the phantasms of love and honor.

1686–7. Zeig'. The mood is sarcastic: 'Come now, show me your wonderful trees,' etc. In C. M. (Scheible, II., 84) we read that 'Faust's pleasure-garden was almost like paradise; for the foliage and grass, min-gled with all sorts of trees, kept green the whole year long. The trees too would suddenly, in a moment, put forth fruit different from their natural fruit.'

1691. was Guts, 'something good'; i. e., something really satisfying and not a mere sham or phantasm.

1692. Faulbett, 'bed of ease,' 'lazy couch'; 'Laying one's self upon a bed of ease' is a symbol of perfect satisfaction with the egoistic pleasure of the moment.

1694. mich .... belügen, 'beguile me with blandishments.'

1698. Topp, 'agreed'; usually **Topp.** — **Schlag auf Schlag** means 'shake again.' Faust offers his hand twice.

1700. Verweile doch, 'pray tarry.' Faust uses these words in l. 11582, but not to the *passing* moment and not while stretched upon a 'bed of ease.' — On the compact, cf. Intr. pp. lxxi, lxxii.

1705. der Zeiger fallen. Some of the early water-clocks were so constructed that the hour-pointer would rise steadily along a bar for twenty-four hours and then drop back. The 'falling of the hand' thus marked the end of a fixed period.

1710. Wie ich beharre, = sobald ich beharre, 'as soon as I stagnate' — I am a slave anyway, i. e., no longer a free, self-determining man.

1712. Doctorschmaus; the supper given by a student on taking his doctor's degree. As the text stands, we are left to imagine the scene; but in Par. p. 11 ff. we find a sketch of a doctoral disputation, which would naturally have been followed by a **Schmaus.** This was one of the professional scenes at one time contemplated by Goethe and then dropped; for the reason, probably, that a third episodical picture of university life (in addition to the Wagner dialogue and the student scene) appeared unnecessary. Or perhaps he found that the scene did not work out well.

1714. Um .... willen; a formula used in asking for a written agreement, and meaning, according to Grimm Wb., VI., 417, für alle Fälle, i. e., 'to provide for all contingencies,' 'to guard against accidents.'

1716–30. The logic of this difficult passage seems to be this: The word of a *man* is as good as his bond. It is indeed strange that we should be held to our course, in the tempestuous flood of this life, by so slight a thing as a promise, but so it is. This curious notion of honor is implanted in us, and I have no desire to be rid of it. It pays to follow it at any cost. But most men reverence a formal document; very well, then, how will you have it? — The formal written agreement is made much of in the Faust-books, in Marlowe, and in the puppet-plays. So also Faust's honesty is emphasized. An Erfurt legend (Scheible, V., 488) makes a certain monk named Klinge endeavor to convert him at the last, promising to say mass for him. Faust replies: 'Mass begone! .... The devil has honestly kept

his word with me, and so I will also keep my word and written agreement
with him.' Whereat Scherer, *Faust-Buch*, p. XII, is reminded of the saying
of Tacitus: 'So great even in a bad cause is German tenacity. They themselves call it fidelity.'

1719. **ſchalten** (mit), 'govern,' 'be a law unto.'

1722. **dieſer Wahn**, 'this strange conceit'; i. e., this sense of honor,
of **Treue**.

1728. **Das Wort . . . . Feder**, 'the word dies in the very act of writing.' The somewhat fanciful thought is, that when an agreement is 'reduced to writing,' the seat of potency is at once transferred in the minds
of men from the impalpable word of honor, where it ought to be, to the
parchment on which it is written and the wax with which the document is
sealed.

1737. **Tröpfchen Blut.** So in the legend and the puppet-plays; but
the custom of confirming solemn agreements with blood is much older than
the Faust-legend. Loeper says that its use in compacts with the devil is
a parody of the blood in the Christian sacrament.

1739. **Fratze**, 'mummery.' The thought is: Let the farce be carried
out.

1741–59. Faust would in a sense 'break the agreement,' if he were to
hold back and give the devil no chance to satisfy him. So he gives his
assurance that he will do his best to carry out his part of the program;
i. e., that he will cut loose from his present existence and engage with all
possible fervor in the business of 'seeing what life is.'

1748. The sense is: As thinker I have reached the end of my course.

1752–3. The thought is: Produce your marvels; I'll take them as
they come and not play the rationalist with you.

1759. **Nur . . . . Mann**, 'without any cessation the (true) man keeps
doing.' **Der Mann** here = **der echte, tüchtige Mann**, as in **Da rühre ſich
der Mann**. Cf. the numerous examples in Grimm Wb., VI., 1562. The
general thought is well illustrated in a saying of *Dicht. u. Wahr.*, *Werke*,
XXVII., 12: **Er hätte mir nur ſagen dürfen, daß es im Leben bloß auf's
Thun ankomme, das Genießen und Leiden finde ſich von ſelbſt. — Nur**
limits **raſtlos**; 'not otherwise than restlessly,' i. e., without any cessation
whatever.

1763. The thought is: May the program which so pleases you now in
anticipation suit you when you come to carry it out.

1765–75. Faust hastens to correct the impression, very natural from what he has just been saying, that he hopes for enjoyment from the new career. It is to be a wild 'reel' through the world in quest of experience, the painful as well as the pleasant. He expects to be bored and to suffer, but he will accept that as a part of his destiny, for his desire is to feel in his own being all that men have ever felt anywhere. Cf. Intr. p. l.

1766–7. ſchmerzlichſtem .... Verdruß. The triple oxymoron contains this sense: I will play the rôle of pleasure-seeking sensualist and suffer pain and hate myself in so doing. Soulless sensuality indulged in, as a matter of experience, by a man capable of deep feeling, becomes 'enamored hate' rather than love, and 'exhilarating disgust' rather than true enjoyment.

1770. With this line Fgm. begins abruptly, though a large part of what precedes must also have been in existence in 1790. As to Goethe's probable reasons for publishing the lines 1770–1867, while suppressing what goes before, see Intr. p. l.

1774. erweitern. This idea of infinite self-expansion was a favorite conception with the youthful Goethe. Cf. the lines, addressed to Nature, from his poem *Künstlers Abendlied*, written in 1774:

> Wirſt alle meine Kräfte mir
> In meinem Sinn erheitern,
> Und dieſes enge Daſein hier
> Zur Ewigkeit erweitern.

So also in *Prometheus*, I., the hero says: Vermögt ihr mich auszudehnen, zu erweitern zu einer Welt? Cf., again, *Faust*, ll. 641, 3285, and 3289.

1775. Zerſcheitern. On the meaning of this word in relation to the compact, cf. Intr. p. lix.

1776–84. To Faust's grandiose talk of a world-embracing experience, Mephistopheles replies humorously that he has been acquainted with the world a long time and has discovered that only God can know it as a whole. Other beings must be content with limitations. The hopeless task of knowing the world as a whole he conceives under the image of attempting to digest a mass of indigestible leaven ('sour dough').

1784. Und euch .... Nacht, 'and for you only day and night (i. e., the alternation of day and night) is suited.' Düntzer quotes from *Meister*,

Werke, H., XVII., 372 : Wo ist vor ihm (Gott) etwas Hohes oder Tiefes, etwas Helles oder Dunkles? Wir nur haben ein Oben und Unten, einen Tag und eine Nacht.

1785. Das läßt sich hören, 'that sounds plausible.'

1789–1800. The thought is : The only way to be all-things-in-one is to become the theme of a poet.

1792. Ehren-Scheitel, 'honorable pate'; *vertex honoratus,* says Grimm, Wb.

1804. Menschheit . . . . erringen. To 'win the crown of humanity' is evidently from the context, only a new phrase for Faust's dream of partaking personally in the experience of all mankind.

1816–7. ihr seht . . . . sieht, 'you see things as people just *see* them'; i. e., you see things as they *appear*, you take a superficial view. The logic of what follows is : Out upon your repinings over human limitations ! To be sure, you have the bodily organs of a man, and you can not be anything but a man. But, after all, that is *yours* which serves your pleasure, and pleasure, not speculation, is what life is for.

1825. die meine ; for the rime's sake instead of die meinen.

1830. Kerl der speculirt. Cf. Scherer, *Goethe's Frühzeit,* p. 69, who quotes from Herder : Speculation als Hauptgeschäfte des Lebens — welch elendes Geschäfte !

1832. bösen Geist. It is familiar Germanic folk-lore that animals may be bewitched by elves and dwarfs. See Grimm, D. M., I., 381.

1837. Die Jungens. The Low German plu. in *–s* (see Brandt, § 60) occurs several times in *Faust.* Cf. Fräuleins in l. 3020, and Mädels in l. 3525.

1838. Nachbar Wanst, 'neighbor Paunch'; Mephisto's name for a commonplace, fat and self-complacent pedagogue.

1840–41. Because he would be driven from his position for heterodoxy. There is evidence that Goethe at one time thought of representing Faust as suffering in that way. Cf. ll. 590–3. 6230–8, and Intr. p. xxxi.

1842. Gleich, 'this moment.'

1844. wartet lange. Apparently the boy has but just arrived. We are to imagine, probably, that he had called earlier and been asked to wait outside until Professor Faust should be at leisure.

1851–67. On this soliloquy cf. Intr. p. li. It has underlying it the early conception of Mephistopheles, and was written before the compact had taken shape. The devil that speaks here is a tormentor who is quite sure of his victim and not at all concerned to *win* Faust by satisfying him. His program is not to satisfy, but to stupefy. In retaining the soliloquy, Goethe of course counted upon the interpretation that Mephistopheles here speaks his true character, having been playing the hypocrite hitherto. The fact is, however, that we shall hear very little henceforth of the devil who speaks here, or of the program that he lays down for himself.

1852. allerhöchſte Kraft. The devil of the Prologue (l. 284) thinks, or professes to think, that man's 'reason' is a delusion.

1861. Unbedeutenheit, 'insignificance'; for Unbedeutendheit, after the analogy of Anweſenheit, Beklommenheit, etc.

1862. zappeln, ſtarren, kleben, 'struggle, relax effort, stick fast.' The verbs denote three stages in the progress of a man becoming gradually accustomed to contact with something vile or dangerous.

1863. Unerſättlichkeit. The dat. means 'for' in the sense of 'for the delusion of,' 'as a decoy for.'

1866. übergeben. The Faust of the early plan was to 'give himself over' to the devil, but the Faust of the compact simply makes a wager with the devil.

1867. The meaning is: A man of such insatiable and ungovernable desires must have gone to ruin, even without a formal surrender to the devil.

1868–2050. On the early version of this scene and the revision for Fgm., cf. Intr pp. xxxix and li; also p. l, footnote. Otto Pniower, in V. L., IV., 317, makes it appear probable that the original scene, as it appears in U., consists of two parts separated in their composition by a considerable interval, the juncture being at what is now ll. 1903–4. The first part was comparatively vulgar and *burschikos*, while the second dealt more with the intellectual side of student life and contained satire of a higher order. On the revision, this first part was in the main omitted and the second considerably expanded. These changes have left traces upon the text as it now stands. For the original text of U. see Appendix II.

1868. allhier = hier. The word was archaic even in Goethe's youth. The student tries to talk like a book.

1874. Habt ihr .... umgethan, 'have you been about elsewhere,' i. e., have you called on any other professors? U. has hier, i. e., in this city, instead of ſonſt.

1875. The student, full of his momentous errand, does not answer the question put to him.

1879. was Rechts. Cf. l. 371, note. — **hieraußen,** 'out here.' The student comes from another 'land' (kingdom, duchy, principality) than that in which the university is situated.

1896–7. In U. this question comes much later (after a dialogue about the besetting dangers and trials of student life), and the boy in reply announces that he is going to study medicine. Here he replies more vaguely so as to give an opportunity for a satirical review of all four faculties.

1901. Wissenschaft und Natur, 'science and nature,' correspond roughly to what we should now call the historical and the natural sciences. But the student does not himself know just what he means.

1903. The thought is: You must not waste your time.

1904. dabei, 'in for it.'

1908. der Zeit. The gen. with **gebrauchen,** common in the classics, is now well-nigh obsolete.

1909. Ordnung, 'system.' As Leipzig freshman writing to his friend Riese (*Briefe*, I., 14), Goethe prefaces a list of his dissipations with the remark: **Ich brauche Kunst um fleißig zu sein.**

1911. Collegium Logicum, 'course in logic.' Mephistopheles here gives the 'correct' professorial advice. Logic was at this time regarded as a drill study of especial value as a general propædeutic. In U. this whole speech comes right after the student's announcement that he is to study medicine.

1913. spanische Stiefeln. The plu. is now usually strong. The 'Spanish boot' was an instrument of torture that found favor with the Inquisition (hence the name 'Spanish'). It consisted of an iron case which enclosed the leg and compressed it, wedges being driven between the leg and the boot.

1914. bedächtiger, 'more deliberately.'

1916. die Kreuz und Quer, 'hither and thither'; a fem. substantive made by taking the adverbs **kreuz** and **quer** together as one word and forming from them a noun upon the analogy of **die Quere.** The construction is acc. of the way, with **hinschleiche.**

1918–41. The point of the satire is that logic, while parading itself as the science of thought, does not teach one to think new thoughts, but only to unravel the thoughts one already has. ‘ In logic it struck me as odd,’ writes Goethe in speaking of his Leipzig experiences, ‘that I was expected thus to pull to pieces, simplify and, as it were, destroy those mental operations which I had performed from youth on with the greatest ease, and to do this in order that I might understand the right use of them’; *Werke*, XXVII., 53.

1919. **auf einen Schlag,** ‘at a stroke,’ i. e., all at once, without any analytic process.

1934. **aller Orten,** ‘everywhere’; adv. gen. of place, **Orten** being the old weak plu.

1935. The thought is: Logic makes unravelers, not weavers.

1940. **Encheiresin naturae,** ‘nature’s encheiresis,’ i. e., procedure, *modus operandi*, Gk. ἐγχείρησις. The provenience of the phrase was long a puzzle until Lippmann showed conclusively in the *Chemiker-Zeitung* for 1907, p. 461, that Goethe here borrows from the *Institutiones Chemiae* of J. R. Spielmann, who was his teacher at Strassburg (cf. *Werke*, 27, 238). In discussing chemical analysis Spielmann makes a distinction between ‘products’ and ‘educts,’ the latter being ‘parts’ which were present in the original substance but were held together by a ‘bond’ (*vinculum*) of which nothing is known except that it is ‘not mechanical.’ This ‘bond’ (chemical affinity), which Boerhave called *spiritus rector*, is ‘driven out’ by the analytic process, and only the ‘parts’ remain. Wherefore, says Spielmann, it is futile and presumptuous for chemists to suppose, since ‘nature has many encheireses for uniting substances,’ that they can duplicate her process by manipulating the ‘parts’ without the ‘bond.’

1941. **spottet ihrer selbst.** U. has **bohrt sich selbst einen Esel,** ‘makes a fool of itself.’ The idea is that the chemists only make themselves ridiculous by supposing that they can lay bare the ultimate secret of chemical union by a purely analytic process. There is something, namely, the ‘bond,’ which they can ‘drive out,’ but can not put back.

1950–53. The thought is that metaphysic is a matter of high-sounding names for ideas so very profound that the human brain can not understand them.

1955. **Nehmt wahr,** ‘take note of’, ‘give heed to’; **Ordnung** gen.

1956. **habt ihr**; not 'you have,' but 'take,' i. e., I advise you to take. U. has **nehmt**.

1959. **Paragraphos**; the sections or paragraphs into which the text-book is divided. The form is a Lat. acc. plu., to be pronounced **Para'= graphos**.

1961. **er**; the lecturer. We have to think of academic lectures consisting of comment upon a printed text-book.

1962–3. It was one of Goethe's grievances at Leipzig that he was expected to listen to and write down what he already knew.

1963. **der Heilig' Geist**; an archaic phrase preserving the old uninflected adj. There is really no elision.

1972–79. These lines upon the study of the law are not found in U. Cf. Intr. p. li. The charge is that jurisprudence is the study of precedents rather than of justice or natural right. The student must occupy his mind with laws that originated far away in time and space (German jurisprudence is based upon the Roman law) and have survived the conditions that gave them birth; so that legislation which was once reasonable and beneficial may be absurd or even harmful. The nature of the study here described appears clear from a passage of *Dicht. u. Wahr.* (*Werke*, XXVII., 235), in which Goethe speaks of the contrast between the universities of Leipzig and Strassburg. At the latter his mentor said to him: 'It is not asked (here in France) how and where a law originated and what was the inner or outward occasion of it; we do not inquire how it has been modified by time and custom, or how far it may have been actually perverted by false interpretation or wrong judicial usage. In such investigations the learned quite properly spend their lives; but we concern ourselves with that which is at present.'

1972. **Gesetz' und Rechte**, 'statutes and laws' (*leges et jura*).

1986. **verborgnes Gift**, 'hidden poison'; heterodox views which the student is in danger of absorbing into his system unawares.

1998. **bereiten,** 'prepare,' 'devise.'

2000. **Jota**; a dissyllable.

2008. **Läßt .... fühlen,** 'one can the sooner feel his own way further.'

2012. **groß' und kleine Welt**; here simply a phrase for 'all the universe.' In l. 2052 it is used more definitely.

2019. **noch,** 'moreover.'

2024–6. The meaning is that woman's ills all have their seat in her sexual nature. — It is here that Mephistopheles begins to 'play the genuine devil' (l. 2010).

2029. Ein Titel; i. e., you must first become an M. D.

2031. Zum Willkomm' .... Siebenfachen, 'then by way of welcome (i. e., at the very outset) you have only to reach out your hand for all sorts of favors.' Goethe conceived Willkomm' as an abbreviated Willkommen.

2039. Grün, goldner. The colors seem contradictory, but Goethe is fond of using golden in the sense of 'lovely,' 'precious.' Thus Frau von Stein is addressed as goldne Frau. Grün is, of course, the color of the living tree, as grau is that of ashes and death.

2048. Eritis .... malum, 'ye shall be as God, knowing good and evil'; part of the serpent's promise in Gen. iii. 5, where, however, the Vulgate has dii, 'gods,' instead of Goethe's Deus. Schröer supposes the change due to Luther's translation, which has: Ihr werdet sein wie Gott.

2049–50. The meaning is: Let yourself be beguiled by the devil (as Adam and Eve were) into forming fine hopes of the wonderful knowledge you are to acquire, and you will be disappointed as they were. The lines can be scanned after a fashion as hexameters, but the rime indicates that they were not consciously intended for hexameters. Bartsch, G.-J., I., 133, is probably right in calling them defective alexandrines.

2051–72. These lines, not found in U., were inserted in Fgm. to furnish the needed introduction to 'Auerbach's Cellar.'

2052. Die kleine .... die große Welt. The 'little world' is the world of common life, the 'great world' the Emperor's court.

2055. bei, 'with.' Fgm. has mit.

2056. leichte Lebensart, 'easy way-of-the-world,' savoir vivre.

2069. Feuerluft, 'hydrogen'; the 'inflammable air' of Cavendish's early experiments. The first hydrogen balloon was sent up at Paris Aug. 27, 1783, in which year Goethe's letters several times allude to his interest in the new art.

Auerbachs Keller.

For the original form of this scene, see Appendix II.; respecting
the revision of 1790, see Intr. pp. xxxix, li. On the strength of a letter
(*Briefe*, II., 292), in which Goethe speaks of having just 'made' a scene
of *Faust*, and in the same connection compares himself to a poisoned rat,
it has been supposed that 'Auerbach's Cellar' was written Sept. 17, 1775,
the date of the letter referred to. But the prose of the scene as it appears
in U., its crude art, its vivid Leipzig reminiscences, above all its undevel-
oped Faust, who is simply the self-complacent magician of the legend, all
point to a much earlier date for the composition of the scene. The letter
just spoken of may mean only that a part of the scene, say the rat-song
itself, was written at this time, or that the poet now first committed to
paper what he had long been carrying in his mind. Or it may refer to an
entirely different scene.

Auerbach's Hof as known to Goethe was a large, old building (it was
begun in 1530) designed especially for the accommodation of traders who
came to the great Leipzig fair. The 'Keller,' which still thrives under the
old name, was a wine-room in the basement. Just how old the tradition
is which connects Faust with this place, can not be stated. The Spies
book of 1587 does not mention Leipzig among the places visited by Faust.
In Widman, however, who is copied by C. M., we find (Scheible, V., 499)
a story of Faust's visiting the Leipzig fair with several companions. They
pass a wine-cellar (name not given), where some workmen are trying to
get up a cask of wine. Faust's party laugh at their efforts, whereat the
men become angry and abusive. Then the host promises the cask to any
one who will bring it up alone. At this Faust seats himself on the cask,
rides it up out of the cellar, and then taps it for the benefit of his friends.
This exploit was soon localized by the saga at Auerbach's Keller, where in
Goethe's time, as still to-day, various mementos of the famous ride are
preserved. Chief among these are two pictures, one showing Faust astride
the cask in presence of his wondering friends, the other representing the
subsequent drinking-bout.

Widman (Scheible, II., 511) also tells the story of the wine conjured
from four gimlet-holes bored in the edge of a table, but describes the

occurrence as taking place at the house of a friend of Faust at Erfurt. The trick of the grapes is not reported by Widman, but is found in the *Centuriae* of Philip Camerarius, which appeared in 1602. From this Latin work it found its way into various books, some one of which must have been known to Goethe. The substance of the story in Camerarius is that Faust, being once in a company of revelers, who ask to see a specimen of his powers, promises to make a vine full of ripe grapes grow out of the table. After charging them to remain quiet until he shall permit them to cut off the grapes, he produces his illusion. They all draw their knives and wait for the word. Then Faust breaks the spell, and they find they have prepared to cut off each others' noses.

2072+. **Zeche luſtiger Geſellen.** That the 'jolly fellows' are students is not expressly stated, but so we must doubtless regard them. In U. Altmayer is called Alten, and Siebel is referred to as a married man.

2074. **lehren Geſichter machen.** The thought is: Out upon those solemn faces of yours! **Ich will dich lehren** is a formula of reproach. Thus Goethe writes to his sister, *Briefe*, I., 32: **Ich will dich lehren ſo unfleißig zu ſein**, i. e., 'fie upon your laziness!' So in Eng. an angry parent says: 'I'll teach you to disobey me,' meaning, 'I'll teach you not to.'

2076. **lichterloh,** 'with bright flame'; from **lichter Lohe** taken as gen. of manner.

2079. **doppelt Schwein,** 'doubly hog'; viz., once for the 'stupidity' of the trick and once for its 'nastiness.' U. has **Eſel! Schwein!** To which Frosch replies: **Muß man mit euch nicht beydes ſeyn.**

2082. **Runda.** The word is a musical summons to 'join in' a song (**Rundgeſang**). Several old German songs have the refrain 'runda, runda, runda, dinella.'

2088. **A tara lara da;** a sort of preliminary do-mi-sol-do.

2091. The lack of unity and cohesion in the Holy Roman Empire was a favorite theme for satire in Goethe's day.

2099. **Qualität;** an obscene allusion to the legend of Pope Joanna and the precautions taken in the college of cardinals after her time to prevent the election of a woman to the papal chair. Cf. V. L., II., 596.

2101-2. An old folk-song begins with the exact words of l. 2101, and another runs:

Nachtigall, ich hör' dich singen,
Grüß' mein Schätzchen tausendmal.

2105–7. These lines seem to be Goethe's own. The waiting lover entreats admittance to the room of his sweetheart, who is to bolt the door after his departure in the morning.

2112. auf einem Kreuzweg. A cross-road is, in German folk-lore, an uncanny place. Cf. Schiller, *Jungfrau*, l. 112 :

.... tritt auf den Kreuzweg hin und pflegt
Geheime Zwiesprach mit der Luft des Berges.

2113. Blocksberg; the Brocken, to which on Walpurgis-Night (cf. note to the scene of that name) witches ride on the backs of devils (Buhlteufel) in the form of rams, he-goats, etc.

2120. ich weiß zu leben, 'I know what's what.'

2122. nach Standsgebühr, 'according to the requirements of (their) position.' The song is to be a love-song for lovers.

2123. Zur guten Nacht, 'as hoping for a jolly night.' Brander does not intend a good-night song thus early. The zu is used as in trinken wir eins zur glücklichen Reise. — On zum Besten geben, cf. l. 119, note.

2138. thät; indicative. The form is a dialectic survival of M. H. G. *tete* > *tet* (1. and 3. sing. pret. ind.). The a of the modern that belonged originally only to the plu. For other examples of thät as ind., cf. ll. 2145, 2869–70, 3578.

2139. genung. Goethe often uses genung, instead of genug, not only in verse where the rime requires it, but in his letters; e. g., *Briefe*, I., 231, 253.

2147. pfeift .... Loch. Auf or aus dem letzten Loch pfeifen is a figure derived from blowing a flute, and means 'to be at the end of one's wind,' 'to be at the last gasp.'

2172. ein klein Paris. In Goethe's time the Leipzig people plumed themselves on their refinement and *savoir vivre*. The city is called ein klein Paris in a book on Leipzig published in 1768 by a theological student who styled himself Baron von Ehrenhausen. See *Leipzig und seine Universität vor hundert Jahren* (Leipz.: Breitkopf u. Haertel, 1879), p. IX.

2174. Bei einem vollen Glase ; not a form of asseveration. Frosch means that one glass will loose the tongues of the two strangers and enable him to 'pump' them, i. e., find out where they come from and what their business is.

2184. hinft. The devil has one human foot and one horse's foot (cf. ll. 2490 and 2502), which makes him limp. Or, his lameness is due to his fall from the sky. Hinkebein, Lame-leg, is one of his names; cf. Grimm, D. M., II., 829. So Goethe's Satyros is a hinkender Waldteufel. Hephaestus-Vulcan was also lame.

2189. Rippach; a village a few miles southwest of Leipzig. In Goethe's day its name was used like our American 'Wayback.' Hans, or Hans Arsch von Rippach is John Lubber of Lubberton. The jest is at least as old as 1710; cf. G.-J., I., 435.

2192. das letztemal, i. e., on occasion of our last preceding visit.

2214. Sohn; to be pronounced Soh, thus riming with Floh. The dropping of the n is South German dialect. Cf. mei Soh, for mein Sohn, quoted in Zelter's letter to Goethe of Oct. 11, 1827.

2237. wir; i. e., we common people, who are not bound by court forms, or subject to the tyranny of parvenu court-favorites, — we can get rid of the fleas that trouble us.

2243. fein, 'deftly.'

2255. auch recht = schon recht; schon recht voll, 'right well filled.'

2256. Altmayer takes the strangers for wine-dealers from the Rhine.

2293-4. To be taken, seemingly, as the beginning of a catch familiar to the company. — Kannibalisch wohl, 'savagely, inordinately, happy.'

2304. Er; cf. note to l. 548.

2305. The sense is: I should think we'd better quietly get rid of him.

2323. hab' ich. In view of war in l. 2322 one might expect hatte. But we must suppose that Brander and Siebel hold each other's noses a second longer than the other pair, and that these words are spoken *during* the Auseinanderfahren of l. 2321+.

2332. Mein, 'well now'; a common exclamation of wonder. Grimm Wb., VI., 1919, supposes it to come from mein Geselle. But other phrases, like mein lieber Freund, or mein Gott, may also have had to do with its origin.

2336. eins; = jemand. So again in l. 7196.

Hexenküche.

THE relation of this scene to the general plan of the poem is discussed in Intr. p. xlvii. The only occasion for the scene, from a dramaturgic point of view, was to explain the astonishing change that was to take place in the character of Faust. It is easy to see, however, that the love-philtre did not necessitate a long and elaborate scene like the one we have. Mephistopheles might have been made to furnish the magic potion himself, as is hinted in ll. 2367 ff. But, since the brewing of love-potions was looked upon by popular superstition as peculiarly the business of witches, and witches are servants of the devil, it seemed plausible to take Faust to a witch for the needed elixir. This idea once adopted, the poet gave the rein to his fancy and worked out a very simple dramatic motive into an elaborate genre-picture. It suited his humor to abstract himself from the associations of classical art in Italy and let his imagination disport for a time among the grotesque superstitions of the North.

The details owe nothing whatever to the Faust-legend, but are the work of Goethe's imagination aided only by the general literature of witchcraft, and also, as commentators think, by certain paintings of the Flemish artists Teniers and Breughel. The 'baboons' of Teniers were famous, and in one of his pictures some of these animals are depicted as rolling a huge world-ball. There is no considerable amount of genuine folk-lore connecting apes with witches; but since the devil caricatures the works of God, and the ape is a caricature of man, it seemed logical to regard the ape as belonging to the devil's kingdom. So Goethe's apes imitate men, and, naturally enough, their talk and actions contain here and there a touch of satire. But we are not called upon to ponder very deeply over this satirical mimicry, or the glass ball, or the witch's multiplication-table. Goethe had from youth on a propensity for humorous mystification. He was fond of dressing up nonsense, or mingling sense and nonsense, in such a way as to convey a suggestion of portentous wisdom. The reader of *Faust* needs often to be on his guard against finding too much 'meaning' in the play of its author's poetic humor.

2338. **genesen,** 'recover.' Imagine Mephistopheles to have been saying that Faust's brooding reserve is a malady that requires a magic cure.

2342. **dreißig Jahre.** See Intr. p. xlvii.

2347. **klug,** 'sensibly'; because at the last (ll. 2345–6) Faust seems disposed to take the question of rejuvenation more seriously.

2349. **andern;** 'other' than that of magic.

2351–61. This somewhat irrelevant banter means that 'nature' (cf. l. 2345) provides no way of making a man young except to make him and keep him a child in experience. One who leads a simple, eventless life under primitive conditions remains 'young' until he is ready to die.

2358. **acht es .... Raub,** 'do not feel above.' **Für Raub achten** means 'to regard as a robbery, i. e., derogation, from one's dignity.' In Luther's Bible it translates the Gk. ἁρπαγμὸν ἡγεῖσθαι of Phil. ii. 6. Goethe writes to Schiller, Apr. 29, 1798: **Freund Meyer wird es auch für keinen Raub achten, zu dieser barbarischen Production (Faust) Zeichnungen zu verfertigen.**

2361. **Auf achtzig .... verjüngen,** 'to (make and) keep you young to your eightieth year.'

2369. **Brücken.** The devil of Germanic folk-lore builds bridges, sometimes that he may reach some object of his lust, sometimes at the request of men, in which case his reward is the soul of the first, or of every thirteenth, person that crosses the bridge. Cf. Grimm, D. M., II., 853.

2392. **Bettelsuppen,** 'soup for beggars.' The point of the satire appears from a passage in a letter of Goethe to Schiller, written July 26, 1797, in which he speaks of a then popular play as 'genuine beggars' soup, such as the German public loves.' Whence we see that **breite** means 'thin,' 'watery.'

2397. **schlecht ist's bestellt,** 'it (i. e., the distribution of wealth) is badly ordered.'

2398–9. The ape means that he only needs money to give him a reputation of 'sense.'

2401. **in's Lotto setzen,** 'take a risk in the lottery.'

2410. **Ich bin lebendig,** 'I am alive,' i. e., lively, spry. The ape jumps out of the way of the ball and advises his son to do likewise, lest it burst and kill him.

2417–8. These lines allude to the art of coscinomancy or divination by means of a sieve. It was employed commonly in Germany in the 16th and 17th centuries for the detection of thieves. A witch or other expert would take the sieve between the two middle fingers, speak an incantation, and pronounce the names of suspected persons. At the mention of the right name the sieve would begin to turn. There were also other methods. Cf. Grimm, D. M., II., 927.

2428. in Seſſel; for in'n, i. e. in den Seſſel. The contraction does not occur elsewhere in *Faust*, but is found in *Götz* repeatedly; e. g.: Ihr warft ſie dem Feind an Kopf; ſollſt du nicht in Streit — both from the first act.

2429–40. himmliſch Bild. Mephistopheles seeks to excite Faust's sensuality by showing him a vision of female beauty. There is no occasion to think of Helena, much less of Gretchen.

2442. bravo; in allusion to Gen. i. 31.

2452. leimen. The crown is as yet only cracked. The apes want the play-monarch to mend it, just as real monarchs mend their broken crowns, with sweat and blood — those of their subjects.

2464. aufrichtige. The ape-poets are called 'honest' because of their frank admission that ideas are with them a secondary consideration, a matter of luck. They chatter and rime, and may *happen*, now and then, to express a thought. The lines are aimed at jingling rimesters who have nothing to say.

2483. Was hält .... zu; = was hält mich davon ab, daß ich zuschlage. Cf. l. 1020.

2491. Raben. The Norse god Odin had two ravens, Huginn and Muninn (Thought and Memory), who brought him tidings of what was going on. Mephisto's ravens actually appear further on, in l. 10664.

2504. Junker Satan. Cf. l. 1535, note.

2507–9. A side thrust at the Age of Enlightenment. Men look on Satan as a myth; they have got rid of the Evil One, but not of the evil ones.

2518. schafft; the weak verb schaffen, in the sense of befehlen, is South German dialect.

2540–52. From behind her ape-pulpit, with ape-candelabra on either side, the witch, as priest, declaims from her big Bible — unctuous nonsense.

2543. gleich, 'even' i. e. an even number.

2556. manche Zeit; an unusual expression for viel Zeit.

2561–2. The devil refers here to the doctrine of the Trinity. Said Goethe to Eckermann, Jan. 4, 1824, in speaking of the world's reception of his ideas : ' I believed in God and nature, and in the victory of the noble over the bad. But that was not enough for the pious souls; I was also to believe that three are one and one three. But this was opposed to my instinctive feeling for truth.'

2563–6. The logic is : So they babble on, and no one interferes with them, because it is the nature of man to assume, when he hears words spoken, that they must have some meaning, though he does not understand it.

2567–72. The witch, still parodying the priestly tone, insists that her wisdom is not the wisdom of the world, but transcends reason. No use to *think* about it, it must be received by faith.

2581. Graben ; the taking of a ' degree ' would naturally be followed by conviviality. The thought is : He is no novice in the matter of strong drink.

2591. Lied. The witch gives Faust an incantation which will intensify the effect of the potion.

2601. Muster aller Frauen; the Helena of the legend. But of course *Goethe* was thinking of Gretchen.

2604. Helenen. Goethe makes the name He′lene, as here, or Hele′ne, according to the exigency of the meter.

Straße.

WITH regard to the Gretchen scenes in general, their earliest form and sequence, the names ' Margarete ' and ' Gretchen,' the omissions of Fgm., and the revisions and additions of the final version, see Intr. pp. xxv, xl, xlii–iv, lii–iv, lxii–vii, and lxxx–ii. The scenes are nowhere distinctly localized, but we may suppose that Goethe had in mind his native city.

2606. Meinen Arm und Geleit. Present approved usage would require Meinen Arm und mein Geleit. U. has Mein, i. e. Mein'n. — Respecting Ihr as pronoun of address, cf. note to l. 548.

2607. Fräulein. For Gretchen the word means ' fine young lady.' It was formerly applied only to persons of noble rank or high station. When its use was extended, gnädiges was prefixed to give the implication formerly given by Fräulein alone. — Weder .... weder, for weder noch, is colloquial.

2611. sitt= und tugendreich, 'modest and virtuous'; a very dubious compound = sittsam und tugendreich. There is no such word as sittreich, while sittenreich would not give the required meaning.

2614. die Tage der Welt, 'while the world lasts'; acc. of duration.

2617. kurz angebunden, 'snappish'; an expression derived, according to Grimm Wb., from the practice of giving savage animals a short tether. 'To be tied short' thus came to mean 'to be cross and unapproachable.' It is thus much the same as schnippisch above.

2623. vorbei. U. has herbei, giving the sense of 'crept up by,' instead of 'crept past.' The first seems better since he would hardly hear so much in merely creeping past.

2628. Hans Liederlich, 'Jack Profligate.' The adj. occurs in various phrases as the name of a dissolute person, i. e., Bruder Liederlich, Frau Liederlich, Monsieur Liederlich.

2630. dünkelt ihm, 'he fancies conceitedly'; a denominative verb from Dünkel, 'conceit.'

2633. Magister Lobesan, 'Master Worshipful.' Lobesan, changed from Lobesam, 'laudable,' was appended to a title at first as a serious, or mock serious, title of respect. Thus, Herr Ritter Lobesan (Wieland), Kaiser Rothbart Lobesan (Uhland), ein junges Weibchen Lobesan (Bürger). Magister Lobesan early became stereotyped as a sarcastic form of address to an academic graduate who showed himself inclined to dogmatize and 'lay down the law' (cf. Gesetz in l. 2634).

2639. was .... mag, 'what is possible.'

2642. sieben Stunden. U. has sieben Tage. The ground of the change and the nature of Faust's pressing business are not apparent.

2650. Brimborium, 'fol-de-rol'; a Latinization of Fr. *brimborions,* 'trifles,' 'knick-knacks.'

2652. wälsche Geschicht' ; in allusion to lubricious French novels, or perhaps to Italian tales in the manner of the Decamerone of Boccaccio.

2654. ohne Schimpf .... Spaß, 'joking and jesting aside'; an old alliterative phrase preserving the original meaning of Schimpf, i. e., 'jest,' 'pleasantry.'

2659. **Engelsſchaß,** 'heavenly creature'; one fit to be the sweetheart of an angel.

2674. **reüſſiren,** 'succeed'; Fr. *réussir*.

2677. **revidiren,** 'reconnoitre'; Lat. *revidere*.

Abend.

2699. **heil'gen Chriſt,** 'Christmas gift.' The German fiction is that the gift comes from the Christ-child, so that the gift itself is called a **heiliger Chriſt,** or **Chriſtkindchen;** so we sometimes speak of a child's Christmas-gift as his Santa Claus.

2706. **den Sand kräuſeln;** in allusion to the practice of sprinkling sand on the floor after scrubbing. Dainty house-keepers make ornamental patterns of the sand, — hence **kräuſelt.**

2709. **Wonnegraus,** 'rapturous awe.'

2711–2. **Hier bildeteſt (du) .... aus,** 'here (i. e., in the bed) thou didst bring to perfection the angel born here'; **eingeboren** in the sense of *innatus*, 'native' to a particular place.

2716. **entwirkte ſich,** 'wrought itself out.' The preceding **Weben** designates the silent, mysterious formative process by which the work was accomplished. It is doubtful whether a metaphor of weaving a tapestry-figure is intended.

2727. **Der große Hans,** 'the grand gentleman.' The phrase was much used in the 16th and 17th centuries in the sense of 'rich man,' 'gentleman,' in contrast with **kleiner Hans** or **Kleinhans,** 'common man.' Here it is sarcastic in the sense of 'big fellow,' one who puts on grand airs.

2732. **wo anders,** 'in another place.' Mephistopheles makes a mystery of the source of his treasures.

2736. The sense is clear from U., which has

Um eine Fürſtin zu gewinnen.

2737. **Zwar.** The logic seems to be: With such costly trinkets you might win a high-born 'child' (all women being children in their love of finery), instead of a humble, ignorant girl. To be sure, though, one is as good as another for our game.

2748. ſeht drein; not, 'you look on,' but simply, 'you look.' The verb is often so used by Goethe, e. g., in l. 2797. Cf. Grimm Wb., II., 773.

2759–82. In *Dicht. u. Wahr.*, *Werke*, XXVIII., 287, Goethe says that he recited 'The King of Thule' to Jacobi in the summer of 1774 as one of his 'latest ballads.' The poem was published, with music by Seckendorff, in 1782, the text agreeing in the main, but not exactly, with that now found in U., in which the first two stanzas run:

> Es war ein König in Tule
> Einen goldnen Becher er hett
> Empfangen von ſeiner Bule
> Auf ihrem Todtesbett.
>
> Der Becher war ihm lieber
> Trank draus bey jedem Schmaus.
> Die Augen gingen ihm über
> So offt er trank daraus.

These two stanzas, it will be seen, underwent a radical revision for Fgm., the others remained substantially unchanged.

2759. Thule; the *ultima Thule* of the Romans, best identified with Mainland of the Shetland Isles.

2763. Es ging .... darüber, 'he prized nothing more highly.'

2790. Schau'; South German dialect for ſieh.

2791. mein' Tage, 'in my life'; acc. of duration.

2800. man läßt's auch ſein, 'people pass it all by just the same.'

Spaziergang.

In U. the scene is headed Allee.

2806. daß ich's fluchen könnte; not 'curse it,' but 'use it to swear by.'

2808. So kein Geſicht = kein ſolches Geſicht.

2817. gar einen feinen = einen gar feinen.

2824. Befängt, 'makes befangen,' i. e., 'perturbs,' 'deprives of peace.' — **Zehrt auf,** 'consumes,' is to be taken literally. The mother believes that the possession of ill-gotten gains causes the body to wither.

2828. halt; a South German expletive having such meanings as frei-lid), bod), eben, wohl, gewiß, or, in Eng., 'indeed,' 'to be sure,' 'you know,' 'don't you see?' — **Geschenkter Gaul.** The German adage of the 'gift-horse' runs : Einem geschenkten Gaul sieht man nicht in's Maul.

2835. An allusion to Rev. ii., where blessings are promised 'to him that overcometh.'

2838. **übergessen.** Gessen, for geessen, is the earlier pple. of essen, gegessen having come into use as late as the 17th century. The form used here presupposes a separable sich überessen, pres. ich esse mich über ; but ich überesse mich is usual.

2843. **Strich ein ;** from einstreichen, 'to bag.'

2857. **mach',** 'hurry!' So in Lessing's *Nathan :* mach', erzähl', erzähle.

2858. **Häng' dich an ;** like our colloquial 'get in with.'

2859. **Brei.** Porridge is thick and moves slowly.

Der Nachbarin Haus.

2868. **auf dem Stroh ;** she is a 'grass-widow,' Strohwittwe.

2880. **Thät's ;** here subjunctive.

2882. **du.** Cf. note to l. 548.

2890. **Leuten sehen läßt.** The dat. is a Gallicism, Fr. *faire voir à quelqu'un.*

2892. **man macht . . . . vor,** 'we can also invent some story for her.'

2894. **Es geht . . . . Dingen,** 'there's something wrong about it'; more literally : 'It does not happen with things that are right.' Cf. *Clavigo,* act v.: Es müßte mit dem Teufel zugehen, 'the devil would have to be in it.'

2895+. **Vorhängel ;** the curtain before the peep-hole in the door.

2906. **Fräulein ;** cf. l. 2607, note.

2926. **Antonius.** The finest of the Paduan churches is the famous basilica of St. Anthony, where the bones of the saint rest in a splendidly decorated chapel. Hence the humor of giving the drunken vagabond Schwerdtlein a resting-place close to St. Anthony.

2933. **Schaustück ;** = Schaumünze, 'medal.'

2936. **bettelt.** Supply als es weggibt.

2954. **baß er . . . . hätte,** 'that he would deserve a worse fate still.' **Etwas auf der Zeche haben** is 'to have something on the score' against one. **Hätte** is potential subj. The sense is : He found that if he were to have his deserts he would be 'booked' for a worse fate than dying on a bed of filth.

2970. **euch ;** ethical dat. U. has instead **recht herzlich.**

2981. **ein schönes Fräulein ;** i. e., a courtesan. The following lines are a gross allusion to the 'Neapolitan evil' as the cause of Schwerdtlein's death.

2982 . **Napel,** from Italian Napoli, is used by Goethe also in *Tasso*, l. 3137, and in the *Römische Elegien.* The usual form is **Neapel,** from Νεάπολις.

2991. **Visirte** = **ausspähen,** 'I should look around.'

3020. **Fräuleins.** Cf. l. 1837, note.

Straße.

3025. **Will's fördern,** 'is it going to work?'

3028. **Nachbar' Marthen ;** i. e., **Nachbars Marthen,** which is the reading of Fgm. This manner of designating a neighbor's wife (or daughter) is common in popular speech. Thus Freytag writes : **Haft bu heut vielleicht Nachbars Röschen gesprochen?** And Matthison : **Den Hag, wo Nachbars Lotte zur Veilchenlese kam.** U. has **Nachbaar Marthen.**

3030. **Zum . . . . Zigeunerwesen,** 'for the business of a gypsy go-between' (hendiadys). The gypsy fortune-tellers were consulted especially in love-affairs.

3037. **Sancta Simplicitas,** 'sacred simplicity'; the words spoken by the martyr Huss when, at the stake, he saw an old woman throwing a fagot into the flames.

3040. **Da wärt ihr's nun,** 'in that case you would be one indeed,' i. e., if you were to insist on going to Padua.

3050. **Sophiste.** Mephisto's sophistry consists in his implication that the honest mistakes of the theological professor are on a par with deliberate falsehood.

3056. **Wird ;** supply **bie Rebe sein.**

3069. **Recht behalten,** 'to maintain that one is right,' 'to have the last word' in an argument.

3072. **weil ich muß.** In saying that he 'must' consent to the false-hood, Faust means that he is so under the domination of his passion for Gretchen that he can not help himself. He *must* have her, can not live without her; and as the proposed deceit promises to accomplish his desire, he can not allow himself to be balked by scruples of conscience.

Garten.

3081. **Incommodirt .... nicht,** 'don't put yourself out' by conde-scending to kiss such a hand.

3089. **raschen,** 'active.'

3098. **der Freunde häufig,** 'many friends.' The construction is rare, if not unparalleled, and seems due to a blending of **die Freunde** (acc.) **häufig** (i. e., **haufenweise,** 'in large numbers') **haben,** and **der Freunde viele haben.**

3114. **accurat,** 'economical.'

3116. **regen,** 'make a stir.'

3118. **vor der Stadt,** 'in the suburbs'; but Gretchen and her mother *live* in the city.

3122. **meine liebe Noth,** 'my blessed trials.' **Lieb** is used with a touch of irony in various phrases, like **die liebe Gewohnheit,** 'blessed habit,' **das liebe Einerlei,** 'the blessed routine.' So Goethe writes, *Briefe,* I., 233 (he has been speaking of his past illness and the trouble it gave to his friends: **Doch ich verdiente Mitleiden; ich hatte auch meine liebe Last.**

3173. **Es schien .... anzuwandeln,** 'it just seemed to come over him all at once.'

3174. **g'rade hin zu handeln,** 'to act his pleasure,' 'do as he pleased.'

3176. **begonnte.** In Goethe's youth this was the preterit form of **beginnen** that came most naturally to him; in the latter part of his life, **begann.** Cf. Grimm Wb., I., 1297.

3188–94. On the prose cf. note to ll. 468–74.

3198. niemand nichts. The double negation is colloquial, but is sometimes used by Goethe in dignified prose; e. g., in the *Campagne in Frank-
reich, Werke*, H., XXV., 60: In diesen Augenblicken, wo Niemand nichts
zu essen hatte u. s. w.

Ein Gartenhäuschen.

This scene is really a part of the preceding one, the summer-house
being in Martha's garden. Escaping, half in frolic, half in maidenly alarm,
from Faust's passionate declaration (ll. 3188–94), Gretchen runs into the
summer-house, and is at once followed by Faust. There is no change of
time, place or actors. That the scene has a separate heading (which it
has in U. also) is probably due to the fact that it took shape as a dramatic
picture by itself. There are also two other indications that, when it was
composed, the garden scene was not vividly present to Goethe's conscious-
ness. (1) In l. 3206, instead of von Herzen lieb' ich dich, Gretchen is made
to say, in U., schon lange lieb ich dich. (2) At the end of the scene, ll.
3213–4, Gretchen chides herself for standing 'abashed' before Faust and
saying 'yes' to all his wise talk. In fact, however, Faust has not talked
'wisely' at all (as he does later in the following scene), and *she* has been
loquacious. It is Faust who has said 'yes' to her. One is hardly satisfied
to call this a touch of nature and say that Gretchen only imagines that she
has appeared stupid. As to the textual change, Goethe would hardly have
put the comparatively neutral and tame von Herzen in place of the more
significant schon lange, had he not felt the latter as an incongruity, in view
of the close sequence of the two scenes.

Wald und Höhle.

The idea and genesis of this scene, its original position after the scene
'At the Well,' its later transposition to where we now find it, and the difficulties thus created, are discussed at some length in Intr. liii–iv and lxii–iii.

3217. Du gabst. This 'giving' can not of course refer to the occasion
of the Spirit's appearance in ll. 482–513, where nothing is given or prom-

ised. Nor is it likely that Goethe, so late as when these lines were written (1788–9), was planning a second citation of the Spirit by Faust. The right understanding of the matter is rather this: The Earth-Spirit is a symbol of nature, who gives to man all things that come to him. For this 'giving,' no appearance in personal form is necessary — just as Goethe thought that the best worship of Nature was a spiritual communion for which no visible symbol was needed. Cf. Intr. p. liii.

3222. **kalt ſtaunenden Beſuch**; the perfunctory visit of the gazing tourist.

3226. **meine Brüder.** The sense of man's kinship with all living things was with Goethe at first a mere poetic sentiment — a part of his youthful nature-worship. Cf. Werther's second letter: 'When I lie down in the tall grass by the falling brook, and, closer to earth, ... feel nearer to my heart the thronging multitude of the little world, the countless, inscrutable forms of worms and gnats, and feel the presence of the Almighty who created us in his image, etc.' — Later, the sentiment became a serious scientific opinion. Cf. the letter to Knebel, of Nov. 17, 1784: 'Man is most closely related to the lower animals,' etc.

3231. **ihrem Fall,** 'at its fall'; a kind of responsive dative.

3238. **ſilberne Geſtalten.** The 'silvery forms of the earlier world' are the oreads (**von Felſenwänden**) and dryads (**aus dem feuchten Buſch**) of the Greeks.

3249. **Genuß.** Cf. Intr. p. lxiii, foot-note.

3254. **Neuen;** *metri gratia* for **Neuem**.

3256. **am guten Tag;** = **an einem guten Tag,** 'on one of my good days.'

3265. **daß er mich ennuyirt,** 'for boring me'; Fr. *ennuyer.*

3268. **Kribskrabs,** 'hodge-podge,' 'confused medley.'

3270-1. The meaning is: If I had not called you away from your life of solitary brooding and morbid introspection, you would have committed suicide ere now. But see also the introductory note to the scene 'Before the Gate.'

3272-3. **Was haſt . . . . verſitzen,** 'what is the matter with you to be sitting out your days like an owl'?

3277. **Doctor.** A 'doctor' might be spending his time thus in the interest of science.

3285–90. On the imagery, cf. ll. 614 ff.

3286. mit . . . . burchwühlen, 'permeate with bodeful impetuosity.'

3287. Alle sechs Tagewerf'; i. e. 'all creation.'

3290. ber Erbensohn; nominative absolute.

3294. gesittet; to be taken as adj. with pfui. The sense is: It's all very well for you to pronounce your high-moral 'shame!'

3298. Gelegentlich . . . . vorzulügen, 'to delude yourself a little now and then'; namely, with these grand self-communings in the woods.

3300. abgetrieben, 'exhausted.' The word is sometimes applied to a horse tired from over-driving, or a wild beast exhausted by the chase. The idea is that human wit can not endure very long a life of solitary brooding and Faust is already 'again' (i. e., as in ll. 1544–1606) at the point of exhaustion.

3301. aufgerieben, 'used up.' The meaning is: You will be reduced to sheer insanity.

3312. ließ' es, 'it would become.'

3313. affenjunge; quoted in Grimm Wb. only for this passage and defined blutjung, i. e. 'very young.' It would seem as if bas affenjunge Blut were a comical transposition of ber blutjunge Affe, 'the young ninny.' In l. 3521, Gretchen is called a Grasaffe.

3318. Wenn ich . . . . wär'; the beginning of a well-known folk-song which continues:

> Unb auch zwei Flüglein hätt',
> Flög' ich zu bir.

3325. Gelt, 'indeed!' 'right you are!'

3334. Leib bes Herrn; the holy wafer of the sacrament.

3337. Zwillingspaar; in allusion to Song of Solomon iv. 5.

3345–69. These lines occur in U. in another connection, being spoken by Faust when on his way to visit Gretchen at night — the visit which was to result in Valentin's death.

3346. Laß; conditional imperative.

3352. bumpfen 'dim,' 'vague.'

3360. mußte. On the original implication of the tense cf. Intr. pp. liv, lxiii.

3367. Geh ein. When it was first written this meant 'go into Gretchen's house'; now it means 'go into the city.'

3369. **er;** i. e., Kopf, implied in Köpfchen. U. has es.
3371. **eingeteufelt,** 'diabolized.'

Gretchens Stube.

These stanzas are probably to be taken as a lyric monologue rather than a song. They seem to have been written originally as one in a *crescendo* of such monologues picturing Gretchen alone with her shame and sorrow; for the lines read naturally only on the presupposition that Gretchen has already fallen and been, at least temporarily, deserted by her lover. This desertion is now sufficiently provided for by 'Forest and Cavern,' and this may have been one of the reasons for inserting that scene where we now have it. On the other hand the scene stands in U., as in the final version, just before the 'catechization'; which requires it to be read under the presupposition of Gretchen's innocence. It appears possible that the scene was given its position originally in order to break the succession of three scenes in Martha's garden.

Marthens Garten.

In writing this scene the poet evidently presupposed a longer acquaintance between Faust and Gretchen than is implied in what precedes. Gretchen has had opportunity to find out that her lover does not go to church and is not devout in her way. She has 'long' been troubled (l. 3469) at seeing him in the company of Mephistopheles, etc.

In what Faust here says of religion we of course hear the youthful Goethe. In Kestner's *Goethe und Werther*, p. 35 ff., there is a description of Goethe as he appeared to Kestner after a short acquaintance at Wetzlar in the summer of 1772 — a description which, so far as it concerns religion, coincides remarkably with Faust's utterances. For example, Kestner writes: 'He doesn't go to church nor to communion (cf. ll. 3423–5); he is not what is called orthodox, but not from pride or caprice . . . . he does not like to disturb others in their settled ideas (cf. l. 3420); he honors

the Christian religion (cf. l. 3424), but not in the form in which our theo-
logians present it (cf. ll. 3428–9); he is eager for the truth, but cares more
for the feeling than the demonstration of it' (cf. ll. 3451–8). All this suggests (one can hardly say proves) that the catechization may be a poʼ
rendition of religious conversations at Wetzlar, with the imaginary tɪ
Faust-Gretchen-Mephistopheles replacing the real one Goethe-Lotte-Mercɪₑ
Cf. Mertens in G.-J., IX., 237.

3414. Heinrich. In the legend Faust's name is Johann, but this name
had been made vulgar and ridiculous by the associations of the popular
Faust-drama and the puppet-plays. See Intr. p. xx. Hence the change
of the name. The choice of 'Heinrich' is either purely arbitrary or, perhaps, a compliment to Goethe's friend Friedrich Heinrich Jacobi. Cf.
Minor in G.-J., VIII., 232.

3415. wie haſt du'ß mit, 'how do you feel about'?

3422. Wenn ich . . . . könnte, 'if I could influence you a little'; =
wenn ich etwas über dich vermöchte.

3428–30. The meaning is that the 'priest' or 'sage' will answer with
formal statements, propositions, names etc., which are all ridiculously in-
adequate to express the infinite content of *feeling* that ought to be implied
in the word 'God.' This and the following speech of Faust need to be
read in the light of Goethe's first letter to Auguste Stolberg, written Jan.
26, 1775. It begins: Meine Teure — ich will Ihnen keinen Nahmen
geben, denn was ſind die Nahmen Freundinn, Schweſter, Geliebte, Braut,
Gattin, oder ein Wort das einen Complex von all denen Nahmen begriffe,
gegen das unmittelbare Gefühl? . . . . Ich fühle Sie können ihn tragen,
dieſen zerſtückten, ſtammelnden Ausdruck, wenn das Bild des Unendlichen in
uns wühlt. Und was iſt das als Liebe!

3434. glaub' ihn; = glaub' an ihn. Thus also in *Meister* Goethe
writes: So glauben Sie kein Schickſal?

3438–58. The thought may be paraphrased in plain prose thus: The
Infinite is all about us and within us, — in sky and earth and star and in
the mysterious thronging emotions of our hearts. If we but *feel* the greatness of this omnipresent Divinity, that is enough. Names and formulae are
are of no importance. On this passage cf. G.-J., I. 201.

3451. ſo groß es iſt, i. e., your whole heart.

3460–1. The priest says also that God is omnipresent and that religion
is a matter of the heart.

3488. nichts keinen. Cf. l. 3198, note.

3511. Fläschchen. The only natural presumption is that Faust has brought the opiate in order to be prepared for this very contingency.

3512. in ihren Trank; supply gegossen.

3521. Grasaff'. Cf. l. 3313, note. The lexicographers do not explain the word, but it seems to have been suggested by monkeys frolicking in the grass. Heyne Wb., quoting this passage, calls it a Schimpfwort, but Goethe sometimes uses it as a term of jocose endearment, applying it, e.g., to Lili as married woman and to the children of Frau von Stein. Translate 'kitten.'

3523. wurden; 'plu. of majesty,' with a title. Cf. Brandt § 311, 2.

3524. Ihnen. Mephistopheles addresses Faust with du, Er, or ihr, but never elsewhere with Sie. The latter is used here only on account of the preceding Herr Doctor wurden.

3525. Mädels. Cf. l. 1837, note.

3532. heilig; to be taken in the dialectic sense of sehr, ganz besonders — like Eng. 'awfully.'

3536. Spottgeburt; = Spott erregende Geburt, 'monstrous progeny.'

Am Brunnen.

The final revision of *Faust* requires us to presuppose for this scene that on the night mentioned in l. 3541, Gretchen carelessly gave her mother too much of the opiate (l. 3511) and so caused her death. This scene takes place after a lapse of some time, during which Gretchen has led a quiet life (l. 3545) alone with her shame and remorse. When the scene was first written, however, the presupposition was somewhat different. See the introductory note to the scene 'Cathedral.'

3546. Sibylle; probably the name of some girl friend.

3556. Curtesirt, 'courted.'

3560. Geschleck'; vulgar for Geküsse.

3561. Blümchen; the flower of maidenhood, Lat. *flos*.

3569. Sünderhemdchen, 'sinner's smock'; an allusion to the practice of requiring public penance, *deprecatio publica in templo*, in a garb symbolical of humiliation.

3575. reißen; in the sense of zerreißen.

3576. Häckerling, 'chopped straw' instead of the flowers which a chaste bride would receive.

3581. schwärzt's noch gar. 'I actually even made it black.'

3584. der Sünde bloß, 'given over to sin'; bloß in the sense of bloßgestellt, preisgegeben. See Grimm, Wb. II., 146.

Zwinger.

The term 'Zwinger,' applied first to the space between the main wall of a castle or city and the encompassing moat, means here the unoccupied space between the wall and the nearest buildings within. In the wall is a shrine containing an image of the Sorrowing Mother gazing at her Son upon the cross, her heart pierced by a sword (Luke ii, 35). At this shrine Gretchen is wont to worship.

With reference to the final revision of *Faust* we may suppose this scene either to follow very closely upon the preceding or to be separated from it by an interval of weeks. Originally, however, there can be little doubt that it was meant to be taken as expressing Gretchen's first agony of remorse on finding that she had caused the death of her mother. Cf. the introductory note to the scene 'Cathedral.'

Writing Oct. 11, 1775, to Frau La Roche, who was just then anxious about her son, Goethe uses the expression: 'Alas that fate thrusts such swords at the hearts of mothers!' This has led to the conjecture that the scene 'Zwinger' may have been of contemporary origin with the letter. Cf. D. Jacoby in G.-J., I., 187.

3599. Was: cognate acc. with the intransitive bangen. The meaning is: Thou only knowest my poor heart's distress, its trembling, its longing.

Nacht.

On this scene cf. Intr. pp. lii and lxiii. Only the opening ll. 3620–45 and the ll. 3650–9 are found in U., but the greater part of the scene is quite certainly of early origin. (1) The general style in its vivid, popular realism is that of Goethe's pre-Weimarian period; (2) specific phrases point to an early date of composition (cf. the notes to ll. 3706, 3760); (3) Faust is here an uneasy libertine on his way for one of his habitual visits to his paramour (ll. 3674–5). On the other hand the reference to Walpurgis-Night, in l. 3661, is undoubtedly a late intercalation.

3620. **fo,** 'you know,' 'as I often did.'

3622. **Flor,** 'blooming beauty.'

3623. **laut gepriefen vor.** Construe: Wenn .... die Gefellen .... laut vorgepriefen hatten.

3624. **verfchwemmt,** 'washed down'; the construction like that of gepriefen.

3633. **Waffer reicht;** like our idiom 'hold a candle to.'

3634. **Top!** is an expression of approval = 'right you are.' **Kling! Klang!** describes the clinking of glasses in token of assent.

3638–9. The sense is: It's enough to make one tear out one's hair and (try to) rush up the walls, as a caged beast does in his impotent rage.

3644. **zufammenfchmeißen,** 'smash their heads together.'

3650. **Sacriftei.** The dialogue is to be thought of as taking place while the speakers walk along the streets of the city on their way to Gretchen's house. **Sacriftei,** usually 'vestry-room,' but here apparently a chapel pertaining to some church, probably the 'cathedral' of the next scene.

3651. **ew'gen Lämpchens;** an altar-lamp burning night and day.

3655. **fchmächtig,** not 'lean' but 'languishing,' in a coarse sense. M. H. G. *smahtec* meant 'hungry.'

3656. **Feuerleitern,** 'fire-escapes.'

3659. **Rammelei,** 'lustfulness.'

3661. **Walpurgisnacht.** Since the Walpurgis-Night comes on the eve of May-day, the date of this scene, in view of übermorgen in l. 3662, is April 29; and since the action of *Faust* begins at Easter all the preceding scenes must be thought of as taking place in the month of April. But see the introductory note to the next scene.

3664. **Schatz.** German folk-lore taught that a phosphorescent light near the ground betokens a subterraneous treasure just below; or, as Goethe here conceives the superstition, that a treasure is trying to make its way up to the surface.

3669. Löwenthaler, 'lion-dollars'; in allusion to the 'dollars' first coined in Bohemia, in the 15th century. They were called Joachimsthaler from the Joachimsthal where they were first made, and Löwenthaler because stamped with the royal lion of Bohemia.

3682–97. The song is adapted from Ophelia's song in *Hamlet*, IV., 5. Of this innocent theft Goethe said to Eckermann, Jan. 18, 1825: 'Thus my Mephistopheles sings a song of Shakespeare, and why shouldn't he? Why should I take the trouble to invent one of my own, when Shakespeare's was just the thing and said what was needed'?

3698. bei'm Element; a very common imprecation which no lexicographer has explained.

3699. Rattenfänger; possibly suggested by Shakespeare's 'Tybalt, you rat-catcher, will you walk?" in *Romeo and Juliet*, III, 1.

3702. an der .... halten; = darauf ist nichts zu halten, 'that's of no use.'

3706. Flederwisch, 'duster'; a cant term for 'sword.' In Goethe's *Claudine*, as finished in April–June, 1775, are introduced 'three vagabonds standing at a table and playing dice.' One of these, Crugantino, with sword at his side and cithera in hand, sings a song in which occur the words:

> 'Raus, feurig, frisch
> Den Flederwisch!

This points to an early origin for the Faust-Valentin encounter. Cf. Jacoby in G.-J., I., 197.

3714–5. The meaning is, according to Loeper, that Mephistopheles can trick the police, they being a purely human institution; but the criminal court (Blutbann), having jurisdiction in capital crimes and deriving its authority from God, is harder for the devil to manage.

3756–61. See App. III.

3760. Jammerecken; the old weak acc., M. H. G. *ecken.*

3769. Vergebung reiche Maß. Maß is the obsolete fem., die Maß 'measure,' and the construction a sort of appositional acc.; as one might say in Eng. 'forgiveness plenty,' for 'abundant pardon.' But reiche Maß really performs the function of the adverb reicher Maßen.

Dom.

On this scene cf. Intr. pp. lii and lxiii ff.   As is there noted, the scene has in U. the heading 'Obsequies of Gretchen's Mother,' which fact, taken with ll. 3790–3, shows that the swoon in the cathedral can not have been thought of at first as occurring soon after the time referred to in l. 3542. The chronology was rather conceived in this way : Gretchen's first trial of the opiate was to leave the mother uninjured, and then the experiment was to be repeated at subsequent visits.   There would then be an interval during which Gretchen, conscious of her shame, would 'go but little among people' (l. 3545), and here would come the scene 'At the Well.'   After a lapse of months there was to be a visit of Faust, in anticipation of which Gretchen, now perhaps grown careless, should give too much of the poison and so cause her mother's death.   On the morning of the next day but one would come the scene 'Zwinger' with Gretchen's agonized prayer to be saved from 'shame *and death*,' and then, on the day of the funeral, the scene 'Cathedral.'   This was then to be followed by the visit which should result in Valentin's death (for in U. the Valentin scene comes after 'Cathedral') and give occasion for Faust's flight and long absence.   The 'dismal day' of the prose scene would then be a day of the ensuing year.

On the final revision, however, this chronology was hopelessly confused, so that it is not now possible to make the love-tragedy read naturally on any supposition whatever.   The confusion seems to have had two sources : first, the introduction of the fixed dates, Easter and Walpurgis-Night; and, secondly, a purpose never thoroughly carried out, to ennoble the character of Gretchen by letting it appear that she had sinned but once.   Cf. Intr. p. lxiii.   Goethe's final intention seems to have been to have it understood that the opiate proved fatal on the first night.   Then, since the scene 'Cathedral' presupposed a considerable lapse of time, he omitted the heading which told that the occasion was the funeral of the mother.   Moreover, since the Valentin scene was to prepare the way for the Walpurgis-Night, it had to come before instead of after 'Cathedral'; and this adjustment being made, l. 3789, with its allusion to Valentin's death, was intercalated in the final draft.

But now these presuppositions require us to assume that Gretchen in the scene 'At the Well' is already burdened with the guilt of her mother's death; which makes her gossipy conversation with Lieschen appear unthinkable. Again, 'Cathedral' can not on account of ll. 3790–3, come naturally before Walpurgis-Night; unless indeed it were to be the Night of the ensuing year, a supposition which is made impossible by the über= morgen of l. 3662.

3775+. **Gretchen unter vielem Volke.** U. has, instead, **Gretgen alle Verwandte.** The **Böser Geist** is a tormentor conceived like the biblical 'evil spirit'; cf. 1 Sam. xvi.

3779. **vergriffnen,** 'well-worn' from handling. U. has **verblätterten.**

3780. **Gebete lalltest,** 'prattled prayers.' U. has **deinen Gebeten nachlalltest.**

3791. **Regt sichs . . . schon,** 'is there not already a quickening stir?'

3792. **sich.** The child is assumed to share and to increase the mother's agitation.

3796. **mir,** 'for me,' i. e., 'in my mind': a loose dat. of interest.

3797. **Wider mich,** 'accusing me.'

3798–9. **Dies irae . . . favilla.** 'Day of wrath, that day shall dissolve the world in ashes'; the opening lines of the famous 'sequence' *Dies Irae*, composed by Thomas Celano in the 13th century.

3800–7. The Evil Spirit here voices Gretchen's dread of the resurrection.

3806. **Wieder aufgeschaffen,** 'brought forth anew.'

3810. **den Athem versetzte,** 'were choking me.'

3813–5. **Judex . . . remanebit.** 'When therefore the Judge shall be seated, whatever is hidden shall appear, nothing shall remain unpunished.'

3821. **Verbirg dich;** ironical, 'Wouldst hide thyself?'

3825–7. **Quid sum . . . securus.** 'What then shall I say in my wretchedness? What protector shall I invoke when scarcely the just man shall be secure?'

3833. As Düntzer observes, it is not obvious why the chorus should repeat the preceding stanza instead of beginning the next one. Probably a mere inadvertence on Goethe's part.

3834. **Fläschchen,** 'smelling-bottle.'

Walpurgisnacht.

Cf. Intr. pp. lxiv. ff. A dated manuscript in the Royal Library at Berlin indicates that this scene was begun in November, 1800, and 'continued in February, 1801.' It was never really finished at all. As we can see from the Paralipomena, there was to have been, after the Intermezzo, a scene which would have apprized Faust of Gretchen's impending fate. But this was never written — with the result that the so-called 'Intermezzo' appears not as an intermezzo at all, but as the end of the Walpurgis-Night. We are left to imagine what follows between that and the prose scene as best we may.

Walpurgis, or Walpurga, was an English nun who died Feb. 25, 779, as abbess of a Bavarian convent. As her calendar-day fell on May 1, her name came to be associated with the old rites and festivities of the May-time (cf. D. M., II., 878), and finally with the superstition of an annual conclave of witches on the Brocken, the highest point of the Harz Mts. This summit, Lat. *mons Bructerus*, rises some 3600 feet above sea-level. It is covered at the top with granite blocks (whence probably the popular name 'Blocksberg') among which the tourist is still shown a *Hexenkanzel* or *-altar*, a *Hexentanzplatz* and a *Hexenwaschbecken*.

The Faust-legend does not connect its hero in any way with the May carnival; but a poem on the Walpurgis-Night, published in 1756 by J. F. Löwen, introduces Dr. Faust on the Brocken and gives him a seat at the left hand of Beelzebub. As Goethe refers to Löwen's poem in the 6th book of *Dichtung und Wahrheit*, he may have got from it the suggestion of taking his own Faust to the Blocksberg festival, but there is no evidence that a Blocksberg scene was part of his early plan. From several visits, the first in 1777, Goethe was very familiar with the Brocken region. On his literary sources see App. III.

3834+. Schierke und Elend. These are two neighboring villages lying southward from the Brocken. From Schierke, the higher of the two, it is an easy walk of about two hours to the summit.

3851-2. On Feb. 26, 1824, Goethe said to Eckermann, that while he had been able to portray Faust's world-weariness and Gretchen's love by 'anticipation,' it required some observation of nature to write these two lines.

3855. Irrlicht. The *ignis fatuus*, Eng. Jack-o'-Lantern or Will-o'-the-Wisp, is regarded in Germanic folk-lore as an evil spirit that delights in luring travelers from their way and leading them to destruction. It is thus, naturally, a minion of the devil.

3863. Mephistopheles means that Will-o'-the-Wisp's zigzag is patterned after the devious course of men through life.

3871–3911. The distribution of the solos was not indicated by Goethe, and has been matter of much discussion. The third clearly belongs to Faust and the fourth to Mephistopheles. The fifth, on account of the allusion to the irren Lichter, which would hardly be so noteworthy to Irrlicht himself, seems also best assigned to Faust. As to the first, the scheint es of l. 3872 seems to indicate a mental uncertainty, which would not be expected of Mephistopheles, who must be supposed to know the locality perfectly. On the other hand, the mandatory führ' uns of l. 3873 suggests Mephistopheles rather than Faust. In any case, the second strophe must be assigned to Will-o'-the-Wisp. The songs represent a swift transition by magic, just as in ll. 9078 ff.

3876. Seh'; i. e., ich sehe.

3880. schnarchen. Two granite rocks near Schierke have long borne the name of die Schnarcher, 'the Snorers.'

3885–6. Faust sings in elegiac tone, as if 'those heavenly days' of youthful hope and love were far away, as they actually were for the poet who penned the lines. The words, like the whole scene, were written with little concern for the inner requirements of the Gretchen-tragedy. Cf. Intr. p. lxv.

3889. Uhu! Schuhu! here an imitation of the night-owl's hoot. The words are also onomatopoetic names of the owl.

3892. Molche. We may think either of actual salamanders abroad, as minions of the devil, on the uncanny mountain, or only of something that *looks* like salamanders. The idea of the song is, in part at least, to voice the weird fancies one has in going through a wild region in the night. Thus the mice of l. 3900 may be the moonbeams glancing here and there upon the ground. But bright-colored mice belong to the devil's kingdom. Cf. l. 4179.

3898. belebten derben Masern, 'from massive living tree-warts.' Belebt means that they *seem* like living things.

3906–11. The trio have been moving swiftly by magic; as they 'slow down,' Faust is giddy and confused.

3913. ſo ein Mittelgipfel, 'one of these mid-way peaks.' They are not yet at the top.

3916–31. Cf. the note to l. 3664 for the idea of subterraneous gold manifesting its presence by a light above ground. So Mammon, conceived on account of the familiar personification in the New Testament (Matt. vi. 24), as a devilish Lord of Wealth, is represented as lighting up his mountain-palace for the great festival.

3919. wittert er hinein, 'penetrates with its gleam.'

3936. Windsbraut; a very ancient (O. H. G. wintes brût) and not fully explained name for 'tempest,' 'whirlwind.' See Grimm, D. M., I., 525.

3950. übertrümmerten; bridged over with the débris of fallen trees.

3959. Urian; a name for the devil. It is the same as Urhans, 'Old Jack.'

3962. Baubo; a nurse of Demeter, who tried to divert the goddess from her sorrow by obscene antics. The story can be found in Arnobius. In *Werke*, H., XVI., 328, Goethe applies the name to an immodest merry-maker in the Roman carnival. As a type of bestial shamelessness, Baubo is an appropriate leader of the ribald witches.

3968. Ilſenſtein; a high rock a few miles northeast of the Brocken.

3977. So great is the crowd that the unborn child is squeezed to death and the mother to bursting.

3987–9. In these witches that wash and wash but remain sterile and so can not mount into the air, we have a bit of nonsensical mystification, which it is hardly worth while to try to interpret seriously. Cf. introductory note to ' Witch's Kitchen.'

4003. Halbheze. A 'half-witch' seems to be a person who would like to be a witch, but cannot.

4023. Voland ; a name for the devil; M. H. G. vālant. The word is thought by Grimm to be a pres. pple. of a verb meaning 'to seduce.'

4033. beliebig, 'at will,' i. e., 'capriciously.'

4076–91. These gentlemen, who have withdrawn from the crowd, are different types of the old fogy, the *laudator temporis acti*, who can see no good in the new generation.

4095+. Trödelheze ; a witch who deals in Trödel, i. e., old curiosities. Taylor has ' huckster-witch.'

4119. Adams erſte Frau. According to a rabbinic tradition, Adam's first wife, the 'female' of Gen. i. 27, was named Lilith. Being superseded by Eve, she became a ghost-like being that delights in seducing men and doing harm to children. The word occurs in the Hebrew Bible in Isaiah xxxiv. 14, where it is rendered, in the King James version, 'screech-owl,' with the alternative 'night-monster.'

4121. einzig; as if an adj. with Schmuck.

4143+. Proktophantasmiſt, 'rump-visionary.' The name and the following lines to l. 4175 allude to Friedrich Nicolai, who, though at one time the friend and co-laborer of Lessing, afterwards made himself somewhat ridiculous as an apostle of common sense in literature. Goethe and Schiller looked upon him as the type and embodiment of tedious dictatorial mediocrity. In 1799 Nicolai read to the Berlin Academy a paper entitled 'Example of the Appearance of Several Phantasms.' In this paper he reported how he had been troubled with visions, and had been cured by the application of leeches to that portion of his person called by the Greeks πρωκτός.

4159. aufgeklärt. The Age of Reason, i. e., the age of Voltaire and Friedrich the Great, is called in German das Zeitalter der Aufklärung.

4161. Tegel; a place near Berlin, the home, in Goethe's time, of the brothers Humboldt. In the above-mentioned paper of Nicolai he discussed a ghostly apparition reported to have been seen at Tegel in 1797.

4169. Reiſe. Among Nicolai's tedious commonplace writings was a long-winded book of travels entitled *Beschreibung einer Reise durch Deutschland und die Schweiz.*

4173. ſoulagirt, 'gets relief'; Fr. *se soulager.*

4179. rothes Mäuschen. According to Grimm, D. M., II., 905, there is folk-lore to the effect that red mice sometimes run out of the mouths of sleeping witches.

4181. doch nicht grau; i. e., it was not an ordinary mouse.

4182. Schäferſtunde, 'amorous hour.'

4186. geschloſſ'nen, 'fettered.'

4190. Idol, 'phantom'; Gr. εἴδωλον.

4194. Meduſe; the Gorgon whose serpent hair changed all who looked at it to stone.

4211. Prater; the name of a famous park at Vienna.

4214. **Servibilis**; a servant, or 'super,' employed about the stage.

4220. **Mich bilettirt's**; patterned comically after It. *mi diletta*, 'it delights me.'

Walpurgisnachtstraum.

INTERMEZZO.

The 'Walpurgis-Night's Dream' is the 'new piece' mentioned in l. 4215 as just about to be performed at the dilettante theatre — which is the sum total of its connection with *Faust*. The title was suggested by Shakespeare's *Midsummer Night's Dream*, in which Oberon and Titania, the king and queen of the fairies, after having quarreled about the possession of an Indian boy and become alienated from each other by jealousy, are at last reconciled. Goethe introduces them as celebrating their golden wedding, which is conceived, at the same time, as a festival of reconciliation. The orchestra consists of buzzing insects, frogs, crickets, etc. As guests or spectators and critics we have a multitude of persons and personifications who give vent to their feelings in the form of comment upon what they see and hear. Goethe's diary, *Tagebücher*, II., 72, shows that he was working on the 'Golden Wedding' June 5, 1797. But it was not then connected in his mind with *Faust*. In the summer of 1796 Goethe and Schiller began together the composition of a collection of epigrams to which they gave the ancient name of *Xenia*, or 'gifts of hospitality.' Some four hundred were published at once in Schiller's *Almanach*. The next summer Goethe sent in a fresh collection of similar character under the title of *Oberon and Titania's Golden Wedding*. Schiller saw reasons for not publishing them (see his letter of Oct. 2, 1797), whereupon Goethe, having now doubled the original number of verses, decided to make a place for them in *Faust* (letter of Dec. 20, 1797).

This decision is to be regretted, because, with the suppression of the scene which was to come after it, the Intermezzo no longer deserves its name. Furthermore, it does not help on the action in any way, and the verses are not very interesting in themselves.

4224. **Miedings.** Mieding was a highly esteemed stage-decorator who died at Weimar in 1782.

4227–30. The thought is that it is the reconciliation rather than the lapse of fifty years which makes the festival 'golden.'

4239. 𝕬𝖗𝖎𝖊𝖑; the Ariel of Shakespeare's *Tempest*.

4247. 𝖌𝖗𝖎𝖑𝖑𝖙, 'is freaky.'

4257. 𝕾𝖈𝖍𝖓𝖊𝖈𝖐𝖊𝖘𝖈𝖍𝖓𝖎𝖈𝖐𝖊𝖘𝖈𝖍𝖓𝖆𝖈𝖐; a word coined to describe the music made by the soap-bubble bag-pipe.

4259–62. Whether these lines are to be understood as spoken by the inchoate 'Geist' himself or by some one of the performers about him, is uncertain. So is the 'point' of the nonsense, if it has any.

4273. 𝕲𝖔̈𝖙𝖙𝖊𝖗 𝕲𝖗𝖎𝖊𝖈𝖍𝖊𝖓𝖑𝖆𝖓𝖉𝖘. In 1788 F. L. Stolberg published a narrow-minded attack upon Schiller's poem *Die Götter Griechenlands*, charging the author with blasphemy, etc.

4274+. 𝕹𝖔𝖗𝖉𝖎𝖘𝖈𝖍𝖊𝖗 𝕶𝖚̈𝖓𝖘𝖙𝖑𝖊𝖗. Here one thinks of Goethe himself who was actually planning a journey to Italy, when the lines were written.

4279–82. The 'purist' as we see is a typical stickler for propriety.

4294+. 𝖂𝖎𝖓𝖉𝖋𝖆𝖍𝖚𝖊. The 'weather-vane,' that first praises and then condemns, is evidently a symbol of turn-coats. That anybody in particular is alluded to is at least not clear.

4302+. 𝖃𝖊𝖓𝖎𝖊𝖓. Goethe several times refers to the *Xenia* under the image of annoying insects.

4306+. 𝕳𝖊𝖓𝖓𝖎𝖓𝖌𝖘. Hennings was the editor of the journal *Genius der Zeit*, in which he attacked the *Xenia* violently. This journal, called by Loeper a 𝕿𝖚𝖒𝖒𝖊𝖑𝖕𝖑𝖆𝖙𝖟 𝖚𝖓𝖗𝖊𝖎𝖋𝖊𝖗 𝕯𝖎𝖈𝖍𝖙𝖊𝖗𝖑𝖎𝖓𝖌𝖊, was especially disliked by Goethe.

4310+. 𝕸𝖚𝖘𝖆𝖌𝖊𝖙, 'Leader of the Muses.' Under this name Hennings published, in 1798–9, some numbers of a poetic journal intended to rival Schiller's *Almanach*.

4314+. Ci-devant; 'quondam.' The *Genius der Zeit* was discontinued in 1803.

4318+. 𝕹𝖊𝖚𝖌𝖎𝖊𝖗𝖎𝖌𝖊𝖗 𝕽𝖊𝖎𝖘𝖊𝖓𝖉𝖊𝖗; Nicolai again. See l. 4143, note.

4322. Nicolai was famous for his opposition to the Jesuits. The line is to be taken as a comment by the crowd in explanation of the 'traveller's' continual snuffling.

4322+. 𝕶𝖗𝖆𝖓𝖎𝖈𝖍. The 'crane' is Goethe's old friend Lavater, of whom he said to Eckermann Feb. 17, 1829: 'Lavater was a genuinely kind man, but subject to powerful illusions, and the strict, exact truth was not his affair; he deceived himself and others, whence there came a complete rupture of our relations. His gait was that of a crane, for which reason he appears as ' crane ' on the Blocksberg.'

4326+. Weltkind. In the summer of 1774 Goethe dined with Lavater and Basedow at Coblenz. In a poem suggested by the occurrence are found the lines :

Prophete rechts, Prophete links,
Das Weltkind in der Mitten.

So Goethe himself is probably the Weltkind here on the Blocksberg.

4328. Behikel; ' vehicle of profit,' ' means of grace.'

4334. Dommeln, ' herons'; usually Rohrdommeln. The droning herons are the philosophers who appear below.

4335–8. A dancing master on the stage comments on the approaching crowd of dancing herons.

4338+. Fideler; a puzzling word. Düntzer takes it to be Fidéler, from the adj. fidel, Lat. *fidelis*, used in student-dialect for ' jolly.' The word was certainly familiar to Goethe, but there seems to be no point in introducing a ' jolly good fellow ' here. The connection rather requires a ' fiddler ' to go with the ' dance-master.' There is, as Loeper shows, good and abundant authority for the spelling fideln, Fidel, Fidler, but as a matter of fact Goethe usually wrote Fiedel fiedeln, etc. Schröer thinks Fideler a printer's mistake for Fiedler. Cf. G.-J., I. 435, and II. 439.

4340. das Restchen geben, ' do to death,' ' settle.'

4342+. Dogmatiker; ' dogmatist,' in the sense of a philosopher who bases his doctrine on received dogmas. This ' dogmatist,' however, falls out of his role in the last two lines, since instead of accepting the devil's existence on faith and trust, he proceeds to argue it on the ground that there are ' devils ' among men.

4349. Wenn ich . . . bin. ' Idealist ' is used here in the technical Fichtean sense of one who holds that the Not-Me is the creation of the Me. Thus he is compelled to believe that all he sees on the Brocken is ' Me.'

4359. Sie gehen ; i. e., the supernaturalists, who are likened to credulous persons seeking for treasure from the light it emits. Cf. l. 3664, note.

4366+. Gewandten ; the ' clever ones ' are the lucky dogs who ' get along ' by hook or by crook. They call their army ' sanssouci,' i. e., ' free from care ', because no scruples trouble them. They are pococurantists.

4370+. **Unbehülflichen** ; the ' ne'er do weels ' whom help never helps.

4382+. **Die Massiven,** 'the coarse crew.' **Ein massiver Kerl** is the same as ein **grober Bursche.**

4384. True spirits would not crush the grass (Loeper).

Trüber Tag.

Among the Paralipomena and dating presumably from the period 1797–1801, are found various fragments of a scene that was to come after the Intermezzo and represent the court of Satan on the summit of the Brocken. Cf. ll. 3959, 4037–9, and 4116. Satan was to make a speech from the throne, give audiences, confer fiefs and receive the homage of his subjects. A chorus was to sing his praise. At the end there was to be a symbolical decapitation of the ' eidolon' (l. 4190) with comments by spectators from which Faust was to learn of Gretchen's fate. For some reason Goethe failed to carry out this plan, so we are left to imagine how Faust gets his knowledge and to make the return as best we can from the phantasms of the Blocksberg to the intense realism of the love-tragedy.

The scene ' Dismal Day ' is found in U. substantially as it appears here. Its wild extravagance of diction, the work of a youthful writer who has not yet mastered his art, points to an early origin, probably the year 1772. Cf. Scherer, *Goethe's Frühzeit,* p. 81. The more important dramaturgical questions suggested by the scene are discussed in Intr. p. lxiii ff. Cf. also the introductory note to the scene ' Study,' (1).

6. **ingrimmend** ; = ingrimmig. There is no verb **ingrimmen** and this form is probably unique.

9. **der richtenden gefühllosen** ; = der gefühllos richtenden.

10. **Zerstreuungen.** It is quite doubtful what ' diversions' Goethe had in mind when these words were written.

13. **Wandle ihn.** When this was written the presupposition was that the devil had associated with Faust for a time in poodle form before being given human shape. Accompanying Faust on his evening walks, the poodle would divert his master by rolling in the path in front of pedestrians so that they might fall over him. Scherer, *Goethe's Frühzeit,* p. 81, re-

gards this passage, strangely enough, as evidence that the devil was not to appear first in poodle form.

16. follern, 'roll in a heap,' or 'turn somersaults.'

28. überschnappt, 'snaps from over-tension.'

30. Drangen wir . . . uns? When the scene was written the presupposition was that Faust had taken the initiative toward an alliance with the devil. So in l. 1414 the first suggestion of a compact comes from Faust, though he says in l. 1426: Ich habe dir nicht nachgestellt. But the Prologue gives us to understand that the devil seeks out Faust.

49–50.. des Erschlagenen; evidence that the murder of Valentin and Faust's flight in consequence were a part of Goethe's earliest plan.

57. mit Menschenhand. The assumption is that Mephistopheles can not spirit Gretchen out of her prison-cell by magic. He can take Faust to the spot speedily and can befool the guard, but the removal must be effected by the 'hand of mortal.' **Zauberpferde.** The magic horses, as a means of locomotion, are found only in this early scene. In the later ones the pair usually travel by means of a magic mantle (cf. l. 2065, and l. 6983).

Nacht.

This short scene in rhythmical prose, found in U. precisely as here, falls of course on the night following the preceding 'Dismal Day.' As Faust and Mephistopheles sweep through the air on their black horses, they pass a 'raven-stone,' or place of execution (Rabenstein is properly the 'block' of masonry built under a gallows), at which a bevy of witches are engaged in their characteristic employments of 'cooking,' 'strewing' and 'devoting' to the powers of evil. The scene was conceived as an uncanny picture that should serve to adumbrate the fate of Gretchen. But this is now done sufficiently by the 'eidolon' on the Brocken (ll. 4203–5).

Kerker.

In U. this scene is in prose, (for the text see Appendix II), the substance differing but slightly from what is found here. It was probably written in 1772 or 1773 and put into verse in 1798. See Intr. p. lvi.

4405. längſt entwohnter Schauer. The presupposition is, or was, that Faust has been away from Gretchen several months and during that time has been a stranger to deep, sincere emotion. **Schauer** = 'feeling of awe.' Later Goethe preferred **entwöhnen** to **entwohnen.** Cf. l. 25.

4406. Der Menſchheit . . . . Jammer. Cf. ll. 1770-3, and Intr. p. lxxiii.

4411. zögert . . . heran, 'lingers death more near' (Taylor); an intransitive verb used transitively, as in l. 389.

4412-20. Gretchen in her distraction sings a coarse song as does Ophelia in *Hamlet*. The song itself is based on the Low German legend of the juniper-tree, which is found in Grimm's *Märchen*. The story runs thus: A bad stepmother serves up her step-son as a meal for her husband. A little sister gathers up the bones and buries them under a juniper-tree. The bones become a little bird that sings the song: *Min Moder de mi slacht't, Min Vader de mi att*, etc.

4413. Die; demonstrative.

4417. Bein' = **Knochen.**

4449-50. The meaning is: They mock me by singing an old ballad of a mother that killed her child; who bids them apply it to me?

4489. überdrang, 'came over me.'

4501. auch; unaccented, in the sense of 'really,' 'indeed.'

4512. feucht; in allusion to the killing of Valentin.

4520. übrig bleiben, 'continue to live'; the preceding 'you'll kill me,' being taken literally.

4532. The thought is: I can no longer bring back the old feeling.

4567. Es faßt . . . . Schopfe, 'it's as if a cold hand seized me by the hair.'

4569. wackelt; in recollection of her mother's fatal drowsiness.

4584. Es iſt eben geſchehen, 'it is e'en a thing of the past.'

4590. It was once the custom at public executions to toll the church bell while the culprit was on the way to the block, and also to break a white wand over the condemned person's head in token that his life was forfeit to the law.

4593-4. 𝖅𝖚𝖈𝖐𝖊𝖓 𝖚𝖓𝖉 𝖟ü𝖈𝖐𝖊𝖓 are variants of the same word and both mean 'to move with a flash,' 'to dart swiftly.' The on-looker is supposed to shrink from the fatal blow as if it were meant for his own neck.

4611. Mephistopheles means: She is beyond the reach of judge and executioner; her 'doom' has already come. It was apparently to forestall the possible interpretation 'she is doomed to perdition,' that Goethe added the supernatural 'voice from above' declaring that 'she is saved.'

APPENDIX I.

BIBLIOGRAPHY.

A complete Faust-bibliography would treble the size of this volume. Engel's *Zusammenstellung der Faustschriften* (see under VIII., below) is fairly exhaustive down to the year 1884. For the time since then consult the successive volumes of the *Goethe-Jahrbuch*, edited since 1880 by L. Geiger; also the reviews in the *Jahresberichte für neuere deutsche Litteraturgeschichte*, edited since 1892 by E. Schmidt and others. The following classified list gives a selection of the more important publications under each head, their relative importance being further indicated by the familiar guidebook device of asterisks. For all questions pertaining to the history and recension of the text, manuscripts, and early editions of critical significance, consult the *Lesarten* in vols. 14 and 15 of the great Weimar edition of Goethe's works (see under III., below). Biographies of Goethe are not listed; the most important for their discussion of *Faust* are those of Grimm (1876), Heinemann (1895), Meyer (1895), Witkowski (1899), Bielschowsky (1896-1904), and Geiger (1910). Histories of German literature are ignored, though of course they all have something to say about *Faust*.

I.

The Historical Faust and the Faust Legend.

*Braune, W. Das Volksbuch vom Doctor Faust. Abdruck der ersten Ausgabe (1587). Halle. 1878. Bibliography by Zarncke.

Dumcke, J. Die deutschen Faustbücher. Nebst einem Anhange zum Widmanschen Faustbuche. Leipzig. 1891. Dissertation.

Düntzer, H. Die Sage von Doctor Johannes Faust. Scheibles 'Kloster,' V. (1847), 1–260.

Ellinger, G. Zu den Quellen des Faustbuches von 1587. *Zeitschrift für vergleichende Litteraturgeschichte*, Neue Folge, I. (1887), 156–81.

Faligan, E. Histoire de la légende de Faust. Paris. 1888.

Grimm, H.   Die Entstehung des Volksbuches vom Dr. Faust. 'Fünf-zehn Essais,' dritte Folge. Berlin. 1882. Pp. 192–219.

*Keller, A. von.   Fausts Leben von G. R. Widman. Tübingen, 1882. A reprint of Pfitzer's edition (1674) of the Widman Faust-book (1599).

*Kiesewetter, K.   Faust in der Geschichte und Tradition. Leipzig. 1893.

Kühne, A.   Das älteste Faustbuch. Wortgetreuer Abdruck der Editio Princeps des Spies'schen Faustbuches vom Jahre 1587. Mit Ein-leitung und Anmerkungen. Zerbst. 1868.

Logeman, H.   The English Faust-book of 1592. Gand. 1900.

Milchsack, G.   Historia D. Johannis Fausti des Zauberers. Nach der Wolfenbütteler Handschrift. Wolfenbüttel. 1897.

Nagel, S.   Helena in der Faustsage. *Euphorion* IX (1902), 43–69.

Pfitzer, C. N.   See above under Keller.

Pick, A.   Faust in Erfurt. Eine kulturgeschichtliche Untersuchung. Leipzig. 1902.

*Scherer, W.   Das älteste Faustbuch. Mit einer Einleitung. Berlin. 1884. Facsimile reprint.

Schmidt, E.   Faust und das 16. Jahrhundert. 'Charakteristiken,' pp. 1–37. Berlin. 1886. 2. Aufl. 1902.

Faust und Luther. *Sitzungsberichte der Berliner Akademie* XXV. (1896), 567–91.

Schwengberg, M.   Das Spies'sche Faustbuch und seine Quelle. Ber-lin. 1885.

Szamatólski, S.   Zu den Quellen des ältesten Faustbuches. *Viertel-jahrschrift für Litteraturgeschichte* I. (1888), 161–83.

Das Faustbuch des Christlich Meynenden. Leipzig. 1892. A reprint of the edition of 1725.

Tille, A.   Die deutschen Volkslieder vom Dr. Faust. Halle. 1890.

Die Faustsplitter in der Litteratur des 16. bis 18. Jahrhunderts. Nach den ältesten Quellen. Berlin. 1900.

Widman, G. R.   See above under Keller.

*Witkowski, G.   Der historische Faust. *Deutsche Zeitschrift für Geschichtswissenschaft* I. (1897), 298–350.

Zahn, T.   Cyprian von Antiochien und die deutsche Faustsage. Erlangen. 1882.

II.

The Puppet Plays and the Faust Drama prior to Goethe.

*Bielschowsky, A. Das Schwiegerling'sche Puppenspiel vom Dr. Faust. Brieg. 1882.

Das Alter der Faustspiele. *Vierteljahrschrift für Litteraturgeschichte* IV. (1891), 193–226.

Bruinier, J. W. Zur Geschichte des Volksschauspiels von Dr. Faust. *Zeitschrift für deutsche Philologie* XXIX. (1897), 180–95; 345–72; XXX. (1898), 325–59; XXXI. (1899), 60–89; 194–231.

Faust vor Goethe. Heft 1. Halle. 1894.

Carriere, M. Calderons Wunderthätiger Magus und Goethes Faust. Braunschweig. 1876.

*Creizenach, W. Versuch einer Geschichte des Volksschauspiels vom Doctor Faust. Halle. 1878.

Engel, K. Das Volksschauspiel von Dr. Johann Faust. 2. Aufl. Oldenburg. 1882.

Kralik, R. und Winter, J. Doktor Faust. In 'Deutsche Puppenspiele.' Wien. 1885.

Kraus, E. Das böhmische Puppenspiel vom Dr. Faust. Breslau. 1892.

Petsch, R. Das fränkische Puppenspiel vom Dr. Faust. Würzburg. 1902.

Schade, O. Das Weimarer Puppenspiel. *Weimarisches Jahrbuch*, V. (1856), 241 ff.

Scheible, J. Das Kloster. Stuttgart. 1845–50. Vol. V., pp. 729–922, contains the Geisselbrecht puppet-play and others emanating from Berlin, Ulm, Köln, Strassburg, and Augsburg.

Tille, A. Das katholische Fauststück, die Faust-Komödienballade und das Zillerthaler Doctor-Faust-Spiel. *Zeitschrift für Bücherfreunde* X. (1906), 129–74.

Ward, A. W. Christopher Marlowe: The Tragical History of Doctor Faustus. 4th ed. Oxford. 1901. Contains an excellent introduction.

Werner, R. M. Zur Faustsage. *Goethe-Jahrbuch* XIV. (1893), 245–70.

Zarncke, F. Zur Faustdichtung vor Goethe. 'Goethe-Schriften.' Leipzig. 1897. Pp. 257–308.

III.

EDITIONS OF GOETHE'S FAUST.

Düntzer, H.　Goethes Werke. Zwölfter Theil. Kürschners Deutsche Nationallitteratur, Band 93. Berlin. No date.

Goebel, J.　Goethes Faust. Erster Teil. New York. 1907.

Harnack, O.　Goethes Werke, Band 5, in Meyers ' Klassiker Ausgaben.' Leipzig und Wien. No date.

Hart, J. M　Goethe : Faust, Erster Theil. Edited with an introduction and notes. New York. 1877.

Lévy, M. B.　Faust, Tragédie de Goethe. Avec une introduction et un commentaire. Paris. 1884.

*Loeper, G. von.　Faust. Eine Tragödie von Goethe. Mit Einleitung und erklärenden Anmerkungen. 2. Bearbeitung. Berlin. 1879.

**Schmidt, E.　Goethe's Werke herausgegeben im Auftrage der Grossherzogin Sophie von Sachsen. Bände 14–15. Weimar. 1887–8. Called the ' Weimar edition.'

*Goethes Sämmtliche Werke. Cotta'sche Jubiläums-Ausgabe. Bände 13–14. Stuttgart. 1904–6. Called the ' jubilee edition.'

Schröer, K. J.　Faust von Goethe. Mit Einleitung und fortlaufender Erklärung. Erster Theil, 5. Aufl. Leipzig. 1907. Zweiter Theil, 4. Aufl. Leipzig, 1904.

*Witkowski, G.　Goethes Faust. Leipzig. 1906. ¦ Erster Band : Der Tragödie Erster und Zweiter Teil, Urfaust, Entwürfe und Skizzen. Zweiter Band : Kommentar und Erläuterungen.

IV.

THE GÖCHHAUSEN FAUST (UR-FAUST), THE FRAGMENT OF 1790, AND THE PARALIPOMENA.

Bossert, A.　Le ' Faust ' de Goethe. Ses origines et ses formes successives. In ' Essais sur la littérature allemande.' Paris. 1905.

*Collin, J.　Goethes Faust in seiner ältesten Gestalt. Frankfurt am Main. 1896.

Holland, W. L. Goethes Faust. Ein Fragment. In der ursprünglichen Gestalt neu herausgegeben. Freiburg. 1882.

Kógel, R. Der vorweimarische Faust. *Vierteljahrschrift für Litteraturgeschichte* II. (1889), 545–62.

Morris, M. Die Form des Ur-Faust. ' Goethe-Studien,' erster Band, 2. Aufl. Berlin. 1902. Pp. 1–12.

Die Faustparalipomena. *Ibid.*, pp. 153–232.

Niejahr, J. Kritische Untersuchungen zu Goethes Faust. *Euphorion* IV. (1897), 272–87 ; 489–509. Älteste Gestalt ; das Fragment.

Pniower, O. Einige Faustparalipomena Goethes. *Vierteljahrschrift für Litteraturgeschichte* V. (1892), 408–30.

Raiz, Ä. Goethes Faustredaktion 1790. *Vierteljahrschrift für Litteraturgeschichte* III. (1890), 323–59.

**Schmidt, E. Goethes Faust in ursprünglicher Gestalt nach der Göchhausen'schen Abschrift herausgegeben. 7. Abdruck. Weimar. 1909.

Strehlke, F. Paralipomena zu Goethes Faust. Entwürfe, Skizzen, Vorarbeiten und Fragmente, geordnet und erläutert. Stuttgart. 1891.

Weltrich, R. Goethes Faust in der Göchhausen'schen Abschrift. *Magazin für Litteratur des In- und Auslandes*, 1888. A series of articles.

Witkowski, G. See above under III.

Wohlauer, A. Das erste Paralipomenon und der erste Entwurf zu Goethes Faust. Breslau. 1899.

V.

COMMENTARIES AND EXPOSITIONS WITHOUT THE TEXT.

Baumgart, H. Goethes Faust als einheitliche Dichtung erläutert. 2 Bde. Königsberg. 1893–1902.

Boyesen, H. H. Goethe and Schiller. Their lives and works. Including a commentary on Goethe's Faust. New York. 1882.

Coupland, W. C. The Spirit of Goethe's Faust. London. 1888.

Düntzer, H. Goethes Faust. Erster und zweiter Theil. Zum ersten Mal vollständig erläutert. 2 Bde. Leipzig. 1850.

*Fischer, K. Goethe's Faust. 4 Bde. Heidelberg, 1902–4. Band 1 :

Die Faust-Dichtung vor Goethe. Band 2: Entstehung, Idee und Composition. Bände 3–4: Erklärung des Goethe'schen Fausts nach der Reihenfolge seiner Szenen.

Kreyssig, F. Vorlesungen über Goethes Faust. 2 Aufl. herausgegeben von F. Kern. Berlin. 1900.

*Minor, J. Goethes Faust. Entstehungsgeschichte und Erklärung. 2 Bde. Stuttgart. 1901. Band 1: Der Ur-Faust und das Fragment. Band 2: Der erste Teil.

Petsch, R. Vorträge über Goethes Faust. Würzburg. 1902.

Valentin, V. Goethes Faustdichtung in ihrer künstlerischen Einheit dargestellt. Berlin. 1904.

Vischer, F. Goethes Faust. Neue Beiträge zur Kritik des Gedichtes. Stuttgart. 1875.

VI.

CRITICAL STUDIES AND CONTRIBUTIONS.

Biedermann, W. von. Goethe-Forschungen. Anderweite Folge. Leipzig. 1899. Pp. 7–40: Die angeblichen Faustpläne; Vorbilder zu Faust; die Domscene.

Büchner, W. Fauststudien. Weimar. 1908. Relates mainly to the first three acts of the Second Part.

Collin, J. Die Mittel der dichterischen Darstellung im zweiten Teil von Goethes Faust. *Jahrbuch des Freien Deutschen Hochstifts.* 1895. Pp. 247–63.

Curto, H. Die Figur des Mephisto im Goethe'schen Faust. Turin. 1890.

Cutting, S. W. Faust's first monologue and the Earth-Spirit scene in the light of recent criticism. *Modern Language Notes* X. (1895), 464–75.

Dehio, G. Altitalienische Gemälde als Quelle zum Faust. *Goethe-Jahrbuch* VII. (1886), 251–66.

[Du Bois-Reymond, E. Goethe und kein Ende. Antrittsrede. Berlin. 1883.

Düntzer, H. Die Entstehung der beiden ersten und der beiden letzten Akte des zweiten Theiles von Goethes Faust. 'Zur Goethe-Forschung.' Stuttgart. 1892. Pp. 246–79.

Enders, C. Die Katastrophe in Goethes Faust. Dortmund. 1907.

Gerber, A. The evolution of the Classical Walpurgis-Night and the scene in Hades. *Americana Germanica* III. (1899), 1–26.

Goebel, J. The etymology of Mephistopheles. *Transactions of the American Philological Association* XXXV. (1904), 148–56.

Homunculus. *Goethe-Jahrbuch* XXI. (1900), 208–23.

*Graffunder, P. Der Erdgeist und Mephistopheles in Goethes Faust. *Preussische Jahrbücher* LXVIII. (1891), 700–25.

Harnack, O. Der Gang der Handlung in Goethes Faust. Darmstadt. 1902.

Über die Entstehung des Faust. 'Essais und Studien zur Litteraturgeschichte.' Braunschweig. 1899. Pp. 58–76.

Hartmann, E. von. Der Ideengehalt des Goethe'schen Faust. *Im neuen Reich* II. (1872), 445–508.

Haupt, W. C. Die poetische Form von Goethes Faust. Leipzig. 1909. Dissertation.

Heine, G. Der Erdgeist und Mephistopheles. *Zeitschrift für den deutschen Unterricht* XIX. (1905), 447–53.

Hering, R. Zum Erdgeist in Goethes Faust. Festschrift des Freien Deutschen Hochstifts zu Goethes 150. Geburtstagsfeier. Frankfurt am Main. Pp. 187–208.

Huther, A. Die verschiedenen Pläne im ersten Theile von Goethes Faust. Cottbus. 1887.

Jostes, F. Die Einführung des Mephistopheles in Goethes Faust. *Euphorion* III. (1896), 390–407; 739–58.

Landsberg, E., und Kohler, J. Fausts Pakt mit Mephistopheles in juristischer Beleuchtung. *Goethe-Jahrbuch*, XXIV. (1903), 113–31.

Lichtenberger, E. Le Faust de Goethe. Essai de critique impersonelle. Paris. 1911.

Faust devant l'humanité. *Goethe-Jahrbuch* XXVI. (1905), 101–25.

Lippmann, F. O. Über einen naturwissenschaftlichen Aberglauben. Halle. 1894.

*Morris, M. Goethe Studien, Erster Band. 2. Aufl. Berlin. 1902.

Swedenborg in Faust; die geplante Disputationsscene; die Walpurgisnacht; Faustquellen; Gemälde und Bildwerke in Faust.

Mephistopheles. *Goethe-Jahrbuch* XXII. (1901), 150–91; XXIII.
(1902), 139–76.

Niejahr, J. Die Osterscenen und die Vertragsscene in Goethes Faust.
Goethe-Jahrbuch XX. (1899), 155–96.

Goethes Helena. *Euphorion* I. (1894), 81–109.

Paulsen, F. Schopenhauer. Hamlet. Mephistopheles. Drei Aufsätze zur Naturgeschichte des Pessimismus. Berlin. 1900.

Petsch, R. Faust-Studien. *Goethe-Jahrbuch* XXVIII. (1907), 105–
33, XXIX. (1908), 88–112. Helena und Euphorion; das erste Gespräch
Fausts mit Wagner.

*Pniower, O. Goethes Faust. Zeugnisse und Excurse zu seiner
Entstehungsgeschichte. Berlin. 1899.

Goethe's Faust und das Hohe Lied. *Goethe-Jahrbuch* XIII. (1892),
181–98.

Die Abfassung der Scene ' Vor dem Thor' im Faust. *Goethe-Jahrbuch* XVI. (1895), 149–78.

Roscher, W. H. Ephialtes. *Abhandlungen der sächsischen Gesellschaft der Wissenschaft* XX. (1900), 1–133.

Rössler, C. Die Entstehung des Faust. *Die Grenzboten*, 1883.
A series of articles.

Saran, F. Die Einheit des ersten Faustmonologs. *Zeitschrift für
deutsche Philologie* XXX. (1898), 508–48.

Scherer, W. Aus Goethes Frühzeit. Strassburg. 1879. Herder im
Faust; der Faust in Prosa; der erste Theil des Faust.

Aufsätze über Goethe. Berlin. 1886. Gretchen; Neue Faustkom-
mentare; Betrachtungen über Faust; Fauststudien.

Valentin, V. Homunculus und Helena. *Goethe-Jahrbuch* XVI.
(1895), 127–48. Cf. Gerber's review in *Modern Language Notes* XII.
(1897), 70–79 and XIII. (1898), 204–15.

Die Klassische Walpurgisnacht. Leipzig. 1901.

Volkelt, J. Fausts Entwicklung vom Geniessen zum Handeln in
Goethes Dichtung. *Neue Jahrbücher für das klassische Altertum u.s.w.*
XI. (1903), 508–21.

Wehnert, Dr. Gottvater, Erdgeist und Mephisto. *Zeitschrift für den
deutschen Unterricht*, XXII. (1908), 758–68.

Witkowski, G. Die Walpurgisnacht im ersten Teile von Goethes Faust. Leipzig. 1894.

Der Erdgeist im Faust. *Goethe-Jahrbuch* XVII. (1896), 122–37.

Die Handlung des zweiten Teils von Goethes Faust. 2. Aufl. Leipzig. 1906.

Woerner, R. Fausts Ende. Antrittsrede. Freiburg. 1902. Cf. Michels' review in *Euphorion* XIII. (1906), 633–41.

Wohlauer, A. Goethes Helenadichtung in ihrer Entwicklung. Breslau. 1903.

VII.

GOETHE'S FAUST ON THE STAGE.

Buchholz, R. Goethes Faust. Zweiter Teil für die Bühne eingerichtet. Hamburg. 1881.

Creizenach, W. Die Bühnengeschichte des Goethe'schen Faust. Frankfurt. 1881.

Devrient, O. Goethes Faust. Für die Aufführung als Mysterium in zwei Tagewerken eingerichtet. Karlsruhe. 1881.

Kilian, E. Goethes Faust auf der Bühne. Beiträge zum Probleme der Aufführung und Inszenierung des Gedichtes. München. 1907.

Marcks, A. Goethe's Faust. Zweiter Teil. Nach der Bearbeitung von Dr. Wollheim für die königlich-sächsische Bühne eingerichtet. Dresden. 1880.

Possart, E. Über die Gesammt-Aufführung des Goethe'schen Faust auf dem Münchener Hoftheater. München. 1895.

Schröer, K. J. Die Aufführung des ganzen Faust auf dem Wiener Burgtheater. Heilbronn. 1883.

Thomas, C. The complete *Faust* on the German stage. *The Nation*, April 30, 1906.

Wilbrandt, A. Goethes Faust für die Bühne in drei Abenden eingerichtet. Wien. 1900.

Witkowski, G. Goethes Faust. Erster und zweiter Teil. Für die Bühne eingerichtet. Leipzig. 1906.

VIII.

Miscellaneous.

Bibliography, methodology, Goethe's sources, works of reference, etc.

Arnold, G. Unpartheyische Kirchen- und Ketzerhistorien. Vom Anfang des Neuen Testaments biss auf das Jahr Christi 1688. 2. Aufl. Schaffhausen. 1740–42.

Bekker, B. Die bezauberte Welt. Amsterdam. 1693. Source for the first Walpurgis-Night.

*Biedermann, W. von. Goethes Gespräche. 10 Bde. Leipzig. 1889–96.

Carpzov, B. Practica nova Imperialis Saxonica rerum criminalium. 1635. Doubtful source for the first Walpurgis-Night. See Weimar Goethe XIV, 297.

*Engel, K. Zusammenstellung der Faust-Schriften vom 16. Jahrhundert bis Mitte 1884. Oldenburg. 1885.

Fischer, K. Die Erklärungsarten des Goethe'schen Faust. Heidelberg. 1889.

Francisci, E. Der höllische Proteus. Nürnberg. 1708. A source for the first Walpurgis-Night.

*Gräf, H. G. Goethe über seine Dichtungen. Zweiter Teil, zweiter Band (des ganzen Werkes vierter Band). Frankfurt am Main. 1904.

Grimm, J. Deutsche Mythologie. 4. Aufl. besorgt von E. H. Meyer. Berlin. 1875–8.

Hauhart, W. F. Goethes Faust in England. New York. 1909. Dissertation. Good bibliography of English translations and criticisms.

Hederich, B. Mythologisches Lexicon. Ansehnlich vermehrt und verbessert von J. J. Schwaben. Leipzig. 1770. Goethe's vade mecum for classical mythology.

Horst, J. W. Zauberbibliothek; oder von Zauberei, Theurgie und Mantik, Zauberern, Hexen und Hexenprocessen, Dämonen, Gespenster und Gespenstererscheinungen. Mainz. 1821–25.

Jacoby, G. Herder als Faust. Leipzig. 1911.

Kopp, H. Aurea Catena Homeri. Braunschweig. 1880.

Loeper, G. von. Goethes Werke, Hempel'sche Ausgabe. Einundzwanzigster Theil, pp. 348–51. Contains useful bibliographic notes on the various authors expressly mentioned by Goethe in connection with his early studies of alchemy and magic; viz., Welling, Paracelsus, Basilius Valentinus, Van Helmont, Starckey, Aurea Catena Homeri, Agrippa von Nettesheym, and Boerhave.

Praetorius, J. Anthropodemus Plutonicus. Magdeburg. 1666. Important source for the first Walpurgis-night.

Roskoff, G. Geschichte des Teufels. Leipzig. 1869.

*Schmidt, E. Aufgaben und Wege der Faust-Philologie. *Berichte der Versammlung deutscher Philologen und Schulmänner in München.* 1891.

Strehlke, F. Wörterbuch zu Goethes Faust. Stuttgart. 1891.

Taylor, B. Faust, a tragedy by Goethe. Translated in the original metres. Boston. 1879. Cf. J. Haskell's dissertation, ' Bayard Taylor's translation of Goethe's *Faust*.' New York. 1908.

Thomas, C. The methods of Wilhelm Scherer as a critic of Faust. *Transactions of the Modern Language Association of America* II (1886), 92–106.

Weissenfels, R. Goethe im Sturm und Drang. Halle. 1894.

Witkowski, G. Über den Plan einer wissenschaftlichen Ausgabe von Goethes Faust. *Goethe-Jahrbuch* XXVII. (1900), 144–57.

APPENDIX II.

THE TEXT.

The critical student of the text of *Faust* is referred to Goethe's *Werke*, XIV., 247 ff., where can be found a full account of the manuscripts and prints compared in the recension of the Weimar text, together with a full list of variant readings. The Weimar text is followed in this edition, but it is not thought necessary to reproduce here its entire critical apparatus. The fundamental principle is to follow the *Ausgabe letzter Hand* except where there is clear and cogent reason for departing from it. The purpose of the following notes is twofold: first, to comment briefly on those textual questions that have an important bearing on the sense, and secondly to give in full those passages of U which differ radically from the final version. U means 'Urfaust'; S, the Fragment of 1790; A, the *editio princeps* of the completed First Part (1808); C, the *Ausgabe letzter Hand* (1829).

21. Leib. So AC. The Lied of many later editions is probably a mistaken correction, — trivialisirende Schlimmbesserung as it is called by Schmidt, the Weimar editor — of Riemer, who noted in the back of Goethe's diary for 1809 that Leib was a misprint for Lied. By oversight, seemingly, the reading Lied crept into a few copies of a Cotta print of 1825 and was then adopted in the Riemer-Eckermann quarto edition of 1836–7. The reading Leib in C indicates that Riemer's note was without Goethe's authorization.

379. Würde. U has werde. Cf. introductory note to scene 'Night,'

390. Büchern. US have Bücher. Cf. note.

481+. After Flamme U has in wiederlicher Gestalt. Cf. note.

503. Wehe. USA have wehe; C wehe. Changed apparently on account of the ensuing Weben and Webstuhl, and also for the sake of the parallelism Lebensfluthen: Wall' = Thatensturm: Wehe.

519. U has Nun werd ich tiefer tief zu nichte.   Cf. note.

521. Schleicher. U has Schwärmer.   Cf. note.

532–3. Instead of these lines U has:

> Man weis nicht eigentlich wie sie zu guten Dingen
> Durch Ueberredung hinzubringen.

546–7. In U Wagner's speech consists of the single line:

> Allein der Vortrag nützt dem Redner viel.

to which Faust's reply runs in U:

548–51. Was Vortrag! der ist gut im Puppenspiel
> Mein Herr Magister hab er Krafft!
> Sey er kein Schellenlauter Thor!
> Und Freundschafft, Liebe, Brüderschafft,
> Trägt die sich nicht von selber vor.

596. nur immer fort. US have bis morgen früh.

1867+. In U the heading (cf. Intr. p. l, foot-note) is: Mephistopheles
im Schlafrock eine grose Perrücke auf. Student.

1882–95. These lines are lacking in U, the following being found
instead:

> Sieht all so trocken ringsum aus
> Als säs Heishunger in iedem Haus.

Meph: Bitt euch! dran euch nicht weiter kehrt,
> Hier alles sich vom Studenten nährt.
> Doch erst, wo werdet ihr logiren?
> Das ist ein Hauptstück!

Student.   Wolltet mich führen
> Bin warrlich ganz ein irres Lamm.
> Mögt gern das gute so allzusamm,
> Mögt gern das böse mir all vom Leib,
> Und Freyheit, auch wohl Zeitvertreib,
> Mögt auch dabei studiren tief,
> Dass mirs über Kopf und Ohren lief!
> O Herr helft dass meiner Seel
> Am guten Wesen nimmer fehl.

Mephis: krazt sich. Kein Logie habt ihr? wie ihr sagt.

Student. Hab noch nicht 'mal darnach gefragt.
> Mein Wirthshaus nährt mich leidlich gut,
> Feines Mägdlein drinn aufwarten thut.

Meph: Behüte Gott das führt euch weit!
         Caffee und Billard!   Weh dem Spiel!
         Die Mägdlein ach sie geilen viel!
         Vertripplistreichelt eure Zeit.
         Dagegen sehn wirs leidlich gern,
         Daß alle Studiosi nah und fern
         Uns wenigstens einmal die Wochen
         Kommen untern Absaz gekrochen.
         Will einer an unserm Speichel sich lezzen
         Den thun wir zu unsrer Rechten sezzen.
Student. Mir wird ganz greulich vorm Gesicht!
Meph: Das schadt der guten Sache nicht.
         Dann fordersamst mit dem Logie
         Wüßt ich euch wohl nichts bessers hie,
         Als geht zu Frau Sprizbierlein morgen
         Weis Studiosos zu versorgen
         Hats Haus von oben bis unten voll,
         Und versteht weidlich was sie soll.
         Zwar Noes Arche war saubrer gefacht,
         Doch ists einmal so hergebracht.
         Ihr zahlt was andre vor euch zahlten
         Die ihren Nahm aufs — Haus mahlten.
Student. Wird mir fast so eng ums Herz herum
         Als zu Haus im Colegium.
Meph: Euer Logie wär nun bestellt.
         Nun euren Tisch für leidlich Geld!
Student. Mich dünkt das gäb sich alle nach,
         Wer erst von Geists Erweitrung sprach!
Meph: Mein Schatz! das wird euch wohl verziehn,
         Kennt nicht den Geist der Akademien.
         Der Mutter Tisch müßt ihr vergessen,
         Klar Wasser geschiedne Butter fressen.
         Statt Hopfen Keim und iung Gemüs,
         Geniessen mit Dank Brennesseln süs,
         Sie thun einen Gänse stuhlgang treiben,
         Aber eben drum nicht baß bekleiben,
         Hammel und Kalb kühren ohne End,

>Als wie unsers Herr Gotts Firmament.
>Doch zahlend wird von euch ergänzt
>Was Schwärmerian vor euch geschwänzt.
>Müßt euren Beutel wohl versorgen,
>Besonders keinem Freunde borgen
>Aber redlich zu allen Maalen
>Wirth, Schneider und Professor zahlen.

Student. Hochwürdger Herr das findet sich.
>Aber nun bitt ich leitet mich!
>Mir steht das Feld der Weisheit offen,
>Wäre gern so grade zu geloffen,
>Aber sieht drinn so bunt und kraus
>Auch seitwärts wüst und trocken aus.
>Fern thät sich's mir vor die Sinnen stellen,
>Als wie ein Tempe voll frischer Quellen.

1898-1901. In U the Student's reply runs :
>Soll zwar ein Mediziner werden
>Doch wünscht ich rings von aller Erden,
>Von allem Himmel und all Natur,
>So viel mein Geist vermögt zu fassen.

1941. U has : Bohrt sich einen Esel und weis nicht wie,

2079. From this point on the scene reads in U :

Brander　　　　　　　　　Esel! Schwein!

Frosch　Muß man mit euch nicht beydes seyn.

Siebel. Drey Teufel! ruht! und singt runda! und drein gesoffen drein gekrischen. Holla he! Auf! He da!

Alten. Baumwolle her ; der sprengt uns die Ohren.

Siebel Kann ich davor daß das verflucht niedrige Gewölbe so wiederschallt. Sing.

Frosch. A! Tara! Tara! lara! di! — Gestimmt ist! Und was nun ? [Here ll. 2090-91].

Brander. Pfuy ein garstig Lied! Ein politisch Lied, ein leidig Lied. Dankt Gott daß euch das heilige römische Reich nichts angeht. Wir wollen einen Papst wählen.

Frosch [ll. 2101-2].

Siebel Wetter und Todt. Grüs mein Liebgen! — Eine Hammelmauspastete mit gestopften dürren Eichenblättern vom Blocksberg, durch

einen geſchundnen Haaſen mit dem Hahnenkopf überſchickt, und keinen Gruß
von der Nachtigall. Hatt ſie mich nicht — Meinen Stuzbart und alle Appar-
tinenzien hinter die Thüre geworfen wie einen ſtumpfen Beſen, und das um
— Drey Teufel! Keinen Gruß ſag ich als die Fenſter eingeſchmiſſen!

Froſch (den Krug auf den Tiſch ſtoſſend) Ruh iezt! — Ein neu Lied Kam-
meraden, ein alt Lied wenn ihr wollt! — Aufgemerkt und den Rundreim
mit geſungen. Friſch und hoch auf! [Here ll. 2126–49, but with dashes
in place of Doctor Luther, l. 2129].

Siebel. Und eine hinlängliche Portion Rattenpulver der Köchin in
die Suppe. Ich bin nit mitleidig, aber ſo eine Ratte könnte einen Stein
erbarmen.

Brander. Selbſt Ratte! Ich mögte den Schmeerbauch ſo am Heerde
ſein Seelgen ausblaſen ſehn!

Fauſt, Mephiſtopheles.

Meph: Nun ſchau wie ſie's hier treiben! Wenn dirs gefällt, dergleichen Sozietät ſchaff ich dir Nacht nächtlich.

Fauſt Guten Abend ihr Herren.

Alle Groſen Dank!

Siebel Wer iſt der Storcher da!

Brander. Still! das iſt was vornehmes iukognito, ſie haben ſo was
unzufriednes böſes im Geſicht.

Siebel Pah! Commödianten wenns hoch kommt.

Meph: (leiſe) Merks! den Teufel vermuthen die Kerls nie ſo nah er
ihnen immer iſt.

Froſch. Ich will 'en die Würme ſchon aus der Naſe ziehn, wo ſie her=
kommen! — Iſt der Weeg von Rippach herüber ſo ſchlimm, daß ihr ſo tief
in die Nacht habt reiſen müſſen!

Fauſt Wir kommen den Weeg nit

Froſch. Ich meinte etwa ihr hättet bey dem berühmten Hans drüben
zu Mittag geſpeißt.

Fauſt. Ich kenn ihn nicht. (die andern lachen).

Froſch. Der iſt von altem Geſchlecht. Hat eine weitläufige Familie.

Meph: Ihr ſeyd wohl ſeiner Vettern einer.

Brander (leiſe zu Froſch). Stecks ein! der verſteht den Rummel.

Froſch. Bey Wurzen iſts fatal, da muß man ſo lang auf die Fähre
manchmal warthen.

F a u ſt. So!

S i e b e l (leiſe). Sie kommen aus dem Reiche man ſiehts 'en an. Laſſt ſie nur erſt fidel werden. — Seyd ihr Freunde von einem herzhaften Schluck! Herbey mit euch.

M e p h : Immer zu. (ſie ſtoßen an und trinken).

F r o ſch. Nun Herrn ein Liedgen. Für einen Krug ein Liedgen, das iſt billig.

F a u ſt Ich habe keine Stimme.

M e p h : Ich ſing eins für mich, zwey für meinen Cammeraden, hundert wenn ihr wollt, wir kommen aus Spanien wo Nachts ſo viel Lieder geſungen werden als Sterne am Himmel ſtehn.

B r a n d e r Das verbät ich mir, ich haſſe das Geklimpere, auſſer wenn ich einen Rauſch habe, und ſchlafe daß die Welt untergehen dürfte. — Für kleine Mädgen iſts ſo was die nit ſchlafen können, und am Fenſter ſtehen Monden Kühlung einzuſuckeln.

M e p h : [ll. 2207–8].

S i e b e l Stille! Horch! Schöne Rarität! ſchöne Liebhaberey!

F r o ſch. Noch ein mahl.

M e p h : [ll. 2211–18].

S i e b e l Wohl gemeßen! Wohl! (ſie ſchlagen in ein Gelächter aus) Daß ſie nur keine Falten werfen!

M e p h : [ll. 2223–40.]

A l l e durcheinander. Bravo! Bravo! Schön und trefflich! Noch eins! Noch ein paar Krüge! Noch ein paar Lieder.

F a u ſt. Meine Herren! Der Wein geht an! Geht an wie in Leipzig die Weine alle angehn müſſen. Doch dünckt mich ihr würdet erlauben daß man euch aus einem andern Faſſe zapfte.

S i e b e l Habt ihr einen eignen Keller? Handelt ihr mit Weinen? Seid ihr vielleicht von denen Schelmen aus 'm Reich? —

A l t e n. Wart ein biſſgen (er ſteht auf) Ich hab ſo eine Probe, ob ich weiter trinken darf. (Er macht die Augen zu und ſteht eine Weile) Nun! nun! das Köpfgen ſchwanckt ſchon!

S i e b e l Pah! eine Flaſche! Ich wills vor Gott verantworten und vor deiner Frauen. Euren Wein!

F a u ſt. Schafft mir einen Bohrer.

F r o ſch. Der Wirth hat ſo ein Körbel mit Werckzeug in der Ecke ſtehn.

F a u ſt. (nimmt den Bohrer) Gut! Was verlangt ihr für Wein?

Frosch He!

Faust Was für ein Gläsgen mögtet ihr trinken? Ich schaffs euch!

Frosch. He! He! So ein Glas Reinwein ächten Nierensteiner.

Faust Gut! (er bohrt in den Tisch an Froschens Seite) Nun schafft Wachs!

Alten Da ein Kerzen stümpfgen.

Faust So! (er stopft das Loch) Halt iezzo! — und ihr?

Siebel Muskaten Wein! Spanischen Wein sonst keinen Tropfen. Ich will nur sehn wo das hinaus läufft.

Faust (bohrt und verstopft) Was beliebt euch?

Alten Rothen Wein! Einen Französchen! — Die Franzosen kann ich nicht leiden, so grosen Respeckt ich vor ihren Wein hab.

Faust (wie oben) Nun was schafft ihr?

Brander Hält er uns für'n Narren?

Faust Schnell Herr nennt einen Wein!

Brander Tockaher dann! — Soll er doch nicht aus dem Tische laufen.

Faust Stille iunger Herr! — Nun aufgeschaut! Die Gläser unterge= halten. Jeder ziehe den Wachspropfen heraus! Daß aber kein Tropfen an die Erde fällt, sonst giebts ein Unglück!

Alten Mir wirds unheimlich. Der hat den Teufel.

Faust Ausgezogen!

(Sie ziehn die Pfropfen, jedem läufft der verlangte Wein in's Glas.)

Faust Zugestopft! Und nun versucht!

Siebel Wohl! trefflich wohl!

Alle Wohl! Majestätisch wohl! — Willkommner Gast
(sie trinken wiederholt.)

Meph: Sie sind nun eingeschifft.

Faust Gehn wir!

Meph: Noch ein Moment.

Alle singen [ll. 2293-4.] (Sie trinken wiederholt, Siebel läßt den Pfropf fallen, es fließt auf die Steine und wird zur Flamme die an Siebeln hinauf lodert.)

Siebel. Hölle und Teufel!

Brander Zauberey! Zauberey!

Faust Sagt ichs euch nicht. (er verstopft die Oeffnung und spricht einige Worte, die Flamme flieht.)

Siebel. Herr und Satan! — Meynt er, er dürft in ehrliche Gesellschaft sich machen und sein Höllisches Hokuspokus treiben.

Faust Stille Mastschwein!

Siebel. Mir Schwein! Du Besenstiel! Brüder! Schlagt ihn zusammen, Stoßt ihn nieder! (sie ziehn die Messer) Ein Zauberer ist Vogelfrey! Nach den Reichsgesetzen Vogelfrey.

(Sie wollen über Fausten her, er winckt, sie stehn in frohem Erstaunen auf einmal und sehen einander an.)

Siebel   Was seh ich! Weinberge!

Brander   Trauben um diese Jahrs zeit.

Alten   Wie reif! wie schön!

Frosch   Halt das ist die schönste! (sie greifen zu, kriegen einander bey den Nasen, und heben die Messer)

Faust   Halt! — Geht und schlaft euren Rausch aus!

(Faust und Meph: ab. Es gehen ihnen die Augen auf, sie fahren mit Geschrey aus einander.)

Siebel   Meine Nase! War das deine Nase? Waren das die Trauben? Wo ist er?

Brander   Fort! Es war der Teufel selbst.

Frosch   Ich hab ihn auf einem Fasse hinaus reiten sehn.

Alten   Hast du! Da ist gewiß auf dem Marckt nit sicher — Wie kommen wir nach Hause.

Brander   Siebel geh zu erst!

Siebel   Kein Narr.

Frosch.   Kommt wir wecken die Häscher unterm Rathaus, für ein Trinckgeld thun die wohl ihre Schuldigkeit.   Fort!

Siebel   Sollte wohl der Wein noch laufen. (er visitirt die Pfropfen.)

Alten   Bildt dirs nicht ein!   Trocken wie Holz!

Frosch   Fort ihr Bursche!   Fort! (alle ab.)

2609–10.   U has:

> Das ist ein herrlich schönes Kind
> Die hat was in mir angezündt.

2674–77.   U has:

> Er thut als wär er ein Fürsten Sohn
> Hätt Luzifer so ein Duzzend Prinzen
> Die sollten ihm schon was vermünzen
> Am Ende kriegt' er eine Commißion.

2735–6.   U has:

> Ich sag euch es sind Sachen drein
> Um eine Fürstin zu gewinnen.

2760–64.   Cf. note.

2785.   U has: Was Guckguck mag dadrinne sein?

2814.   Between this and l. 2815 U has:

> Hätt einer auch Engelsblut im Leibe,
> Er würde da zum Heerings Weibe.

3031–2. U has:

Fauſt. Sie iſt mir lieb.

Meph: Doch gehts nicht ganz umſunſt,
Eine Gunſt iſt werth der andern Gunſt.

3346–7. U has:

Das durch erſchüttern durcherwarmen?
Verdrängt es dieſe Seelen Noth.

3483. U has:

Es iſt ein Kauz wie's mehr noch geben.

3775+. The heading is in U: Dom. Exequien der Mutter Gretgens. Gretgen alle Verwandte. Amt, Orgel und Geſang Böſer Geiſt hinter Gretgen.

3780. U has: Deinen Gebeten nachlallteſt.

3791–2. U. has:

Schlägt da nicht quillend ſchon,
Brandſchande Maalgeburt!

4405–612. The text of this scene reads in U:

Kerker.

Fauſt mit einem Bund Schlüſſel und einer Lampe an einem eiſernen Türgen.

Es faſſt mich längſt verwohnter Schauer. Inneres Grauen der Menſchheit. Hier! Hier! — Auf! — Dein Zagen zögert den Todt heran.

(er faſſt das Schloß es ſingt inwendig.) [ll. 4412–20.]

Fauſt (zittert wankt ermannt ſich und ſchließt auf, er hört die Ketten klirren und das Stroh rauſchen.)

Margarethe (ſich verbergend auf ihrem Lager.) Weh! Weh! ſie kommen. Bittrer Todt!

Fauſt (leiſe) Still! Ich komme dich zu befreyn. (erfaſſt ihre Ketten ſie aufzuſchlieſſen)

Marg: (wehrend) Weg! Um Mitternacht! Hencker iſt dir's morgen frühe nicht zeitig gnug.

Fauſt Laſſ!

Marg: (wälzt ſich vor ihn hin) Erbarme dich mein und laß mich leben! Ich bin ſo iung, ſo iung, und zwar ſchön und bin ein armes iunges Mädgen. Sieh nur einmal die Blumen an, ſieh nur einmal die Kron. Erbarme dich mein! Was hab ich dir gethan? Hab dich mein Tage nicht geſehn.

Fauſt. Sie verirrt und ich vermags nicht.

Marg: Sieh das Kind! Muß ich's doch tränken. Da hatt ich's eben! Da! Ich habs getränkt! Sie nahmen mirs, und sagen ich hab es umgebracht, und singen Liedger auf mich! — Es ist nicht wahr — es ist ein Märgen das sich so endigt, es ist nicht auf mich daß Sie's singen.

Fauſt (der ſich zu ihr hinwirft) Gretgen!

Margr: (die ſich aufreißt) Wo iſt er! Ich hab ihn rufen hören! er rief Gretgen! Er rief mir! Wo iſt er! Ach durch all das Heulen und Zähn-klappen erkenn ich ihn, er ruft mir: Gretgen! (Sich vor ihm niederwerfend) Mann! Mann! Gieb mir ihn schaff mir ihn! Wo iſt er!

Fauſt (erfaßt ſie wütend um den Hals) Meine Liebe! Meine Liebe!

Margr: (ſinckt ihr Haupt in ſeinen Schoos verbergend)

Fauſt Auf meine Liebe! Dein Mörder wird dein Befreyer. Auf! — (Er ſchließt über ihrer Betäubung die Arm Kette auf) Komm, wir entgehen dem ſchröcklichen Schickſaal.

Margr (angelehnt) Küſſe mich! Küſſe mich!

Fauſt Tauſendmal! Nur eile Gretgen eile!

Margr: Küſſe mich! Kannſt du nicht mehr küſſen? Wie! Was! Biſt mein Heinrich und haſt's Küſſen verlernt! Wie ſonſt ein ganzer Him-mel mit deiner Umarmung gewaltig über mich eindrang. Wie du küſſteſt als wollteſt du mich in wollüſtigem Tod erſticken. Heinrich küſſe mich, ſonſt küſſ ich dich (ſie fällt ihn an) Weh! deine Lippen ſind kalt! Todt! Antworten nicht!

Fauſt Folge mir, ich herze dich mit tauſendfacher Glut. Nur folge mir.

Margr: (Sie ſetzt ſich und bleibt eine Zeitlang ſtille) Heinrich biſt du's?

Fauſt Ich bin's. Komm mit.

Marg: Ich begreiffs nicht! Du? Die Feſſeln los! Befreyſt mich. Wen befreyſt du? Weiſt du's?

Fauſt. Komm! Komm!

Margr: Meine Mutter hab ich umgebracht! Mein Kind hab ich ertränkt. Dein Kind! Heinrich! — Groſer Gott im Himmel ſoll das kein Traum ſeyn! deine Hand Heinrich! — Sie iſt feucht — Wiſche ſie ab ich bitte dich! Es iſt Blut dran — Stecke den Degen ein! Mein Kopf iſt verrückt.

Fauſt. Du bringſt mich um.

Margr: Nein du ſollſt überbleiben, überbleiben von allen. Wer ſorgte für die Gräber! So in eine Reihe ich bitte dich, neben die Mutter den Bruder da! Mich dahin und mein Kleines an die rechte Bruſt. Gieb mir die Hand drauf du biſt mein Heinrich.

Fauſt (will ſie weg ziehen) Fühlſt du mich! Hörſt du mich! komm ich bins ich befreye dich.

Margr: Da hinaus.

Fauſt Freyheit!

Margr: Da hinaus! Nicht um die Welt. Iſt das Grab draus, komm! Lauert der Todt! komm. Von hier in's ewige Ruhe Bett weiter nicht einen Schritt. Ach Heinrich könnt ich mit dir in alle Welt.

Fauſt. Der Kerker iſt offen ſäume nicht.

Margr: Sie lauren auf mich an der Straſe am Wald.

Fauſt. Hinaus! Hinaus!

Margr: Ums Leben nicht — Siehſt du's zappeln! Rette den armen Wurm er zappelt noch! — Fort! geſchwind! Nur übern Steg, gerad in Wald hinein links am Teich wo die Planke ſteht. Fort! rette! rette!

Fauſt Rette! Rette dich!

Margr: Wären wir nur den Berg vorbey, da ſizzt meine Mutter auf einem Stein und wackelt mit dem Kopf! Sie winckt nicht ſie nickt nicht, ihr Kopf iſt ihr ſchweer. Sie ſollt ſchlafen daß wir könnten wachen und uns freuen beyſammen.

Fauſt (ergreift ſie und will ſie wegtragen)

Margr: Ich ſchreye laut, laut daſſ alles erwacht.

Fauſt Der Tag graut. O Liebgen! Liebgen!

Margr: Tag! Es wird Tag! Der lezte Tag! Der Hochzeit Tag! — Sags niemand daſſ du die Nacht vorher bey Gretgen warſt. — Mein Kränzgen! — Wir ſehn uns wieder! — Hörſt du die Bürger ſchlür-pfen nur über die Gaſſen! Hörſt du! Kein lautes Wort. Die Glocke ruft! — Krack das Stäbgen bricht! —.Es zuckt in iedem Nacken die Schärfe die nach meinem zuckt! — Die Glocke hör.

Meph: erſcheint. Auf oder ihr ſeyd verlohren, meine Pferde ſchaudern, der Morgen dämmert auf.

Marg: Der! der! Laſſ ihn ſchick ihn fort! Der will mich! Nein! Nein! Gericht Gottes komm über mich, dein bin ich! rette mich! Nimmer nimmermehr! Auf ewig lebe wohl. Leb wohl Heinrich.

Fauſt ſie umfaſſend. Ich laſſe dich nicht!

Margr. Ihr heiligen Engel bewahret meine Seele — mir grauts vor dir Heinrich.

Meph: Sie iſt gerichtet! (er verſchwindet mit Fauſt, die Thüre raſſelt zu man hört verhallend) Heinrich! Heinrich!

APPENDIX III.

377-9. Paracelsus writes thus of magic: Magia ift an ihr felbft bie verborgenfte Kunft und größte Weisheit übernatürlicher Dinge auf Erden; und was menfchlicher Vernunft unmöglich zu erfahren und zu ergründen ift, das mag durch die Kunft Magia erfahren und ergründet werden. — As this passage is quoted in Arnold's *Kirchen- und Ketzerhistorien* it may well have fallen under Goethe's eye.

392-6. One is reminded here of Goethe's tribute to Ossian in *Werther* (*Werke*, XIX., 124): Welch eine Welt, in die der Herrliche mich führt! Zu wandern über die Heide, umfauft vom Sturmwinde, der in dampfenden Nebeln die Geifter der Väter im dämmernden Lichte des Mondes hinführt. Zu hören vom Gebirge her im Gebrülle des Waldftroms halbverwehtes Ächzen der Geifter aus ihren Höhlen u. f. w.

422-5. The doctrine of the 'cabbalists' was that each heavenly body, including the earth, was controlled by a spirit, and that these spirits form an interconnected hierarchy of 'correspondences': they 'correspond' with one another and also with men. By natural magic, which was conceived not as a sinful black art, but as the highest kind of science, a man's nature could be so exalted and illuminated that he could not only converse with these spirits, but could become like them and understand the whole system of things by direct cognition. But this wonderful power could not be attained by reasoning or 'dry reflection'; it was a matter of 'divine compassion,' of strengthening the *vis imaginationis*. Swedenborg writes in the *Arcana Coelestia:* Inde est quod non solum omnia et singula apud hominem correspondeant, sed etiam omnia et singula in universo: ipse sol correspondet, et quoque luna, nam in coelo est dominus sol et quoque luna .... quia correspondentia est cumprimis hominis cum coelo, et per coelum cum Domino. Another passage of the same work runs: Quia ex divina Domini misericordia mihi aperta sunt interiora et ita loqui datum est cum illis qui in altera vita..... Locutus sum cum spiritibus et angelis.

442–6. Scherer, *Aus Goethes Frühzeit*, p. 71 ff., argues that the 'wise man' is Herder, whose *Älteste Urkunde* (1774) contains a rhapsodical account of the influence of the dawn-cult among primitive races. 'Come forth, young man,' says Herder, 'into the open fields and give heed. The most ancient, most glorious revelation of God appears to thee every morning as a fact.' Witkowski notes that the dawn plays a rôle in the Faust-legend, since we read in C. M. that Faust, wenn die Sonne früh Morgens aufgienge, das sogenannte Crepusculum matutinum gebrauchte. But Goethe's Faust is operating successfully in the middle of the night. We can then hardly suppose him to conclude, as the essence of wisdom, that the dawn is the only time, or even the best time, for a spirit-revelation. In that case we should expect him to wait until morning. It is obviously better to take Morgenroth figuratively as the morning-dawn of a better insight, a higher wisdom.

The case for Swedenborg is most fully stated by Morris, *Goethe-Studien*, I²., p. 13 ff., who finds this whole passage to be saturated with Swedenborgianism. The citations show many striking parallels. Swedenborg is continually 'talking' with spirits and about them. Planetary spirits appear to him as bright flames which change to birds and flit about his head. They exercise a 'species of suction or attraction' (speciem suctionis seu attractionis), which causes local pain. It will be noticed that Goethe reverses the direction of the force and makes Faust 'suck' at the sphere of the Earth-Spirit. Swedenborg's spirits 'wander through the universe.' They talk with men, as with one another, by immediate transference of ideas. In heaven they live in a 'state of peace,' which is the celestial counterpart of the terrestrial dawn. So the dawn is for Swedenborg, says Morris, 'a symbol of the highest, holiest, most ineffable.'

All this makes a strong case for Swedenborg in *Faust*, especially when we know that Goethe in his youth was considerably interested in the Swedish ghost-seer. On the other hand, it should not be forgotten that Swedenborg's spiritistic ideas did not originate with him, and that similar conceptions can be found in older writers who were either certainly or probably known to Goethe.

447-53. For the beneficent Himmelskräfte that ascend and descend Goethe may have been indebted to Van Helmont's *Paradoxaldiscurse oder Ungemeine Meinungen von dem Macrocosmo und Microcosmo* (1691), who says, as quoted by Witkowski: Dieſer Weg iſt kein andrer, kann auch kein ander ſein, als welcher durch Jacobs Leiter vorgeſtellet worden: Denn gleicherweiſe wie auff derſelben die Engel Gottes auff und nieder ſteigen, alſo ſteigen die weſentlichen lebendigen Kräfte oder geiſtlichen Leiber der himmliſchen Lichter unabläßlich von oben herab durch die ätheriſche Luft zu dieſer unteren Welt, als von dem Haupt zu den Füßen; und hernach, wenn ſie ihre Aus= würkung vollbracht, ſo ſteigen ſie zu ihrem eignen Nutz und Verbeſſerung wieder von unten aufwärts zu dem Haupt, mit demſelbigen wieder vereiniget. . . . . Und dieſes Auff= und Niederſteigen der himmliſchen Kräfte, und die ſtetige Verbeſſerung und Verherrlichung, die daran henget und darvon her= kommt, wehret und beharret ohn Unterlaß, und muß nothwendig alſo thun.

As to the perplexing 'golden vessels' (l. 450), Goebel quotes a passage from J. P. Faber's *Chymische Schriften* (1713), in which the author de-scribes the wonderful character of the Eymer oder Becher in which the alchemists prepare the philosopher's stone: dieſer Eymer iſt auch das Licht der Natur, welches in der Höhe ſublimieret worden aus der erſten Materie der Welt . . . . weßwegen ſie denen Ländern eine ſehr große Feuch= tigkeit, folglich eine große Fruchtbarkeit und einen Überfluß von allerhand Früchten mittheilen. This is certainly suggestive for the ſegenduftende Schwingen.

'459+. Just how the triangular relation between the Earth-Spirit, Faust, and Mephistopheles was conceived by Goethe in his early musings has been the subject of endless discussion; see Bibliography under VI. The problem is still further complicated by the later introduction of the Lord in the Prologue, who must of course be understood as overseeing and directing all that happens. Probably the original idea was somewhat as follows. Faust dreams of a spiritual new-birth by means of natural magic. To this end he must 'be like,' must 'comprehend,' the being with whom he presumes to speak as one spirit to another. But the Earth-Spirit, whom he succeeds in evoking, is too great for him. Only by the largest experience can he comprehend a being who knows and does all things terrestrial. Thus far, however, Faust has had experience only of books and dust and dead men's bones. Hence, the Spirit can only repel Faust's presumptuous advances.   Yet he is not unkindly disposed, and hence sends a subordinate spirit whom Faust *can* comprehend, and by whose aid he may find out what the world is really like.

Just how Goethe intended to end this experience-drama, directed by the Earth-Spirit through the agency of Mephistopheles, can not now be definitely made out.   We can hardly avoid supposing, however, that at the end of Faust's earthly life the Earth-Spirit was in some way to reappear and pass judgment on his strivings ; perhaps to speak of him benignly as one who had exhausted the possibilities of a carnal existence and was therefore fit to pass on to the higher life of an incorporeal being. This, however, is sheer guess-work. What is plain is that Goethe's early conception had little to do with traditional notions of God and the Devil, of heaven and hell. As time passed Goethe drifted away from the spiritistic ideas that had possessed him in his youth. His mystic cabbalism came to seem unreal and unfruitful. A passion for 'clearness' took hold of him. And so it came about that he dropped his original plan, whatever it may have been, and decided to let his drama rest on the more solid ground of tradition.

1112. In Bekker's *Bezauberte Welt*, a book known to have been in Goethe's hands in February, 1801, he may have read of the Manichæans Sie halten gar dafür, daß jeder Mensch zwei Seelen habe, deren eine allezeit wieder die andere streite. But the two-souls theory is found in Xenophon's *Cyropedia* and in several modern writers.   Cf. Pniower, G.-J. XVI., 165.

1118 ff. Geister in der Luft. Goethe appears to have got his spiritlore mainly from the Pfitzer Faust-book, which he drew from the Weimar library in 1801. Pfitzer, p. 193 of Keller's reprint, tells how 'the devil's kingdom extends toward the east, the south, the west and the north.'   The spirits wohnen gemeiniglich unter dem schwarzen Gewülcke und düsterer Luft, vermengen sich nicht selten unter die Donner, Blitz und Ungewitter, und erwarten, wenn es ihnen Gott verhenget, damit sie solches Geschoß zu einem und andern Verderben abgehen lassen. They also richten giftige Nebel, Reiffen und anderes an, da Seuchen und Kranckheiten entstehen. On p. 250 ff. there is more about them. Pfitzer argues that it is possible for magicians to be carried through the air by evil spirits, and tells how Faust himself once bore three men to Munich, the vehicle being a magic mantle.   It may be added that Bekker (see note above) also has much to say of air-spirits. He describes them, quoting Plutarch, as filling the world and acting as mediators between men and gods — warum fie auch zwifchen Himmel und Erde, nemlich wie gefagt wird, in der Luft und alfo zwifchen den himmlifchen Göttern und den irdifchen Menfchen gefetzet find.

1347. The cabbalists conceived of man, the microcosm, as a reflex on a small scale of the macrocosm. Welling observes daß alfo der Menfch, die kleine Welt, die einzige Verfammlung ift diefes ganzen Univerfi, der großen Welt, darinnen alle ihre Ausgeburten, fo unzählbare Formen und Geftalten, wiederum vereiniget zufammenkommen.

3756–61. An old city ordinance of Frankfurt, reprinted in 1765 and known to have been read by Goethe, runs : Es follen auch die gemeinen armen Dirnen und fuft offent. bulerin in diefer ftadt keine gülbener oder vergülte ketten, auch keinen fammet, atliß und damafker . . . . tragen, auch in der kirche in keinem ftule fteen.

3835–4222. For the orgies of the Blocksberg Goethe drew on certain books from the literature of witch- and devil-lore — books in which gross superstition fairly outdoes itself in filthy imaginings. This literature, so far as it is known to have been used by Goethe, is conveniently reviewed by Witkowski in *Die Walpurgisnacht im ersten Teile von Goethes Faust*, Leipzig, 1894. The more important of these literary sources were, it would seem, two works of J. Praetorius, namely, *Anthropodemus Plutonicus* (1666), and *Blockes-Berges-Verrichtung* (1668), and Francisci's *Höllischer Proteus* (1708). From Praetorius came the 'red mouse' of l. 4179, the seductive *Buhlteufelin* Lilith, Adam's first wife (ll. 4119 ff.), and the will-o'-the-wisp as talking minion of the devil (ll. 3855 ff.). Praetorius also tells of the salve used by witches, of the vehicles on which they ride to the Brocken (ll. 4008 ff.), and of their lewd dances. He remarks further on the greater appetency of women for evil (ll. 3980 ff.), and mentions a 'theater' as one of the lures of the witches' sabbath. In Francisci Goethe found additional matter about Lilith and the will-o'-the-wisp, observations on the malodorous lascivious goat-devil, and the idea of a phantom with a bloody line about the neck — eine rothe Korallen-Schnur von Blut — signifying decapitation.

These are but examples. To give more is the less necessary because, unlike the original works, Witkowski's booklet is easily accessible.

Mch 2   p. 92 — 121

" 9   p. 132 — 156

" 16   p. 157 — 188

" 23   p. 188 — 230
           (omit p. 194 — 197   l. 3955 - 4005
             p. 199 - 201   l. 4022 - 413
             p. 202 - 204   l. 4136 - 417
             p. 207 - 215)